The Political Economy of Economic Freedom

The Political Economy of Economic Freedom

Alan Peacock
David Hume Institute

Edward Elgar
Cheltenham, UK • Lyme, US

Published by
Edward Elgar Publishing Limited
8 Lansdown Place
Cheltenham
Glos GL50 2HU
UK

Edward Elgar Publishing Inc.
1 Pinnacle Hill Road
Lyme
NH 03768
US

A catalogue record for this book
is available from the British Library

Library of Congress Cataloguing in Publication Data
Peacock, Alan T., 1922–
The political economy of economic freedom/Alan Peacock.
Includes bibliographical references.
1. Free enterprise. I. Title.
HB95.P33 1997
330.12'2—dc21 96–48251
CIP

ISBN 1 85898 535 8

Printed and bound in Great Britain by
Biddles Limited, Guildford and King's Lynn

Contents

Preface

Some years ago when I was asked to prepare an entry in *Who's Who in Economics* (eds. M. Blaug and P. Sturges, 1983), the editors requested a statement on one's principal contributions to Economics. With some misgivings I wrote that perhaps I had a knack of hitting on interesting problems in public sector economics and the economic analysis of government for which others found elegant solutions. I am not sure that I can still make this claim for, in reviewing the contents of this collection of (mostly) recent contributions to political economy, I sense that I have become an observer of rather than a participant in the intensely competitive markets in which my *confrères* seek to make and to retain their professional reputations. I find this role congenial enough and, as I have been asked several times to prepare a collection of this sort by those whom I respect, I suppose that critical observation has still some part to play in professional discourse.

I have brought together mainly articles which have a bearing on my views on economic freedom, including its underlying philosophy, its influence on the critique of economic policy and the problems encountered in expanding it. (The format is further explained in Chapter 1.) They represent a diversity of experience ranging from academic speculation to close involvement with policy issues. The collection is not entirely representative of my recent output. In recent years I have indulged myself by writing on economic questions concerning the arts and culture, partly as a result of six years' service as a member of the Arts Council of Great Britain and as Chairman of the Scottish Arts Council. The results appear in a series of articles in the *Journal of Cultural Economics* and in a book entitled *Paying the Piper* (Edinburgh University Press, 1993). I have, however, included two articles based on my experience as Chair of the Home Office Committee on Financing the BBC, broadcasting being an area in which freedom of choice is an important issue. I have resisted the idea of prefacing the work with a personal autobiography but have introduced each reprinted article with some background material on its intellectual origins.

I hope that this selection will appeal to those in business and government who have to comprehend what their economists are talking about, and to professional social scientists and philosophers who encompass political economy in their deliberations, as well as to economists not so taken up with mathematical refinement of economic theories and new methods of testing them that they have no time to consider other ways of improving our knowledge of economic phenomena. I do occasionally use 'eine kleine Mathematik' where it seems sensible for my purpose, but I suppose I should warn those economists who suppose that their main preoccupation is to transact ideas only with each other that I rely mainly on their second language.

Several colleagues have been most helpful in the exploration of some of the ideas presented below. I must first of all thank Martin Ricketts and Ilde Rizzo, tolerant and able collaborators, for allowing me to reproduce joint articles. Graham Bannock, Norman Barry, Mark Blaug, Herbert Giersch, Keith Lumsden, Charles Rowley, Keith Shaw, David Simpson, Hans Willgerodt, Alan Williams and Thomas Wilson are owed my grateful thanks for friendly comment and criticism. I am likewise very much indebted to Ralph Harris and Arthur Seldon who recruited me as a member of the Institute of Economic Affairs over thirty years ago and who, as with many others, offered valuable professional advice, constant encouragement and an entrée to participation in public discussion.

Many thanks are due to the Wincott Foundation for a grant towards the preparation of the manuscript and to the David Hume Institute, especially Kathy Mountain, Personal Assistant to the Directors, for secretarial help. I am also extremely grateful to Edward Elgar and his staff and to Margaret Christie for editorial work.

I must single out for special mention two old friends and colleagues, Francesco Forte and Jack Wiseman. Francesco is a man of many talents which have been recognised nationally by his position as a government adviser and former Minister of Cabinet rank on top of his meteoric career in Italian academic life, and internationally by his many assignments with international agencies and professional organisations. I have benefited enormously from his intellectual prowess and continue to enjoy our mutual adventures into unwonted areas of economic investigation. The untimely death of Jack deprived me and many others of the pleasant ordeal of running the gauntlet of his critical appraisal and of a plan to round off our studies of the growth in public expenditure. Although we engaged in a form of creative tension over a period of 35 years, which he most generously acknowledges in his *Cost, Choice and Political Economy* (Edward Elgar, 1989, Chapter 1), it is only latterly that I have come to realise how crucial his views on costs and choice have become in my own thinking about the functions of markets. He concluded Chapter 1 of this last work with the words 'academics are lucky people', but this is only true if you have known colleagues like Francesco and Jack himself.

Alan Peacock

Acknowledgements

The author and publishers wish to thank the following who have kindly given permission for the use of copyright material.

Aberdeen University Press, Aberdeen for: Chapter 7, 'Foreword to David Hume's *Political Discourses*' from Douglas Mair (ed.) (1993), *The Scottish Tradition in Economic Thought*, pp. 233–48.

Atlantic Economic Journal for: Chapter 9, 'The LSE and post-war economic policy', *Atlantic Economic Journal*, **10** (1), (1982), 35–40; Chapter 12, 'The disaffection of the taxpayer', *Atlantic Economic Journal*, **10** (1), (1982), 7–15.

Economic Journal for: Chapter 22, 'The credibility of economic advice to government', *Economic Journal*, **102** (September 1992), 1213–22.

Elsevier Science Publishers, Amsterdam for: Chapter 5, 'Liberalism and economic growth' from A. Szirmaie, B. van Ark and D. Pilat (eds) (1993), *Explaining Economic Growth: Essays in Honor of Angus Maddison*, pp. 413–27.

D.C. Heath, Lexington, Mass. for: Chapter 19, 'The political economy of devolution: the British case' from Wallace E. Oates (ed.) (1976), *The Political Economy of Fiscal Federalism*, pp. 49–63.

Institute of World Economics, Kiel, with the support of the Bertelsmann Stiftung, the Heinz Nixsdorf Stiftung and the Ludwig Erhard Stiftung for: Chapter 10, 'The justification for progressive taxation' from Horst Siebert (ed.) (1996), *Sozialpolitik auf dem Prufstand*, J.C.B. Mohr (Paul Siebeck), Tübingen, pp. 197–223.

International Review of Law and Economics for: Chapter 14, 'Bargaining and the regulatory system' (with Martin Ricketts) (1986), *International Review of Law and Economics*, **6**, 3–16.

Korean Society for Journalism and Communication Studies and Seoul Broadcasting Foundation, Seoul for: Chapter 21, 'The political economy of public service broadcasting' from (1995), *The Future of Broadcasting: Policies, Programming and Management*.

Longman, London and New York for: Chapter 6, 'Welfare philosophies and welfare finance' from Thomas Wilson and Dorothy Wilson (eds) (1991), *The State and Social Welfare,* pp. 37–54.

Macmillan, London for: Chapter 2, 'Economic freedom' from (1987), *The New Palgrave: A Dictionary of Economics, Volume 2,* pp. 88–93; Chapter 4, 'The value of freedom of expression' from Ali El-Agraal (ed.) (1993), *Public and Industrial Economics: Essays in Honour of Hiro Shibata,* St Martin's Press, pp. 10–19; Chapter 8, 'Keynes and the role of the state' from D. Crabtree and A.P. Thirlwall (eds) (1993), *Keynes and the Role of the State,* St Martin's Press, pp. 3–32.

OECD, Paris for: Chapter 18, 'Designing tax reform: identifying the problems' from (1991), *The Role of Tax Reform in Central and Eastern European Countries,* pp. 267–72.

Public Choice for: Chapter 23: 'The utility-maximising government economic adviser: a comment', *Public Choice,* **80** (1994), 191–7.

Public Finance for: Chapter 16, 'Government debt and growth in public spending' (with Ilde Rizzo), *Public Finance,* **XXXXII** (2), (1987), 283–90.

Royal Bank of Scotland for: Chapter 20, 'The "politics" of investigating broadcasting finance' from *Royal Bank of Scotland Review* (March 1987), 3–16.

Springer Verlag, Berlin and Heidelberg for: Chapter 11, 'The rise and fall of the Laffer curve' from D. Bos and B. Felderer (eds) (1989), *The Political Economy of Progressive Taxation,* pp. 25–40; Chapter 15, 'Public X-inefficiency: informational and institutional constraints' from Horst Hanusch (ed.) (1983), *Anatomy of Government Deficiencies,* pp. 125–38.

Wayne State University Press, Detroit, Michigan for: Chapter 13, 'Economic analysis of problems of government selective aid' (with Martin Ricketts) from (1989), *Public Finance and the Performance of Enterprises,* Proceedings of the 43rd Congress of the International Institute of Public Finance 1987, pp. 197–209; Chapter 17, 'Fiscal theory and the "market" for tax reform' from F. Forte and K. Roskamp (eds) (1981), *The Reform of the Tax System,* pp. 11–20.

Every effort has been made to trace all the copyright holders, but if any have been inadvertently overlooked, the publishers will be pleased to make the necessary arrangement at the first opportunity.

Introduction

1. The promotion of economic freedom

I. INTRODUCTION

In 1979 I published a collection of papers under the general title of *The Economic Analysis of Government*. It followed the golden rule of tripartite form. The first part was essentially a defence of liberalism against the predations of Paretian welfare economics which I had previously explored with Charles Rowley in our book, *Welfare Economics: A Liberal Re-Interpretation* (1975), and the second part offered analyses of actual government policies using the common discourse amongst economists. The third part had an institutional economics flavour about it because it described my experiences as a government economic adviser, i.e. as a decision-maker maximizing a welfare function (which included professional pride as an argument!) subject to political and administrative constraints. The reviews were surprisingly favourable and I particularly savour the comment of the anonymous reviewer in *The Economist* that my essays would 'help to restore the subject's good name' when many economists might have claimed that my incursions into political questions did precisely the opposite. My publisher put me in my place when he finally decided that the book might be risked in a paperback edition for he was 'constantly surprised by how well my books sold'. (Remember that he was an economics publisher for whom 'success' probably meant a sale reaching four figures!)

I follow the same format in this volume, but the content requires me to be more specific about how I view my position as a liberal (in the British sense) economist. This is because, compared with twenty years ago, we are now two-a-penny. It was not difficult then to differentiate one's product at the risk of being regarded as eccentric. One has only to examine the attitudes to those in policy debate in the UK and elsewhere to the productions of the Institute of Economic Affairs, a body with which I have been connected for over thirty years. Thirty years ago, press and political comment on the IEA's work offered, with outstanding exceptions, ritualistic excoriation of its criticisms of the operation of the welfare state, the size and efficiency of government, the lack of commitment to competition etc. and of its championship of the liberty of the individual. Today, if the IEA has a problem it is that of being the victim of its own success. The acceptance of liberalist ideas amongst professional economists, politicians and governments is almost an embarrassment. Moreover, intellectual support rolls in from moral philosophers – a breed of intellectual animal almost rendered extinct by its own efforts at self-destruction – and converts to such policy measures as privatisation extend to the entire globe. One may be forgiven for feeling like the don in Evelyn Waugh's *Scott-King's Modern Europe* who was a little known authority on an obscure Balkan poet. When the poet was adopted as the national hero of an emerging Communist state, the don's work came into great prominence, and his reaction was to feel that this was a gross intrusion into his privacy. Or, as speculative thinkers have warned one over the centuries, when your ideas become popular, consider the strong possibility that they are wrong!

It would be immoral to desert one's liberalist ideals because they had, perhaps only temporarily, become popular, but the fact of their popularity must lead one to consider how far one has something distinctive to say about economic freedom which is so closely associated with a liberalist position and about the problems encountered in establishing a society which embodies liberalist principles. In what follows, I have emphasized, albeit indirectly, that, no longer on the defensive, liberal thinkers must avoid three temptations which I illustrate largely in respect of economic problems, that is within the compass of my trade.

II. THREE TEMPTATIONS

The first temptation to avoid is clothing oneself in the trappings of triumphalism which can so easily lead to the adoption of an illiberal position in intellectual discourse on fundamental ideas. Crusading under the banner that 'those who are not with us are against us' is understandable when there is a threat to the dissemination of liberal ideas, but when credibility is well established, there must always be open and well-tempered discussion with sceptics. This must be so for the very good reason that when content is given to liberal ideas, particularly in respect of the 'good society' that is seen as desirable, there is room for disagreement amongst liberals themselves, and the individual freedom that is at the core of liberalism entails tolerance of voluntary adherence to illiberal – and usually hierarchical – institutions within that society. I discuss this matter further, with respect to economic freedom, in Chapter 2.

The second temptation is to rely on the moral authority now accredited to liberalist ideas in order to dispute the need for most forms of government intervention in the market and to bias the production of analytical and empirical evidence to demonstrate it. I could hardly be accused of ignorance of the limitations of government action, and several of the chapters in Part II use rigorous economic analysis to demonstrate the dimensions of government rather than market failure. I place particular emphasis on the need to use models which postulate bargaining situations which arise in the interaction between those in charge of implementing government measures and the individuals and organisations that these measures are designed to influence. At the same time, I am critical of attempts to prove that economic freedom, defined broadly in terms of the degree of government intervention, inevitably induces a superior performance in the economy, as such performance is conventionally measured. More particularly, I have taken a very critical view of attempts to prove that there is some unique relation between tax rates and tax yields which would support the famous Laffer curve, which has excited those seeking some automatic means of limiting the size of tax revenue as a means of controlling the growth in government expenditure. It might fairly be claimed that I have biased my selection of papers to those which emphasize the limitations of government action, particularly those plagued by the problem of asymmetric information, but that is the result of the forces of demand rather than supply. Most of the papers in this collection were responses to requests to write on specific issues and not exercises in speculative production running the gauntlet of the rigorous refereeing of professional journals. By his scepticism of the efficiency of government shall ye know him. I attempt to remedy this bias somewhat in later sections of this chapter.

The third temptation is found in the argument that one has no responsibility with respect to the implementation of the policies that one advocates. The campaign for limiting the size of government in the name of economic freedom stops, as it were, when the thinking behind it is in the public domain, through publication widely available to those who form opinion and those most affected by the proposals themselves, the public at large. There is certainly a strong argument based on the doctrine of comparative advantage that this gives political economists enough to do, for it assumes that they not only have ideas but are both willing and able to promulgate them in a palatable form. Long may this remain so. This argument may be buttressed by the recognition of the high opportunity cost attached to monitoring the progress or lack of it in the acceptability of one's proposals and in trying in some practical way to implement them at the invitation of those who may be in a position to do so. No criticism is advanced here of those who do not have the stomach for this activity. But people I admire greatly, such as James Buchanan, the late Harry Johnson and Arthur Seldon, have regarded close involvement in the design of policy measures compatible with their ideas as tantamount to treating with the enemy and risking being corrupted by the wily ways of bureaucrats and politicians. I not only do not share this view but, as I have already indicated, I believe that if one has at least the occasional opportunity to be involved in policy design, where one's skills and experience may be influential, then refusal on grounds of the risks of being compromised is to give in to the worse temptation of denying one's commitment as well as to claim that political economists necessarily lack the moral fibre to hold their own. I offer evidence below that economists have skills which enable one to help to delineate the path as well as the goal of particular policies, but this is not to say that they should commit themselves to the path actually chosen and to compromises which take it in the wrong direction (see Chapters 22 and 23). It may be claimed that one is bound to lose both the battles and the war against bureaucrats when one's policy measures demand reduction in the scope of their activities, but better to have advised and to have lost than not to have advised at all.

While these themes are illustrated in later chapters, it may be useful to consider somewhat further the general issues that they raise about the promotion of economic freedom and personal freedom in general, most of which require a survey of one's views about the relation between the government and the performance of the market. However convinced one may be, like the author, that the promotion entails a major extension of the use of the market as a guide to the structure and development of the economy, it is rather disturbing to find such exaggerated claims being made for the 'victory over socialism'. It is contrary to the Classical liberal tradition which adopts a position of no more than cautious optimism about the achievements of any human institution. That tradition also emphasizes that there are important preconditions for the successful operation of the market economy which might even require positive action by the government itself. Their views have been amply justified in the difficulties encountered with privatization of state monopolies without adequate provision for ensuring that competitive conditions can be created through freedom of entry or can be simulated in a sensible fashion. Another way of 'differentiating' my product is in examining more closely the implicit assumption in attempts to increase economic freedom giving greater scope to market forces so that when it falls down on the task, the market itself promotes methods by which its own failures are removed. I shall now develop this theme with reference to 'standard' objectives that are identified by liberals themselves as elements in a 'freedom index' such as the sovereignty of the consumer, the pursuit of economic growth and the distribution of income.

III. THE SOVEREIGNTY OF THE CONSUMER

Let me begin with an old friend: the maximization of consumer satisfaction. There are two dispositions of liberalist economists which illustrate their attacking spirit. The first is that maximization of consumer satisfaction is largely identical with consumer sovereignty – consumers are the best guardians of their own interests. This is an old argument, but it keeps cropping up in unwonted places. It has become central to the recent debate on broadcasting, in which I have been closely involved, concerning the extent to which listeners and viewers should be free to watch what they want. The erosion of the paternalist position has not been effected simply by the winning of a philosophical argument about the capabilities of the consumer, but by the analytical attack on bureaucracy by public choice theorists. The modelling of bureaucratic motivation coupled with empirical testing has been designed to demonstrate that, far from being the impartial spectators able to identify our interests for us and the guardians of our economy and culture motivated solely by public-spiritedness, public servants seek their own personal ends. It would be awkward if this were wholly true because if, as it implies, there are circumstances in which consumers themselves recognise that state intervention is necessary, i.e. there is some market failure, how is 'government failure' to be prevented?

Consumer choice exercised through the market is normally identified as the instrument for achieving sovereignty but in this instance, too, liberalist economists have attacked very strongly those who have assumed that their position entails a policy directed towards attaining some static general equilibrium position with perfect competition. For example, 'New Left' writers have responded to the problem that they have had to face as a result of events in Eastern Europe by claiming that the Walrasian equilibrium is both undesirable and unobtainable, with the underlying assumption that such an equilibrium represents an optimal position for supporters of the free market. This is a common error not confined to the New Left and it is all the more paradoxical that liberalist writers also regard a general equilibrium position similarly if for different reasons. This, position is unobtainable because the spur of competition to match what consumers want with what producers can supply can only operate through a process of disequilibrium in which ever-changing preferences of buyers of products and services require entrepreneurs to continually adjust their actions to survive as profit takers. It is undesirable because such adjustment would not be achieved unless entrepreneurs are stimulated to introduce process and product innovations through the threat of potential competition, in which firms are not simply passive adjusters to price. This rehabilitation of an essentially Austrian position changes the emphasis in competition policy away from preventing or regulating monopolies and mergers with reference primarily to market shares towards improving opportunities for reducing the costs of contestability in their markets through, for example, promoting freedom of entry. This has become a particularly important element in ensuring that privatization of public utilities does not simply substitute private for public monopoly.

Even those critics of free markets who have emphasized that microeconomic analysis of markets understates the importance of transaction costs have been bypassed by a subtle argument. Margaret Thatcher, for example, has had strong support from moral philosophers who have emphasized the ethical foundations of markets. Contractual arrangements over time and space, involving countless individuals and organizations who may never meet, presuppose mutual trust, the keeping of promises and common interest in resolving disagreements and disputes. Indeed the spur of competition and the need to minimise costs have stimulated Voluntary Dispute Resolution (VDR) so eliminating the necessity for recourse to expensive court actions, and relying more on a 'moral contract' to abide by arbiters' decisions.

Why then am I somewhat uneasy about the attempt of free market economists to capture the moral high ground? The clue lies in this last reference to VDR. Most of the discussions I have seen about the moral foundations of capitalism relate to contracts between those who are roughly equal in economic power, who have continuing economic relations with each other and see reputation for probity as good commercial sense. But this is a relationship characteristic of business to business contact. Does it apply in the case of relations between producers and final consumers?

There are respectable arguments which support the view that, provided that there is competition assured by freedom of entry, consumers will be adequately protected, even when explicit contracts with producers are too difficult or too costly to draw up. Consumers make mistakes in matching their preferences to their purchases, but these can be eliminated quickly in the case of repeated purchases, such as those made every day, and where misspecification of the product causes the consumer to be dissatisfied, then, with alternative sources of supply, the consumer can punish the producer by taking custom elsewhere. But in the cases described the search costs may be low and the information received a reasonably accurate guide to future purchases.

There are clearly purchases of a 'lumpy' character that do not fit with this description. The consumer is at a double disadvantage with 'once-and-for-all' purchases where the information on their contribution to consumer welfare is difficult to assess in advance of purchase and the financial commitment may be a large part of current income. In such a category may be placed the very goods and services that those in favour of privatization of government services would want to be purchased through the market rather than financed out of taxation. If consumers are urged to own their own homes financed by mortgages, to make their own pension and life assurance provision instead of relying on state insurance systems, to pay directly for education and health services, and to invest in share capital – in return, of course, for lower taxes – then costly, even tragic, errors may be made if they rely on rectifying mistakes through learning solely from experience.

Consider the privatization of social security. Lifetime saving to provide income protection and to cover dependants is much encouraged by supporters of the market economy, but the financial commitment can be large, and contracts with insurance providers will cover long periods of time over which there will be uncertainty about the value of the investment and the ability to meet contractual premium payments out of uncertain future earnings. The insuree is highly dependent on information and advice, but evaluating that information is difficult when its quality will not be apparent until the insurance policies are activated. In competitive situations, insurers will have an incentive to provide information as a joint product but have no incentive to offer such information on rivals' products. The insuree is highly dependent on indirect evidence, notably the reputation for quality and fair dealing of the suppliers.

Writers of a liberalist stamp with Neo-Austrian sympathies, myself included, may argue that 'the market abhors a vacuum', and that where situations of the kind described arise, the 'gap' in the market will be filled by spontaneous institutional innovations designed to encourage trust and confidence in provision of goods and services and to improve consumer knowledge at minimum cost. Producers may find it in their own interests to agree on codes of conduct designed to increase consumer confidence, which seems desirable unless any such agreement is used as a barrier to entry. Consumers may combine together in co-operative enterprises or support consumer organisations which test and advise on products as a means for reducing the risk of unfortunate choices.

The removal of 'market failure' by market forces themselves is likely to take place only gradually and the period of adjustment necessary is unlikely to coincide with the short time horizon of those whose expectations have been disappointed and with that of the policy-makers whom they will expect to rectify matters. Not surprisingly, as public choice analysis would predict, the survival of governments committed to privatization on a considerable scale requires them to enclose their market creations in a regulatory framework which is often as complex as it is strict. Such short-term reactions to the sluggishness of market forces are fully understandable and their consequences need to be closely analysed by liberalist writers. They should first of all analyse the effects of regulation, with a view to recommending regulatory regimes which minimise side effects, such as costs of compliance, and investigate how eventually such regimes may be dispensed with or at least turned into self-regulatory systems. Such unglamorous activities hardly appeal to those who derive professional satisfaction and possibly reward from examining profounder issues in political economy which may specify some noble end but not the stony path to reach it. However, perhaps market forces will come to dictate that fewer economists will be required to spend their time on high theory requiring more of them to seek employment where they will have to dirty their hands!

IV. GROWTH AND MARKET PERFORMANCE

It could be argued that the object of achieving some 'satisfactory' rate of economic growth is not a necessary element in the list of desirable aims consistent with a liberalist position. Growth is simply an outcome of individual work and savings patterns. Indeed, any idea of an 'optimal rate of growth' has no meaning. Individuals should not be accountable to 'society' for their actions, once the rule of law is established. It is contrary to a liberalist philosophy to impose some collective saving objective which would be necessary to pursue some target rate of growth set by government.

However, even if a liberalist point of view denies the necessity for defining a collective goal in the form of growth targets, it is interesting to observe how much more confident free market economists have become that, in the long run, economic freedom is a necessary condition for achieving high rates of economic growth. In our professional lifetime, international organisations such as ECE produced evidence of much higher rates of growth in Eastern Europe than in Western Europe, which buttressed theories of economic growth that emphasized the size of the capital stock as the crucial factor. Though the data and its interpretation might be suspect, this produced the defensive reaction that a higher standard of living produced by forced saving and labour was too high a price to pay by those who value economic and political freedom.

Broadly speaking, growth models became a casualty of practical action taken in their name, notably in attempts to raise the investment ratio and in lowering the capital/output ratio without regard to the need to put in place measures to promote efficiency in the use of resources. A professional reaction in favour of models that reflect the aims and actions of economic actors was therefore inevitable.

I say 'reaction', but, in essence, a liberalist view of the growth process has existed since Adam Smith analysed the process by which profit-seeking entrepreneurs look for investment opportunities and exploit endogenous improvements in technology, spurred on by competition. One can demonstrate that his model competes in sophistication with modern growth models, but is much more specific about the role of government: (i) remove barriers to competition, notably barriers to communication; (ii) keep the growth of the public sector in check to prevent the reduction in saving through increasing tax burdens; and (iii) relate effort to reward in the public as well as the private sector. I consider the liberalist view of growth modelling in Chapter 5 below.

We owe to Herbert Giersch a formidable elaboration of the Classical doctrine, an English version of which may be found in his Wincott lecture, published by the Institute of Economic Affairs in 1986, 'Liberalisation for Faster Economic Growth'. Although tied to the discussion of faster growth in the EC, his recommendations apply in a much wider context: (i) competition is the spur to economic progress in a world of uncertainty and imperfect knowledge; and inducements to make product and process innovations must be kept in place whatever the perceived short-term gains from encouraging or allowing firms to merge or to cartelize in order to achieve economies of scale. It follows (ii) that free international competition must be fostered and forces to weaken competition, such as industrial subsidies which supposedly support innovations (which would be undertaken anyway), must be eliminated; and (iii) official 'growth targets' of an overall or sectoral nature are unnecessary and should be left to individual concerns; and likewise within an EC context (iv) countries should be left with freedom to choose their mix of direct and indirect taxes, presumably provided that these were not designed to distort international competition. These proposals reflect analytical rigour and a clear programme of action, which is more than can be said about 'growthmanship' in general. (See further Chapter 5 below.)

An implicit assumption in the argument for competition as the engine of growth is that the capital market works efficiently. The tendency in 'grand design' models of economic growth is to make the actors in this market into shadowy figures. There are individual investors who supply individual entrepreneurs with capital, whereas in reality capital is supplied by institutional investors who muster the savings of individuals, and its transformation into capital is organized by managers rather than by its owners. Once again one encounters the 'agency problem' in markets, a problem which exercised Adam Smith in his strictures on the operations of joint stock companies. For example, the monitoring of managerial activities of firms employing shareholders' funds in order to minimize managerial rent-seeking requires the identification of the appropriate information which acts as a check on these activities and appropriate control mechanisms. Shareholders may neither have the expertise to identify relevant information nor be willing to incur the costs of acquiring it. Additionally, seeking control through voting rights encounters the further costs of organising a change in management.

Can a potential 'market failure' of this kind be automatically corrected by the market? Clever financial economists assure us that competitive forces are sufficiently strong to control managerial rent-seeking, because if capital is being inefficiently used, companies will be threatened with takeover. If one wants a good example of 'triumphalism', it may be found in the highly sophisticated analysis, backed by empirical studies, of takeovers which have influenced governments in their attempts to free international capital markets from extensive control. The official British government view, for example, is, broadly speaking, that takeovers are a 'sign of economic vitality' and the only major policy issue to which they give rise is whether takeovers and associated mergers reduce the degree of competition.

British experience may not be typical, but a series of investigations, including one which I conducted fairly recently, offers little evidence that takeovers operate as a superior form of monitoring device. There is a double agency problem because, as well as the uncertainties attached to putting more efficient management in place, the motives of institutional investors may be mixed, notably in preferring to make short term gains in share values rather than to use their power to ensure that the capital resources that they supply will be efficiently used.

I am not arguing that there should be extensive regulation of capital markets, other than that necessary to prevent fraud and to promote fair dealing. On the contrary, market economists should devote more attention to such matters as company law and taxation measures which exacerbate the agency problem by favouring corporate enterprises. In particular, their own emphasis on the importance of contestability of markets suggests removing barriers to entry by new and growing firms, so challenging the position of entrenched companies relying on takeovers for expansion. Again, I have to emphasize that investigations leading to suitable proposals require skills which are at a discount with those who would prefer to be working at the frontiers of economic knowledge!

V. EQUITY AND THE MARKET

I need hardly repeat the arguments that are mustered against equality in the distribution of income and wealth by liberal economists – the principle itself is 'unjust' because effort is divorced front reward, its achievement in practice would destroy incentives to produce wealth (killing the goose that lays the golden eggs) and involves draconian redistributory measures that inflame class conflict and destroy individual freedom and initiative. There are many variations on these themes but the interesting point about their contemporary repetition is their articulation within the context of social policy by a wide spectrum of social scientists, including even sociologists!

However, when it comes to identifying what liberals are 'for' rather than against, so far as income distribution is concerned, they hardly speak with one voice. A useful starting point in this discussion is to view the market as a distributing agent. One recalls how at the end of the nineteenth century, influential economists considered that justice in income distribution was attained when factors were rewarded according to their marginal productivity. This got them into a lot of trouble for they were according ethical status to what was essentially an analytical proposition about microeconomic behaviour under competition. No wonder that they were regarded as apologists for capitalism. Something of the spirit of this approach survives in the 'broader-gauged approach to economic justice' advanced by Kirzner and others, which attaches particular significance to the nature of and necessity for profits as a reward for the 'primordial' efforts of entrepreneurs, offering then, as it were, a prior claim on the 'cake'.

It is clear that if we followed this position through to its logical conclusion then the problem arises about the 'reward' to be attributed to those who cannot market their skills in the market or are unwilling to do so. To imply that they deserve nothing and should starve must surely shake the confidence of even the most committed marginalist to marginal productivity as an ethical principle. One answer, of course, is to argue that the 'original' distribution resulting from the marginal rule does not determine the final distribution, which will depend on how individuals allocate their income, which can include voluntary redistribution through private charities. The market, as it were, does not correct market failure, but can be the effective instrument for reflecting individual, voluntaristic impulses to help the unfortunate.

There is an implicit acceptance in this argument that any market distribution of income must somehow be modified to provide at least a minimum standard of living. The basic question over which reasonable persons can differ is whether and to what extent this requires state intervention – an old but still important issue. Voluntary redistribution is too haphazard a method and, if it reflects the tastes and preferences of the better-off individuals, major gaps would be left in the provision for the unfortunate. Those who benefit may do so not solely because of the merits of their case but because of the skills of public relations consultants employed by charities to raise money. Furthermore, unless the charity is in the form of a co-operative in which poorer persons can help themselves, voluntary effort can veer towards being solely a way of relieving poverty and not become a positive force to help people to get out of the poverty 'trap'. Finally, what have been called 'charity contracts' with the poor are not binding on the relatively rich, who may 'free-ride', enjoying the benefits of help by others given to the less fortunate while not being obliged to pay; and, in a large nation-state, relative anonymity ensures that no one need know that they are not paying!

It is very easy to reject this argument, and to demonstrate conclusively that liberalist political economy is compatible with quite radical policy measures, with growing emphasis on lifetime income distribution through the creation of individual 'savings accounts' partly funded by government and by liberalization of pension provision so that individuals have more freedom in the time pattern of premium payment and can take out private pensions of a prescribed standard. The name of the game is 'self-reliance with a helping hand', and it appears to be in vogue even with those who have been strong supporters in the past of the welfare state.

However, we should not be diverted from considering the long-term aims of a liberalist society, namely that individuals are given as much opportunity as possible to plan their lives and to exploit their talents with as little help as possible from the public authorities, though with the guarantee that such help is forthcoming where it is strictly necessary. This points towards two vital areas in which the market can play a crucial role.

Measures of income distribution used in the debate on vertical equity normally only consider income at a point in time, and this 'snapshot' view clearly gives very little indication of relative economic circumstances. In the UK the 'poverty line' is conventionally fixed at household incomes which are below half the mean income, but this places in poverty a large part of the student population who borrow and/or are supported by relatives thus increasing their disposable income and in the expectation that investment in education will pay off in higher lifetime incomes and/or more satisfying employment. Similarly, a fair proportion of self-employed starting in business or those making temporary losses are to be found below the poverty line. While there must be those who never get out of the poverty trap, it is clear that those in the categories mentioned see the market as the principal method for implementing individual plans to reallocate their resources through time. Therefore, it is reasonable to claim that the more efficiently the market works, the greater the opportunity that exists for 'upward mobility'. Policies designed to remove restrictions on entry into industrial and professional occupations, designed, that is to say, to make the market cure what is commonly regarded as a market failure, have some role to play, alongside social 'rescue operations'. Of course the market penalizes failure as well as rewarding success, but at least making it work more efficiently should raise living standards generally, offering the prospect of more resources available to help the unfortunate.

Notwithstanding the scepticism concerning private voluntary redistribution as the counterpart to a market solution to achieving an equitable income distribution, institutions offering help' to those in need, and which offer the opportunity for those who seek income protection to help themselves, still act as an important supplement to statutory means for relieving poverty. Indeed, their activities have stimulated some economists to argue that, had the welfare state not taken over a large part of their functions, such institutions would have been more effective instruments for social policies designed to relieve poverty and to stimulate lifetime saving, because they would be more knowledgeable of and sensitive to individual circumstances and aspirations. The market in the narrow sense as way of co-ordinating economic decisions may not correct its own failure to guarantee minimum standards of living, but it can still be an effective instrument through which preferences can be expressed to help the poor and unfortunate and to promote self-help by the funding and management of voluntary bodies. In the UK, where considerable concern has been expressed by both politicians and the professions directing and administering social policy at the insensitivity endemic in a social security system which has to work to general rules, much more attention has now to be paid to the role of voluntary organizations such as housing associations, mutual insurance companies and religious foundations – not only as suppliers of supplementary support but as the monitors of the state system itself; and now it is being suggested that such organizations should take over a large part of the administration of the state-financed system through 'contracting-out' arrangements. Such pluralism of institutions is an essential element in a liberal society, and it is worth passing mention that the lack of a broad spectrum of them in a country like Russia is a major worry. Radical economic reform is all very well but it produced major changes in the distribution of income and wealth which a centralized social security system with a constrained budget cannot rectify to the extent necessary to make such reform minimally acceptable. There are no non-governmental institutions of the kind described to deal with abject poverty or to help those who might avoid it by setting up a small business. When I chaired the UN Mission to Russia to advise on this problem, it was striking to find that the Orthodox Church had no tradition of social service and that the nearest but hardly equivalent institutions were the Communist Party and the Army, i.e. centralized institutions designed to look after only previously privileged sections of the community.

VI. CONCLUDING REMARKS

I have indicated that I am very sympathetic to the proposition that the market can be a signalling device of much greater sophistication than the mathematical modelling of much of contemporary microeconomic analysis suggests and one which can reveal quickly where corrective action may be required to overcome 'agency problems'. My experience as a government adviser, such as it is, also makes me sceptical of much analysis which identifies market failure and then postulates corrective action by government based on the naive assumption that action by the latter is devoid of the very agency problems that it is designed to solve. At the same time, I have given instances of cases where the spontaneous action by the market to rectify its own failures cannot produce solutions in which there are 'prizes for all' and where the length of the 'rectification' lag may be longer than those affected by market failures may be prepared to tolerate. The obvious case is that of Russia, where the distributional changes alone have been underemphasized by Western advisers and suppliers of capital, and have been sufficient to make capitalistic solutions manifestly suspect by the public.

However, it does little to promote the case for economic freedom to claim a minimalist role for government, and to avoid facing up to the problems created by the process of privatizing public utilities and government services to achieve that end. This would not only be contrary to the tradition of Classical Political Economy which, in willing the end of 'natural liberty', envisaged situations where, in certain circumstances, which could change through time, the means for achieving the end would require positive action by government. The contemporary importance of this is illustrated in the sophisticated choices that are expected of individuals precisely as a consequence of privatization in respect of the education of their children, and the provision made for housing, sickness, unemployment and old age in times when job security may be a thing of the past. As I have emphasized, reducing the information and learning costs associated with the growing sophistication expected in individual decision-making can justify regulatory provisions at least in the short term. The challenge to liberalist thinkers is how to ensure that, when these provisions have served their purpose, they can be dismantled, and to determine how this can be done. Insofar as I have considered these matters in this volume, I make no claim to know precisely how this should be done, other than in areas in which I have some personal experience. I am all too well aware, as those chapters concerned with regulatory matters indicate, of the difficulties encountered.

Promotion of economic freedom entails a view to be taken about persuading people of its benefits. Moreover the very essence of liberalism is that measures to promote economic freedom should be based on consent. Obtaining that consent must not be based on a crooked prospectus which claims that Nirvana is round the corner if individual choice is expanded. Also, the laying out of an honest prospectus by those of a liberal disposition must carry with it the obligation to point towards alternative economic philosophies or at least not to indulge in 'percussive advertising' designed to induce the reader to 'avoid worthless substitutes', but this will no doubt be regarded as a counsel of perfection. Above all, an honest prospectus must emphasize that an economic doctrine only offers a rough-and-ready guide to the institutional arrangements that further its ends. The most important task in promotion is to improve the disposition towards a society relying more on its members engaged in voluntary co-operation to solve its economic and social problems. As Anthony de Jasay has said, very wisely, 'the most one can hope for in this respect is to improve the odds' (*Choice, Contract, Consent: A Restatement of Liberalism*, IEA, 1991, p. 123).

PART I

Political economy

2. Economic freedom

(I owe it to the reader to offer a definition of economic freedom. This I have done as succinctly as possible in this chapter, the word limitation of which was decided by the editors of The New Palgrave. *I am grateful to them – and so may the reader be – that I had to undergo this test of brevity. Confining myself to what I regard as the essential elements in economic freedom saves me unnecessary repetition in later chapters when I expand some of the issues raised here. In any case, the unsatisfied reader may care to explore some of the references given at the end of this chapter, including, possibly, my earlier work with Charles Rowley on welfare economics. But much has been written about the dimensions of freedom, including economic freedom, since I penned this piece. I recommend in particular Anthony de Jasay's splendid* Choice, Contract, Consent: A Restatement of Liberalism *published by the Institute of Economic Affairs, London, in 1991, which I have already quoted in Chapter 1.)*

Economic freedom describes a particular condition in which the individual finds himself as a result of certain characteristics in his economic environment. Taking a simple formulation of decision-making in which it is assumed that the individual maximizes his satisfaction both as a consumer of private and government goods and services and as a supplier of factor services, his position may be depicted as follows:

$$\text{Max } U^i = U^i(x^i, q_k, a^i) \tag{2.1}$$

subject to

$$p_k^c \cdot x^i + T_k^i = Y^i = \varphi(a^i) = p_k^a \cdot a^i \tag{2.2}$$

where x^i is a vector of 'private goods', q_k is a vector of goods supplied by government, a^i is a vector of factor inputs, p_k^c is a vector of product prices for private goods, p_k^a is a vector of factor prices, T_k^i is net tax liability of individual ^{i} (tax obligation *less* transfers), Y^i is personal income before tax of individual ^{i} and subscript k denotes an exogenously determined variable.

Assuming the budget constraint (2.2) is exactly satisfied, the individual maximizes his satisfaction solving for the vector of private-goods consumption in terms of their prices, disposable income and predetermined levels of public goods available for consumption, where goods prices and factor prices, quantities of factor inputs and tax liabilities are either known or predicted by the individual.

Economic freedom requires that the various terms in the budget constraint reflect the absence of 'preference or restraint' (Adam Smith) on the individual. Therefore p_k^c is a vector of product prices which result from the operation of competitive market forces with the individual being free to choose between alternatives. Similarly, p_k^a must be characterized by competition in the factor market with the individual being 'free to bring both his industry and capital into competition with those of any other man or order of men' (Adam Smith). There is less certainty concerning the constraints placed on T_k and q_k. Some writers would argue that economic freedom requires a pre-established limit on the values of T_k and q_k either expressed or implied in a country's constitution (Nozick's 'minimal state'; see Nozick, 1974). Others would argue that within a system of democratic government it should be possible to devise voting systems through which individuals express their preferences for values of T_k and q_k which simulate if they do not replicate the competitive market in the private sector (see Buchanan, 1975). All agree, however, that economic freedom is not compatible with large values of T and q in relation to values of x^i, mainly because a large public sector increases the monopoly power of public servants both as suppliers of public goods and factor services to produce them and encourages the growth of private monopolies as a defence against public monopsony buying.

ECONOMIC FREEDOM AND LIBERTARIAN PHILOSOPHY

There are features of this attempt at a 'technical' definition which may be called in question and which must be considered later, but it will be recognizable to those economists who have elevated economic freedom to an important goal in its own right and have claimed that it is the most important means of ensuring that the economy develops at the right 'tempo'. Discussion of the usefulness of the concept of economic freedom, therefore, centres on these two libertarian propositions.

The first proposition is contained in a striking passage in Book III of J.S. Mill's Essay on Liberty:

> He who lets the world, or his own portion of it, choose his plan of life for him, has no need of any other faculty than the ape-like one of imitation. He who chooses to plan for himself, employs all his faculties. He must use observation to see, reasoning and judgment to foresee, activity to gain materials for decision, discrimination to decide and, when he has decided, firmness and self-control to hold to his deliberate decision

> ... It is possible that he might be guided on some good path, and kept out of harm's way, without any of these things. But what will be his comparative worth as a human being? It really is of importance, not only what men do, but also what manner of men they are that do it. (Mill, 1859)

The passage captures the essence of the libertarian view of the good society, clearly implying that it requires that individuals should accept the necessity for choosing and for recognizing their responsibility for making choices. It must simultaneously require that, to develop the capacity for choosing. individuals must have the widest possible freedom of choice in the acquisition and disposal of resources. Two further conclusions follow.

The only restriction on economic freedom experienced by the individual should be when such freedom harms others.

The individual is not accountable to society for his actions and this, together with the different and changing preferences of individuals, makes libertarians distance themselves from attempts to establish a 'social welfare function' (cf. Rowley and Peacock, 1975).

The second proposition maintains that economic freedom brings the added bonus of promoting the economic welfare of both the individual and of society. Economic freedom encourages the individual to 'better his condition' (Smith, 1776) by exploiting opportunities for specialization and gains from trade which will be fully realized through the spontaneous emergence of markets. Not only is economic freedom regarded as the only material condition compatible with human dignity but it is also a necessary condition for the economic growth of the economy and for its adjustment to the changing preference structures of its members in response to market forces. The market is a 'discovery process'(Hayek, 1979) in which participants adjust to change, giving rise to the notion of the 'invisible hand' which co-ordinates human economic actions automatically without recourse to government intervention. *Pace* Hahn (1982) and others, libertarians do not attach importance to a general equilibrium solution, attained by the operation of competitive market forces (cf. Barry, 1985). Indeed, though some exceptions will be noted below, it is claimed by supporters of the doctrine of economic freedom that disturbance of the natural process of exchange by government intervention assumes knowledge of the intricacies of the economy which is vouchsafed to no one, but there is no guarantee that officials, who maximize their private interests like everyone else, would be willing to maximize some social optimum even if they knew how to do so.

It was clearly recognized, by Hume and Smith for example, that for markets to work efficiently there must be a well-defined system of property rights and that costs of contracting between individuals in order to benefit from gains-from-trade would need to be minimized. The promotion of market efficiency was therefore bound to require some government intervention. No specialization or gains-from-trade would take place in a society in which there was no machinery for settling disputes and for preserving law and order. Acceptance of coercive intervention, however, requires that the 'rule of law' prevails. The law must be prospective and never retrospective in its operation, the law must be known and, as far as possible, certain, and the law must apply with equal force to all individuals without exception or discrimination. The state could also have a role in reducing the costs of contracting both by the removal of barriers to trade and to factor mobility and by the positive encouragement to the reduction in the costs of transport. In this latter respect Adam Smith supported reduction in the 'expense of carriage' by state financing of road building and supervision of financial methods to promote road maintenance and improvement.

At no stage therefore in the development of the doctrine of economic freedom, as understood by economists, was it regarded as synonymous with 'laissez-faire'. At the same time, the role of the state in respect of the promotion of economic freedom was and has remained strictly limited in libertarian thinking. Indeed, some modern libertarians devote much discussion to the possibilities of 'privatizing' even such traditional functions of the state as the maintenance of law and order.

SOME PROBLEMS RAISED BY THE CONCEPT OF ECONOMIC FREEDOM

The most obvious question posed to libertarians by those who are sceptical of their position is that the system of economic freedom is silent on the question of the distribution of property rights. In terms of our simple model, what principle should determine the values of $Y^1, \ldots, Y^i, \ldots, Y^n$ which, when aggregated, would describe some initial distribution of income as measured, say, by the shape of the Lorenz Curve? What reason have we for supposing that the 'optimal' distribution of income would emerge from the process of economic exchange between individuals?

The answer to this question does not find libertarians speaking with one voice. The problem is not one of principle, for the ultimate test to them is how far any government intervention represents a restriction of freedom. The problem is one of interpretation. It would be difficult today to find libertarians who would object to government intervention designed to assure protection to those who are severely deprived. Thus Hayek has argued that so long as 'a uniform minimum income is provided outside the market to all those who, for any reason, are unable to earn in the market an adequate maintenance, this need not lead to a restriction of freedom, or conflict with the Rule of Law'. This still leaves room for much disagreement among libertarians as to the precise level of the minimum and how to decide on who is entitled to receive it. Some supporters of the libertarian position, including the present author, would go much further and argue, along with J.S. Mill, that concentrations of wealth sustained over lengthy time periods can endanger economic freedom, not to speak of political freedom, by the association of such concentrations with the concentration of power of wealthy individuals over the less fortunate.

If the concept of economic freedom cannot embrace some precise guidance about the extent to which economic exchanges should be interfered with, it certainly places limits on the form of that interference. Thus libertarians, to the extent that they accept the need for a state-guaranteed minimum standard of living, prefer the use of money transfers to individuals rather than the provision of social services below or at zero cost, that is to say the economic condition of individuals in receipt of state support should be reflected in reduction in T_k^i (whose value may have to be negative) rather than an increase in q_k. Thus it is argued that individuals then retain responsibility for the purchase of goods and services designed to promote their own welfare and that the power of the state over the individual by bureaucratic dictatorship of preferences and by the lack of incentives in the public sector to economize in resource use is circumscribed.

A more severe test for the practicality of libertarian measures, designed to permit some redistribution without increasing the power of the state, arises in the case of any attack on the concentration of wealth. Clearly, a system of inheritance taxation which results in the transfer of capital from the private to the public sector would not conform to libertarian thinking, not only because this would discourage private saving but also because it would build up the power of the state. A system of taxation would have to be devised which not only did not discourage accumulation of private capital but also simultaneously encouraged legators to disseminate capital in favour of those with little capital. It is a long time since libertarians have plucked up the courage to try to develop such a system, given that eminent public finance specialists have failed in their attempts to fulfil these requirements.

The second major question arises from the persistent objection of Marxists and other socialist writers that the system of economic freedom, as depicted by the libertarians, fails to solve the problem of 'worker alienation'. It may be that the system of economic freedom can allow employees alone or in combination with others to influence the price of factor inputs (p_k^a)and the work/leisure combination (a^i), variables which play a crucial part in individual welfare. The fact remains that the system of property rights, which libertarians support, includes the individual ownership of capital and the use of capitalistic methods of production which imply an authority relationship between employer and worker. The hierarchical order at the place of work seems at complete variance with the independence of economic action attributed to the individual by the supporters of economic freedom.

Reactions to this argument by libertarians are sometimes reminiscent of the Scots preacher who, on recognizing a theological difficulty in his sermon, recommended his congregation to look the difficulty squarely in the face and pass it by. However, even socialist writers, notably the prominent Marxist Ota Sik (1974), have recognized that the alternative to market capitalism – collectivist production – does not solve the problem for it is not synonymous with democratization at the shop-floor level. In other words, the basis of alienation is technological and not institutional. Some libertarians, notably Mill, have made common cause with socialists by arguing that alienation must not be taken to be an inevitable consequence of productive activity. Mill sought one solution in the encouragement of firms owned and managed by the labour force, but still subject to competition. Utopian socialists have claimed that the only solution is to reject altogether the technology which imposes hierarchical relations in the first place. Both 'solutions' are still the subject of lively debate in both the professional and political arena.

REFERENCES

Barry, N.P. (1985), 'In Defense of the Invisible Hand', *The Cato Journal* 5(1), Spring, 133–48.

Buchanan, I.M. (1975), *The Limits of Liberty: Between Anarchy and Leviathan*, Chicago and London: University of Chicago Press.

Hahn, F. (1982), 'Reflections on the Invisible Hand', *Lloyds Bank Review*, 144, April, 1–21.

Hayek, F.A. (1979), *Law, Legislation and Liberty,* Vol. 3, London: Routledge & Kegan Paul; Chicago: University of Chicago Press.

Mill, J.S. (1859), *Essay on Liberty*, Oxford: Oxford University Press, 1942; Chicago: H. Regnery, 1955.

Mill, J.S. (1871), *Principles of Political Economy*, Book IV, ch. VII, Toronto: University of Toronto Press, *1965*.

Nozick, R. (1974), *Anarchy, State and Utopia*, Oxford: Basil Blackwell; New York: Basic Books.

Peacock, A. (1979), *The Economic Analysis of Government and Related Themes*, Oxford: Martin Robertson, chs 5 and 6; New York: St. Martin's Press, 1980.

Rowley, C. and Peacock, A. (1975), *Welfare Economics: A Liberal Restatement*, London: Martin Robertson.

Sik, O. (1974), 'The Shortcomings of the Soviet Economy as seen in Communist Ideologies', *Government and Opposition*, 9(3), 263–76.

Smith, A. (1776), *An Inquiry into the Nature and Causes of the Wealth of Nations*, Book IV, ch. 9 and Book V. Ed. R.H. Campbell, A.S. Skinner and W.B. Todd, Oxford: Clarendon Press, 1976; New York: Liberty Press, 1981.

3. Ethics, economics and the liberal order

I. INTRODUCTION

The export of ideas from West to East about the virtues of the market economy compared with the vices of Communist regimes was made with all the enthusiasm associated with a religious revival. The impression could easily have been gained that a rapid transition from collectivism to a market economy was not only desirable but also practicable. No person of liberal persuasion would wish to harbour the thought that the Russian people might not, eventually at least, appreciate the benefits of allocation of resources through efficiently working markets, but initially far from sufficient account was taken in Western-inspired schemes for economic reform of the high incidence of economic hardship that would result. It was certainly clear at the time of the introduction of the first privatization measures that there would be radical shifts in the distribution of income resulting from the opening up of markets.

Early in 1992, I headed up a UN Mission to Russia faced with the task of preparing, at breathtaking speed, an outline scheme designed to identify what measures of social protection might be necessary to accompany the rapid evolution of a market economy. (For details on terms of reference, membership etc., see Hay and Peacock, 1992.) It was taken for granted by the Mission that such measures would have to be devised so as to be compatible with increasing reliance on market forces. One would have to be able to demonstrate that the benefits of a freely working price system would benefit ordinary people by creating conditions in which individuals could help themselves. We would have to indicate how those who were casualties of economic change could be helped by a de-centralized system of social security which would give scope for voluntary action. In short, it would be impossible to engineer an acceptable transformation of the economy 'from above'. (For the controversy over methods of transformation, see Rodrick, 1996.)

What the Mission feared would happen, has happened. The market may have provided excellent opportunities for entrepreneurial initiatives, but it has also been associated in the public mind with Mafia-type operations which have besmirched the name of liberalist economics. Public opinion polls taken in 1992 at the time our Mission went to Moscow indicated majority support of a 'social market economy' of a Swedish or German type and therefore a critical acceptance of a liberalist economic and political regime, but now (1996) it is not clear that even that position might not eroded by those who have played on the fears of the Russians that Western ideas and practice are alien to their traditions and even their religion. Nor have Russian opponents of the market economy been slow in picking up the prevalent theme in the West that 'Thatcherism', while it may have struck a chord with ordinary people by emphasis on individual initiative, has become identified as a philosophy of greed reflected all too often in dubious practices. While that is hardly a fair assessment, the business world in the West has become sufficiently defensive about its operations, particularly those which involve the purchase and sale of companies, to support the fashionable intellectual discipline of business ethics. Prominent businessmen in the UK support government measures to regulate even their own business practices, though this may lead one to harbour the suspicion that meeting the costs of compliance with such regulations raises the costs of entry to potential competitors. On a somewhat higher intellectual plane, the New Left economists do not regard themselves as blown off course by events in Eastern Europe. While references to the historical inevitability of the collapse of capitalism seem to have disappeared from the professional literature, the attack on the market has continued in the form of its emphasis on opportunistic behaviour at the cost of trust and reciprocity (see, for example, Bowles and Gintis, 1993).

What can an economist of liberal persuasion say about these events and the criticisms of the market economy that are associated with them? An answer requires one to explore the relation between economics and ethics, which is the subject of Section II of this chapter. Then one can turn to the question of the liberalist perspective on ethics and its bearing on the appraisal of the market economy (Section III). I shall not attempt to compete with those who have cast doubt on the singling out of business as an activity in which ethical issues are of greater consequence than in other walks of life, notably in the incisive attack by Norman Barry (1991). I am more directly concerned, in the light of our attempt to outline a scheme of social protection for Russia, with the role of the market in the relief of poverty. I set my views, in Section IV, against the formidable criticisms of the market's performance made by Amartya Sen (1987), who has argued so persuasively for exploring the ethical dimension of human behaviour.

II. ECONOMICS, ETHICS AND POLITICAL ECONOMY

Economics claims to be a science. Hypotheses are formed about human behaviour concerned with the acquisition and disposal of resources. These hypotheses are regarded as testable. In essence, economics is 'value-free' and to be an economist does not entail the acceptance of any ethical position. An economist need not be precluded from evaluating how individuals and governments conduct their economic affairs, but the process of evaluation requires making judgments about the 'good society' which are not derived from economic analysis itself. Whether such judgments, embodying statements about human values, are themselves capable of being derived from 'objective analysis', which can be submitted to scientific methods of proof, is a matter for further discussion.

A liberal view of the organization of the economic system, broadly speaking, shows what roles are to be assigned to the individual and, by some system of consent, to the state. One must make clear what this view is, that is to say, one must clearly differentiate statements about values from statements about economic arrangements which reflect these values. This is normally described by economists as a distinction between 'normative propositions', which are non-verifiable, and 'positive statements' which, in principle, can be verified. I shall argue that this distinction has to be carefully explored if my purpose is to be achieved. The preliminary point may be made that the scientific validity claimed for economics itself depends on the acceptance by all economists of the moral precept of intellectual honesty, i.e. evidence must not be consciously suppressed or distorted.

The tradition of 'political economy', which forms a link between ethics and economics, has an honourable history. It may be claimed that it has been a major motive force in the development of economics as a scientific discipline. It is beyond the scope of this chapter to verify this statement, but it is incontrovertible that improvements in economic analysis have often been stimulated by the urge of economists to find a solution to some problem about the good society which worried them.

Ethics is concerned with the identification of human actions as 'right' and 'wrong'. The classification of actions in this way is often made with reference to some broad statement of principle about the goals of individuals as members of a society, such as 'we should aim for the greatest happiness of the greatest number' or 'individuals should be wholly responsible for their own actions', or 'God's will must be done'.

Clearly, individuals acting alone or in concert pay attention to moral precepts so that the study of ethics has a descriptive and analytical element to it. In other words, one can study ethical systems without having to evaluate them. The distinction is illustrated by the story of the Harvard Professor of Law who owned a summer house in Maine in a small community. It was some time before he was regarded as a fully-fledged member of the community and the signal to be such was to be invited to put his feet on the stove when a community meeting was held in the local general store. Eventually it was indicated to him that on a particular evening he might be so invited and, very excited, he arrived for the occasion to discover that a heated argument was in progress on the subject of baptism. Some were in favour and some very much against. He saw the dilemma approaching him. If he declared for one side or the other, he would give offence and be denied the final accolade of acceptance – putting his feet on the stove. At last, the question was put to him: 'Do you believe in baptism?' and all eyes turned towards him. He replied 'Believe in it? I have seen it done!' He was allowed to put his feet on the stove.

The typology of moral or ethical systems must certainly add to our knowledge of society and their systems of government. Indeed, an obvious link between ethics and economics is forged by the study of the influence of ethical conduct on the use of resources. It is interesting to note that the emphasis on an ethical dimension in the way individuals allocate their resources was a particular concern of liberal Classical economists, notably Adam Smith. In modern parlance, it is frequently contended that, in devising a utility function for an individual maximizing his/her satisfaction, we would miss a vital element in human behaviour if we did not embody an argument reflecting the satisfaction derived from concern for others. Therefore, to generalize the point, identifying economics with the study of 'materialist' behaviour is a mistake. Economists are bound to recognise that an individual's motivation is influenced by both the opinion of others and the effects of one's actions on others. However, a word of warning is necessary. To describe an 'interdependent utility function' as evidence of ethical behaviour may be to go too far. Further evidence is required as to whether an individual is following some moral imperative, such as 'we must help others', when there is an inter-personal transfer of resources. A more profound question still is what are the individual's motives for subscribing to the moral imperative itself and how these are to be evaluated with reference to some moral code. Is my behaviour 'more moral' if I conform to the code because of my conviction that it is right when I may conform simply because it is convenient or advantageous? Such a question is well outside the scope of economic investigation and is not an essential part of a study merely of the content of ethical systems. Nevertheless, it is one which has to be addressed.

The fact that what is regarded as moral behaviour appears to differ between societies and between groups within a given society seems to offer sufficient reason for accepting that value systems are subjective. However, a respectable line of argument used by some philosophers is that these differences may be more apparent than real. It could be claimed that at least the general objectives of ethical systems have distinct similarities as, for example, in the prevalence of the precept 'do as you would be done by'. The difference may lie in identifying the appropriate human actions which accord with these general objectives and which are manifested in differences in social and economic structure between societies. Although it may seem a superhuman task, it is possible to imagine that close investigation of these differences might lead to their resolution, in the same way as discovery of new facts and analytical developments are designed to resolve disagreements amongst scientists about cause and effect.

However, it would be a false step to argue that resolution of differences about moral ends and means for achieving them would confer any objective status on the result. We may detect a coherent pattern in human striving to achieve some moral end, but we could only conclude from the 'scientific' study of moral values that this might represent a *consensus*. However, the goal itself is independent of whether human beings seek to reach it or do not. Agreement about the goal and how to reach it merely represents a situation where the subjective judgments of individuals about moral goals happen to coincide.

Economists, understandably, on the whole have kept clear of philosophical discussion of the nature and status of value judgments. The result has been interesting. Although it has become widely accepted that statements about the 'welfare' of individuals in a community are normative, attempts have been made to confer a special status on particular value judgments, notably those associated with Paretian welfare economics. Thus a form of Paretian welfare economics has been supported (e.g. by Archibald and Hennipman – see Blaug, 1980) because it appears to *minimize* the normative propositions that need to be made. One 'trick' used by such authors is to argue that we do not need to invoke the assumption of 'consumer sovereignty' as a normative postulate in judging any particular economic arrangements. It is simply assumed that 'self-chosen' preferences are the ones that 'count', and we do not even have to argue that such preferences are translated into choices which reflect the 'real' interests of consumers. With this assumption before us, positive statements can be made about which economic arrangements conform to this preference system. Such is 'positive welfare economics' whereas actually doing something about this, such as invoking government policies to remove tariffs and promote competition, must be based on normative recommendations – such measures 'ought to be instituted'. It is not clear what purpose is served by this process of 'minimization', so long as it is agreed that policy recommendations are clearly labelled as value judgments. It is also entirely a subjective matter what weight is to be put on each component of a 'bundle' of value judgments representing 'good' policy objectives. An attempt to remove some of them from the 'bundle' does nothing to render the 'bundle' more 'value-free'.

Even if 'minimization' of the number of value judgments does nothing to fuse positive and normative economics in a form which would be universally acceptable, to economists at least, the view that Paretian postulates about welfare have some 'special' status is still widespread in writing on welfare economics. Thus it is claimed that the three basic postulates of Paretian welfare economics – consumer sovereignty, individualism of social choice and unanimity – are self-evidently 'common sense' and are (ought to be?) widely accepted amongst economists. What needs to be noted here is that economists who take this line can easily fall into the trap of confusing consensus with objectivity.

As Blaug argues, uncontroversial value judgments are value judgments nevertheless (Blaug, 1980).

III. ETHICS AND CLASSICAL ECONOMIC LIBERALISM

Consider a popular view of economic liberalism. This view is that economic liberalism regards the 'free market' not simply as a mechanism by which individuals obtain the 'best value' in stating their preferences but that, in following their own materialist ends – maximizing their profits and maximizing their satisfaction from use of their resources – the market performs some 'higher' function. The famous doctrine of the Invisible Hand by which the market co-ordinates the 'selfish' decisions of individual buyers and sellers and in doing so benefits all is given as an instance where 'materialistic' ethics are claimed to dominate. The attacks on the 'materialistic' bias in the doctrine are well known. At one extreme, it is claimed that the 'narrow' behavioural assumptions are simply incorrect. At the other extreme, it is held that the market itself, in some inscrutable way, *causes* the actors in the market to act in a materialistic fashion. The corrupting influence of the market is contrasted with the ennobling influence of a properly-run Socialist Commonwealth, in which human beings come to realize how much they love their fellow men. The extremes both support the conclusion that economic liberalism, by worshipping the market, is at best amoral and, at worst, corrupts human nature. It has no ethical foundations. These criticisms emanate primarily from moral philosophers. Economists, notably Sen (1987, 1994), have concentrated on the 'failure' of the market to lead to a 'just' distribution of income which would be instrumental in fulfilling a moral obligation to help the relatively ill-off (see Section IV below).

Any ethical perspective on liberalism must be based on a set of propositions which fully reflect a liberalist position, but, as the role of the market is a crucial element in the application of liberalist principles to the conduct of the economy, it must be demonstrated that the above criticisms are misconceived. In the first place, the market paradigm which is attacked is one which would be unrecognisable to economists who have closely observed how the market functions. The false paradigm may be caricatured as one in which the market is dominated by producer monopolies who exploit both factors of production, particularly labour, and consumers who are held up to ransom. If this were the sole and accurate representation of the way the market works, liberals, as opponents of concentration of power, would not countenance the market as an economic arrangement. (Actually, when such situations arise, they are frequently the result of deliberate government intervention.) However, a much more accurate picture of the market is as a dynamic process – the Austrian view – in which a myriad of transactions take place between buyers and sellers at a point of time and over time, stimulated by entrepreneurial actions designed to make profits and where product and process innovations continually come on stream because these are necessary for market survival. In the long run, only those survive who satisfy the ever-changing preferences of those who buy products and services.

In the second place, the market, as liberals would have it operate, cannot do so without firm ethical foundations. The process of buying and selling, often conducted between persons and organizations who never meet and located at vast distances from one another, must rest on the expectation that, in the main, promises are kept about the specification and the price of the goods and services, and that contractual arrangements can be entered into in which any dispute or disagreement can be satisfactorily resolved, that is to say arbitration or legal decisions will be complied with. The bedrock of a liberalist market system must be trust. Of course, this is not to say that behaving honestly may not be derived from expediency. Cheating and lying may simply not pay. Moral philosophers could argue, as we have suggested earlier, that a propensity to behave morally can be accorded a 'higher' ethical status when individuals act in accordance with their 'conscience' and not because of the pressures which would be exerted against them if they did not so act. However there is nothing unique or special about the mixture of motives which may impel individuals to behave morally, and which requires us to single out market behaviour as exceptional.

IV. THE MARKET AND 'FREEDOM TO CHOOSE'

Sen has pioneered the revival of ethical considerations as part of the mainstream of economics discussion. He has developed his views in a series of brilliant papers and books. He has also combined philosophical speculation with intense concern with the problem of world poverty, which has led him on several occasions to question the value of free markets as policy instruments. Let me say at the outset that I agree with his general stance on the subject-matter of economics, which leads me, like him, to question the value of the 'welfarist' approach to policy questions. However, I do not share his value judgments and have a rather different view of the nature and function of the market. What follows is largely based on a comment on Sen (1994).

First of all, Sen considers how we are to judge the market. I agree entirely with his approach by which the market is not some 'mortal God' which needs to be worshipped with the fervour one associates with extreme 'liberals'/conservatives; but it is a mechanism. Whether and in what form one should employ that mechanism depends on normative judgments. I am also at home with his proposal to consider the role of the market in relation to the promotion of individual freedom.

I want first of all to explore his important point that 'the perspective of freedom is *motivationally* quite different from that of "welfarist" approaches underlying standard assessments of the market mechanism'. Charles Rowley and I (Rowley and Peacock, 1975) explored this difference in detail some years ago at a time when non-acceptance of Paretian welfare economics was regarded as a cardinal sin. I am glad that Sen has accepted our primary contention of the *separate natures* of liberalist philosophy and Paretianism. His emphasis, however, is different from ours. Agreeing with John Hicks, he rightly stresses that pursuit of economic efficiency is not the first item in the ordering of liberal priorities. In contrast, we emphasize that the achievement of Pareto preferred or optimality positions, in the presence of externalities, is based on a 'Nirvana' view of the use of government intervention.

To elaborate, government intervention to take account of externalities by regulation or public provision of goods and services removes the discipline of market forces and can result in the achievement of neither allocative nor 'X' efficiency. Even if one accepts the narrow Paretian criteria, any supposed inherent deficiencies in a free market solution should not be compared with some idealised alternative. More important still, implementing the consumer sovereignty element in Paretian welfare economics by devising political institutions which reflect citizens' choices does not guarantee 'liberal' results which would exercise firm control over the growth of the public sector (see Peacock, 1992). This was why the Classical economists held that the franchise should only be extended as property became more widely distributed. A modern liberalist view regards equality of voting rights as an essential principle, which means that only persuasion may be used to reduce voters' support for ever-increasing public expenditure.

Sen makes a distinction between 'freedom to act' and 'freedom to achieve'. There is a sophisticated exploration of this distinction, but it really comes down to identifying the circumstances where one is free to allocate what resources one has and to transact and bargain in such a way as to alter that allocation as one thinks fit in contrast to the circumstances where the ability to choose is restricted because of lack of physical or human capital.

Sen accepts that the market mechanism is a necessary condition for freedom of choice, but this view must be qualified by two circumstances. The first is obviously the hollow ring of 'freedom of choice' to those whose domain of choice is severely restricted by poverty or misfortune. The second is where freedom of choice leads to conflicts of interest, as demonstrated in negative externalities. I shall follow Sen in ignoring the latter circumstance, interesting though it would be to discuss 'liberal' solutions to internalizing externalities (see particularly de Jasay, 1991).

Sen argues that the defence of the market rests primarily on the freedom to transact and exchange, restrictions which are 'ethically very limiting indeed'.

I find this contention unhelpful. (If the opportunities to transact and exchange are limited because of inequalities of ownership, the market can hardly be to blame. This is like blaming the gun for murder. It is another thing altogether to pass judgment on those who create or tolerate a situation where ability to choose may be limited to the relatively few. Furthermore, as I have argued above, the efficient working of markets characterised by a myriad of transactions in time and space, involving millions of persons who may never meet, presupposes a high degree of mutual trust and honesty.

Sen reserves most of his doubts about the market's performance for an examination of 'freedom to achieve'. His analysis has two parts.

In the first, major differences in resource endowment between persons are ignored. Then the process of achievement might be depicted very much along the lines of traditional welfare economics with the market facilitating the maximization of personal welfare by re-allocation of one's resources to provide the most preferred combination. I do not dispute the legitimacy of this approach. Nor do I dispute that persons with similar material endowments may differ in their opportunities for 'freedom achievement' if they differ in their personal and environmental characteristics. Sen considers the situation of a disabled person with more command over resources than a fit person, the former having 'less freedom to achieve' though being conventionally better off.

In the second part, Sen emphasizes that the market can do little to help those who are poor as well as disabled in some way. They may suffer from the double disadvantage of low resource endowment and lack of the capability of using what resources they have to the best advantage.

It is important to note that Sen's position relies on his particular description of the market. He implicitly accepts the welfarist view that the sole function of the market is to enable individuals to maximize utility, subject to resource constraints. I offer a very different view of the market's functions which includes the opportunities it gives to individuals to lessen these constraints so as to 'better their condition', as Adam Smith maintained. This entrepreneurial function is only made possible because the real world is characterised by market imperfections which stimulate the discovery of ways of removing them. The relevance of this view of the market here is that, in contrast with dirigiste systems, it offers the poor and uneducated the chance to exploit entrepreneurial skills, and in so doing to pull themselves out of the poverty trap. Sen knows better than I do that this argument forms the basis of a powerful counter-attack on the conventional wisdom of development planning by those who claim that 'poor' countries fostering the market economy will have a better chance of removing the resource constraints governing the economic dimensions to freedom of choice than those relying on government intervention.

Sen's analysis is designed to support the proposition that if 'freedom to achieve' is an important dimension of freedom, then control of market forces will be necessary in order to rectify the imbalance in access to that freedom brought about by inequality. Sen is not diverted into an argument about conflicts between freedom and economic equality but concentrates on the special though not unusual case of severe hardship caused by famines. Most of us will probably accept that the market by itself can neither prevent the onset of famine caused by some natural disaster nor operate so quickly that destitution and starvation are prevented. What system can cope with such conditions in an adequate fashion? This is not to deny that preventive as distinct from remedial measures of the kind associated with rural development in poorer countries may crucially depend on government participation in educational programmes and in extensive support for irrigation and technological improvement in agriculture. A good argument could be made for the view that these are preconditions for the efficient operation of a market system which is not to be riddled with imperfections, such as local monopolies of means of subsistence.

Towards the end of Sen's contribution he recognises what he describes as the 'commissioning' role of the market. Private markets are the conduit which offers an efficient response to consumer demands for the necessities of life. However, the sin of omission of the market is that it does not generate income and purchasing power which enables potential victims of famines to exercise this freedom to choose. A 'discriminatingly activist' government is necessary to create income opportunities for the 'disentitled' population, and to offset manipulation of the market by monopolistic traders by some form of counter-speculation devices. Alongside his own well-known investigations of the appropriateness of this complementary arrangement between the public and private sector, he reminds those who claim to be lineal successors of the Classical economists that such an approach is endorsed by Turgot, Smith and Condorcet. He bases his case on an important study of these economists by Rothschild (1992).

I would emphasize a different aspect of the Classical analysis. As Rothschild shows, the need for public intervention was perceived as being necessary, not simply because the initial endowments of the poor were such that destitution would follow from scarcity resulting from famine, but also because opportunities for entrepreneurial activity within competitive markets were severely restricted by government regulation of commerce. Clearly, their view of the market was very different from those who would judge its performance by the achievement of Pareto optimality. The market was an essential condition for the promotion of thrift and enterprise on which the relief of poverty must ultimately depend, though reasonable men might differ about the extent to which government intervention might be necessary to remove imperfections. I suppose that Sen would argue that the market might remove poverty but that would not satisfy his ethical stance which would favour a much more radical attack on economic inequality. Furthermore, this process would take a much longer period of time than would be tolerable to the poor in poor countries. However, even if one agrees with Sen that at least some state intervention will be necessary to create compatibility between ethical norms and removing poverty – a position that liberals will accept to a greater or lesser degree – it is a separate question whether such intervention necessarily entails the use of methods of support which set aside the market and restrict freedom of choice of individuals. The importance of this question is not denied, but is better treated separately, as I endeavour to do in Chapter 4 below.

V. CONCLUSION

I have argued that the market is a mechanism and that the pattern of the transactions which it facilitates is a reflection and not a determinant of human behaviour. If moral obloquy attaches to what takes place in the process of market exchange, this must be pinned on individuals characterized by what Hume called our 'narrowness of soul'. Such narrowness is surely not a characteristic confined to those who spend their lives investigating market opportunities. The implication in the arguments of those who believe that the market is a corrupting influence is that some other institutional arrangements will produce a moral transformation and this is a chimera, as the study of Utopian schemes designed to produce the perfectibility of man makes only too clear.

REFERENCES

Barry, N. (1991), *The Morality of Business Enterprise*, Edinburgh: The David Hume Institute.

Blaug, M. (1980), *The Methodology of Economics*, Cambridge Surveys of Economic Literature, Cambridge: Cambridge University Press, Chapter 4.

Bowles, S. and Gintis, H. (1993), 'The Revenge of Homo Economicus: Contested Exchange and the Revival of Political Economy', *Journal of Economic Perspectives*, Vol. 7, No. 1.

Hay, M. and Peacock, A. (1992), *Social Policies in the Transition to a Market Economy: A Report of the United Nations Mission to the Russian Federation*, Edinburgh: The David Hume Institute.

De Jasay, A. (1991), *Choice, Contract, Consent: A Restatement of Liberalism,* London: Institute of Economic Affairs.

Peacock, A. (1992), *Public Choice Analysis in Historical Perspective* (The Mattioli Lectures 1989), Cambridge: Cambridge University Press.

Rodrick, D. (1996), 'Understanding Economic Policy Reform', *Journal of Economic Literature*, Vol. XXXIV, March, 9–41.

Rothschild, E. (1992), 'Commerce and the State: Turgot, Condorcet and Smith', *Economic Journal*, Vol. 102, 1197–1210.

Rowley, C. and Peacock, A. (1975), *Welfare Economics: A Liberal Restatement*, London: Martin Robertson.

Sen, A. (1987), *On Ethics and Economics*, Oxford: Basil Blackwell.

Sen, A. (1994), 'Markets and the Freedom to Choose', in Horst Siebert (ed.), *The Ethical Foundations of the Market Economy*, Tübingen: J.C.B. Mohr (Paul Siebeck), pp. 123–38.

4. The value of freedom of expression

(Economists are often accused of harbouring imperialistic designs on other branches of learning, and this chapter might be regarded as an intrusion into the field of ethics. I would regard it as a simple attempt to explain why I believe that economic analysis may assist in the clarification of the issues surrounding the vexed question of how much freedom of expression should be allowed. I avoid the central questions of ethics associated with what John Mackie called 'inventing right and wrong' by nailing my colours to the libertarian mast. Having adopted the initial value judgment that people should be allowed to choose to use their resources and talents in the way which they regard as being in their own best interests, it is at least possible to prepare an agenda of issues which may help to answer the question about the extent to which freedom of expression should be controlled. Why I should have made this attempt is explained in the text, and whether I have succeeded in my modest task is for the reader to judge. At least, the fumblings of an economist in trying to work out an agenda may have an anthropological interest!)

PREAMBLE

It is a personal pleasure and privilege to offer this short essay on an unusual subject in honour of Hirofumi Shibata, an esteemed former colleague and friend, and an expert on public economics. He knows all too well how difficult it is to devise schemes of collective action which fulfil the requirement of maximizing the sovereignty of the individual in matters of choice.

How I came to address the problem of this contribution may be of interest. In 1985 I was appointed by the British government as chair of a committee investigating the future financing of the British Broadcasting Corporation and we duly reported our findings the following year. The government accepted and implemented several of our more important recommendations which were designed to make the British broadcasting system more responsive to consumer preferences. The government were initially rather startled at the radical nature of our proposals and one in particular appears to have worried them. Our final proposal, entirely in keeping with our conclusions, was that only the normal laws of the land concerning obscenity, blasphemy, sedition and similar matters should be applied to TV and radio broadcasting and that there was no necessity for pre-broadcast vetting of programmes or instructions to broadcasting companies to avoid political controversy. To quote para. 695 of the Report, 'the end of all censorship arrangements would be a sign that broadcasting had come of age'. Instead of following the spirit of our other proposals which promoted de-regulation of broadcasting, the Government, to my regret, tightened up regulations and actually appointed a Broadcasting Standards Council with the task of drawing up a 'moral code' for broadcasters.

I and others have vigorously opposed this development, without success, and have risked being regarded as supporters of licentious and violent behaviour. Of course the charge is unfounded, but, insofar as the debate is conducted in a rational manner, it is as well to examine the logic of one's own position. This is what I have tried to do here, and I believe that I have demonstrated in a modest way that economic analysis offers useful guidance on how to approach the subject.

FREEDOM OF CHOICE AND FREEDOM OF EXPRESSION

My starting point embodies a value judgment, which is that people should be allowed to choose to use their resources and talents in the way which they regard as being in their best interests. This is not to say that they necessarily know where their best interests lie, but, if they do not, then equally this is not to say that others should decide for them how to act and behave. It means that individuals who are uncertain about their choices, because they are not sure of the relationship between their wishes and what might satisfy them, should have an incentive to seek advice and information and to experiment in the exercise of choice. Nor does it mean that all choices have to be made in isolation. Individuals may choose to act collectively, but free choice must mean that they agree to the rules governing the making of collective choices.

This initial value judgment means that free individual choice will attach a positive value to the dissemination of information about the choices open to them, to activities which enable them to judge whether they might wish to reconsider how to spend their time and resources. However, freedom of expression implies something much more than allowing as free entry as possible into the supply of a market in information and advice. It means allowing individuals or groups of individuals to present ideas which question how society is organized and to put forward proposals which may attempt to engineer major changes in how we think and feel.

Freedom of expression, therefore, is an important component of individual freedom, but it must be recognized that sometimes the value which individuals will attach to particular forms of freedom of expression may be negative. I may be repelled by the noise of rock music which my neighbour insists on playing very loudly in the next garden, though he regards it as an adjunct to the removal of his restrictive inhibitions. Under what circumstances, if any, should he be prevented from playing rock? Are the costs of negotiating with him to turn his radio down or to restrict the noise to agreed hours worth incurring in order to obtain peace and quiet?

An even more fundamental question is whether freedom of expression extends to expressing views which support ideas about the organization of society which might entail that freedom of expression should be carefully controlled. I shall not envisage circumstances where such a view would prevail to the extent that the community is willing to vote in a government which will restrict the right of freedom of expression to those forms of expression of which it alone approves. We must nevertheless be aware that this can happen.

These preliminary ideas point towards an agenda containing three items: (i) defining and illustrating the conditions which will ensure that freedom of expression has a positive value; (ii) considering the circumstances in which conflicts may arise as a result of freedom of expression; and (iii) considering how such conflicts ought to be resolved.

CONDITIONS FOR ENSURING FREEDOM OF EXPRESSION

It must be realised at the outset that all attempts at freedom of expression on offer to society entail some form of persuasion. The suppliers are concerned to persuade us to 'buy', as it were, some idea. Sometimes the acceptance of the idea brings with it the expectation that the persuaded will buy some product for which they are willing to pay. Sometimes, all that is hoped by the persuaders is that their ideas alone are accepted, but that they entail a change in the preferences of the persuaded which will increase the utility of the persuaders. Of course, the distinction is a fine one. Thus acceptance of a religious or political opinion which is novel to the persuaded may entail offering material support in the form of gifts of money to a religious order or political group and, in the latter case, to accepting the tax regime which they introduce if they become the government in power.

However, if freedom of expression is to have a positive value to a community in which it is assumed that persons have the right to accept or to reject the goods and services on offer, its members must have the opportunity for testing the product. The usual way in which we do this is to 'sample' the product until we are sure that the persuaders have fulfilled their promises. But the process goes further than that. A vital part of the testing process consists in being able to compare alternative products which satisfy the same 'need' In short, the positive value of freedom of expression to the 'buyer' entails free competition in the presentation of ideas.

The importance of competition soon becomes obvious. It not only facilitates the testing process in appraising 'contingent' persuasion, i.e. where being persuaded means parting with money. It applies equally in the realm of 'ideological' persuasion, i.e. it entails competition between political parties, intellectual movements, and religions. But competition has another vital function to play in a world in which freedom of expression is to be valuable to the community. It is likely to encourage the 'sellers' of ideas to provide full information on their content, for, if they fail to do so, they will be at a disadvantage compared with rivals who will be only too willing to indicate where the gaps in information are to be found. In short, competition reduces the cost to the buyer of ideas of obtaining the requisite information upon which an intelligent choice can be based.

Two examples may be helpful here. First of all, take a common form of 'contingent' persuasion – the advertising of some domestic product. It is in our interests for the car salesman to extol the virtues of a new Toyota and he must be given the same freedom to express his views as the car salesman making a pitch for a Nissan. If we already have experience in driving cars, we have some check on these views, but what we cannot expect is that he will extol the virtues of the rival product and we would be right to be suspicious if he attempts to 'knock' his rival's product. Fortunately, his rivals are only too willing to point out the differences between their products and that being 'pushed' by the Toyota salesman. However, if there were no competition for cars, there would be no incentive for the sales representative of the monopoly firm to reveal much about the product and the costs of obtaining information by the customer would be made much more difficult.

Exactly the same reasoning can be applied to the 'sale' of political or religious views. Competition with freedom of entry into the 'ideas' market must encourage the 'sellers' to be much more specific about the content of their 'product' and how it is to be differentiated. With 'freedom of expression' under conditions where different views can be expressed there is at least some prospect that 'the wool will not be pulled over our eyes'.

Let me now try to deal with two objections. The first concerns the nature of the experience of new ideas and concepts, whether contingent or not. The examples I have given emphasize rational calculation on the part of the 'buyer' of ideas and the right of those who seek information to be able to trace the connection between that information and their needs. However, often our experience of new ideas, as when we visit the theatre, the concert hall or museum, leaves us questioning our own ideas about life and work. We become confused, though perhaps elated. Sometimes we may be outraged and angry. We may not be sure whether our welfare has been increased. Does this not entail that 'freedom of expression' as found in the arts must have some separate justification other than its contribution to what we perceive as being our welfare?

There are two answers to this objection. The first is that anyone who does not wish to risk the discomfiture of being shocked and startled by artistic endeavours is not forced to submit themselves to the 'ordeal'. The second is that it is usually possible to obtain full information on the nature of the 'happening' which could change one's preference structure. In other words, the presuppositions for a rational calculation are there if we want to take advantage of them.

The second objection relates to circumstances where the nature of the choices we have to make cannot offer the opportunity to repeatedly sample the product as a test of the veracity of those who produce it. I may consider it desirable that everyone who is able to offer me a hip operation should have the right to inform me about the relative merits of their surgical skills. However, in the absence of technical knowledge, who am I to believe? And if I make a wrong decision, I cannot learn from my mistakes, for the mistake cannot be rectified if the operation cannot be repeated in the event of failure. Freedom of expression, in the form of freedom to give information about the nature of the service, may encourage suppliers to take advantage of the ignorance of buyers when there is no learning curve for them to move down.

Ignorance may make us vulnerable to freedom of expression which embodies a false prospectus, as with unscrupulous doctors, lawyers and, say, fortune tellers and clairvoyants, but this is not to say that a gap in our knowledge cannot be filled or if it cannot be filled very easily that we are totally at the mercy of the clever propagandist. If a sufficient number of people suffer from ignorance with potentially awful consequences, then the media will have a strong incentive to investigate such situations. Professions faced with public exposure of their activities will see that it is in their interests to enforce acceptable standards, quite apart from any satisfaction which individual members will derive from behaving honestly and efficiently towards their clients. Gaps in the information system may also be filled by consumer organizations to which the 'ignorant' can subscribe in return for guidance on the performance of those who supply them with 'one-off' purchases. In short, one important function of freedom of expression by the press is to facilitate monitoring of the performance of those providing services which cannot be adequately tested by consumers themselves.

EXTERNALITY PROBLEMS

So far the discussion has viewed freedom of expression as a service like any other available to those willing to pay for it and capable of rejection by those who are unwilling to do so. However, as with other services, the welfare effects may not be confined simply to the transactions made directly between seller and buyer. As with many other goods and services, individuals in the community who are not parties to the transaction may have their welfare affected, either as unwilling consumers or unwilling producers.

I consider 'unwilling consumption' first of all, or what economists term 'consumption externalities'. Let us take a concrete example in the form of the famous controversy about the publication of Salman Rushdie's *The Satanic Verses*. This is advertised as a novel by a very well-known writer, which could be bought like any other novel, and presumably buyers expected to, and clearly did, obtain enjoyment from reading it. However, certain passages brought to the attention of the Moslem community were regarded as blasphemy, that is to say any perceived benefits by readers of a positive kind were counterbalanced by the 'disbenefits' suffered by those outraged at its blasphemous utterances. The reaction in Iran was so extreme that Rushdie has been condemned to death and has had to hide from the world. Even in countries in which there is no theocracy, there have been requests that the book should be banned or at least removed from public display. The *Satanic Verses* affair is only one in an endless succession of 'scandals' about freedom of expression derived from public attitudes to blasphemy and obscenity.

Consider now 'unwilling production' or 'production externalities'. If freedom of expression entails public exposure to criticisms not only of doctrines held by individuals but also of their personal conduct, this usually entails access to details of their private life. The individuals concerned or their relatives and friends are frequently, if not always' unwilling 'factors of production' in the process of public exposure. The technical means now available to the 'paparazzi' – to take the more sensational purveyors of exposure – have improved enormously with 'zoom' lens TV and camera techniques, not to speak of listening-in devices, alongside more traditional means such as bribery of colleagues and servants and blackmail. Even if individuals may have property rights in privacy and in the use of private possessions such as the letters of the dead, these rights may be difficult to enforce. While our reaction is likely to be that such activities are a travesty of 'freedom of expression', even the most objective and incorruptible writer exposing personal conduct, who may himself not be interested in sensationalism for its own sake or in the pecuniary gains of his activities, imposes 'negative external benefits' on those who are the object of his enquiry. However we weigh the pros and cons of his activity, freedom of expression is not affording a positive gain to all those exposed to it, and some sort of balance has to be struck.

Thus even if one is a convinced libertarian, one has to recognize that there are conflicts between different sorts of freedom – in this case between freedom of expression and freedom of privacy. I shall look at the way a libertarian should approach such conflicts later on. What we have to note here and now is that resolution of these differences cannot be achieved by some technical means. For example, counting heads of gainers and losers would not help very much. First of all, this would entail a census – an expensive operation if every instance of conflict required one – of attitudes and it may not be always in the interests of all individuals to give their true view of how they are affected. Even if they did, what account would one want to take of the 'intensity' of feeling that individuals had for or against allowing freedom of expression or its suppression in particular instances? Even if the issue could be decided by a majority vote, this is not to say that even those who claimed to have experienced negative gains would necessarily believe that the majority decision rule was fair and reasonable. Finally, to say that a majority had decided that the gains were negative tells us nothing about whether any action should be taken to prevent the 'offending' practice. It could even be the case that faced with this information, those using this practice might voluntarily cease to use it. In short, while technical information, such as a census, may be useful in helping a community to make a decision, the decision itself will rest on the tastes and preferences and therefore the value judgments of its members.

CONFLICT RESOLUTION AND COLLECTIVE ACTION

The resolution of a conflict of freedoms appears to call for some form of collective action. However, a libertarian would want to be very careful about concluding from this that this action should take the form of state censorship of freedom of expression backed by the force of the criminal law. It may come to that, but not before one has examined very carefully the various forms that collective action could take.

We would agree, I suppose, that freedom of expression which took the form of propagandistic activities which would actually lead to civil disturbance and dissolution of civilized behaviour must be prevented. However, it is far from easy to trace the quantitative connection between the output of such activities and the undesired result. The very assurance that entry into the ideas market was free might prevent any connection at all, for the preaching of revolution would be swamped by alternative views. Put in another way, a society committed to freedom of expression, subject to negative externalities, presupposes the existence of a populace trained in the civic virtues of tolerance and understanding of different points of view and the resolution of conflict by agreement. If these virtues are absent, then there is no way that conflict could be resolved.

Where freedom of expression imposes a substantial negative externality on a sizeable proportion of the population, it may be an overreaction to accede to state intervention to ban such activities. The extent of the externality might be minimized in some way. Thus active propaganda for pornography may have to be restricted in some way, but those who perceive benefits from watching pornographic displays can conduct their activities in private.

Where freedom of expression, as in the attack on the behaviour of a specific individual or organisation, is perceived by those attacked as damaging their interests, this seems an issue best dealt with under the law of libel and slander. I agree that this tells us nothing about the scope of the law and the severity or otherwise of the damages awarded if the case is won. Communities have very different evaluations of the nature and extent of damage. A colleague of mine who wrote a book on Greek philosophy was described in a Californian newspaper reviewing his book as a well-known homosexual. He and his British lawyers considered that this statement was libellous and warranted heavy damages, but were amazed to find that in California the statement would not be so regarded and that it might even be taken as something of a compliment!

It must be conceded, however, that some general rules need to be formulated about what forms of freedom of expression are allowable and what are not. The presence of general rules must imply some method of enforcing them, but we are not yet at the stage of arguing for criminal legislation.

One reason for proceeding with caution is that the public recognition of the detriment suffered by victims of self-expression may influence those who have attacked them and those who are tempted to follow their example to adopt a system of self-regulation. Thus professional organizations see that it is in their own interests to lay out a code of conduct for members accompanied by a disciplinary code laying down penalties for non-adherence to the code of conduct. Likewise, in the UK, advertisers have to submit themselves to an Advertising Standards Authority and the Press to a Press Council both of which are financed by a levy on members of the appropriate professions.

The analogy here with the detriment suffered from cigarette smoking is perhaps relevant. Smoking is not expressly forbidden but a succession of obstacles are put in the way of smokers which are designed to get them to stop or at least not to inconvenience non-smokers. Smokers are first of all warned about the possible consequences of their activities, and cigarette packets have to be marked with a government health warning. The negative externalities suffered by non-smokers are reduced by the growing number of 'no-smoking' areas in public buildings and vehicles. Finally, the smokers' pockets are hit through discriminatory taxation on tobacco.

It is reasonable to claim that my argument points to much more specific action by government than incentives offered to private organizations and warnings to 'put their house in order'. So far as I am aware, Western countries have legislation designed to control quite severely obscene and blasphemous publications and latterly to prevent the screening of comparable material by means of TV and the cinema. I do not think that there can be any hard and fast rule about the content of such legislation which has to be framed very carefully so that it does not conflict with constitutional rights to freedom of speech. What is permissible and on what terms very much depends on public opinion and how far such opinion exercises political influence. The only point I would make is that there is a case for automatic review of such legislation, rather along the lines used in voting for the annual budget, though annuality is perhaps too stringent a requirement. Every three years, say, the legislation on control of freedom of expression' might lapse automatically and its continuance, in whatever form, would require a new act of legislation which, if appropriate, could be an amendment of the previous enactment or simply the replication of the previous legislation.

CONCLUDING REMARKS

I have argued from rather unusual premises that 'freedom of expression' is an integral part of a free society. I have illustrated this theme with reference to economic transactions. At its simplest, freedom of expression is the provision of information which is essential in a free economy, and competition itself offers some likelihood that there is an incentive to provide accurate information. But freedom of expression is itself a necessary adjunct to the presentation of commentary and criticism of our society. Here, too, the individual has the right to accept or reject new ideas and concepts, and freedom of expression must be presented in a form where acceptance or rejection is feasible. That is to say that 'negative externalities' in the presentation of opinions must be avoided in so far as that is possible.

One would like to think that in a free society, the state of education encourages people to resolve conflicts between freedom of expression and other freedoms, e.g. privacy, so that individuals can seek redress by voluntary action within a properly prescribed set of individual property rights. If these rights are violated, one would prefer resolution of conflict through civil action rather than through the criminal code. Any such code, especially if it extends to the specification of criminal offences, should be subject to periodic automatic review.

REFERENCE

Home Office (1986), Report of the Committee on Financing the BBC (Peacock Report), Cm. 9824, London: HMSO.

5. Liberalism and economic growth

(An economist with a specialized interest in public finance and with the opportunity to offer economic advice to countries at very different stages of economic development could hardly be unaware of the impact of the enormous literature on economic growth models on the devising of policy instruments designed to improve growth prospects. My textbook with Keith Shaw, The Economic Theory of Fiscal Policy (1976), *based on both our professional articles and experience in advice-giving, explored the analytics of fiscal policy and growth in some detail, but, in the end, a strong note of scepticism governed our conclusions about the desirability of using fiscal tools in order to influence economic growth and employment.*

Further experience derived from three years (1973–1976) as Chief Economic Adviser to the UK government's Department of Trade and Industry convinced me that 'big push' growth theories which advocated government discrimination in favour of large-scale manufacturing investment were misconceived. The missing element in such theorizing lay in the neglect of the motivation of entrepreneurs, stimulating their perceptions of investment opportunities which would be sharper, the more that they were subjected to competitive forces. This profoundly unoriginal observation leads back to the economic system as perceived by Adam Smith and Schumpeter. Certainly modern growth models have been forced to come to grips with the role of management and organisation as important elements in the growth process.

My professional links with Angus Maddison and a long friendship made it impossible to resist making a contribution to his Festschrift *though I had misgivings at being asked to offer a liberal view of economic growth. However, it turned out to be surprisingly easy to explain the liberal 'slant' on the growth process within the conventional growth model framework, and it was also fortuitous that I was writing at a time when the claim has been made that economic freedom and growth go together, though no liberal thinker need be committed to the view that growth is the overriding aim of economic policy. I am not convinced that this claim has been fully substantiated – for an attempt to do so, see* Economic Freedom of the World, 1975–1995 *(The Fraser Institute, 1996) – mainly because of the difficulty mentioned below about quantifying the role of regulatory measures. I hope that any reader interested in this debate will at least derive some guidance about the issues involved by reading this chapter.)*

> Little else is required to carry a state to the highest degree of opulence from the lowest barbarism, but peace, easy taxes, and a tolerable administration of justice; all the rest being brought about by the natural course of things. (Adam Smith in 1755 as reported in Dugald Stewart, *Account of the Life and Writings of Adam Smith LL.D.* (1793), reprinted in Adam Smith, *Essays on Philosophical Subjects,* edited by W.P.D.J.C. Bryce and L.S. Ross, Oxford University Press, 1980, p. 322.)

I. INTRODUCTION

Liberalism is a political creed which embraces a distinct economic philosophy or 'political economy' using the term liberalism in the Anglo-Saxon sense. The political economy of liberalism therefore comprehends a particular stance towards society's objectives, a particular view about the way the economic system works and therefore a particular view of the role of government in relation to liberalist objectives.

My agenda is based on this threefold division between objectives, economic constraints and policy instruments. So far as objectives are concerned, I must try to achieve the impossible and encapsulate liberal economic philosophy within a few sentences; for it does turn out to be necessary to recognize that the place of growth in the list of objectives and the 'trade-off' between these objectives is quite distinct (see Section II below). I then consider what will be more familiar to 'growthmen', namely the particular emphasis placed by Adam Smith and his followers on economic freedom as a factor in promoting economic growth (see Section III below). I can then consider how far liberals have been correct in their claim that the role of the state in promoting growth should be a much more restricted one than that promoted by growthmen in general (see Section IV below).

I must warn the reader that liberalism is a wide-ranging political philosophy and that disagreement between liberals about the precise content of economic policy towards growth is quite common. I have not explored these differences in detail but consider that a synthetic view of liberalism does not give an entirely misleading picture of the liberalist position and enables me to proceed directly towards issues more germane to the theme of this conference volume. What I can say is that, whatever one's political philosophy, the profession owes an immense debt to Angus Maddison for his long devotion to the study of comparative economic development which combines the talents of economist, statistician and historian to a unique degree. My own debt to him will soon become apparent.

II. THE GROWTH OBJECTIVE

Liberalism embodies an important initial proposition – the comprehension of how the economy behaves or ought to behave cannot be understood without reference to the actions of individuals. There is no society which is independent of the individuals who compose it. The basic model of the economy is derived from the study of individuals' tastes and preferences which lead them to try to 'better their condition', as Adam Smith put it, within the limitations imposed by resource constraints, by lack of knowledge and information and by the uncertainties surrounding the attempt to overcome these limitations. We shall examine later how this view influences liberalist growth models as a contribution to positive economics, but must first of all note that underlying the concept of the individual acting to further his/her own interests is an ethical principle – individuals are the best judges of their own welfare. Such a principle certainly does not rule out co-operation between individuals in order to resolve conflicts between them about the distribution of property rights and about how further matters of collective interest are to be decided. The 'decision rules' to be applied in cases where voluntary transactions between individuals do not achieve individuals' aims are themselves subject to the liberal prescription that they must minimize the use of compulsion. Where state action is regarded as necessary, all must have an equal share in making the law and there must be equality before the law (for further discussion, see Barry, 1986).

Given this individualist philosophy, one cannot derive from it a commitment to economic growth as an objective which requires collective action. Growth is not an end in itself. It is simply the outcome of individual work and savings patterns. The idea of an optimal growth rate has no meaning. Moreover the individual is not accountable to 'society' for his actions, once the rule of law is established. Consequently, it is illiberal to seek to impose some collective saving objective which would be necessary in order to pursue some target rate of growth set by government.

Of course, if one strand of liberal philosophy requires that there is an equal share in making the law, then it could be that one outcome of a voting system which conformed with liberal principles could be strong support for a government that wished to encourage a 'satisfactory' rate of growth. In short the economic policy paradigm need not be one in which the government simply dictates the policy agenda by identifying 'desirable' movements in target economic variables such as the rate of growth, the unemployment rate and the rate of inflation and specific trade-offs between them, if appropriate. The policy paradigm becomes one in which a bargaining situation exists between those who supply policies, the politicians, and those who demand them, the voters. Is it contrary to liberal philosophy if voters demand that the government specifies for them a collective growth target which, when voted upon, has their full support?

There are two ways of answering this question. The first is to agree that liberal support for a political system which seeks to reflect individual preferences as nearly as is possible does not guarantee that illiberal policies will not be introduced. However, this does not mean that those who regard liberalism as identified with individual self-reliance would wish to 'force men to be free'. If the liberalist political process produces support for collectivist action, then the only course open to the liberal idealist is to try to persuade voters to change their minds (see Rowley and Peacock, 1975).

The second way of answering this question is to enquire further what forms of intervention are necessary in order to achieve a 'satisfactory' rate of growth. Indeed, the liberal idealist placed in the position of persuader need not adopt a defensive stance. First of all, he/she could emphasize that consumption and not growth (as measured by GDP per head) is the object of most interest to individuals; and their welfare functions can sensibly include concern for the consumption opportunities of the less fortunate and for the endowment of resources which protect the consumption standards of future generations. Second, he/she could emphasize that the pattern of consumption at a point of time and through time is an important argument in individual welfare functions. Third, if the liberal perception of human action is correct then there is a strong presumption that market economies characterized by limited state intervention will be better able to achieve a satisfactory rate of growth and consumption per head than those which capture a large proportion of annual output for government use. This last proposition leads naturally to an analysis of a liberal perception of the growth process.

III. LIBERALISM AND GROWTH MODELS

The 'liberal slant' on the comparative growth performance of countries is evident at the very beginning of the professional discussion of long-term economic growth. Indeed it could be argued that the father of economic liberalism, Adam Smith, first put forward a coherent growth model of a kind which is readily translatable into the aggregate production function form commonly found in modem growth theory.[1] I use a stylized version of Smith's model in order to bring out the points where this distinct liberal slant may be detected. Of course, Smith did not adopt a mathematical formulation even of the simple kind presented below; the input of scholarship which would justify this formulation has been prodigious and may be found in the references cited in note 1.

The Smithian aggregate production function can be specified as follows:

$$Y = f(L,K,N,T), \text{ where } f_l, f_k, f_n, f_t, > 0 \qquad (5.1)$$

where

Y = output;
K = capital stock;
L = labour force;

N = 'natural resources'; and
T = level of technique.

Y is an increasing function of capital and labour input and natural resources and the state of technology with partial second derivatives of each factor negative. I shall follow other writers and regard N as a 'bit of a nuisance' (Higgins) and treat it as part of the capital stock. This makes no difference to the general argument though it would be important to consider N separately if one were closely concerned, as I am not, with highlighting all the main characteristics of Smith approach (for critical discussion, see Reid, 1989).

The particular contribution of Smith in the specification of the aggregate production function which attracts attention is his treatment of T. Smith rather dismisses philosophy and speculation as an important influence on T and concentrates on endogenous influences. Imagine that, for reasons to be gone into later, K increases relative to L. Y/L may increase initially but, *cet. par.*, diminishing returns to capital must eventually set in, the capital/output ratio rises, and the process of growth is halted. However, T is itself a function of the extent of the market (Y/L) and the capital/labour ratio (K/L). The growth in the extent of the market facilitates specialization, offering greater opportunities for learning by doing which pays off in greater efficiency. The increase in capital per head

Figure 5.1 Technological change according to Adam Smith

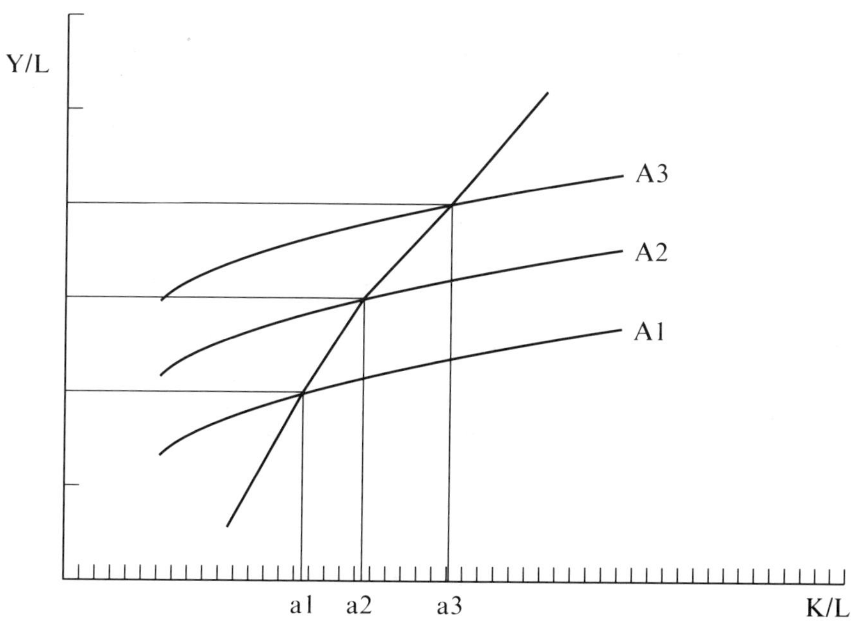

is associated with an increase in the number of production processes and therefore with an extension of experience of specialization. It follows that:

$$T = T(Y/L, K/L), \text{ where } t'(Y/K),\ t'(K/L) > 0 \tag{5.2}$$

We can represent the Smithian process of growth which is *technologically possible* as being self-sustaining over some range of output (Figure 5.1). Curve A1 represents the relationship between an increase in capital per worker and output per worker for a given state of technology. For given L, Y/K increases but at a decreasing rate, i.e. the capital/output ratio rises, Curves A2 and A3 are similarly drawn for successively higher levels of T. Given equation (5.2), the potential growth path can be represented by a locus of points on successive A curves, as T increases in response to market expansion (Y/L) and the increase in capital per worker (K/L). Expressed in this way Smithian analysis recognizes the distinction between a growth effect produced by some permanent increase in K/L and a level effect produced by endogenous technical change (cf. Lucas, 1988).

It is hardly necessary for our argument to go into detail on the length and timing of the process of growth. Sufficient to say that Smith places primary emphasis on capital accumulation. The reaching of a maximum Y/L with a subsequent stationary state or even a decline in Y/L is closely related to the motives for capital accumulation. This is not to neglect the limitations that might be placed on the growth process from growing scarcity of that 'bit of a nuisance', land, or what was to become famous as the Malthusian effect, namely that population growth could be a function of growth in income per head.

The liberal slant in growth modelling first becomes evident in the insistence on understanding the micro-foundations of the growth process. What makes a society start moving along a growth path? The answer cannot be provided by specifying a technological relationship but depends on individual motivations. As we have already observed, Adam Smith put great emphasis on men's desire to 'better their condition'. Human action is both purposive and rational, a theme which is endlessly repeated in liberal political economy. With capital accumulation playing such a major part in Smith's model, how do we translate individual motivations into an increase in K/L? By an increase in resources set aside from personal consumption, in short by frugality. Indeed, Smith's prime example of bettering one's condition is that of saving, 'a desire which, though generally calm and dispassionate, comes with us from the womb, and never leaves us till we go into the grave'. The intended result is an increase in wealth and 'an augmentation of fortune is the means by which the greater part of men propose and wish to better their condition' (Smith, 1776/1976, p. 341).

In short:

$$S = s(Y),\ s'(Y) > 0 \tag{5.3}$$

$$S = \delta K$$

where S = Saving and δK = the increase in capital stock.
It follows that if saving increases with income, so will investment, so does the capital stock and with it T increases, as previously explained.

The next element in the liberal slant is to define the conditions which will favour an increase in K without an offsetting rise in K/Y, the capital/output ratio. It is important that entrepreneurs envisage investment opportunities which offer profits over and above compensation for risk.[2] Smith is the first of many liberal writers to emphasize the importance of good government and particularly institutional arrangements which favour security of property and the legal enforcement of contracts. Stable and wise government would be a necessary but not a sufficient condition for growth. A further condition would have to be some incentive to use capital efficiently so as to maximize profits. Competition which would allow freedom of entry into new markets at home and abroad and which would encourage process innovation would be an important supplement. Stern (1991, p. 128) actually observes that it goes 'beyond the standard theory' to add management and organization as an argument in the aggregate production function. Maybe; but this is an important theme in Smith who observes that 'monopoly ... is a great enemy of good management, which can never be universally established but in consequence of that free and universal competition which forces everybody to have recourse to it for the sake of self-defence' (Smith, 1776/1976, pp. 163–4).

The liberal slant is carried over into the Smithian recommendations regarding the role of the state in promoting growth. His is not an extreme laissez-faire position, as the following list clearly indicates:

(i) Remove barriers to competition, such as granting of monopoly privileges and – constantly emphasized – barriers to communication. Good roads, canals and navigable rivers are means for breaking down local monopolies. These require state action to remove barriers to private provision and even financial support by government – but not a state-run communications system.[3]
(ii) Keep the growth of the public sector in check to prevent reduction in saving through increasing tax burdens;
(iii) Insofar as the state has to provide services which promote good government, try to relate effort to reward in public as well as in the private sector.

Again, it should be noted that Stern states that it goes beyond the standard theory to pay attention to infrastructure, in the widest sense, highlighting such impediments to growth as slow, costly and hazardous transport and corrupt and inefficient bureaucracy as impediments to growth, but credit for emphasizing such matters, which appear frequently in Smith, is only attributed to writings first published in the 1980s!

Smith's emphasis on good government as a precondition for growth and limited government as a cardinal element in maintaining it ran into trouble long before more sophisticated models appeared as rival products in the intellectual marketplace. The doubts and reservations are well known and I only briefly mention those that emanate from liberal writers.

The first set of criticisms is associated with the Classical debate about whether or not economies would reach a stationary state. In this respect, the most that Smithian limited measures of intervention would achieve would be to postpone the day when the standard of living would gravitate to the subsistence minimum, even taking account of the benefits which could accrue from extending the market through encouragement of free trade. Smith's critics did not, however, envisage any solution which rested on further state intervention, and had different views about when the exact moment would come when, in Mill's words, 'the condition of the poorest class sinks, even in a progressive state, to the lowest point which they will consent to endure' (Mill, Toronto Edition, 1965, p. 753). It is worth parenthetic mention that Mill broke ranks amongst those who had an 'unaffected aversion' for the stationary state: 'I confess that I am not charmed with the idea of life held out by those who think that the normal state of human beings is that of struggling to get on; that the trampling, crushing, elbowing, and treading on each other's heels ... are the most desirable lot of human kind, or anything but the most disagreeable symptoms of the phases of industrial progress' (Mill, *loc. cit.*), adding later: 'the best state for human nature is that in which, while no one is poor, no one desires to be richer, nor has any reason to fear being thrust back by the efforts of others to push themselves forward'. Many liberals would say 'Amen'.

The second set of criticisms offers different reasons for the inadequacy of Smith's views on 'natural liberty' as the mainspring of economic growth. I need hardly dwell on Marx's attempt to use the stationary state of argument to demonstrate that the inevitable emergence of intolerable inequalities of income and employment opportunities would bring about the demise of capitalism. The influence of Marx on Schumpeter, a liberal convert, is manifest. Schumpeter accepted Marx's view that 'internal forces' would bring about a transformation of capitalism, though not as Marx predicted. The transformation to socialism would be gradual rather than violent. Increasing industrial concentration would separate ownership from control and remove the mainspring of capitalism – the proprietary interest in the use of capital. In its place would emerge state socialism fostered by the bureaucratic attitudes resulting from the organizational changes in large business enterprises. Schumpeter, unlike Marx, did not relish what he believed would come to pass.[4]

Nevertheless, what is striking about Smith's approach is that important vestiges of it still remain in the modern growth literature, though this is not the result of the passing down of a Smithian torch from one generation of liberals to another.[5] The intellectual battle between liberalist and socialist economists changed its form in the later nineteenth century and concerned such questions as the determination of factor shares according to the principle of marginal productivity and whether market socialism could be made to conform with principles of allocation based on consumer sovereignty. Indeed, I know of no specifically liberal model of economic growth to lay alongside the many variants of aggregate production models of the post-World War II era. That is not to say, as we shall soon observe, that there is not a liberal disposition towards such models, and particularly towards some of the policy conclusions that have been drawn from them. Thus, the Solow-type growth models adapted to include endogenous technological change have a clear affinity to the Smithian model, although the role of the entrepreneur is often not spelt out in the detail which Smith and later Schumpeter considered necessary.

The crucial question is whether the growth theories of today require liberals to modify their view about the Smithian conception of the role of the state in promoting economic progress. In the case of the Solow-type models with variable capital/output ratios and flexible factor and product prices, clearly the Smithian 'canons' are preconditions for the growth process to take place, but, in the primary version of the model, with no 'built-in' technological progress, no fiscal or monetary measures can influence the growth rate, in the long run anyway. Keith Shaw and I (Peacock and Shaw, 1976) have shown that if consumption rather than income per head is taken as the target variable, the fiscal policy could influence its growth rate; and it is well known that fiscal policy models have been produced to show how the natural rate of growth can be reached more swiftly by compensatory finance. But these are not much more than theoretical curiosities.

Once the model is developed along Smithian lines with technological improvements made a function of the growth in capital stock, then fiscal stimuli, so it is claimed, could raise the natural rate of growth and could do so within the time horizon which would make such a policy of interest to vote-maximizing governments (see Streissler, 1979; Peacock and Shaw, 1976). 1 suspect that liberals, assuming that they accepted that evidence supported this position, would be divided on the desirability of buttressing the Smithian 'canons' with fiscal stimulation. Those who considered growth as the most important argument in some widely agreed welfare function might consider that liberal principles would not be violated. Others would argue that the fiscal policy was in effect promoting the collectivization of saving for raising the rate of capital formation would imply a rise in the rate of saving above that sanctioned by a freely working capital market. The additional argument might be used that stimulation of investment by tax reliefs and grants would take the pressure off entrepreneurs to be efficient and innovative.

However, the recent emphasis on knowledge and therefore on research and education and training as a cardinal factor in growth (cf. Romer, 1986; Solow, 1991) presents a more interesting challenge to liberal thinking. Entrepreneurs may only have a limited interest in investment in knowledge and education because of the claimed difficulties of capturing the benefits. This leads to the familiar argument that the externalities created by research and knowledge require public support if not public production. The additional twist provided by Romer is that, even if externalities can be internalized, the introduction of increasing returns to scale throws doubts on the encouragement of competition, notably through trade liberalization, as a measure which would promote economic growth. It is beyond my competence to pass any judgment on the strength of this line of argument. What can be said is that a liberal who was convinced by the argument and accompanying evidence would wish to look very closely at how far the externalities created by knowledge required public support, and the efficiency of the delivery systems for education, training and research relying on such support; unless, of course, (s)he judged that such collective action would be contrary to liberal principles in the first place, whatever growth benefits might follow from it.

I have probably given the impression that the liberal position vis-à-vis growth economics is that of the critical bystander; and to some extent I believe that to be the right description. There is one area, however, in which liberal economists have been very much on the attack, namely with regard to growth models which assign a large role to collective action in raising growth rates in 'developing' countries. This attack is of more than passing interest because liberal thinkers, notably Bauer (1969) and Lachmann (1973), have questioned the very existence of a phenomenon labelled 'growth' and 'historicist prophecies' (Bauer) which claim to be able to map its progress and identify the forces which promote it. For example, Bauer argues:

> (M)any of the concepts used ..., notably capital output ratios, are exceedingly vague. But even if they were more precisely defined they could not serve as the basis for scientific prediction as they are only simple descriptions of past occurrences and not variables between which functional and causal relationships have been established. And casual collection of a few statistics is not serious historical study, nor does simple extrapolation of arbitrarily chosen trends reflect scientific activity. (Bauer, 1969)

Latterly, liberal economists have been less 'Austrian' and more 'Smithian' in their attitude to macroeconomic modelling. It has become accepted that national income accounting and input-output analysis have considerably improved our knowledge of the workings of developing countries, though themselves originating in the need for development plans which have been, so it is claimed, conspicuously unsuccessful. Indeed, it is maintained by Deepak Lal, in a phrase which encapsulates the growing acceptance of the importance of efficient markets in development countries, that 'efficient growth which raises the demand for unskilled labour by "getting the prices right" is probably the most important means of alleviating poverty' (Lal, 1983, p. 102). Space prevents me adumbrating further the precise policy measures implicit in Lal's prescription of 'getting the prices right'; sufficient to note that his conclusion is that administrators in developing countries have much to learn still from 'that oft-neglected work, *The Wealth of Nations,* both so relevant and so modern' (Lal, 1983, p. 108). Adam Smith still lives and not only in Chicago!

IV THE SIZE OF THE STATE AND ECONOMIC GROWTH

The corollary of the Smithian prescriptions must be that, whereas it will be generally accepted that some state intervention is a necessary condition for long-term growth, an increase in the proportion of resources absorbed by government will exercise both a negative effect on the rate of economic growth and growing misallocation of resources. The latter proposition has been extensively investigated by public choice liberals employing the theory of rent-seeking. The former has received less attention though it has received more prominence with the marriage of hypotheses with empirical testing.

That well known proposition known as Baumol's Law postulates that the opportunities for employing new technologies in service sectors (notably in government) are limited whereas wage rates in these sectors are not likely to fall out of line with those in manufacturing sectors, if the normal forces of competition operate in the labour market. It follows that, even if the proportion of real resources absorbed by government is constant, government expenditure will rise as a proportion of Gross National Expenditure (GNE). It follows further that if the proportion of real resources rises, a progressive rise in the ratio of G to GNE will be associated with a lower rate of economic growth than would otherwise be the case.[6]

The proposition that purely technological factors account for the differences in economic performance of the public and private sector seems suspect. I would not deny that welfare and environmental services, commonly produced within the public sector, contain a large element of personal service so that the physical presence of labour input is a necessary constituent of output. However, I refuse to believe that, in the age of 'info-tech' and computers, the technical limitations on factor substitution are of paramount importance in the public sector. A more plausible argument for the existence of labour-intensive public services lies in the barriers that can be erected to prevent or to control the speed of introduction of new technologies. In the private sector, given competition, product and process innovation are necessary for firms to survive. The pressures to introduce new technologies are much less in circumstances where, as with government undertakings, there is a monopoly or near-monopoly of the output of a particular service and the product is not sold on the market. The barriers to improving productivity in the public sector therefore reflect the behaviour of rent-seekers, particularly bureaucrats, and do not have their origin in technological constraints.

My criticism of Baumol's thesis has been elevated into a more general hypothesis that echoes Adam Smith's complaint of 'want of parsimony' in public spending. Buchanan (1980) argues that the incidence of rent-seeking and the associated diversion of resources is a function of the increased size of government resulting in a decline in economic growth. The effect is cumulative, for the growth in the relative size of the public sector itself reduces incentives in the private sector through higher and higher taxes. In other words, the more an economy moves away from the Smithian ideal of limited government input to promote free trade, the lower its rate of growth; if this were true, then the economic prescriptions of Classical liberalism should command wide appeal.

Table 5.1 Growth rates of real GDP per capita in relation to the share of government expenditures in GDP, 1960–1980

	Compound growth rate of real GDP per capita (CAPGWTH)	
	Equation 1	Equation 2
Constant	.0467	.0372
	(7.04)	(6.70)
Change in capital/labour ratio		.4752
1960–1980 (KLGWTH)		(7.61)
% share government expenditures in	–.1123	–.0889
GDP 1960 (GOVT60)	(3.15)	(3.05)
Change in government expenditure	–.1140	–.0871
share 1960–1980 (CHGGOVT)	(3.66)	(3.41)
R^2	.1007	.4039
(N)	(115)	(115)

Notes:
CAPGWTH = Compound growth rate of real per capita GDP, 1960–1980. KLGWTH = Compound growth rate in the capital/labour ratio, 1960–1980. GOVT60 = Government expenditures as % of GDP, 1960.
CHGGOVT = Government Expenditures as % of GDP, 1980 – GOVT60
Student t values are in parenthesis below the coefficients.

Source: Scully (1989), p. 156.

This hypothesis should be testable and, indeed, there is an attempt by Scully (1989) to do so. Here I only report his results in summary form (Table 5.1). He uses World Bank data for 115 market economy countries which record economic growth, as measured by the growth rate of real GDP over the period 1960–1980, alongside the growth in the share of government in GDP. The relation between government share and economic growth was estimated using linear OLS and the error term is assumed to be normally distributed, it being claimed that tests for heteroscedasticity validate this assumption. In equation (1), the 'simpliste' version of the hypothesis is presented, in which only the government share variables appear as regressors. Both the size of government share (GOVT 60) and the change in that share (CHGGOVT) are of the right sign, which accords with earlier studies. However, as Scully points out, account has to be taken of the change in the capital/labour ratio over the relevant period. Public investment has a positive effect on the growth rate, though less productive than private investment. To neglect this factor may be to overstate the negative effect of the government share on growth. In equation (2) the compound rate of growth in the capital/labour ratio (KLGWTH) is introduced as a regressor but GOVT60 and CHGGOVT still have the correct sign and are statistically significant in a one-tail test at better than the 1 per cent level.

I have only reproduced the results which are sufficient to further discussion of the economics, and certainly not the econometrics, of such an approach. Here are the points for discussion that occur to me:

(i) As Scully recognizes, his approach really requires that the economy-wide growth rate should be a weighted average of the growth rates of each sector, with separate production functions estimated for both private sectors and the public sector. The increased size of the government sector and its effect on the growth rate could then be directly measured. Scully rejects this approach, simply because data are not available. There is a much more important problem than this. Ignoring any attribution of the relation between growth in public investment and output in the private sector, how is one to measure the real output of public sector services which are not priced? Conventional measures based on input changes 'adjusted' to take account of productivity changes are notoriously arbitrary.

(ii) Government expenditure as a percentage of GDP cannot embrace all the influences of government actions on the private economy. As is often argued, government by statute and regulation can exercise a major effect on private incentives and the allocation of resources. At the very least, any complete empirical study should take account of non-budgetary forms of government intervention. It cannot be assumed that growth in regulation is complementary to the growth in overall government expenditure. It could be; but account would then have to be taken of the influence of the composition as well as the amount of government expenditure on the complexity of the regulatory system. Matters are further complicated by the propensity of Western governments embarking on privatization programmes to subject privatized concerns which were previously public monopolies to strict regulatory control. The size of the public sector relative to the rest of the economy will decline, *cet. par.*, but will its influence be diminished?

(iii) One should be careful not to conclude that a Western-type economy which embarked on a vigorous programme of cutting government services in order to improve growth prospects would necessarily achieve its aim. As Maddison (1991, pp. 79–80) has emphasized, extensive state action to equalize the primary distribution of income has been a prerequisite for widespread acceptance of capitalist property relations and the operation of market forces, making them more legitimate by removing most of the grievances which motivate proponents of a socialist alternative. This is not to deny that potential efficiency gains would not accrue from reductions in social transfers and subsidies with disincentive effects on individuals and firms respectively, but the perceived distribution effect could engender strong opposition to major cutbacks. While it is arguable whether Maddison is right in claiming that the efficiency losses from the growth in public spending are likely to be insignificant, one can certainly agree with him that they are modest in comparison with those experienced in command economies where the level of state intervention has been very much higher.

V. CONCLUDING OBSERVATION

The thing that strikes me most about conducting this review of the liberal stance towards economic growth both as an objective and as a variable which may be influenced by policy is the change in the intellectual climate. When growth economics became a fashionable subject in economic theory in the 1950s, anti-Keynesianism was so strong amongst Continental and some, but by no means all, Anglo-Saxon liberals that friendly discourse was almost impossible. I can even recall being accused by Ludwig von Mises at a liberal meeting in 1958 of being tainted with 'national socialism' because I used the term national product! An appeal to the 'Introduction and Plan' of *The Wealth of Nations*, which starts with a definition of a nation's annual produce, fell on deaf ears. That has all changed, I am glad to say, and it may be worth saying a word or two as to how this has come about.

Firstly, whatever one's views on policy, any fair-minded economist could not fail to be impressed by the careful empirical work which has vastly improved our knowledge of the process of growth and thrown light on its determinants. This work has been influenced by and has influenced growth modelling. Angus Maddison has played a major part in this comparatively recent development.

Liberal speculation on the effects of public sector growth on economic development has been given a much better focus by growth accounting.

Secondly, it has become accepted that any macroeconomic theory that deserves the name has to have firm microeconomic foundations; and this applies to growth models as well as to short-term forecasting models. As I have argued, the methodological bias in liberal economics towards the importance of individual motivation has made us all more wary of models which treat economic actors as automatons.

Lastly, economists of very different persuasions with experience of advice-giving have been brought face to face with the harsh realities of political action. Growth policy cannot be based on the presupposition that correction of market failure is simply a matter of choosing the right policy instruments. Whatever the value judgments underpinning the approach of public choice theorists, the move towards an economic analysis of government which studies the motivation of politicians and bureaucrats and their relations with firms and individuals must influence our attitude to the feasibility of growth policies that rely on large-scale government intervention. Government failure is a reality to be faced and not an uncomfortable fact to be ignored. But then that is one of the most important messages to be found in *The Wealth of Nations* which we are in the process of re-learning.

NOTES

1. See, for example, Adelman (1961), Simpson (1983), Reid (1989), Stern (1991) and, of course, Maddison (I991).
2. On this point, see the excellent discussion by Adelman (1961).
3. For further discussion, see Peacock (1979).
4. For further discussion, see Schumpeter (1950).
5. For detailed discussion, see Reid (1989), Chapter 9.
6. For a simple proof, see Peacock (1979).

REFERENCES

Adelman, I. (1961), *Theories of Economic Growth and Development,* Stanford: Stanford University Press, Chapter 3.

Barry, N. (1986), *On Classical Liberalism and Libertarianism*, London: Macmillan, Chapter 5.

Bauer, P. (1969), 'Development Economics: The Spurious Consensus and its Background', in Erich Streissler (ed.), *Roads to Freedom. Essays in Honours of Friedrich A. von Hayek*, London: Routledge and Kegan Paul, pp. 5–46.

Buchanan, J. (1980), 'Rent Seeking and Profit Seeking', in J. Buchanan, G. Tullock and R. Tollison (eds), *Toward a Theory of a Rent Seeking Society*, Texas: A. and M. University Press.

Lachmann, L. (1973), *Macro-Economic Thinking and the Market Economy*, Hobart Paper, No. 56, London: Institute of Economic Affairs.
Lal, D. (1983), *The Poverty of 'Development Economics'*, Hobart Paperback, No. 16, London: Institute of Economic Affairs.
Lucas, R.E. (1988), 'On the Mechanics of Economic Development', *Journal of Monetary Economics*, Vol. 22, pp. 3–22.
Maddison, A. (1991), *Dynamic Forces in Capitalist Development*, Oxford University Press.
Mill, J.S. (1848/1965), *Principles of Political Economy*, Toronto Edition, ed. V. Bladen and J. Robson (1965), University of Toronto Press, Book IV, Chapter VI.
Peacock, A. (1979), *The Economic Analysis of Government*, Oxford: Martin Robertson, Chapter 3.
Peacock, A. and Shaw, G.K. (1976), *The Economic Theory of Fiscal Policy*, Revised Edition, London: Allen and Unwin, Chapter V.
Reid, G. (1989), *Classical Economic Growth: An Analysis in the Tradition of Adam Smith*, Oxford: Basil Blackwell.
Romer, P. (1986), 'Increasing Returns and Long-Run Growth', *Journal of Political Economy*, No. 94, pp. 1002–37.
Rowley, C. and Peacock, A. (1975), *Welfare Economics: A Liberal Restatement*, London: Martin Robertson.
Schumpeter, J. (1950), *Capitalism, Socialism and Democracy*, 3rd edition, New York: Harper, Preface.
Scully, G. (1989), 'The Size of the State, Economic Growth and the Efficient Utilization of National Resources', *Public Choice*, Vol. 63, No. 2, November, pp. 149–64.
Simpson, D. (1983), *The Political Economy of Growth*, Oxford: Basil Blackwell, Chapter 4.
Smith, A. (1776/1976), *An Inquiry into the Nature and Causes of the Wealth of Nations, 1776*, R.H. Campbell and A.S. Skinner (general eds) (1976), Clarendon Press, Book II, Chapter 3.
Solow, R. (1991), 'Growth Theory', in *Companion to Contemporary Economic Thought*, D. Greenaway, M. Bleaney and I. Stewart (eds), London: Routledge, Chapter 19.
Stern, N. (1991), 'The Determinants of Growth', *Economic Journal*, Vol. 101, No. 404, January, pp. 122–33.
Streissler, E. (1979), 'Growth Models as Diffusion Processes', *Kyklos*, Vol. 32, pp. 251–69 and pp. 571–86.

6. Welfare philosophies and welfare finance

(I was 'blooded' in statistical analysis of public finance in 1949 when I assisted Frank Paish, my senior colleague at LSE, and, like me, an ardent member of the Liberal Party, in preparing a negative income tax scheme which involved the amalgamation of the UK social security and income tax systems. This stimulated me to write my first book, The Economics of National Insurance *(1952), which 'exposed' our social insurance scheme as a piece of fiscal legerdemain. As a result of this and related work I was promoted to Reader in Public Finance at the LSE in 1951, which required me to broaden my interests and diverted me away from specializing on welfare problems. Had I not done so, I might have become Reader in Social Policy at the LSE, having been offered the post informally by Richard Titmuss ; but a divinity must shape our ends. I doubt if Richard would have tolerated my antipathy towards certain features of the welfare state, and, in any case, he appointed instead Brian Abel-Smith, a much-missed, admirable person, willing to countenance friendly argument about his, to my mind, mistaken views on the functions of social policy.*

I return from time to time to the question of the dimensions of the state's involvement in welfare. In this chapter, I have tried to set out clearly the derivation of social policies from alternative sets of philosophical principles and to explain why principles and practice differ. The recent 'conversion' of the British Labour Party to the ideas of the 'social market economy' may make section V somewhat outdated by events, but, as I argue, the link between ideas and events is often a tenuous one and we have yet to see whether the 'conversion' will influence actual policy measures if and when Labour is returned to office. In the interim, the actual experience of linking philosophy with practice in the Thatcher years gives plenty of food for thought about the famous question – which is more important, ideas or interests, in the institution and evolution of social policy?)

I. INTRODUCTION

This chapter concerns the choices open to governments in devising financial arrangements which are designed to fulfil the objectives of the 'welfare state', or, more particularly, of the social security element in it. I distinguish between four choices:

(i) the choice between an absolute or relative poverty line;
(ii) the choice between universality or selectivity in the provision of social benefits;
(iii) the choice between types of benefit provision – tax allowances, money transfers and communal consumption;
(iv) the choice between general taxation and earmarked contributions as a method for financing benefits.

It is as well to begin with the realization that the most that we can expect from an analysis of the financial arrangements is to see how these categories of choices can be made consistent with one another. There are many ways in which this consistency can be achieved, depending on the initial value judgments chosen to govern the aims of the 'welfare state'. There is therefore no point in following the conventional pattern of classifying the 'pros' and 'cons' of any combination of choices. The ranking of the choices is derived solely from the particular value system chosen as the point of departure of the discussion. It follows that it is fruitless to attempt to derive a logic of choice solely from the conditions for economic efficiency in Paretian welfare analysis buttressed by some view of equity objectives. There need therefore be no consensus amongst economists about the 'proper' choices.[1]

These propositions suggest a procedure for developing the exposition which follows in this contribution. First, categorize the more influential political philosophies from which 'operational' value judgments may be derived in order to specify the objectives of the welfare state. This will make clear the initial disagreements about aims. Secondly, translate these 'operational, judgments into policy prescriptions regarding financing arrangements. Thirdly, consider how far differences between the various philosophies are derived from (i) the philosophy itself, (ii) the models of human behaviour and their reflection in economic modelling, and (iii) differing judgments about the practicality of financial arrangements designed to fulfil the policy aims.

This typology of welfare state philosophies may then be used in order to review recent government attempts to change the thrust of welfare policy.

II THE LIBERTARIAN POSITION

It is absurd, of course, to talk about 'the' libertarian position, but there are sufficient common elements in libertarian writing for us to be able to construct a view about society's obligations which involve transfer of resources between individuals.

A useful starting point is Nozick's view on 'entitlement'.[2] The only claim we have on resources is that based on our own efforts and abilities. Our entitlement is to be able to exert effort and to use our abilities in any way we choose provided this does not limit any other individual's entitlement to do the same. It follows that no one has a prior right to a particular standard of living, such as a minimum level of subsistence. This does not carry the implication that people will be left to starve, as it would be wholly consistent with a society in which people could use their own resources as they think fit, for a large proportion of them do, in fact, wish to see poverty eradicated. The motives, as always, may be mixed. Some may wish to see poverty eradicated because they would suffer from feelings of guilt and repugnance or because they are empathic; others may be worried about possible social unrest and attacks on their own perceived entitlements. In short, the relief of poverty would reflect some contractual relationship between members of the community and would not be legitimized by an appeal to some principle of distributive justice.

The translation of this philosophical position into the designing of institutions to give effect to any wish to relieve poverty seems to be regarded as a rather secondary matter by social philosophers; or perhaps they realize that the translation is far from easy. The only general guidance given is that one must minimize the intervention of the state as much as possible and, by implication, the degree of compulsory income distribution. All that an economist can do is to identify the kind of institutional arrangements which would appear to be compatible with the 'minimalist' position.

So far as the poverty line is concerned, it is doubtful if libertarians could accept the concept at all, for poverty is not capable of exact measurement. They are usually the first to complain about the false precision given to the term by poverty action groups. Nevertheless, there is a clear commitment in the libertarian literature to a community responsibility to prevent starvation, however caused. Thus Hayek,[3] after referring to the brilliant success of the capitalist countries in creating the means to eradicate poverty, quotes with approval the words of the famous Poor Law Commissioner and economist, Nassau Senior:

> to proclaim that no man, whatever his vices or even his crimes, shall die of hunger and cold, is a promise that in the state of civilisation of England, or of France, can be performed not merely with safety, but with advantage, because the gift of mere subsistence may be subjected to conditions which no one will voluntarily accept.[4]

The commitment clearly only extends to the relief of absolute poverty. Hayek's view is probably representative of this position:

> poverty in the relative sense must of course continue to exist outside of any completely egalitarian society; so long as there exists inequality, somebody must be at the bottom of the scale. But the abolition of absolute poverty is not helped by the endeavour to achieve 'social justice'; in fact, in many of the countries in which absolute poverty is still an acute problem, the concern for 'social justice' has become one of the greatest obstacles in the elimination of poverty. ...
>
> Misfortune, however, cannot create a claim for protection against risks which all have had to run in order to attain the position they occupy. The very language in current use which at once labels as a 'social problem' anything which causes dissatisfaction of any group, and suggests that it is the duty of the legislature to do something about such 'social injustice', has turned the conception of 'social justice' into a mere pretext for claims for privileges by special interests.[5]

In order to understand the libertarian attitude to universality versus selectivity of benefits, it is necessary to consider the 'minimalist' position about the responsibility of the individual to make provision for himself or herself against the possibility of becoming poor. The initial presumption is that individuals might be able to insure against various calamitous events or predictable conditions (e.g. old age) which would destroy or at least reduce their income earning power. If individuals cannot be relied upon voluntarily to take out such insurance this does not make a case for some compulsory state scheme, but it does suggest some form of government regulation which would make a minimum level of provision through private sector insurance compulsory. However, even assuming that such a regulation would be enforceable, this would not guarantee the eradication of absolute poverty. Firstly, it is quite probable that a fair proportion of insurees would have to pay annual premiums which would leave them with an annual disposable income below the poverty standard and there will be a residuum of persons who cannot provide for themselves anyway. (It is often claimed that poorer people are worse health risks than richer persons so that compulsory insurance premiums could be regressive.) Secondly, loss of earnings resulting from unemployment is uninsurable. (Now it is true that some form of insurance against temporary unemployment is provided indirectly through extension of credit under hire purchase agreements and temporary suspension of mortgage payments, but lenders will expect some form of security, e.g. other physical assets and investment in skills, which can only be supplied by the relatively well-off.) Unemployment is virtually uninsurable because of (i) the adverse selection problem – the insuree can control the incidence of unemployment; and (ii) the risks are not separate and independent – unemployment can hit a large number of persons at once.

The minimalist position, therefore, recognizes that inducing or compelling individuals by regulation to re-allocate their income through time would not eliminate poverty, and that some form of payment from public funds would be required – the form of which is yet to be discussed. Clearly, however, given the overriding requirement that compulsory redistribution of income must be minimized, such payment must be targeted to those who are not able to cover the risks of poverty for themselves and targeting must be related to the particular cause of poverty, such as sickness, old age, housing conditions or unemployment. The inevitable concomitant to targeted benefits must be means testing.

So far as the form of benefits is concerned, there must be a presumption that the libertarian position would entail a preference for money transfers. Individuals who receive some form of subsidized income would be paid in money in order to cover their minimum needs during periods of sickness, unemployment or old age. Such devices as food subsidies, and health provision at zero cost rather than by payment through compulsory health insurance, would be frowned upon, because these would interfere with market forces.[6] It would also be emphasized by libertarians that transfers-in-kind would inhibit the preservation and development of basic household management skills which would enable poorer persons to make the most of scarce resources. At the very most, libertarians might tolerate the issue of vouchers designed to effect payments for particular services, particularly those which protect the interest of minors, such as housing and education. This would still enable a free market to operate in the provision of 'social services' through rent allowances, education vouchers and the like paid directly to recipients of income support and redeemable by private suppliers and targeted to the 'desired' components of a minimum standard of living.

There is, finally, the question of financing the various elements in the provision of income support. The principle in operation which complements the minimizing of compulsory transfers is that of relating benefit to cost so far as possible. Therefore, in an ideal libertarian world, individuals, as we have seen, insure against the incidence of poverty. Taking a longer view, the incidence of poverty might be reduced by investment in human capital, which suggests that somehow a market in educational and training investment should be created with the offer of loan finance. If the absolute minimum payments simply make it impossible for all individuals to pay the premiums or amortize the loans, then the next step would be to subsidize the premiums and loans on a means-tested basis. The important point to note is that while insurance would have to be compulsory, there is no argument deployed in support of a state monopoly in insurance provision. The one important exception would be unemployment, which cannot be insured against, though it is sometimes claimed that any state provision might be financed primarily from a payment by each industry in proportion to the incidence of unemployment 'generated' in it.[7]

Controversy must obviously surround the feasibility of such a system of income and its very compatibility with other principles dear to the heart of minimalists. The onus of proof of entitlement to support would presumably rest with the individual or the head of the family, and it seems impossible to avoid major difficulties in deciding on levels of support and in carrying out detailed enquiries into means. This presents policy-makers with a dilemma. On the one hand, if information is to be supplied solely by those demanding support, claimants may exaggerate their needs – the adverse selection problem. On the other hand, obtaining accurate information might entail rigorous methods of enquiry and heavy penalties for non-compliance which might appear incompatible with a libertarian disposition.

There has been some recent discussion about the prospects for devising an administrative system which would enable a government to differentiate between 'self-provision' requirements and the residuum of financial support which would be targeted towards those who cannot meet the minimum standard of individual and family provision. One such scheme[8] is derived from the principle of taxation according to benefit developed by Wicksell. Each individual is given a social security account by the public authorities. Premium payments are recorded on the credit side on evidence supplied by the individual, who may claim partial or complete exemption depending on evidence of means. Social security payments are recorded on the debit side, with some such payments (e.g. education vouchers, family allowances) also recorded as loans. A separate loan account records loans taken up and records interest and amortization payments. The account is normally 'closed' when the individual reaches pensionable age with provision made for 'early closing' in the event of death before retirement or emigration. Depending on the individual's circumstances, any deficit on the account may be written off, the resultant loss being covered by taxation. Of course, such a scheme does not rule out strategic behaviour by individuals, who may work less and save less, in contemplation of the likelihood that the government will always provide for them. However, if they have a deficit against their name, then they will have to pay up, though they would always be left with a subsistence level of pension.

This kind of scheme raises a basic question about the operation of any social security system, even if it is confined to minimum income support. Unless there is some compelling reason for operating a separate compulsory social insurance scheme run by the government, it would seem logical to integrate the social security account with the individual's 'account' with the tax authorities. Only then would it be possible to have full information on the impact of government transfers and taxes on the disposable income of the individual. Full consideration of proposals to amalgamate social security and income tax administration will be given when proposals for tax credit or negative income tax schemes are examined in Section III below.

III. THE SOCIAL MARKET ECONOMISTS

The 'social market economy' (*Soziale Marktwirtschaft*) was a term invented by the German economist and senior government adviser Alfred Müller-Armack to denote a reconciliation of the free market economy with the demands of distributive justice.[9] It is a useful term to describe the attitudes of a regiment of economic and social thinkers who have extended the concept of 'entitlement' to cover the right of every individual to a 'basic' standard of living and also to access to resources in order to develop their latent talents, for example through investment in their education and social environment (health and housing). At the same time, the choice of means for giving effect to these 'rights' should recognize the importance of developing individuals' capacity to choose for themselves and of expressing these choices through an efficiently operating market economy.

Space does not allow a discussion of the different approaches leading to the delineation of this extension of the concept of entitlement. It is sufficient to say that whether these entitlements are derived from a utilitarian view of economic welfare, based on the assumption that marginal utility falls as income rises, or from a Rawlsian view of social justice, based on maximizing the welfare of the least advantaged person (which does not require inter-personal comparisons of utility), the constraint of minimizing income redistribution no longer applies. This follows directly from the more positive commitment both to a basic standard of living and also to the funding of services designed to promote investment in human capital.

If there is any distinction to be made between the various social market economists, it lies in their view of the organization of production; and this is germane to the choice of practical measures matching their value judgments. One group does not specify in any detail how production should be organized, except to state that competition must be preserved within the market economy – how this is to be done is a separate question. There is another group, following John Stuart Mill, which would argue strongly in favour of much more equality in the ownership of capital. In Mill's case this extended to the proposition that the future of the market economy depended on the growth in labour-managed firms – 'an association of the labourers themselves on terms of equality, collectively owning the capital with which they carry on their operations and working under managers selected and removable by themselves'.[10] The most distinguished contemporary exponent of attempts to reconcile conflicts between capital and labour is James Meade,[11] who has developed a scheme based on joint holdings of risk capital in a company by both 'capitalists' and workers. However, the sharing of risks by labour and capital presupposes, according to Meade, an automatic entitlement by all individuals to 'a certain and reliable tax-free Social Dividend'.[12] Social security income becomes the essential source of stable income alongside the fluctuating capital and wage income received by the worker.

As before, an attempt will be made to trace the connection between the philosophy of the welfare state and the level of benefits. The removal of the constraint on compulsory redistribution immediately suggests that social market economists (SMEs) would be more sympathetic to a minimum level of subsistence which depends on the growth in real GDP; in other words the 'poverty line' is a relative concept. (This is a logical necessity in the case of the utilitarian theory of income redistribution, provided that pre-tax/transfer income distribution remains unequal.) A more difficult question is how far SMEs are committed to a much more radical requirement, namely some proportional relation between income levels and benefits, as in the case of earnings-related pension schemes. The usual argument supporting the claim that such benefits should be earnings-related rests on the supposed 'consensus' between political parties in several European countries which lies behind the 'dynamic' pension schemes operating in such countries as Germany, Italy and the UK. 'Consensus' does not however imply that there is any logical connection between the SME's position and what happens to be agreed, if in fact it is, between different political factions. A more likely explanation of consensus is that offered by Barry,[13] namely that, with no constitutional limitations, public expenditure decisions are taken which commit future generations. Earnings-related pensions become an 'electoral bribe' on a large scale and one which works because of the opportunities open to governments to disguise the long-run economic costs of pensions provision.

A more obvious difference between libertarians and SMEs lies in the firmer commitment of the latter to 'access' by poorer persons to education, health and housing facilities, which can, of course, be justified on the grounds that, in the long run, investment in human capital may reduce the incidence of poverty. This extension of 'entitlement' must be important in the devising of appropriate government measures to give effect to the objectives of policy, but it is difficult to give any precision to terms such as 'access' or 'entitlement' in trying to translate them into resource requirements. On such matters there is room for considerable variations in points of view amongst SMEs.

Turning to the choice between universality or selectivity of benefits, we observe again no logical necessity why SMEs should vote for one or the other, as a matter of principle. Indeed, much of the discussion concerns the danger that selectivity may defeat its own purpose by offering no incentive to beneficiaries to acquire the skills or make the effort to be able to fend for themselves; and this must be an empirical matter which can only be resolved, if at all, by scientific investigation. However, the more explicit commitment of SMEs to income redistribution removes a major objection to the use of universal income provision, e.g. some form of 'Social Dividend' for all, as a major means for eliminating poverty. Therefore, apart from the argument advanced above for a Social Dividend based on the need for a 'certain and reliable' component of income, the claims of the Social Dividend are extended as a way of remedying the perceived deficiencies of selective benefits.

It might be thought that the extension of the definition of welfare provision and the more relaxed attitude to income redistribution would point towards major differences between libertarians and SMEs over the types of benefit provision, but this is not so. Tax allowances (or expenditure) were not specifically mentioned in Section II above, though it is conceivable that the libertarian position would support tax relief granted to charities directed at helping poorer persons. However, such relief becomes of some importance in the SMEs' scenario. This applies particularly to earnings-related pensions. Given the SMEs' interest in combining their views on social justice with an efficient market economy, there is no necessity for such a pension scheme to be nationalized. A pensions standard must be laid down, which could be either contribution-based or final-salary-based, and the employee could be a member of either an occupational or a personal pension scheme. It is an open question how much tax relief should be given alongside the compulsory requirement to meet the pension standard, and it must be borne in mind that such tax relief has to be given at the cost of either raising taxes elsewhere, given the level of public expenditure, or reducing the level of public expenditure, unless the government wishes to face the consequences of a growing public debt. There are three arguments in favour of tax allowances. The first is that SMEs are likely, as a matter of general philosophy, to wish to encourage private saving even at the cost of a reduction in government saving. Second, encouraging competition in the provision of pensions would fit with the SMEs' disposition to support the market economy. (This, of course, would suggest, in strict logic, preference for 'portable' personal rather than occupational pensions, which may be specifically designed to reduce occupational mobility.) Third, although this point is the subject of much argument, a state monopoly of pension provision runs the risk of being highly bureaucratic and therefore slow-moving and costly, because not subject to market pressures.

Clearly, money transfers are a major instrument of SME social policy particularly one wedded to a Social Dividend approach. The more interesting area of discourse on benefits concerns access to educational, health and housing services. The difference between libertarians and SMEs is more one of degree than of kind. For SMEs there is no reason why these services should have to be provided at zero cost by government institutions. Even if it is believed that some form of consumer protection is necessary because of the perceived inability of citizens to make sensible choices regarding education, health and housing, there is no case for turning them over to the government. Consumer protection can be afforded by regulation and by advisory services, with the latter if need be receiving public subsidy. The difference with libertarians will arise over the *degree* of 'entitlement' to such services, and is likely to be reflected not in the form of provision but in the method of financing. We should therefore expect SMEs to be in favour both of money transfers and also of educational, health and housing voucher systems, with the production of the associated services being left partly if not wholly in private hands, and perhaps with a bias towards co-operatives and non-profit-making institutions as suppliers.

Whereas the libertarian position takes 'the insurance principle' as the starting point and modifies it only to the extent necessary to prevent absolute poverty, the SMEs' positive emphasis on distributive justice severs the nexus between contribution and payment, at least in any strict way. SMEs may support the proposition that, as a matter of principle, every citizen should pay something towards the provision of public services, but there is no presumption that such payment should be earmarked for the payment of social security and associated services. At most, labelling finance of social security as 'contributions' or 'premiums' is only a sales pitch, and may contain the danger of deluding contributors into believing that they are paying in full for the benefits received.[14] It therefore comes as no surprise to find that SMEs have been closely concerned with attempts to amalgamate the personal tax and social security systems, particularly if some form of Social Dividend scheme is to become the cornerstone of the social security system. As is well known, if they are not amalgamated or at least not closely co-ordinated, those who move out of entitlement to benefits because they have become fit or have found jobs may be faced with such high marginal tax rates that they are worse off than if not working.[15]

To sum up this section, there is some consonance between the libertarian and SME position, as found, for instance, in the wish to channel income support through the individual or family and to avoid collectivizing the services designed to alleviate poverty. However, the kind of 'life-cycle accounting' suggested above (pp. 65–6) as a logical consequence of libertarian financing arrangements would presumably be regarded by SMEs as neither desirable nor necessary. Individuals suffering from poverty are not considered as being 'in debt to society' as a result of being in this condition. Furthermore, in so far as individuals move from being poor to being better off, they acknowledge any 'debt to society' by the payment of a greater proportion of their incomes in taxes as they move up the income scale. This argument is only subject to dispute amongst SMEs if we adopt such a broad definition of social policy as to include access to higher education. Some would continue to argue that those undergoing higher education should not have to bear the cost, even if as a result their income prospects are enhanced – if that were the result then the fortunate graduates would pay higher taxes anyway. Others recognise a problem of horizontal equity between those obtaining free access to capital if they invest in themselves and those who have to borrow the capital if they invest in a business and initially are at the same income level. Here, the 'life-cycle accounting' concept seems to make sense, with students paying off loans used to finance their studies, though repayment might take into account the economic circumstances of the graduate.[16]

IV. THE COLLECTIVIST POSITION

The common characteristic of the previous positions has been the emphasis on public financing as distinct from public provision of welfare services. Redistribution is regarded as a means by which poorer persons are enabled, as far as possible, to help themselves. In the last analysis, if there were no poverty, then the 'welfare state' would disappear. Hence my previous prescription that 'the proper function of the welfare state … is to teach people how to do without it', and the associated conditional projection that, if it were so desired, in the long run the welfare state could wither away.[17] This position, however, is not acceptable to a wide range of influential writers on welfare state problems, though few economists appear to occupy their ranks.

The modern debate out of which the general differences between individualistic and collectivist positions emerge has centred in medical care. Let us assume that A fulfils his obligations to government under a libertarian regime and insures against illness, as he is required to do, whereas B evades his obligations. If they both fall ill with a similar complaint, A receives better treatment than B because the insurance company will pay up. This is unjust, it is claimed, because such an important service as medical care should be allocated according to people's needs and not according to their means. The fact that B chose to evade his obligations does not alter the situation. The general point being made is that equal access to consumption of 'priority' goods such as medical care fosters the ideal of fraternity and emphasizes interests held in common rather than the diversity of interests and viewpoints which libertarians believe to be the important characteristic of individuals in society. Diversity of interests, so it is held, particularly if matched by income inequality, make for a divided society. This idealist point of view is associated in recent times, of course, with Richard Titmuss.[18] In his view, there was at least a minimum of priority goods and services which must be enjoyed in common, such as health and education. Ryan puts it thus:

> the market can be left to give beer to beer drinkers and champagne to champagne drinkers but not to give blood to those who need transfusions. Both sorts of appeal rely on the belief that there are morally valuable side effects from communality of consumption; the Spartans thought they got extra loyalty and comradeship, Green … and Titmuss … thought they got extra altruism on the one side, and gratitude and a sense of belonging on the other.[19]

Even a brief résumé of the 'communality of consumption' position makes it clear that concentration on the concept of a 'poverty line' is misplaced. However, our previous distinction between social security provision in the narrow sense and social services may still be useful. In the collectivist position, the emphasis shifts from 'entitlement' to some minimum standard of living to the fact of inequality of income distribution. Recalling the utilitarian argument, if in one situation every income receiver was at the margin of subsistence and then the situation changed and half of the income receivers increased their incomes twofold and the rest remained at the margin of subsistence, this would represent an improvement in welfare, though it would almost certainly not represent an *optimal* position to utilitarians. However, the fact that inequality had increased might warn the collectivist that a divisive element had been introduced into society. In short, instead of meeting a poverty standard subject to minimizing income redistribution, it must be shown why any income equality is necessary in the first place – something like the position taken by Rawls. However, this only takes us to the position of requiring positive income redistribution from rich to poor which, other things being equal, need only mean a redistribution of purchasing power as between individual citizens who would then be responsible for their own welfare. An essential element in the collectivist position is that the redistribution must take a form which furthers the aim of equal access to 'priority' goods such as health, housing and education. While redistribution must be reflected to some extent in government transfers, the main impact on the national accounts will appear in an increase, not in individual disposable income, but in a rise in expenditure on consumption goods and services by government.

It follows that the issue of universality versus selectivity of benefits is hardly an issue to collectivists, at least in its traditional context. The categorizing of the different causes of poverty may seem necessary, if only to determine the differing 'needs' in each condition, with benefit payments fixed by reference to these needs for each category as perceived by, say, social administrators. At the same time, a 'Social Dividend' payable in cash may be thought too insensitive an instrument to take account of the differing needs of the ill-off, and one which in any case could be overshadowed by payments in kind, which must now be considered in more detail.

Sufficient has been said so far to explain why collectivists would favour benefits in kind, but it is worth considering further the philosophical basis of this change of emphasis away from the simple provision of cash to the ill-off. First of all, the question of the form of redistribution must be discussed before its provision and extent are considered. The libertarian and, to some extent, the SME positions emphasize the important 'negative freedom' valued by individuals in the sense of freedom from outside interference in their exploitation of their preferences. It has been argued, however, that 'social justice' involves a 'natural right' to certain commodities such as food, shelter and medical care. It is interesting that this argument has been deployed by Dasgupta[20] as consonant with the pursuit of the idea of freedom – not simply freedom from want but a right which would guarantee individuals' access to particular forms of consumption. A familiar argument is the paternalist one – the ability of individuals to make choices that will 'better their condition', as Adam Smith might have put it, diminishes with the degree of poverty. Even if choice is constrained by a voucher system, the ill-off may have neither the courage nor the skill to make the right choices among competing suppliers. There is a touch of this in Dasgupta's argument, but its main thrust is that the variability in needs is difficult to ascertain by the government and that if it polls individuals on what their needs are, it faces the prospect of non-truthful disclosure. The best that the government can do is to assume that individuals have equal needs. Then he adds his bull point. If incomes are more-or-less equally distributed, the deviation from the mean 'demand' for such needs would be negligible and a voucher system would achieve the aim of 'positive freedom'. If incomes are unequally distributed, then the rich would top up their vouchers and receive more than their 'natural rights'; only a state rationing system would achieve the desired aim of equal access.

The term 'equal needs' is clearly ambiguous, but what Dasgupta is concerned to emphasise is that for certain social services the collectivist is not demanding *minimum* but *uniform* standards of provision. This view is fully consonant with Titmuss's precept that there should be communality of consumption, for the most efficient way for the state to provide uniform standards of provision is to set aside the price mechanism and itself to provide the services in kind.

It follows from this argument that, whereas social security transfers would still remain an integral part of the welfare state, tax allowances would be frowned upon. Encouraging individuals to 'contract out' of state provision of health and education services by offering them tax relief on payments made to private suppliers would undermine the moral foundations of the welfare state. Not only would such individuals be denying that they had something in common with others, but they might prefer to be 'more equal than others' by purchasing more of these services than would otherwise be available to them through state provision. The real test of the pure collectivist argument, however, is whether it entails prohibition of any private provision of such services, whatever the tax regime. The logic of the Dasgupta position suggests that the answer is 'yes', in which case another look has to be directed at the definition of freedom. Are people to be prevented from travelling abroad in order to seek some preferred private provision of health and education services?

With the collectivist position, we move even further away from the 'insurance' principle in which there is some close relation between benefits and contributions. In the case of state-provided social services at zero cost, there is clearly no need for any form of earmarked taxation. The amount and composition of expenditure must be decided on 'scientific' lines without reference to any form of hypothecated revenue. So far as transfers, such as pensions, are concerned, collectivists might support the idea of the payment of a minimum contribution as a kind of 'badge of citizenship'. However, why have so many collectivists supported an entirely state-run pension scheme with benefits related to final salary or wage when this would provide a different standard of pension provision according to income?

Various explanations are possible, but none of them can be derived from the logic of 'communality' in social provisions, which would appear to support only uniform pensions for all. I hazard the view that collectivists are not generally in favour of draconian methods for creating income equality and consequently would have to be prepared to accept that diversity of preferences and incomes would produce diversity in the pattern of saving for the future, for example through private pension schemes. The damage that this creates for 'communality of purpose' in the welfare state can be limited by making it compulsory for individuals to join a *state* pension scheme with earnings-related benefits. A variant of this explanation would add the cynical observation that such a scheme would offer the opportunity for the state to build up reserves which could be used as a powerful control by the government over the capital market[21] – what Hugh Dalton once called 'a gun to shoot bears'.

One major institutional difference between the collectivist position and the others is clearly the large proportion of the production of services which is under the direct control and operation of the public sector. Teachers, doctors, dentists and nurses, construction workers (in the case of publicly produced housing) and housing administrators are no longer subject to the pressure of the market. The challenge that this affords to the practical implementation of their ideals is clearly formidable. Writers such as Titmuss[22] expected that the professional classes, not subject to the pressures of the market, would be better infused with the spirit of 'communality' and better able to devote themselves single-mindedly to public service. For those who are aware of the economic analysis of non-profit-making institutions and their propensity to be designed to maximize the interests of the producers but which nevertheless support public provision of social services, the challenge consists in devising substitutes for market forces in order to promote efficiency, such as controls over performance.

V. IDEOLOGIES, INTERESTS AND IMPLEMENTATION OF CHANGE

There is clearly a close correspondence between Labour Party ideology and the collectivist position and between the libertarian wing of the Conservative Party and the 'minimalist' position. This correspondence is not, however, reflected in the composition and structure of the welfare services within the periods when both parties have held office for more than one full term. There is a striking contrast between the 'build-up' of the welfare state in the immediate post-war period during the Labour period of office, and the failure to 'prune' the welfare state during the ten years of Conservative government from 1979. Indeed, as Dilnot (Dilnot *et al.*, 1984) has calculated, in 1978–1988 more than 25 million out of 56 million persons in the UK at any one time were receiving one or more social security benefits. The numbers, in descending order, were 12 million recipients of child benefit, 9.6 million pensioners, 7 million recipients of means-tested housing benefit, and 3 million recipients of unemployment benefit or supplementary benefit. It is interesting to speculate on this contrast.

One obvious source of explanation must lie in the firmness of commitment to ideology, following the familiar adage of Keynes that ideas and not vested interests are the mainspring of political change. There could be something in this argument. Ideological dispute on the broad dimensions of the welfare state within the Labour Party has been minimal. The most effective challenge from within the party in Labour's political heyday came from Crosland's *Future of Socialism* (1956), which questioned the necessity for perpetuation of benefits in kind, such as food subsidies, but certainly did not call for major changes in the provision of health and education services. In contrast, prominent Conservative ideologists have expressed strong doubts about the privatization of education and health services and the destruction of an income-related pension scheme[23] as steps towards the perceived improvements associated with the 'Thatcherite' position. However, this division of opinion is not reflected in the range of proposals discussed at Cabinet level and which have reached at least the Green Paper stage, and even in government measures which have reached the statute book. The difference in commitment seems, therefore, to offer at best a small part of the explanation.

The influence of ideology on political events has been strongly challenged in recent years by public choice theorists as at most a necessary but not a sufficient condition for political change.[24] Put very briefly, and inevitably superficially, public choice analysts emphasize the constraints governing the implementation of policy, which are reflected in the way different interest groups view the effect of policy changes on their economic position. When these changes conflict with the interests of a particular group, they will use alternative instruments of political participation – voting strength, lobbying, negotiation with officials and so on – to protect their position. The 'easy way out' for governments is to buy off political opposition by expansion of government services which improve the welfare of organized interest groups and to rely on some form of 'tax illusion' effect to diminish the perceived costs of expansion. This expansion will itself increase the immunity of relevant interest groups from the rigours of the market. When expansion of public services meets increasing taxpayer resistance, expressed in avoidance and evasion, then a government may still be able to retain interest group support by recourse to exemptions from the application of the law or by some comparable form of legal privilege.

The public choice explanation accordingly would emphasize that a post-war Labour government would face little resistance from trade union, consumer and professional interest groups to a social policy which appeared to offer prizes for practically everyone. The atmosphere of a positive-sum game was also maintained by exploiting the prevalent under-consumptionist, left-wing, Keynesian view of economic prospects which claimed that expansion of government expenditure through provision of social services was a particularly appropriate way of maintaining the economy on a full employment growth path. The social opportunity cost of the growth of the public sector could be presented as zero. By the time the welfare costs of expansion of the public sector became apparent, professional groups such as doctors, nurses, teachers and administrators had been able to unionize and to obtain recognition of their bargaining rights with government. Therefore, any government trying to reduce the relative size as well as alter the composition and funding of welfare services is in a 'game' probably perceived by the players as 'zero-sum' rather than 'positive-sum'. In such a game each interest group will try, either individually or by forming coalitions, to throw the costs of change onto others.

It may also be a game of considerable uncertainty if, as is the case with health and education services, the benefits may be broadly assignable, but the financing of them is a quite separate operation. Thus if it is decided to charge for health and education services and to offset charging by a reduction in taxes, individuals' welfare loss from having to pay for the services can be clearly perceived by them, but the benefits from tax reduction may be widely diffused and hardly perceptible. In short, 'players' enjoined to enter a game of this kind perceived as zero-sum (possibly negative-sum), non-co-operative and beset by uncertain outcomes, will have a strong incentive to use political action designed to destroy the game itself.

VI. CONCLUDING REFLECTIONS

It is ironic that the predictions derived from public choice theory, which draws its inspiration from both the philosophical and technical analysis of classical libertarianism, should come to the conclusion that currently influential liberal ideas have such a slim chance of practical implementation in the case of welfare policy. For those such as the present author, who are broadly sympathetic to the 'minimalist' position (save on questions of wealth distribution), such a pessimistic conclusion presents a challenge rather than an admission of defeat. As Norman Barry has put it: 'ideas about economics and politics must, in some ultimate sense, influence politicians and legislators irrespective of group pressure. Otherwise, how would change occur (except by revolution)?'[25] There is no lack of ideas floating around about the adaptation of government institutions to further ultimate goals. In practice also, perhaps something has been achieved in Britain in the partial dismantling of the state pension system. The severing of the iron link between compulsory pension provision and final salary and the move towards personal pensions, combined with a growth in many alternative private sector sources of supply, go some way towards a reduction in the collectivist element in the British welfare state.[26] Public choice analysis would probably account for this by the fact that there was a discernible link between changes in benefits and in their financing. No prizes are offered for an answer to the 'riddle of the voucher'[27] and why the long and sustained campaign to introduce choice and competition in schooling failed to be regarded as anything more than an attractive idea.

NOTES

1. Charles Rowley and I deal with this matter *in extenso* in Rowley and Peacock (1975). For economists' varying attitudes on welfare state questions, see Ricketts and Shoesmith (1990).
2. Nozick (1974) has been followed by a considerable number of (predominantly) US writers, as in the representative collection of writers in Letwin (1983).
3. See Hayek (1976) for one of his several statements on this issue.
4. Hayek (1976), p. 190.
5. Hayek (1976), p. 140.
6. As we shall observe later, the libertarian position on this issue is widely accepted by economists.
7. This issue has been fully investigated, and, not surprisingly, is found to be a very complex and difficult one, as examined for example by Diamond (1977).
8. See Söderström (1989).
9. See Muller-Armack (1989).
10. See Mill (1871). I have examined Mill's views in more detail in Peacock (1979).
11. See Meade (1989), which is an extended statement of his long-standing commitment to this position.
12. See Meade (1989), app. B.
13. See also Meade's 'public choice' analysis of pensions, in Peacock and Barry (1986).
14. One recalls the quip by Lewis Meriam (Meriam *et al.*, 1950, p. 21) that 'adoption of the term "insurance" by the proponents of social security was a stroke of promotional genius'.
15. For demonstration of this effect, see Barr (1987), Chapter 11.
16. See Peacock and Wiseman (1964). For a detailed working out of a scheme closely related to the present-day debate see Barr (1989).
17. See Peacock (1961). For a detailed criticism of my position see Wilson (1985).
18. See Titmuss (1976).
19. The reference is to T.H. Green and not to David Green! See Ryan (1989), p. 59, for a penetrating analysis of Titmuss's position.
20. See his controversial essay, Dasgupta (1989).
21. For a detailed examination of the scheme, see Peacock (1957).
22. See Titmuss (1970).
23. A good example is David Howell (1986), Chapter 15.
24. For a useful examination of the debate see Barry (1984).
25. Barry (1984), p. 64.
26. The author was a member of the Fowler Committee on Pensions but recommended the total abolition of SERPS. For a criticism of the government's final position, see Peacock and Barry (1986).
27. The rejection, after considerable government discussion, of the educational voucher system was one of the great disappointments for liberal economic thinkers. For a full account of the argument between the academics and the Department of Education and Science see Seldon (1986).

REFERENCES

Barr, N. (1987), *The Economics of the Welfare State*, London: Weidenfeld and Nicolson.

Barr, N. (1989), *Student Loans. The Next Steps*, David Hume Paper no. 15, Aberdeen University Press for the David Hume Institute, Edinburgh.

Barry, N. (1984), 'Ideas versus Interests: The Classical Liberal Dilemma', in Hayek, F.A. (ed.), *'Serfdom' Revisited.* Hobart Paperback no. 18, London: Institute of Economic Affairs.

Crosland, A.R.C. (1956), *The Future of Socialism*, London: Jonathan Cape.

Dasgupta, P. (1989), 'Positive Freedom, Markets and the Welfare State', in Helm, D. (ed.), *The Economic Borders of the State*, Oxford: Oxford University Press, Chapter 5.

Diamond, P. (1977), 'Insurance Theoretic Aspects of Workers' Compensation', in Blinder, A.S. and Friedman, P. (eds), *Natural Resources, Uncertainty and General Equilibrium Systems*, New York: Academic Press.

Dilnot, A.W., Kay, J.A. and Morris, C.N. (1984), *The Reform of Social Security*, Oxford: Oxford University Press.

Hayek, F.A. (1976), *Law, Legislation and Liberty*, Vol. 2, *The Mirage of Social Justice*, London: Routledge and Kegan Paul.

Howell, D. (1986), *Blind Victory*, London: Hamish Hamilton.

Letwin, W. (ed.) (1983), *Against Equality*, London: The Macmillan Press.

Meade, J.E. (1989), *Agathotopia: the Economics of Partnership*, Hume Paper no. 16, Aberdeen University Press for the David Hume Institute, Edinburgh.

Meriam, L. *et al.* (1950), *The Cost of Financing Social Security*, Brookings Institute, Washington DC, USA.

Mill, J.S. (1871), *Principles of Political Economy*, University of Toronto Press Edition, 1965.

Müller-Armack, A. (1989), 'The Meaning of the Social Market Economy', in Peacock, A. and Willgerodt, H. (eds), *Germany's Social Market Economy: Origins and Evolution*, London: Macmillan.

Nozick, R. (1974), *Anarchy, State and Utopia*, Oxford: Blackwell.

Peacock, A. (1957), 'The Economics of National Superannuation', *Three Banks Review*, September.

Peacock, A. (1961), *The Welfare Society*, Unservile State Paper no. 2, London: Liberal Party Publications.

Peacock, A. (1979), *The Economic Analysis of Government*, Oxford: Martin Robertson, Chapter 5.

Peacock, A. and Barry, N. (1986), *The Political Economy of Pension Provision*, Hume Occasional Paper no. 2, Edinburgh: The David Hume Institute.

Peacock, A. and Wiseman, J. (1964), *Education for Democrats*, London: Institute of Economic Affairs.

Ricketts, M. and Shoesmith, E. (1990), *British Economic Opinion*, London: Institute of Economic Affairs.

Rowley, C. and Peacock, A. (1975), *Welfare Economics: A Liberal Restatement*, London: Martin Robertson.

Ryan, A. (1989), 'Value Judgements and Welfare', in Helm, D. (ed.), *The Economic Borders of the State*, Oxford: Oxford University Press.

Seldon, A. (1986), *The Riddle of the Voucher*, Hobart Paperback 21, London: Institute of Economic Affairs.

Söderström, L. (1989), 'Almost Genuine Insurance Schemes as an Alternative to Tax-Financed Pensions and other Social Security Benefits', in Chiancone, A. and Messere,

K. (eds), *Changes in Revenue Structures*, Detroit: Wayne University Press, for International Institute of Public Finance.

Titmuss, R.M. (1970), *The Gift Relationship*, London: Allen and Unwin.

Titmuss, R.M. (1976), *Essays on the 'Welfare State'*, 2nd edn, London: Allen and Unwin.

Wilson, T. (1985), 'The Unwithered Welfare State', in Greenaway, D. and Shaw, G.K. (eds), *Public Choice, Public Finance and Public Policy: Essays in Honour of Alan Peacock*, Oxford: Blackwell.

7. Foreword to David Hume's *Political Discourses*

(Before I retreated from full-time academic employment at the beginning of 1985, I wrote a memorandum to Gerald Elliot, Chairman of Christian Salvesen plc, inviting his views on the possibility of setting up a 'Think Tank' in Edinburgh, an unusual location far from the southern metropolis where Tanks now abound. It would derive its inspiration from the Scots tradition in political economy and particularly the combination of interests of David Hume in political philosophy, jurisprudence and economics. I owe Gerald a tremendous debt of gratitude, for he greeted the idea with enthusiasm and devoted a lot of his time to fundraising as well as putting forward a host of ideas on subjects of policy interest. The early history of what became The David Hume Institute is described elsewhere – see The David Hume Institute: The First Decade *(edited by Nick Kuenssberg and Gillian Lomas), 1996 – and the publications of the DHI certainly bear witness to the influence of Scotland's most famous philosopher. A by-product of my activity as its first Executive Director was that I became instantly labelled as an authority on Hume, a source of some embarrassment to an economist with only a working knowledge of the history of economic thought. I was spurred into action to extend my acquaintance with Hume's work by an invitation to write a Foreword to the production of a facsimile edition of his* Political Discourses *published by the German periodical,* Wirtschaftblatt, *and it duly appeared in German translation.*

In Writing this Foreword I had no scholarly pretensions. I simply read and re-read the Political Discourses *and asked myself the question, what would anyone with an interest in contemporary economic questions gain from studying Hume? I hope that the reader will share with me the view that the answer is – a great deal, not least because of what a colleague of mine has called Hume's 'well-tempered eloquence'. As our first Honorary President, the Nobel Laureate George Stigler, used to remind us, the Classical Economists should be read as literature and not simply as manuals of instruction.*

Finally, one should note that the most recent Chicago School Nobel Laureate in Economics, Robert Lucas, thinks Hume's views on money are sufficiently important to warrant particular attention in his Nobel Lecture on monetary neutrality. See Journal of Political Economy, ***104*** *(4), August 1996, 661–82.)*

I. INTRODUCTION

There is wide agreement amongst British philosophers that the Scotsman David Hume (1711–1776) is the greatest of them all; and his international reputation as a philosopher likewise places him amongst the giants. In his own day, however, his domestic reputation was based on his work as a historian and it was only in France that his philosophical work seems to have had an immediate appeal. His memorial stuck on a crag overlooking the centre of Edinburgh has inscribed on it 'David Hume: Historian' and it comes perhaps as a surprise to find that in the Authors' Catalogue of the London School of Economics and Political Science, where his name is revered, he is still classified as a historian! His reputation as a historian was well deserved and it will soon be seen how important a part his knowledge of history played in his economics.

It must also seem paradoxical today that his *Treatise of Human Nature* (1739), which revolutionized philosophical thinking, in his own words, 'fell deadborn from the Press', whereas his *Political Discourses* (1752) was an instant success both at home and overseas. Yet the latter work is frequently neglected in recent surveys of his intellectual contribution and stature, possibly because the lead in such surveys is inevitably taken by philosophers without a training in economics. Furthermore. the general neglect by economists themselves of the intellectual history of their subject, springing from fear that 'scholarship' is less prestigious than 'original thinking', has contributed to a lack of interest in Hume, who is frequently classified as a mere precursor of Adam Smith.

There are at least three reasons why the *Political Discourses* deserves to be brought to the attention of the modern reader. In the first place, anyone interested in the history of economic ideas who wants to avoid, in Lionel Robbins's words, 'provincialism in time' cannot fail to be struck by the power of Hume's intellect. Likely as not, if the reader is unfamiliar with Hume, he will find his application of his own technique of thinking to economic problems a useful approach to the more fundamental philosophical ideas concerning the analysis of human nature. In the second place, if the reader has a basic knowledge of modern economic analysis, he will find some intriguing pre-echoes of this analysis in Hume's theories of money, interest and international trade – to name only three related topics in the *Discourses* – and some timely reminders of the fallacies underlying the all-pervasive doctrine of national self-sufficiency which renewed its hold on politicians in major industrial countries about a century ago. Lastly, like his younger friend Adam Smith, Hume's writings can be enjoyed as English literature, and, indeed, the bulk of his works were written for an educated but general public and not solely, as so often today, for some inner circle of specialists – some 'peer group'. For example, he was so anxious that his *Treatise of Human Nature* should not be forgotten that he wrote a fascinating *Abstract* of it, published in 1740 anonymously and only identified as Hume's work as late as 1938 and then by none other than Keynes himself, together with the Italian economist Piero Sraffa. Keynes who wrote what might be regarded as one of the last great works of literature in economics, his *General Theory*, clearly recognized how important this short volume is as an 'essay in persuasion'.

This foreword elaborates the points made in this last paragraph with the purpose of making it easier for the reader to appreciate that these essays on widely different subjects are bound together by Hume's general approach to analysing human action. However. before examining Hume's treatment of economic subjects, some account must be given of his life and character. This is not simply because our interest may be aroused by the prospect that great thinkers may have led interesting lives – sometimes this is far from being the case. Rather it is because Hume himself placed so much emphasis on personal impressions and experience as the foundation of our knowledge of both the physical and social world about us that his own impressions and experience give us interesting clues to his methods of reasoning.

LIFE AND CHARACTER

David Hume, the son of the owner of a small estate near the south-east corner of Scotland, was born in Edinburgh on 26 April 1711, the date being midway between the Union of the Scottish and English Parliaments which ended the political independence of Scotland in 1707 and the start of the first Jacobite rebellion (1715) in Scotland aimed at restoring the House of Stewart. Both these contiguous events were to exert a considerable influence on Hume's life. The Union of the Parliaments required Scots with political and intellectual ambitions to make themselves understood in both written and spoken English. Hume was to become a master of the English language and to be a vigorous opponent of 'Scotticisms' in literary works. This accounts for the curious list of Scots words which were to be avoided by his countrymen in their writings printed at the end of the *Political Discourses.* Hume's family were opposed to the Jacobites, as was Hume himself, but his impartiality as a historian led him to take a more balanced view of the Catholic House of Stewart than was considered proper by the churchmen who supported the ruling House of Hanover who were of course Protestants.

Hume was brought up on the small family estate very close to the small town of Duns in Berwickshire. There is a peculiar irony in the fact that the most famous Scots philosopher in Europe before Hume was the medieval theologian John Duns Scotus (*c.* 1265–*c.* 1308) who was brought up in Duns and was noted throughout the medieval world for his subtle proofs of the existence of God, whereas Hume was to become branded, misleadingly, as the philosopher of atheism. This locational affinity of Hume and Duns Scotus, if Hume was conscious of it, would not have been regarded by him as other than a chance event, though it is surely not devoid of interest. If the air of the Scottish Borders was congenial to study and speculation it was soon clear to Hume and his family that David would have to make his own way in the world and he dutifully enrolled at Edinburgh University at the age of 11 (not uncommon in the eighteenth century) but never took his degree (also not uncommon then) and studied law but without qualifying as an advocate. By the age of 18 he had already resolved to become a 'man of letters' but did not wish to be a burden on his family.

He was then on the brink of developing his famous theory of causation. He abandoned the law, and, after a brief and unsuccessful incursion into business in Bristol, settled in provincial France where he could live on his very modest income. The last two years of his three years in France were spent in the small town of La Flèche in Anjou where the greater part of his *Treatise of Human Nature* was written. It is again ironic that he was stimulated by friendly argument with the Jesuit Fathers who allowed him to use their foundation's extensive library. They may not have been entirely aware that their young genial Scots friend had embarked on an intellectual adventure designed to undermine the influence of their College's most famous alumnus – René Descartes, the author of the famous *Discourse on Method* (1637).

The relevance of the *Treatise* for his economic thinking will be explored below. In a biographical context what is interesting is how this work affected Hume's contemporary position as a thinker. Looking at his philosophic speculations through the eyes of his contemporaries, here was an unknown young man from an isolated part of Northern Europe, who had the temerity to argue that in making even the simplest prediction, such as the relation between the length of time an egg is in boiling water and its texture, we generalize from past experience and can never be certain that the future will replicate the past; who stood Descartes's philosophy on its head by claiming that the motive force of man's actions was his tastes and preferences – his 'passions' – and that man's reasoning ability did and ought to serve his passions; who claimed, therefore, that moral actions could not be derived from reason, and, who, worst of all, could find no grounds for supporting the Christian belief that Christianity had a monopoly of religious truth. Such speculations could be ignored but, *pace* Hume, they were not, for his opponents could see that they were formidably presented, as were his subsequent essays on moral philosophy, politics and economics which were soon to follow in 1742. Then in 1744 came the vital test when Hume presented himself as a candidate for the Chair of Ethics and Pneumatical Philosophy which had fallen vacant at Edinburgh University. The town authorities were swayed by a theological faction, including the Principal of the University, who charged Hume with atheism.[1]

He was not appointed, and the same fate befell him six years later when the theologians at Glasgow vetoed his appointment to the vacant Chair of Logic.

The only teaching appointment that Hume was ever to hold was that of tutor to the Marquess of Annandale who turned out to be mad, and that lasted but a year.

Hume's problems of finding employment consonant with his wish to pursue his literary and philosophical activities was partly solved in other ways. Life amongst a coterie of Scots intellectuals in Edinburgh did much to restore his spirits and, as *Political Discourses* bears witness, he became a literary as well as a social success, despite the persecution by the Church which lasted all his life. His friends secured him the appointment of Librarian of the Faculty of Advocates in 1752, which gained him a useful small addition to his money income and a substantial addition to his real income in the form of access to the library's excellent book stock. The use of this library, which he was allowed to retain after his resignation from the post in 1757, was an essential prerequisite for the preparation of Hume's great *History of England.* Modest but tangible success as an author and refusal to waste his energies battling with his bigoted opponents had bought him time to become the man of letters which he desired to be.

The *History* may not be read much today, but it is a landmark in eighteenth-century historiography. Before Hume, history was mostly written as narrative and often as an encomium of the ruling royal house. In keeping with his philosophy, he examines human motivation and the causes of change in society and with unusual detachment. Voltaire was to describe the work as 'perhaps the best ever written in any language' and to applaud 'a mind superior to his materials; he speaks of weaknesses, blunders, cruelties as a physician speaks of epidemic diseases'. The flavour of Hume's historical method can be savoured in several of the essays in *Political Discourses,* notably 'Of the Populousness of Ancient Nations'.

No later influences in Hume's life bear on the production of *Political Discourses*, for the second and last revision of the work appeared later in the same year as the first. Hume's later life, however, has an interest of its own and some consideration of his character has a bearing on his economic analysis.

It may be said that while Hume saw Edinburgh as the base of his intellectual endeavours, he consciously sought to gain experience from travel and even employment abroad. He made extended visits to London to test reactions to his work and to bargain with publishers of his works and those of Scots colleagues. He had many admirers south of the border and gained the respect of his intellectual antagonists but although Adam Smith, now a firm friend, and Hume contemplated settling in London, they were never entirely at ease in a city where Scots were still regarded as potential rebels and where literary success depended so much on soliciting favours from the great aristocratic families. Today, it is easier for Scots to acquire the protective colouration which enables them to pass for Englishmen and even to market their abilities as professional Scots who are 'rough diamonds whom London polishes well'. Justifiable doubts remain amongst Scots intellectuals about the patronizing attitude of some of their English counterparts and the curious blend of 'metropolitan parochialism' which 'foreigners', other than themselves, often remark upon.

Hume bought a house in Edinburgh in 1762 with the clear intention of settling there for a life of quiet contemplation. That was not to be. Local opposition to his work was now accompanied by professional jealousy. The following year, when diplomatic ties were renewed between the French and British after the Seven Years' War, Hume received an unexpected invitation to join the staff of the British Ambassador, Lord Hertford, with the prospect of becoming Secretary to the Embassy in Paris. After some hesitation he accepted, perhaps aware that the appointment had been made with at least the connivance of his growing number of French admirers. He found himself a great celebrity and 'le bon David', as they called him, was a distinct success both socially and professionally. He was not to return to settle in Edinburgh until 1769 for he was promoted to Under-Secretary of State (Northern Division), a post which included conduct of diplomatic negotiations with the Court of Catherine the Great of Russia. Another ironic twist to his career emanates from his duties which included writing the Royal Speech delivered annually by the King's representative to the General Assembly of the Church of Scotland! The more moderate members of that Church had cause to be grateful for his personal influence though one wonders how far they deserved it.

The final return to Edinburgh is marked by his serenity and detachment and by the somewhat tardy recognition by his colleagues of his pre-eminence. This period is remembered best by economists for his close ties with Adam Smith whose *Wealth of Nations* appeared as the philosopher was dying, and delighted him greatly. In the face of death he wrote *My Own Life*, a tantalizingly short but astute analysis of his own character and development. His moral courage in dying is on a par with that of Socrates. He quietly put his affairs in order, disturbing the morbidly curious James Boswell by his lack of fear that his own philosophy postulated that 'it was an unreasonable fancy that we should exist for ever'.

When, on 29 August 1776. his coffin was being carried out of his home, one of the large crowd was heard to remark, 'Ah, he was an Atheist'. A companion added, 'No matter, he was an honest man'.

In *My Own Life* Hume sums up his own character as follows:

> I was ... a man of mild dispositions, of command of temper, of an open, social and cheerful humour, capable of attachment but little susceptible of enmity, and of great moderation in all my passions. Even my love of literary fame, my ruling passion, never soured my temper, notwithstanding my frequent disappointments. My company was not unacceptable to the young and careless as well as to the studious and literary; and as I took a particular pleasure in the company of modest women, I had no reason to be displeased with the reception I met with from them ... I cannot say that there is

> no vanity in making this funeral oration of myself, but I hope it is not a misplaced one; and this is a matter of fact which is easily cleared and ascertained.

When the facts are ascertained from contemporary accounts of friends, colleagues and even intellectual opponents, it is clear that David Hume knew himself very well, which is not typically the case with great men. Space does not permit the documentation of views of contemporaries but Adam Smith, his special friend, is only a shade more generous than others when he closed a famous account of Hume's last days with the words: 'I have always considered him ... as approaching as nearly to the idea of a perfectly wise and virtuous man, as perhaps the nature of human frailty will permit.'

THE METHODOLOGY OF *POLITICAL DISCOURSES*

Having noted that Hume himself was motivated by a desire for literary fame, the initial question raised by the *Political Discourses* is how was such a work to accord with this desire? What was Hume's marketing strategy?

The *Treatise on Human Nature* appeared anonymously and, although in time it was a *succès d'estime*, it was hardly a literary success. His next major venture, *Essays: Moral and Political* (1742), appears to be modelled on the famous essays published in the London literary journal *The Spectator* by Joseph Addison (1672–1719). Like Addison and later Samuel Johnson (1709–1784), Hume writes his own marketing copy. In his essay 'On Essay Writing', he decries the separation of the world of learning from the conversible world, that is the world of the literary salon. The learned scholars lose by 'being shut up in Colleges and Cells, and secluded from the World of good Company'. The conversationists suffer from confining their attention to trivial and ephemeral issues. So Hume is going to bridge the gap by dealing with serious issues but using a manner of exposition which will appeal to the intelligent if not intellectual members of society. Like Johnson, he recognized that an appeal to the ladies was an essential part of the marketing strategy. He wrote in the same Essay: 'I am of Opinion, that Women of Sense and Education are much better Judges of all polite Writing than Men of the same degree of Understanding'. As we know, his strategy paid off, and, by all accounts, he had a distinguished female following!

In 'Of Commerce', the first essay in *Political Discourses*, Hume makes the same marketing 'pitch', but, encouraged no doubt by the success of his earlier essays, the tone is less ingratiating and the author exudes confidence. Hume attacks the 'shallow thinkers' who 'will never allow anything to be just which is beyond their own weak conceptions'. This is particularly true in the case of economic questions where generalizing from individual experience is a particular weakness, as we are all touched by commercial and financial matters. What is clearly needed is some guidance from an 'abstruse thinker' but one, of course, endowed with a good style and a clear mind. In order to disarm his critics in advance, Hume adds: 'there will occur some principles which are uncommon, and which may seem too refined for such vulgar subjects (i.e. commerce etc.). If false, let them be rejected: but no one ought to entertain a prejudice against them, merely because they are out of the common road.'

Hume's marketing problem is therefore similar to that of an economist today writing for the 'intelligent layman' in, say, a monthly periodical. He would have to wear his learning lightly in offering views on interesting subjects. There were, however, two important differences compared with a modern exponent of ideas looking for a wide audience. He wrote to convince his intellectual peers as well as an educated public, and, further, his ideas were likely to meet resistance by their very novelty.

Consider how a modern writer might approach such a subject as what causes economic growth to differ between countries. He would probably begin by defining growth, normally in terms of real income per head, presenting data on the growth in real income per head in different economies for a given period of time. He would then build a model of economic growth in which the most important constituent would be the motivation of individuals to accumulate the resources in order to produce growth, notably the accumulation of physical capital and human capital and the quantity of labour input. He would be bound to consider how far the organization of human institutions, notably the system of government and the system of production, might hinder or promote growth. He would then test his explanation of growth against the data, with reference perhaps to econometric investigations. This methodology would also underpin a popular exposition even though the audience would have to be spared the agony of following the intricacies of economic analysis found in the professional economics journals!

It is clear that Hume could not call upon an elaborate set of national and international statistics produced by governments and international agencies. Historically, such data became available as a by-product of the administrative process in government, and there might not even exist any incentive to make public the data itself. The first detailed statistical analysis of his own country, Scotland, did not take place until after his death and was a mammoth *private* undertaking by the Scottish landowner, Sir Archibald Sinclair, who used the parish Ministers of the Church as his rapporteurs. This is not to say that Hume was not interested in descriptive statistics. On the contrary, the longest essay in *Political Discourses*, 'Of the Populousness of Ancient Nations', is an exhaustive investigation of a wide variety of classical sources designed to disprove the thesis that the ancient nations were more populous than those of Hume's day. If, therefore, survival and growth of population were taken as an indicator of human well-being – a proposition supported, incidentally, by Adam

Smith – then comparisons between some past golden age and a 'desolate' eighteenth century were false. The use of population growth as an indicator of economic welfare was to be a subject of much controversy in the nineteenth century during the famous Malthusian debate, and Hume anticipates Malthus by his appeal to the available data.

The much more striking part of Hume's methodology is the application of his views on human nature which were derived from his *Treatise.* Our actions are derived from our 'passions' – our tastes and sentiments as they are called in the *Abstract* – and our reasoning powers which are developed and sharpened by our knowledge of the world about us are employed in order to promote our happiness. In the preliminary essay in *Political Discourses* entitled 'Of Luxury' Hume argues that human happiness consists of three ingredients, 'action, pleasure and indolence', which are present in all of us though not necessarily in the same proportions. Moreover, these 'passions' are present in people at all times and in all countries. Hume has already laid the foundations on which the modern economic theory of human action is based, though the terminology has changed. We speak today of an individual 'utility function' in which the 'arguments' or determining forces are goods, leisure and work satisfaction. Moreover, his description of the 'passions' does not entail that individuals' satisfaction is independent of that of others. If individuals seeking happiness come into conflict with one another, they cannot change their natures but their reasoning powers sharpen their appreciation of the need to find ways of co-operating in order to resolve conflicts between themselves, otherwise, in the famous words of Thomas Hobbes, life may become 'solitary, poor, nasty, brutish and short'. Hume's views on the origins of government were already developed before the *Political Discourses* and cannot be considered in detail here. Sufficient, I hope, has been said to indicate that his view of human action entails the institution of a system of justice and promotion of security as a precondition for human happiness which is to be anything more than transitory. It is also a view of government which is dramatically different from those who derived principles of justice and security from some moral order, divinely inspired. However, co-operation between individuals was not regarded by Hume as purely a matter of expediency. Individuals derive positive pleasure from helping their friends, from preserving their friends' good opinion of them, and so they have recourse, as the essay 'On Luxury' stresses, to continuous social intercourse once they have progressed beyond barbarism. As it would be put today in an economics treatise, individual 'utility functions' are interdependent, though much economic analysis neglects this rather important ingredient derived from the Classical works of Hume and Smith.

There is no identifiable growth model in Hume's work, as there is in Adam Smith's *Wealth of Nations*, but his emphasis on an examination of human motivation accords well with present-day presentations of the analysis of growth to both professional and lay audiences. The impetus to growth comes from the human desire for action – what Hume in the *Treatise* called the insatiable craving for exercise and employment. Moreover, such action complements the desire for pleasure and continuous pleasure throughout man's life span stimulates the desire to accumulate capital and to improve knowledge. The *Political Discourses* places more emphasis on the self-sustaining nature of the growth process, once resources accumulate. As the standard of living rises above subsistence levels, pleasures become more refined, and this stimulates a diversity of interests which 'carries improvements into every art and science ... men enjoy the privilege of rational creatures, to think as well as to act, to cultivate the pleasures of the mind as well as those of the body'. To Hume, using a crude indicator of growth such as real income per head masks the importance of the pleasures of growing diversity in human society. While Hume argues that it would be impossible for these benefits not to be widely diffused throughout all classes, he is conscious of the need to explain the international differences in the degree of diversity. Why do people in the tropics not attain the degree of 'art and civility' of nations in temperate climates? Presumably, argues Hume in 'Of Commerce', because the tropics encourage indolence. Clothes and houses are less necessary as protection against the elements and the benefits of climate being equally distributed promote more equality of real income. Fewer quarrels are likely to arise between individuals so that a settled system of government is less necessary.

The affinity between Hume's model of human nature and these models encountered in modern economic analysis means that his view would be strongly at variance with that of modern psychologists. Ernest Gellner, for instance, in his profound book *The Psychoanalytic Movement* (1985), pokes gentle fun at Hume who seems to view man as 'a gourmet crossed with an accountant, with a touch of compassionate sensibility thrown in. He conducted his life by studying his palate and seeking to arrange for its greatest satisfaction, and his imaginative sympathy for others inclined him to favour their satisfaction too, if to a lesser degree than his own' (p. 16). It is not that modern psychology would object to Hume's fundamental thesis regarding the dominant role of the passions in human action. The trouble is that Hume's passions are gentle and the impulses that they produce in us are easily brought into harmony with the world around us as our powers of reasoning and observation develop. This view of human nature could hardly explain the facts of history which Hume himself so ably presents, unless its many tragic episodes were caused primarily by natural disasters beyond man's control, which is clearly not the case. Indeed, it could be argued that the treatment of Hume himself by his fellow human beings, examples of which have already been given above, hardly accords with his own depiction of human action! The *Political Discourses* suggests at various points that economic progress offers the firm prospect that men will be more disposed to live in peace and harmony with one another but the evidence points in another direction. The anxieties associated with fear of poverty may disappear in affluent societies, but other anxieties are then more starkly revealed. Hence the grip on our imaginations of the ideas of Nietzsche and Freud which emphasize the dark instinctual drives which propel human beings into conflict with one another, and with themselves.

Economists confronted with criticism of the model of rational calculation embedded in their notion of human action are apt to take refuge in the proposition that they are only concerned with how people act in allocating their scarce resources and not with why they may act in a certain way. Such propositions as 'the quantity demanded of a commodity is sensitive to its price' or 'people's incentive to work depends on what they expect to be paid' contain reasonable hypotheses which are testable. If they fit the facts, then they can be used to explode common economic fallacies and to warn governments of the problems encountered in trying to control individual economic behaviour. It is not necessary to probe the dark recesses of the mind in order to support positive economic reasoning. It is when economists begin to speculate on broader questions such as the consequences of material advance that they are apt to get out of their depth. Hume's own approach to economic growth offers a clear illustration of these observations. In the essay 'Of Interest' he repeats the proposition that there 'is no craving of the human mind more constant and insatiable than that for exercise and employment'. He shows how the desire to accumulate resources leads to economic advance and how economic advance becomes associated with 'low profits and low interest'. His empirical checks may seem by today's standards to be rather casual, but his economic reasoning is both powerful and cogent. Hume is after 'bigger fish' than the majority of economists today, and his own audience certainly expected to learn how he would catch them. He wishes to demonstrate, as already indicated, that the growth of trade and commerce resolves conflicts within society and between nations. The debate on such a matter cannot be settled within the confines of an economic analysis which assumes that men are rational creatures.

THE MAJOR ECONOMIC THEMES

The remarks on Hume's methodology have made it possible to introduce aspects of Hume's treatment of some of the broad issues in economics, as they are treated in *Political Discourses.* Hume's reputation as an economist today rests less on these broad issues, in which he is perhaps overshadowed, unjustifiably I believe, by Adam Smith, and more on his handling of such subjects as the role of money and interest in the economy, international trade policy and the financing of government by taxes and by public debt. At least these are the subjects which warrant him a place in those economic texts which are more than simply teaching manuals designed to minimize the agony of having to pass examinations.

Consider the kind of discussion of the significance of money found in the financial press today. There is a clear agreement that money as a medium of exchange is essential for both national and international trade, for otherwise specialization of production and gains from exchanging products become impossible or intolerably inefficient. Hume makes much of this point towards the end of his essay 'Of Money' but clearly identifies money as an acceptable medium with gold and silver coin (specie) and he is suspicious of paper credit unless clearly convertible into specie. There is also clear agreement that there is some connection between a change in the quantity of money and the change in the level of prices, but disagreement about the transmission mechanism, the precise quantitative relationship between changes in money and changes in prices and the time it takes for the change in money supply to produce a change in prices. These disagreements worry governments who want to use the money supply as an instrument to promote policy objectives such as the control of inflation. Hume is usually given a 'good press' in economic texts for his discussion of such matters. He examines the facts and finds that over long periods of time the supply of specie has risen at a slower rate than the rise in prices. There is therefore a positive relationship established between money and prices, but it is not a proportional one. Why is this so? Because, Hume explains, it takes time for any price adjustment to take place and, in the course of that time period, the increase in demand produced by an increase in money supply may be counterbalanced by alterations in the goods available to be bought. Indeed, the expectation that demand will increase encourages more production, though eventually prices must begin to rise as labour and materials become scarcer.

Hume's policy conclusion is interesting:

> It is of no manner of consequence, with regard to the domestic happiness of a state, whether money be in a greater or lesser quantity. The good policy of the magistrate consists in keeping it, if possible, still encreasing; because, by that means, he keeps alive a spirit of industry in the nation, and encreases the stock of labour, in which consists all real power and riches.

This maxim has an obvious affinity with the common Central Bank maxim that increasing the supply of money is mainly justified by the need to accommodate a growth in potential Gross Domestic Product. However, it should be noted that Hume is describing what is desirable and is not certain that what is desirable is also possible. In his essay 'On Public Credit' he makes it abundantly clear that governments should not rely on the expansion of paper credit as the means for controlling the supply of money. Increasing the government deficit by the issue of public stocks will bring about a lack of confidence in the currency and cause inflation rather than engender an expansion in output. Government can only influence the money supply, that is gold and silver coin, by creating the conditions which enable its citizens to expand and develop its trade with those in possession of specie or who produce gold and silver: 'a government has great reason to preserve with care its people and its manufactures. Its money, it may safely trust to the course of human affairs' (see the essay 'Of the Balance of Trade').

Hume's discussion of money is the point of departure for two further excursions into important economic problems. The first of these is his theory of interest. It was commonly asserted by his contemporaries that one of the advantages of increasing the money supply was that it lowered interest rates. Typically, Hume begins by asking the question: how do we test this proposition? Presumably if the assertion were true, countries with relatively large money supplies would have relatively low interest rates. This is not found to be the case. Then he argues that the assertion is implausible in any case. Doubling the money supply, for example, only means that if you lend me so much labour and so many commodities, I have to repay you the equivalent money value in labour and commodities plus some interest which is a proportion of the equivalent money value. There is no reason to suppose that that proportion of equivalent value would alter simply because the value of labour or commodities had doubled in money terms. Further proof is offered by Hume in the form of historical evidence to back up his 'cross-section' study of countries:

> an effect always holds proportion with its cause. Prices have risen near four times since the discovery of the Indies: and it is probable gold and silver have multiplied much more: But interest has not fallen much above half'. The rate of interest, therefore, is not derived from the quantity of precious metals. ('Of Interest')

Hume therefore uses his knowledge of history to refute a common hypothesis of the time, but turns back to the *Treatise* as the basis of his own explanation of the determination of interest rates. We have to look at the motives for supplying funds and for borrowing them. Concentrating on the fall in interest rates as countries develop, he explains this phenomenon in the following way. Countries develop because of the human desire for 'exercise and employment', as already stated. This is associated with a greater desire to provide for the future by saving. At the same time the 'opportunity cost' of saving diminishes because the growth of commerce produces growing competition amongst merchants which lowers the rate of profit. Accordingly, merchants accept more willingly a lower rate of return on lending. Thus 'an encrease in commerce by a necessary consequence, raises a great number of lenders, and by that means produces lowness of interest'. Space hardly allows extensive discussion of this interesting analysis, but it must be noted that Hume is considering only long-term, gradual changes in the economy. Consider his example of the 'miracle' where every citizen in Great Britain wakes up to find £5 in his pocket. According to Hume, all that would happen is that prices would double and the rate of borrowing and lending would not change. However, Hume has already argued that price adjustments take time, and, if this is so, the extra money could be saved rather than spent unless every person anticipates an immediate rise in the prices of all goods. The extra saving would lower interest rates, though in the longer run, these could rise again as individuals have to pay more for goods. Furthermore, Hume seems to envisage a society where borrowing is used solely in order to finance present consumption and not for the purchase of capital equipment. The level of interest rates simply reflects the degree of advancement of the economy. It does not influence its advancement. There is a good deal of controversy on this point, even today. If the money supply can be used to reduce interest rates, even temporarily, and this were to stimulate the demand for increasing and improving the capital stock, then a change in the interest rate in the short run might affect economic growth in the long run – so the argument goes.

It is a short step from this proposition to the policy recommendation that a government should use monetary policy in order to prevent interest rates from rising, even temporarily, so that capital investment is not discouraged. We can only speculate on how Hume would have replied to this argument. One supposes that even if he were to admit that governments could control the monetary supply, keeping down interest rates by monetary policy would suggest to Hume that the expected rise in prices would raise the costs of investment goods which would counteract any attractions to invest because interest rates had fallen. The debate continues until this day!

The second excursion derived from Hume's view of money is to be found in his analysis of international trade. Hume examines the famous mercantilist view that a country is rich or poor according to whether its stock of specie or precious metals is large or small. This view led naturally to the proposition that a country should aim at amassing gold and silver by maintaining a positive balance of trade with its neighbours, for example by discrimination against foreign imports which would have to be paid for in specie. Hume argues that this policy is both undesirable and impossible to operate in the long run. Suppose, says Hume, a situation where specie flows into Britain as a result of some measure which increases the balance of payments surplus. The increase in money raises prices so that neighbouring countries cannot afford to buy from us whereas their commodities become relatively cheaper. Money flows out. The outflow of money acts as a correcting mechanism for it results eventually in a fall in domestic wages and prices which restores domestic competitiveness. A kind of natural economic law is at work which preserves the money supply in trading countries in proportion to the 'art and industry of every nation' (see 'Of the Balance of Trade'). Of course, a country might attempt to cut itself off completely from other countries and run a siege economy but, Hume argues, this would reduce its standard of living. He illustrates this very graphically by the consequences of the barriers to trade between France and Britain: 'We lost the French market for our woollen manufactures, and transferred the commerce of wine to Spain and Portugal, where we buy worse liquor at a higher price.' Hume was to develop this argument much further in essays written after the *Political Discourses.* His international trade analysis is much admired today by international economists. They argue that if international gains from trade are to be fully realized, then countries who try to manipulate their money supply so that it fails to conform with their command over internationally accepted currency will find themselves facing major adjustment problems as their prices of internationally traded goods fall out of line with those of trading partners. Free trade in internationally traded goods, some of them argue, requires a return to the Humeian 'rules' of expansion and contraction of the increase in domestic money supply according to movements in each country's balance of payments. A continuing surplus in a major country matched by deficits in others would require the surplus country to increase the percentage growth in its money supply, whereas the deficit countries would have to contract their percentages. The reasons why governments act otherwise are not mentioned by Hume, but his own analysis of human nature can easily be used to explore them. The process of adjustment to the 'natural' level of money in any country takes time and is painful to those who have to take cuts in their relative wages and prices in order to regain their international markets. Hume prefers to end on a note of idealism which anticipates that of the founders of the European Economic Community. In a later essay written in 1758 entitled '0f the Jealousy of Trade', he closes with a statement on the consequences of autarkic trade policies:

> were our narrow and malignant politics to meet with success, we should reduce all our neighbouring nations to the same state of sloth and ignorance that prevails in Morocco and the coast of Barbary. What would be the consequence? They could send us no commodities: They could take none from us: Our domestic commerce itself would languish for want of emulation, example and instruction: And we ourselves should fall into the same abject condition, to which we have reduced them. I shall therefore venture to acknowledge, that, not only as a man, but as a British subject, I pray for the flourishing commerce of Germany, Spain, Italy, and even France itself!

The present-day interest in Hume as an economist now extends to the analysis of the government as an economic entity. Although Hume includes in his *Political Discourses* his fascinating essay on 'Idea of a Perfect Commonwealth', the content of this essay concerns the process through which government power should be exercised. To understand Hume's recommendations. it is necessary to go back to his previous essays on the origin of government and the principles which he believes should control its operations. A full discussion of Hume's theory of government would fill volumes. It can only be said here that he traces the origin of government from the need to devise an instrument for resolving conflicts about the use of resources where this cannot be achieved by negotiation in the market. He offers as an example his now famous case of the draining of a meadow which may be generally conceived as mutually beneficial amongst a group of men.

> Two neighbours may agree to drain a meadow which they possess in common, because it is easy for them to know each other's mind; and each must perceive that the immediate consequence of his failing in his part is the abandoning of the whole project. But it is very difficult, and indeed impossible, that a thousand persons should agree in any such action; it being difficult for them to concert so complicated a design, and still more difficult for them to execute it; while each seeks a pretext to free himself of the trouble and expense, and would lay the burden on others. Political society easily remedies both these inconveniences. (*Treatise of Human Nature*, Book III, 'Of the Origin of Government')

Governments, therefore, reduce the transaction costs amongst citizens who perceive that compulsory exactions to finance on indivisible benefit are a lesser evil than the risk that, if there were no government, the benefit could not be realized. This still leaves unresolved three vital questions: who should decide which projects should be undertaken, how can one check on the efficiency of those who undertake and administer them and how should the burden of financing them be divided amongst the beneficiaries? Readers can trace for themselves Hume's answers to these difficult questions in the *Political Discourses*, notably in 'Of Taxes' and 'Of Public Credit' in which he clearly indicates that governments have to be prevented from actions which remove the incentives to save and to invest and which oppress the poor.

POSTSCRIPT: HUME AS AN INSPIRATIONAL FORCE

Reputations of great thinkers fluctuate according to the intellectual fashions and preoccupations of the day. What of David Hume in the 1990s?

The author recently had occasion to test Hume's current reputation in jurisprudence and economics. Returning after many years, as David Hume did, to live in Edinburgh, the author set up The David Hume Institute devoted to the study of policy questions requiring a professional knowledge of law and economics. It is a response to a challenge familiar to Adam Smith and David Hume for it requires the development and promulgation of ideas on policy, but at a long distance from the seat of government. The author made contact with a number of prominent economists and lawyers who had a particular interest in what is now termed 'legal economics', asking them if they would associate themselves with this risky enterprise. They all accepted the invitation and three of them wrote tributes to Hume as one of the major influences on their thinking. What is striking is that all three of them – Friedrich Hayek, George Stigler and James Buchanan – have been awarded the Nobel Prize in Economics. No better evidence need be offered of the power and penetration of David Hume's work and further commendation of it to the reader seems superfluous.

NOTE

1. The views of the bigots might he summed up in a 'clerihew', a peculiarly British form of epigram consisting of two rhyming couplets containing lines of different lengths and concerning some famous figure:

   David Hume
   Made Prelates Fume.
   As a Francophilic Freethinker
   How could he be other than an Insufferable Stinker!

AIDE-MÉMOIRE OF HUME'S LIFE

1707	Union of the Parliaments of England and Scotland.
1711	David Hume born in Edinburgh, Scotland.
1715	First Jacobite Rebellion in Scotland.
1722	Hume enters University of Edinburgh.
1734–7	Hume's first residence in France.
1739	Publication in London of *Treatise of Human Nature.*
1741	Publication in Edinburgh of *Essays: Moral and Political.*
1745	Hume rejected for the Chair of Ethics and Pneumatical Philosophy at the University of Edinburgh.
1745–6	Second Jacobite Rebellion led by Charles Edward Stuart ('Bonnie Prince Charlie').
1746	Hume appointed Judge Advocate to the military forces under the command of General St Clair engaged in an expedition (which proved unsuccessful) to attack the French ports in Brittany.
1751	Hume returns to Edinburgh
1752	*Political Discourses* published in Edinburgh. Hume appointed Librarian to the Faculty of Advocates, Edinburgh, a post held until 1757.
1754	First volume of Hume's *History of England* published in London.
1756–62	Seven Years' War between Britain and France.
1764	Diplomatic relations between Britain and France restored. Hume accompanies new British Ambassador to Paris as Secretary.
1767	Hume returns to London to become Under-Secretary of State.

1769 Final return of Hume to Edinburgh.
1776 Publication of Adam Smith's *Wealth of Nations* in London. David Hume dies.

A BIBLIOGRAPHICAL GUIDE

Life and Times

The standard biography of David Hume is still Ernest Campbell Mossner's *The Life of David Hume*, Nelson, Edinburgh, 1954. Mossner's work quotes extensively from Hume's letters and reproduces Hume's *My Own Life* in full (Appendix A). Essential reading on eighteenth-century intellectual life in Scotland is *A Hotbed of Genius: The Scottish Enlightenment, 1730–90* (edited by Daiches, Jones and Jones), Edinburgh University Press, 1986. This work contains an excellent essay on Hume by Peter Jones and some delightful illustrations. This contribution owes much to both Mossner and Jones for factual information.

Hume's Philosophy

The intrepid reader may wish to consult *A Treatise of Human Nature* (edited by L.A. Selby Biggs), Oxford University Press, 1978. That edition also contains the *Abstract of Human Nature* (1740), which has been separately edited and introduced by John Maynard Keynes and Piero Sraffa, published first in 1938 by Cambridge University Press and now published by Archon Books, Connecticut, USA. 1965. The complete *Essays: Moral, Political, and Literary*, have been reproduced by Liberty Classics, Liberty Fund, Indianapolis, 1985.

Commentaries on Hume's philosophy include A.J. Ayer, *Hume*, Oxford University Press, 1980, and the essay by Peter Jones mentioned above. His position in the development of psychology is most interestingly presented in Ernest Gellner, *The Psychoanalytic Movement or the Coming of Unreason*, Paladin Books, Granada Publishing Ltd, London, 1985.

Hume's Economics

The standard work on Hume's economics is still *David Hume: Writings on Economics*, edited and introduced by Eugene Rotwein, Nelson, Edinburgh, 1955. It contains a useful long introduction by Professor Rotwein, most of the essays contained in *Political Discourses* and relevant extracts from Hume's correspondence concerning economic questions.

Most respectable histories of economic thought now acknowledge the importance of Hume's contribution. Perhaps the most interesting appraisal of his work is still that of Joseph Schumpeter in his monumental *History of Economic Analysis*, Oxford University Press, 1954.

8. Keynes and the role of the state

(As a liberal – I remind the reader that I use the term in the British sense – I have strong affiliations with both the Classical Scots tradition of political economy and with the contractarian approach to the definition of the tasks of government. As an ex-service student at the University of St Andrews, I was subjected to a barrage of harsh criticism of Keynes from my professor, who enjoined us to study in detail Mantoux's The Carthaginian Peace, *a tirade against Keynes's famous* Economic Consequences of the Peace *which had brought him world fame. On my first visit to the USA in 1953, I found that much the same unwillingness to implant Keynesian ideas in the minds of the young was rampant, though it was also my privilege to meet famous intellectual opponents of Keynes who considered his economic analysis independently of his supposed support for collectivism. Latterly, I have been intrigued at the continued prevalence of this contention amongst liberalist friends and colleagues who have held up Keynes as an example of someone who held the naive belief that civil servants were endowed with the wisdom expected of Plato's Guardians. In contrast, liberals who knew Keynes well, such as my friend and mentor Lionel Robbins, took an altogether different view.*

I have always wanted to examine in detail Keynes's views on the role of the state and I was wiser than I knew to wait until his Collected Writings *were published by the Royal Economic Society and to have the groundwork on his philosophical position so thoroughly investigated by a number of writers whose work I consider in this contribution. I was spurred into action by an invitation to deliver the opening paper at the biennial conference on Keynes's work held at Keynes College, University of Kent, in 1991. The result of my considerable labours rather surprised me. Although I adopt a critical stance towards some aspects of Keynes's position, it will soon be apparent to the reader that I have finished up, like so many others, finding it difficult to resist Keynes's spell. I make no apology for offering the contribution as a tribute to him, writing these very words on the fiftieth anniversary of his death.)*

The great trouble with Keynes was that he was an idealist. (Joan Robinson, in Kahn, 1984)

Am I a Liberal? (J. M. Keynes)

I. INTRODUCTION

Those of us who grew up in the shadow of Keynes became used to the shock tactics of Mrs Robinson in trying to persuade us that she was always right, but even those inoculated against her formidable debating skills might be taken aback at the quotation which heads this chapter. Economists have been brought up to believe and may have transmitted the belief that it was Keynes's realism which led him to question so-called 'Classical' views on how the economy behaved and remedies for coping with underemployment of labour and resources. His practical skills and interest in financial matters together with his continuous involvement in public affairs are supposed to have been a major influence on the evolution of his economic analysis; and his growing experience of public life led him to change his mind frequently in the light of national and international events. Indeed, it is part of the conventional wisdom among economists of standing – see, notably, Patinkin, 1982 – that Keynes was *'un homme des affaires'* first and an academic second. In my own case, I had read the *Essays in Persuasion* and *The Economic Consequences of the Peace* before the *General Theory,* and was early convinced by their author that the correct methodological order for an economist was to grasp what were the major economic problems that required solution before seeking out the analysis that might help to solve them. I certainly did not associate Keynes with the broader issues studied by moral philosophers and political scientists, though I was aware that these erupted from time to time, notably in the final chapter of the *General Theory (CW XIV)* in his notes on the social philosophy to which the *General Theory* might lead. But that seemed to me to be the least original part of his *magnum opus.*

A number of factors have produced profound changes in scholarly perceptions of Keynes's work, and go some way to explaining Mrs Robinson's aphorism.

Firstly, as a result of the sterling efforts of the Royal Economic Society employing skilled and experienced editors, we have before us the full panoply of Keynes's writings, which were scattered in many journals and periodicals, together with his extensive professional correspondence and government memoranda. In addition, we have the intriguing memoir of Richard Kahn on The *Making of Keynes' General Theory* (1984), to which Mrs Robinson added a comment from which the above quotation comes. I cannot begin to catalogue the biographical material now available, notable being that provided by Milo Keynes (1975) and Robert (now Lord) Skidelsky (1983). The raw material for scholars is there in profusion, and not only scholars will find much to interest them. Alongside such documents we also have the various government papers covering the period of Keynes's close involvement with the Treasury and Bank of England, and which have been so admirably analysed in Peter Clarke's now standard work on the Keynesian revolution (Clarke, 1990).

Secondly, following this vast increase in documentation, there has been a growing interest expressed by non-economists in Keynes's moral and political philosophy. It is now claimed that the binding force in Keynes's intellectual endeavours was not his pioneering efforts to reform macroeconomics but rather his moral and philosophical ideas. In his stimulating work on *Keynes's Vision* (1988), Athol Fitzgibbons argues that Keynes was possessed of a 'single vision' based on a central core of ethics and moral philosophy. In failing to appreciate this, economists have not only neglected important aspects of Keynes's work but have misinterpreted his intentions as an economist and even his economics. An important exception is O'Donnell (1991), who sees Keynes's philosophy as the major clue to Keynes's view of political action. Although I am not wholly convinced by Fitzgibbons's view, I believe he is right to draw attention to the reasons why Keynes became committed to the search for a third alternative to Marxism and *laissez-faire*. In Fitzgibbons's words:

> Keynes did not himself put morals and economics in separate compartments of the soul, and he formulated his third way in terms that were wide and comprehensive. He declared economics to be a method rather than a set of theories, and he regarded his own method as superior because it alone followed a philosophy of practical action. He believed that Marxism and *laissez-faire* shared a method that was too abstract to capture probabilistic reality and too materialistic to reflect rational values. (Fitzgibbons, 1988, p. 2)

In short, Keynes's position on the role of the state is to be sought in his ideals, at least as much as in his experience of the world.

Finally, albeit with some reluctance, economists in the UK have come to realize that many of the policy measures derived from, if not invented by, Keynes presuppose both that governments are enlightened in their motives and that they can treat private citizens purely as passive adjusters to the policy measures imposed on them. In 1978 the American Nobel Laureate in Economics, James Buchanan, berated an audience invited by the IEA on the baleful influence of nineteenth-century British idealist philosophy. Thus Benthamite utilitarianism 'provided idealised objectives for government policy to the neglect of institutional structure ... and put up barriers against realistic examination of politics' (Buchanan, 1991, p. 30). Keynes does not escape such knocking copy:

> your economists, and notably Lord Keynes ... continued to proffer advice as if they were talking to a benevolent despot who stood at their beck and call. ... British and American economists throughout most of this century continue to seem blind to what now appears to be so simple to us, that benevolent despots do not exist and that government policy emerges from a highly complex and intricate institutional structure peopled by ordinary men and women, very little different from the rest of us. (*Ibid.*)

Latterly, criticism by 'public-choice theorists' has been directed less at Keynes's naivety concerning how governments actually behave and more towards the moral basis of his view of government.

A most forthright attack has been launched by Charles Rowley (1987). After examining Keynes's leading position within the Bloomsbury Group, he argues that 'Bloomsbury fuelled Keynes's fantasies of elitist discretion imbued with pure motives and reliable institutions of the good; and encouraged his attempts to convert such fantasies into a real world expression' (*ibid.*, p. 120; see also Buchanan *et al.*, 1978). The charge that Keynes was naive about government and entertained a Platonic view of the ideal state clearly deserves closer examination.

These worries about Keynes's commitment to what was construed as some form of totalitarianism are not confined to libertarians of the Buchanan School, as I learnt many years ago (1951) in a curious incident during a seminar at the University of Freiburg im Breisgau, where Walter Eucken, the famous German liberal, had established his *Euckenkreis*. I was faced by an audience who had read the German translation of the *General Theory* but were unfamiliar with the expository developments of Keynesian theory such as the famous 45-degree line diagram. I had reached the stage of explaining how equilibrium income was achieved when *ex ante* saving and investment were equal, when an irate lecturer rose to his feet and shouted: 'Diese Abbildung ist nur gültig für eine Planwirtschaft!' ('This diagram is only valid for a planned economy!'). I explained that I had not even introduced any government transactions into the analysis but this satisfied no one – I was denounced as a Keynesian socialist. To understand this emotional reaction one has to go back to the appearance of the German edition of the *General Theory* for which Keynes had written a separate introduction indicating that the then German (Nazi) government would be more sympathetic to his ideas on the employment-creating effects of public works than the British government (*CW XIV*). There is some dispute over whether or not the preface was accurately translated, but the fact remains that prominent German liberals, some of whom had suffered Nazi persecution, were profoundly shocked. After the translation appeared, Wilhelm Röpke, who had to leave Germany in 1933 after refusing to take an oath of allegiance to a Nazi government, expressed grave disquiet (Röpke, 1976) from his 'watchtower' in Geneva, and by 1943 could write to Einaudi that the *Economic Journal* (edited by Keynes) was 'infected with Socialism' (*ibid.*, p. 73). Much has been made by members of the *Euckenkreis* of the point that their considerable influence on the German economic reforms of 1948, which laid aside economic controls, represented defiance of prevailing Keynesian doctrines widely accepted by the occupying powers (see Peacock and Willgerodt, 1989, *passim).* It is ironic that Keynes, who wrote so passionately about how 'abhorrent and detestable' he found the policy of reducing Germany to servitude through reparations after the First World

War, should be subjected to this condemnation after the Second World War. How intelligent and sensitive men could come to think of Keynes in this way merits further investigation.

II. SOME PROCEDURAL MATTERS

Having shown how appreciation and criticism of Keynes's position on the role of government has been extended far beyond his contribution to economics, there must be speculation about what an economist can contribute to the discussion. I believe that the answer lies in adopting the framework of Classical political economy in which I was nurtured, remembering that this tradition is not to be confused with the 'Classical' economists that Keynes attacked because of their *laissez-fairism.* A way into the debate for the economist may be to seek to answer the question which Keynes raised about himself: 'Am I a Liberal?'

To provide a backcloth which could clearly reveal the distinctive features of Keynes's views on the role of the state, one could equally well start by setting out the characteristics of mainstream socialist economic philosophy. Indeed, it might be argued that, ultimately, Keynes's position is so far removed from collectivist socialism that it would stand out more clearly against a disquisition on socialist ideals. I have preferred to follow Keynes himself, who tended to match his views against those of so-called '*laissez-faire* economists'. Even if he recognized that economists whom he respected had severed the nexus between economic analysis and political philosophy, he justified his mode of exposition as follows: 'the guarded and undogmatic attitude of the best economists has not prevailed against the general opinion that an individualistic *laissez-faire* is both what they ought to teach and what in fact they do teach' (*CW IX* 282).

A second procedural matter arises from the fact that what Keynes means by liberalism and its prescriptions for government does not necessarily accord with the meaning of that term today. While Keynes frequently contrasts his political position with *laissez-fair*ism, he associates this doctrine not with the Classical economists such as Hume, Smith, Malthus and J.S. Mill but with their publicists, notably Bastiat, Marcet, Martineau and Whately – see *CW IX* (1972). The economists attending his Berlin lecture on 'The End of Laissez-Faire' in 1926 are likely to have been puzzled by Keynes's lack of reference to any members of the contemporary Austrian School, notably von Mises, whose famous attack on collectivist economic planning had appeared as early as 1908. My procedure is not to pick a quarrel with Keynes's view of liberalism, but rather to offer a synthetic view of liberalism, as would be offered by the heirs to the Classical tradition – the public choice school – and to contrast Keynes's pronouncements with that view. As I am not seeking to rank economists' philosophies of the state, it may be of more interest to proceed in this way rather than to get involved in criticizing Keynes for omissions in his knowledge of liberal thinking.

A third matter concerns Keynes's frequent changes in his ethical position and in his policy perceptions, which led Virginia Woolf to describe him as 'like a piece of quicksilver on a sloping board' (Woolf, 1977). Volumes have been written analysing these changes and I have nothing to add to them. I cannot avoid making some references to changes when these are of a major character, but in trying to convey Keynes's position 'in the round' I am bound to indulge in simplification. On policy questions, I have tended to concentrate on views expressed in his last years.

With these points in mind, let me now draw up my agenda for discussion. I shall start with an account which attempts to derive the broad tasks of the state from liberal principles, but I shall emphasize that the more we try to be precise in the delineation of those tasks, the more we are likely to find differences within the liberal camp. Some of these differences, as I shall demonstrate in Section III, arise from different perceptions of Keynes's own contribution to economic understanding. I then attempt to answer Keynes's own question about himself, but not with reference to his view on what liberalism meant but from the point of view of a modern liberal (Sections IV and V). A concluding section endeavours to assess Keynes's attitude to the role of the state.

III. LIBERAL PRINCIPLES AND ECONOMIC PRACTICE

I begin by trying to distil the essence of the liberal position in a form which I hope will be recognizable to all liberals.

Liberalism begins with an important ontological assumption. There is no society which is independent of the individuals who compose it. Individuals have tastes and preferences and endeavour to 'better their condition', as Adam Smith put it, within the limitations imposed by lack of resources and knowledge and by the uncertainties of life. That is a broad description of reality, to the liberal at least, but underlying this concept of the autonomously acting individual is an ethical principle, namely that the individual is the best judge of his/her own welfare. That being the case, any coercive action can only be justified if by circumscribing the actions of individuals the 'natural liberty' of all is improved. In defining the role of the state, the task is to identify those circumstances in which the actions of individuals conflict and to devise laws which resolve such conflicts but still give individuals equal rights to pursue their own interests. Within the framework of the 'rule of law', the individual is not accountable for his actions to society at large. Therefore, the modern concept of a 'social welfare function' is suspect to liberals – for further discussion, see Rowley and Peacock (1975) and Barry (1986).

In applying these general principles to the problem of the role of the state, there are significant differences of emphasis among liberals, which must now be explored.

The first problem is that not everyone may be persuaded that the rule of law is in their interests. If the natural human condition were, as Hobbes described it, 'war of all against all', then a liberal society would be virtually impossible, but this view is, at least implicitly, rejected by liberals. It will be against the interests of most individuals to conduct a 'war of all against all', and, indeed, it was held by liberals from Hume onwards that the growth of commerce and trade represented a cultural influence which reduced the temptation to use force in resolving international conflict. However, it would be absurd to go to the other extreme and allow individuals the absolute right to defend their property by force or to risk allowing individuals to employ private armies. Defence and law and order were proper functions of government, though one had to be careful not to allow the producers of these services to determine the extent of these services and close attention would have to be paid to the formulation of their tasks. There is clearly room for argument about the amount of resources to be compulsorily acquired in order to perform these functions, but this is not a problem to be faced only by those propounding a liberal philosophy of government.

The second problem concerns the distribution of property rights. On the one hand, why need it be assumed that the optimal distribution of income and wealth would emerge from the process of free exchange? On the other hand, state intervention in order to redistribute income and wealth could be regarded as 'the immoral seizure of legitimately acquired property' (Barry, 1986). There are three liberal attempts to resolve this dilemma, and they are not mutually exclusive. The first is to argue that the problem of inequality, in the long run at least, is not that important. The freely working market system does not manifest some distributional struggle in the form of a zero-sum game, but promotes co-operation which offers the expectation of gains to all. This may not result in growing equality in the distribution of income and wealth, but this is not even accepted as a necessary condition for the achievement of the aims of rival political philosophies. The second argument avers that individuals' perceptions of their satisfaction normally embrace caring for the unfortunate with a consequential wish to allocate part of one's income or wealth to support them. The third argument recognizes that there could be circumstances in which major inequalities of wealth and income would endanger individual freedom through the power of the more over the less fortunate, and this would call for some form of intervention in the distributional outcome of the market process. Again, apart from selecting which particular argument appeals to individual liberals, the problems of implementation of distribution policy are formidable. Even those liberals who envisage a substantial role for the state in distributional aims have disagreed strongly on methods – see Chapter 6 in this volume.

Should the government confine its role to support of private charity, for example through tax relief? At the other extreme, should governments be the main providers of services with a redistributory content, e.g. health and education, and should they offer such services free?

The third problem is an extension of the second. Once it is accepted that government is necessary to enforce the rule of law, then liberals cannot be indifferent to how governments are appointed and how they are to be controlled. The liberal aim is clearly to circumscribe the activities of government, but that cannot be guaranteed if property rights extend to giving all adults the vote. As de Tocqueville predicted, introduction of universal suffrage, coupled with large differences in income between few rich and many poor, is a recipe for a large expansion of the public sector, as the majority, the poor, can exploit their power to transfer resources to them from the rich minority. The Classical economists appreciated the dilemma that this presented. Whereas the concept of economic freedom seemed to suggest political freedom as a necessary complement, there was no guarantee that political freedom, secured through the extension of the franchise, would guarantee votes for free market principles. The resolution of the dilemma was to time the extension of the franchise to match a widening dispersion in the distribution of property as the market economy expanded – for further discussion, see Peacock, 1992. The rent-seeking propensity of voters has stimulated public choice economists, such as the Nobel Laureate James Buchanan, to design constitutional constraints which would restrain majoritarian democracy, constraints which the majority itself would accept as 'fair rules of the game' governing the decision-making process. The classic liberal dilemma remains that a political dimension to personal freedom can be at odds with the preconditions for economic freedom – a small and economically run public sector with minimum interference in the personal and business affairs of the individual.

The fourth problem concerns the possibility that the market economy, by itself, will not generate the preconditions for consumer sovereignty, namely the continuing presence of competitive forces. Liberals have differed among themselves about what is essentially an empirical matter. Some have maintained that a government competition policy is unnecessary and that the best protection for competition is non-intervention in the market, including eschewal of such instruments as tariffs and subsidies. Others, notably members of the *Euckenkreis* already referred to, have maintained that a constitution designed to guarantee individual liberty must contain clauses which outlaw cartels and control mergers.

I have not forgotten that the primary interest of this chapter is in Keynes's position, though, as I have argued, an examination of liberalism is a necessary preliminary. However, Keynes enters the story earlier when we consider the fifth problem encountered by liberals which originates with Keynes himself. Running through our discussion is a transparent thread of argument, namely that liberal support for the state, albeit sometimes reluctantly, arises from the recognition of the 'externality effects', as we call them today, resulting from individual actions which affect others. Whereas some of these effects may be positively beneficial, in the form of gains from trade, others are perceived as negative. Keynes's 'paradox of saving', which some regard as his distinctive contribution to macroeconomics – see Meade, 1975 – is a striking example. According to the Keynes of the *General Theory,* individuals may perceive that they will be better off if they save, having taken account of greater opportunities to consume in the future. However, this is an example of the fallacy of composition. If the aggregate effect is to increase new saving with respect to a given present level of income, then aggregate consumption will fall, which will reduce demand, and therefore investment and ultimately output and employment. Individuals' attempts to 'better their condition' through saving for the future will, in aggregate, leave the community worse off.

The Keynesian 'underemployment equilibrium' thesis confronted liberally minded economists with a major dilemma. If they accepted the diagnosis, then they would be hard put to it not to accept that the cure must lie in further state intervention. If they did not accept the diagnosis, then they would have to come up with an alternative, publicly convincing, explanation of the causes of the Great Depression. The deep divisions between liberal economists have lasted until today. Some like Lionel Robbins bit the bullet and generously agreed that Neo-Classical explanations were at least incomplete. Commenting on his role in presenting Keynesian ideas to Ministers concerned with post-war employment policy in the famous 1944 White Paper, he states.

> I should like to make it clear ... that these functions were very willingly performed. It would not be true to say that then, or at any subsequent period, I had become Keynesian in the sense of accepting *au pied de la lettre* all the analytical propositions of the *General Theory.* Although I had greatly benefited by the intellectual shake-up in studying them, I found many that were confused and wrong-headed in their formulation. ... But if all that is involved by that description is a conviction that, in a free society, the fluctuations in aggregate demand must not be left to look after themselves and that it is an important function of government, national and international, to pay attention to such matters, then indeed that is now my position. I had long realised that my earlier diagnosis of the causes of the Great Depression has missed the mark. ... My activities in connection with the White Paper therefore may be regarded as an attempt at reparation for erroneous advice offered at an earlier period. (Robbins, 1971)

Divested of the more emotional outbursts against Keynes, mainly on the grounds that, as Schumpeter remarked, he was following the profligate ways of a Madame Pompadour by his support for public works, those who rejected his diagnosis and accordingly his policy proposals have argued that Keynes was right to relate the growth of mass unemployment in the late 1920s to the 'over-valued exchange rate', but betrayed the liberal cause by developing remedies other than devaluation which presupposed that the only solution open to government was to exploit economic nationalism. The Neo-Classical theorists he attacked were straw men and the attack levelled against their orthodoxies was an irrelevance (see Johnson, 1975). Today, the more committed libertarians, having recovered their wind, have argued that crises of the kind associated with extremes of inflation and deflation are best avoided by keeping the government budget small and balanced, coupled with the denationalization of money – for a typical expression of this view, see Dowd, 1988. It is ironic that this position is now regarded as both a formidable and a radical attack on Keynesian orthodoxy.

IV. KEYNES AS AN END-STATE LIBERAL

The first stage in identifying anyone's view of the functions of the state is usually to enquire about their objectives. Within the narrower confines of economic policy, this is called identifying the 'arguments' in the social welfare function. Sometimes identification goes further with a statement of the 'trade-off' between these arguments. This sounds like a useful typological device for analysing Keynes's position, were it not that, as we have already warned the reader, the whole concept of a 'social welfare function' is rejected by public choice libertarians of the Buchanan school.

The basic concern of Buchanan (e.g. Buchanan, 1975) is to deny that a libertarian position requires the making of ethical judgments of the kind made by social philosophers who 'play God'. 'My natural proclivity as an economist is to place ultimate value on process or procedure, and by implication to define as "good" that which emerges from agreement among free men, independently of intrinsic evaluation of the outcome itself' (Buchanan, 1975, p. 167). It follows that liberalism is about determination of the 'correct' contractual procedures which will allow individuals to consent to intervention by government. That procedure, if it is to be compatible with an individualist position, requires, so far as is practically possible, unanimous consent. Therefore, the common procedure used by economists to identify a social welfare function which is then to be 'maximized' implicitly rejects the individualistic decision-making process, which is the only mechanism through which individuals both express preferences and have them acted upon. To claim that preferences can be revealed and acted upon by governments, unencumbered by individuals' consent, is to presuppose that they and their officials will always act in an enlightened and wholly disinterested way.

It is a curious paradox that, in the light of Buchanan's distaste for Keynesian elitism (see Buchanan, 1991), there are elements in Keynes's rather fragmentary thinking on political matters which express a sympathy with an individualistic stance. His ethical position, derived from G.E. Moore, put great emphasis on an ideal conception of what constituted 'civilization' – in Moore's view, the pleasures of human intercourse and the enjoyment of beautiful objects. The cultivation of 'good states of mind' need not entail any form of political action. Indeed, the diversion of personal energies into the grubby world of politics could lure individuals towards activities which would be at total variance with pursuing the ethical ends of spending time in civilized company and refining the elements that constitute the good life. The state need have no role in pursuing the goals of civilized society, though, presumably, it was taken for granted amongst The Apostles that it was necessary for their protection.

There is a further distinct element in Keynesian thinking which appears to be in sympathy with the subjectivist elements in public choice theory. The complexity and uncertainties of economic life place major limitations on the individual's ability to achieve his/her ends with given means. The resemblance seems to be superficial, at least when it comes to examining the consequences of uncertainty. For public choice theorists it provides an additional argument for circumscribing state action, because governments cannot possibly acquire the knowledge which would be necessary to maximize any social welfare function. Keynes was conscious of this limitation on government action, which is why, it is claimed, he rejected the notion that we could ever know enough to be able to apply Benthamite utilitarian principles, assuming we wanted to do so (see Skidelsky, 1988). However, if reasons could be found for government action to promote the ends he desired, then, while philosophic doubt might be right and proper, the problems of life could not wait. Economists should not sit on their hands but should organize knowledge so as to assist the intuition of those who had to act.

However, it would be wrong for me to try to bring 'contractarian liberals' into the same camp as 'end-state' liberals – for this distinction see Barry, 1986. An important change came in Keynes's ethical position which authorities seem to agree was the result of the profound effect of the First World War on Keynes and many others who had led sheltered and privileged lives. Put very baldly, it seemed wrong that the benefits of civilized living, which represented all that was good, should be enjoyed by the few. Such benefits should be available to all those who wished to enjoy them. One's view of the functions of the state depended, therefore, on whether the achievement of this aim required government action.

As we shall soon observe, the aim of spreading the benefits of civilized living widely certainly did entail, in Keynes's mind, a crucial role for government. He would certainly have seen nothing particularly controversial in describing the end-state, the goal at which policy should be aimed. Nor do I, although I would wish to define the goal differently. Nor have I ever been able to accept that Buchanan has avoided a normative approach to political action by claiming that it is possible to devise constitutional arrangements which minimize coercion.

This must presuppose that certain kinds of behaviour are the norm. As a minimum it requires that citizens believe that the democratic process is a good thing and accept the moral obligation to abide by the decision rules which are agreed between them – for further discussion of this issue, see Barry, 1986.

Nevertheless, Buchanan's position does raise a major question about end-state liberalism of crucial importance in examining Keynes's position. What if the defined end-state is not one which would be the outcome of the democratic process? Is not the democratic process an essential component of a liberal philosophy? Charles Rowley and I (Rowley and Peacock, 1975) provided a categorical answer in our examination of the 'constitutional' approach. We argued that a corollary of the liberal doctrine that there is equality before the law requires that all individuals, other than minors or lunatics, should have the same share in making the law. The acceptance of majority rule, however, does not require liberals to endorse the outcomes of majority voting which result in illiberal policies. One must abide by decisions arrived at by majority rule, while reserving the right to use all reasonable methods of persuasion, short of coercion, to attempt to alter the preferences of those who would vote for illiberal measures.

A full answer on Keynes's view of this dilemma must wait until we have further examined what action he thought would be necessary to achieve his goals. One can say at this stage that his view of how the democratic system worked, though not expressed in a formal model of the Buchanan–Tullock kind, was very different. In practice, he appears to have seen the public rather as reactors, not necessarily passive reactors, to the agenda presented to them by politicians. I have never come across a passage where he ever suggested that the universal franchise was a positive hindrance to achieving his goals and, *pace* Skidelsky and Fitzgibbons, I do not think it is sensible to produce an undergraduate essay on Burke, however brilliantly written, as evidence to the contrary. However, Keynes believed passionately in the power of ideas in changing preferences. His tactics of persuasion required the concentration of the attack on the minds and souls of politicians and civil servants as the real sources of power. It is fair to say that Keynes avoided the issue that Buchanan raises, but probably would not have thought it one which it was necessary to be bothered about.

V. KEYNES'S PUBLIC POLICY AGENDA

Throughout the inter-war years, Keynes's public policy agenda varied both as a result of the changes wrought in his analytical apparatus and the fluctuating international economic position. This agenda became more stable after the publication of the *General Theory* and its important supplement, *How to Pay For the War.* The wartime discussions of post-war economic policy, in which Keynes took a major part, were carried out within an essentially Keynesian framework in which his macroeconomic modelling together with its statistical complement, national income accounting, became increasingly influential (*CW XXVII passim*). I have based my analysis on what may be described as Keynes's 'final position' – for the evolution of Keynes's earlier views, see, of course, Clarke (1990).

There are several restatements of his *Weltanschauung,* usually appearing as incidental remarks in Treasury memoranda. A good example is contained in a passage commenting on a draft report of the Steering Committee on post-war employment in which he sides with Lionel Robbins against attempts to develop major controls over industry:

> for those who believe that it will be the role of this country to develop a middle way of economic life which will preserve the liberty, the initiative and (what we are rich in) the idiosyncracy of the individual in a framework serving the public good, and seeking equality of contentment amongst all, Professor Robbins's admonitions go to the heart of things. (*CW XXVII* 369)

'Equality of contentment for all' is a resounding phrase, but how is this form of equality to be attained? This was clearly a long-term objective, but Keynes did not believe that it required some grandiose blueprint for society. The first consideration was 'to maintain a steady level of employment and thus to prevent fluctuations' (*CW XXVII* 323). The associated policy measure was control over total investment. The bulk of investment – Keynes varies his estimate between one-half and two-thirds – should be carried out or be influenced by public or semi-public bodies. He was clearly less impressed with anti-cyclical measures that were designed to influence consumption spending, at least as a short-term measure, on the now familiar grounds that spending habits change slowly. While it would be fascinating to reconstruct the macroeconomic model which would throw light on his preferred policy measures and to lay these alongside James Meade's views, which Keynes much admired, the point at issue in his contribution is that no liberalist inhibitions held Keynes back from a proposal which clearly entailed much more public intervention than one which relied on influencing private consumption through taxation. However, one cannot be sure that Keynes regarded global investment control as a permanent fixture. He agreed with Hubert Henderson that a saturation point might be reached in investment when the direction of policy might have to change and move towards 'increasing the scale of consumption or (alternatively) of leisure'. In other words, the long-term economic threat to mustering the resources to produce equal contentment for all was still likely to be underemployment of resources. Keynes alleged that 'short-termism' applied not to the goals he chose for society but to the need for constant adaptation of policy measures to keep on the right path. To change the metaphor: the choice of haven had been taken, but to keep the ship of state moving towards it needed frequent changes in the instructions to the engine room and to the quartermaster at the wheel.

The emphasis on long-term stability as the clue to securing the economic base of Keynes's good society also entailed taking a view of international trade and industrial policy. I have nothing very much to add to what is now so well known. Keynes's own efforts to promote international economic stability were matched by a strong belief that Britain's long-term economic future depended on free international trade (see the famous *Economic Journal* article of 1946 – his last academic contribution). Protection was not entirely ruled out and there is a pre-echo of the left-wing Keynesian view that tariffs and subsidies could be used as devices to protect employment levels (see *CW XVII passim)*, but the difference between Keynes and his left-wing intellectual descendants clearly lies in his view that protection should only be used to cope with the difficulties of transition from a war economy or if there were a complete breakdown in international economic co-operation – see Wilson, 1982. In the case of industrial policy, Keynes was a lifelong opponent of the capture of the 'commanding heights of the economy' by government and latterly of selective intervention in industry. For example, in his many exchanges with Hubert Henderson, he picks on a quotation from the former which 'embodies much wisdom' (*CW XVII* 324):

> Opponents of Socialism are on strong grounds when they argue that the State would be unlikely in practice to run complicated industries more efficiently than they are run at present. Socialists are on strong ground when they argue that reliance on supply and demand, and the forces of market competition, as the mainspring of our economic system, produces most unsatisfactory results. Might we not find a modus vivendi for the next decade or so in an arrangement under which the State would fill the vacant post of entrepreneur-in-chief, while not interfering with the ownership or management of particular businesses, or rather only doing so on the merits of the case and not at the behests of dogma?

I previously observed (in Section III above) that 'the second problem' encountered in defining the practical content of liberal policy concerned income and wealth distribution. Could there not be a close link between 'equality of contentment' and the redistribution of command over resources? It is here that it may seem the easy way out on my part to confine attention to Keynes's final thoughts on this question. If I do, then the answer that Keynes appears to give – 'appears' because there is much that is not clear in his observations – is certainly that the link implied that a *sine qua non* for achieving the goal must be that all should enjoy the fruits of economic advance. For example, Keynes studied the Beveridge Plan in detail, not only supporting its purpose including the precondition of establishing a National Health Service, but also proclaiming its financial viability. His draft speech to the House of Lords on this subject was yet another document emphasizing that

> to make a bogey of the economic problem is. … grievously to misunderstand the nature of the tasks ahead of us. … The real problems of the future are first of all the maintenance of peace, of international co-operation and amity, and beyond that the profound moral and social problems of how to organise material abundance to yield up the fruits of a good life. (*CW XXVII* 260–1)

By 1944, there is not much more to his egalitarianism than commitment to the Beveridge Plan, an element of redistribution involved in financing it (but with due regard to the effects of taxation on incentives) and a capital levy as a once-and-for-all measure to penalize those who had made large capital gains in wartime and to help finance post-war credits. (Keynes credited Hayek with this last proposal!) The capital levy might pave the way for a permanent capital tax 'which would be a valuable addition to our fiscal machinery and has certain important advantages over income tax' (*CW IX* 407). After his death a memorandum to the Treasury on the 1946 Budget was found with some post-Budget reflections. A 'Capital Tax half per cent' is on his list of proposed direct taxes, which hardly suggests some swingeing egalitarian measure.

Although earlier statements of Keynes, notably on the 'euthanasia of the rentier', might support Fitzgibbons's contention that '[t]hose who deny that Keynes was an equalitarian have a far harder case to prove', I cannot accept that it is necessary to seek to prove that case by having to argue that Keynes did not mean what he said. The problem is that, whereas one can accept that Keynes was in favour of a much more equitable distribution of income and wealth in the long run, for this would be a necessary condition for 'equality of contentment', there seems to be a notable reluctance on his part to use the power of the state to move towards this condition by draconian measures. The prospect of economic abundance in the long run, coupled with an investment glut, would be sufficient to relieve a large proportion of the working population from economic necessity and alter the relative shares of labour and capital as the return on capital moved to zero. In technical language, Keynes looked forward to a world in which the factor, pre-tax, distribution of income would become more equal, rather than one in which distributional objectives would be reflected in the post-tax (disposable) income distribution engineered by government. Keynes meant what he said, but, on this issue, he did not say a great deal.

As we have indicated, 'equality of contentment' meant something more to Keynes than a vast improvement in the standard of living of all, as conventionally measured by, say, income per head. Whereas it is a basic tenet of libertarians, if not liberals, that preference scales of individuals cannot and ought not to be ranked, Keynes saw the removal of economic necessity as an opportunity for all to enjoy the cultural benefits which had been handed to him on a plate.

In 'earlier writing', that is before the 1940s, Keynes, having assumed that the economic problem of the ordinary person would be largely solved, asks the question 'how to occupy the leisure, which science and compound interest will have won for him, to live wisely, agreeably and well' (*CW IX* 328). In answering this question, interest centres on what the role of the state would be in achieving this ideal position. Keynes at this stage (1930) does not provide an answer. Rather does he suggest that there is a prospect that the solution of the economic problem would release man from the bondage of instincts and impulses associated solely with money-making. The very realization that the problem has been solved would itself initiate the desired change:

> when the accumulation of wealth is no longer of high social importance, there will be changes in the code of morals. We shall be able to rid ourselves of many pseudo-moral principles which have hag-ridden us for two hundred years, by which we exalted some of the most distasteful of human qualities into the position of the highest virtues. We shall be able to afford to dare to assess the money-motive at its true value. (*CW IX* 328)

... and there is much more of this expressed in equally eloquent terms.

In the field of the arts, at least, Keynes became deeply involved in later life with giving the move towards his cultural nirvana a push in what he saw as the right direction. Apart from his personal aesthetic interests and financial support for all kinds of artistic enterprises, it is extraordinary that he had the time and energy in wartime not only to preside over the foundation of the Arts Council, but to define on what terms government money should be given to artistic enterprises. First, he defines the task of any official body as 'not to teach or to censor, but to give courage, confidence and opportunity' to artistic enterprises, clearly with the aim, as he applied it to broadcasting, 'of enlarging the desires of the listener and his capacity for enjoyment' (*CW XXVIII* 368). Second, he saw the main constraint on the promotion of the arts as the lack of buildings. The restoration of buildings would both enhance the physical environment and provide suitable venues – see Mary Glasgow, 1975, on which this account of Keynes's views is largely based. He was implacably opposed to the public provision of artistic performances, preferring to back established companies against loss or to offer loans. He is reported to have said that if a subsidizing body were 100 per cent successful it would end up spending nothing at all, except on administration. It would choose so well and back such uniformly certain winners that all its loans would be repaid in full and none of its guarantees ever called. As chairman of CEMA (the predecessor of the Arts Council) he expressed his likes and dislikes and followed them through into the composition of funding, rather in contradiction to his public expression of a 'hands-off' approach towards artistic endeavours. It is possible to be dismissive of these efforts, for, alongside the traditional common functions of the state, expenditure on the arts is small beer. However, it is reasonable to suppose that Keynes saw himself as setting an example for other rich lovers of the arts to follow, encouraged by tax reliefs as an alternative method of state support (see *CW XXVIII* 361).

VI. WAS KEYNES A LIBERAL? A PARTIAL ANSWER TO A DIFFICULT QUESTION

At the risk of enclosing myself in a methodological straitjacket, let me try to answer Keynes's question by reference to the discussion of liberalism in Section III above.

Behind the ontological assumption of liberalism, as I have described it above, are two important propositions about the human condition. The first is that the characteristic of self-interest in individuals, which can embrace concern for the interests of others, is independent of time and place. This has become the cornerstone of public choice theory, clearly illustrated in its now-famous economic analysis of bureaucracy which denies that civil servants follow 'higher ideals' than the mean, sensual men who are subject to their regulation. The second is that human beings will always be faced with the dilemma of choice, namely that there is a cost attached to any decision to use resources to promote their individual interests – the alternatives foregone; and one should add that whereas individuals may learn from their mistakes in the course of making decisions, this does not reduce the importance of the unknowability of the future – for a penetrating account of this view and an associated critique of Marshallian economics, see Wiseman, 1989.

Keynes's views seem to deny both propositions. The 'opportunity cost' problem which forces us to make 'tragic choices' would be solved by rapid economic advance. That advance would itself bring about a transformation in human nature. This sounds more like the utterances of utopian socialists looking forward to the day when, with the end of capitalism, 'roast pigeons would fall from heaven into the mouths of the comrades' (von Mises) and the perfectibility of man would be complete. However, a fundamental difference remains between the Keynesian and socialist ideals and in this difference lies the origin of Joan Robinson's aphorism: '[Keynes] thought that when people could understand his theory, could understand how the capitalistic system actually works, they would then behave in a reasonable manner and operate the system in such a way as to produce favourable results ...' (Kahn, 1984, p. 203).

Why should it make any difference to Keynes's position on the functions of the state if he did hold views on human nature and the constraints on human action different from those of latter-day liberals? That question cannot be answered without considering the ethical principle underlying individualism, that the individual is the best judge of his or her welfare. If that principle is accepted, the individual is not obliged to accept any moral imperative, other than that of respecting the interests of others and the resolution of conflicts of interest through an agreed set of rules. If alongside this ethical principle it is held that human beings would always be characterized by what David Hume called 'narrowness of soul' and if resource constraints remained, Keynes's dream would appear to be neither desirable nor possible, unless the power of ideas was so strong that people could be persuaded to change their ways, and provided that, in the interim, they could trust governments to act in accordance with such ideas.

The debate between Keynes and latter-day liberals of the public choice school could be settled, in principle at least, by empirical investigation – in fifty years or so! In this connection, it must be recalled that Keynes entered the caveat that his argument depends on the absence of wars between progressive countries and on there being no population explosion. So far, if we extend Keynes's remit to large industrial countries which have experienced a major increase in their standards of living, it would seem a vain hope to place reliance on a moral transformation which would remove these barriers to progress. Keynes seemed to have a touching faith in the idea that the spread of gracious living and cultural refinement would remove all economic and social conflicts.

The contractarian liberals, as we have seen, place great weight on developing institutions which both support equality of political rights and at the same time direct the employment of these rights towards political support for limited government. No evolution in morals is presupposed, though there must be general acceptance of the constitutional rules of the game. Keynes's position is very different. First one must be sure of one's moral position. As an intelligent person with a conscience one must use all one's power of persuasion to convince as many as possible that this position is right. Finally, the widespread acceptance of the moral position reduces the necessity for being concerned about the precise content of constitutional arrangements. Indeed, one could go further and envisage a situation where self-regulation could supplement government measures. Large corporations would develop a moral conscience and be governed by ethical precepts which would induce them to follow an investment policy which would maximize employment; and individuals could adjust their propensity to save in accordance with the same objective. Here I find Skidelsky's argument instructive, though I am worried by its implications: '[Keynes] means by the state that sector of the polity not working for private self-interest, but for the public good' (Skidelsky, 1988, p. 18). Does Keynes really mean that private self-interest and the public good are antithetic? I prefer an interpretation in which the Keynesian nirvana is one where it is recognized that 'equality of contentment' is not simply what some would prescribe for others but what everyone will perceive as in his or her own interest to embrace.

The most fascinating evidence of Keynes's position is to be found in the well-known letter to Hayek on reading *The Road to Serfdom* (see *CW XXVII*

385 *et seq.*). Keynes writes that 'morally and philosophically I find myself in agreement with virtually the whole of it; and not only in agreement with it, but in a deeply moved agreement'. But having agreed with Hayek on the prime importance of individual liberty and the rule of law, he rejects the notion that 'so soon as one moves an inch in the planned direction you are necessarily launched on the slippery path which will lead you in due course over the precipice'. Keynes maintains that what is needed is not 'no planning' but 'moderate planning', presumably in order to avoid underemployment equilibrium, '[b]ut the planning should take place in a community in which as many people as possible, both leaders and followers, wholly share your own moral position. Moderate planning will be safe if those carrying it out are rightly orientated in their own minds and hearts to the moral issue.'

I have offered sufficient evidence already to indicate that, to the extent that Keynes turned his mind to the other questions of importance – distribution of income and wealth, international economic co-operation to ensure a high level of employment and free international trade, and selective intervention in the economy – there is little to distinguish his position from that of, say, Lionel Robbins or James Meade, both of whom have vigorously defended him from the charge of being a prisoner of collectivism – see, particularly, Robbins, 1971.

It is nevertheless no wonder that contractarian liberals regard Keynes's end-state liberalism as naive. The best evidence of this lies in the remarkable growth in the relative importance of government in the economy since the Second World War, which has been principally a function of the growth in social security transfers and social services coupled with growing centralized control of government. It is simply unreasonable to claim that this growth in government is the *logical* consequence of Keynes's views on the functions of government, as distinct from those of his followers. Also, the pattern of government income and expenditure presupposed by Keynes's measures would have had to be very different. So much for the triumph of ideas which would enlighten politicians about their tasks and convince the public to support them. The meaning of the famous last sentence of the *General Theory* (*CW XVII* 384) should be stood on its head, for all the evidence displayed in the transactions of government supports the thesis that vested interests triumph over ideas. If a man of Keynes's intelligence and perspicacity had spent a bit more time considering the political presuppositions behind his ideas, he would have discovered this for himself. Regrettably, the major influences on his life, notably the patrician stance of his intellectual generation, his remarkable powers of persuasion among his academic and government colleagues, perhaps also the lack of experience of material hardship, deluded him into believing that political structure and organization were not matters which any sensible person would regard as particularly important and, to the extent that it was in place, it could be and should be easily set aside by enlightened administrators advised by persons like himself. At least this is the conventional wisdom amongst contractarian liberals.

No one is obliged to answer the question which Keynes posed to himself solely by reference to the austere propositions of contractarian liberals, but I am prepared to argue that even within the framework set by their propositions, their judgment of Keynes contains methodological faults. These faults are of such a nature that they prevent anyone giving a complete answer to Keynes's question.

In the first place, whereas contractarian liberals share similar values about the importance of constitutional procedures and argue, convincingly in my view, that limited government must be a precondition for preserving individual liberty, that is not to say that they agree in detail about the precise role of the state. Wicksell, the father of public choice theory, paid close attention to the development of voting rules which would maximize individual choice, but he hoped that the result would be strong public support for provision of government services to improve human capital formation and to protect workers from the risks of old age, accident and ill health – see Uhr, 1962. Wicksell believed that these services could be provided without a major expansion in the relative size of government, because 'true' expression of voter preference would result in a shift away from military towards social expenditures while, simultaneously, investment in human capital by government would contribute so effectively towards increasing national income that the government expenditure/national income ratio would not increase. As we have seen, there has always been argument among liberals about the position of 'welfare state' activities in their political philosophy, but what is more interesting here is that no public choice theorist, so far as I am aware, has ever criticized Wicksell's perception of the proper functions of the state. Why then pick on Keynes?

John Gray, certainly a strong believer in limited government, has emphasized that a stable political order requires not only wide diffusion of wealth and equality of opportunity, but also 'a matrix of cultural traditions which is at once legitimate and finds expression in it' (1989, p. 74). The problem is how to ensure that the components of a liberal society are put in place without destroying liberty in the process. In the case of preserving cultural heritage, for example, Gray argues the case for using tax relief on cultural expenditures rather than direct subsidies, exactly as Keynes did just before he died.

In the second place, 'we are all creatures of our time'. No doubt Wicksell could be defended on the grounds that he was fighting for the fundamental right of universal suffrage and for the removal of the ban on dissemination of birth control information, both measures which would redistribute power to the working classes in a legitimate fashion. However, if that defence were offered for Wicksell as a contractarian liberal, it could equally well be offered for Keynes as an end-state liberal. After all, Keynes refused to embrace collectivist planning as a solution to his country's problems at a time when many influential and educated persons were turning their backs on the market economy, particularly those with aesthetic interests which he shared.

Lastly, Keynes was 62 when he died – for me that is young! It is clearly fallacious to assume that policies leading to expansion in the public sector's role and often done in his name would therefore have had his approval – see, further, Hutchison, 1981, Chapter 4. Conjectural history is likewise methodologically suspect, but there is at least some evidence in his last writings that Keynes disapproved strongly of the autarkic policies which were being developed in the immediate postwar period.

My answer must be this. Keynes's liberal dispositions cannot be in doubt. However wrong he may have been about the evolution of morals and the economy, and however unfair he may have been to Classical economics, to regard him as the betrayer of classical liberalism is a charge which cannot stick.

REFERENCES

Keynes's *Collected Writings* have been issued in thirty volumes over a period of years by the Royal Economic Society, published by Cambridge University Press and by Macmillan. For brevity, there are no individual references in this bibliography, but at appropriate places in the text the relevant volume and page number(s) are given. For example, *CW IX* 123 refers to J.M. Keynes, *The Collected Writings of John Maynard Keynes,* volume IX, *Essays in Persuasion* (London: Macmillan for the Royal Economic Society, 1972).

Barry, Norman (1986), *On Classical Liberalism and Libertarianism*, London: Macmillan.

Buchanan, James (1975), *The Limits of Liberty: Between Anarchy and Leviathan*, University of Chicago Press.

Buchanan, James (1991), *Constitutional Economics*, Oxford: Blackwell for the Institute of Economic Affairs, Chapter 3.

Buchanan, James, Wagner, Robert and Burton, John (1978), 'The Consequences of Mr Keynes', Hobart Paper No. 78, London: IEA (reprinted in Buchanan, James (1991), *Constitutional Economics*).

Clarke, Peter (1990), *The Keynesian Revolution in the Making 1924–1936*, Oxford: Clarendon Paperbacks.

Dowd, Kevin (1988), *Private Money: The Path to Monetary Stability*, London: Institute of Economic Affairs.

Fitzgibbons, Athol (1988), *Keynes's Vision*, Oxford: Clarendon Press.

Glasgow, Mary (1975), 'The Concept of the Arts Council', in Keynes, Milo (ed.), *Essays on John Maynard Keynes*, Cambridge University Press, Chapter 25.

Gray, John (1989), *Limited Government: A Positive Agenda*, London: Institute of Economic Affairs.

Hutchison, Terence (1981), *The Politics and Philosophy of Economics*, Oxford: Basil Blackwell.

Johnson, Harry (1975), 'Keynes and British Economics', in Keynes, Milo (ed.), *Essays on John Maynard Keynes*, Cambridge University Press.

Kahn, Richard (1984), *The Making of Keynes' General Theory: The Raffaele Mattioli Lectures*, Cambridge University Press.

Keynes, John Maynard (1971–89), *Collected Writings*, Macmillan and Cambridge University Press for Royal Economic Society, vols VII, IX, XIII, XIV, XXVII, XXVIII.
Keynes, Milo (ed.) (1975), *Essays on John Maynard Keynes*, Cambridge University Press.
Meade, James (1975), 'The Keynesian Revolution', in Keynes, Milo (ed.), *Essays on John Maynard Keynes*, Cambridge University Press, Chapter 10.
O'Donnell, Rod (1991), *Keynes as Philosopher-Economist: The Ninth Keynes Seminar held at the University of Kent at Canterbury 1989*, London: Macmillan.
Patinkin, Don (1982), *Anticipations of the General Theory*, Oxford: Basil Blackwell.
Peacock, Alan (1992), *Public Choice Analysis in Historical Perspective: The Raffaele Mattioli Lectures*, Cambridge University Press.
Peacock, Alan and Hans Willgerodt (1989), *Germany's Social Market Economy: Origins and Evolution*, London: Macmillan for Trade Policy Research Centre.
Robbins, Lionel (1971), *Autobiography of an Economist*, London: Macmillan.
Röpke, Wilhelm (1976), *Briefe 1934–1966* (ed. Eva Röpke), Erlenbach–Zurich: Eugen Rentsch Verlag.
Rowley, Charles (1987), 'John Maynard Keynes and the Attack on Classical Political Economy', in Buchanan, James, Rowley, Charles and Tollison, R.D. (eds), *Deficits*, Oxford: Blackwell.
Rowley, Charles and Peacock, Alan (1975), *Welfare Economics: A Liberal Restatement*, London: Martin Robertson.
Skidelsky, Robert (1983), *John Maynard Keynes (I), Hopes Betrayed, 1883–1920*, London: Macmillan.
Skidelsky, Robert (1988), 'Keynes' Political Legacy' in Hamouda, O.F. and Smithin, J.N. (eds), *Keynes and Public Policy After Fifty Years, Vol. I, Economics and Policy*, New York University Press.
Uhr, Carl (1962), *The Economic Doctrines of Knut Wicksell*, Berkeley and Los Angeles: University of California Press, Chapters 1 and 12.
Wilson, Thomas (1982), 'Policy in War and Peace: The Recommendations of John Maynard Keynes', in Thirlwall, A.P. (ed.), *Keynes as a Policy Adviser*, London: Macmillan.
Wiseman, Jack (1989), *Cost, Choice and Political Economy*, Aldershot: Edward Elgar, Chapter 7.
Woolf, Virginia (1977), *The Diary of Virginia Woolf, Vol. I (1915–1919)* (ed. Anne Olivier Bell), London: Harcourt Brace Jovanovich.

9. The LSE and post-war economic policy

(This short piece was written in response to an invitation to address a symposium on the LSE and its contributions to economics organized by the Atlantic Economic Society and held in the LSE in the autumn of 1981. Two former members of LSE staff were asked to participate, myself and Ronald Coase, now Nobel Laureate in Economics, who spoke on 'Economics at the LSE in the 1930s: A Personal View'. Our papers and those of four other contributors were published in the Atlantic Economic Journal *in March 1982.*

I was a member of the LSE staff for just over eight years from 1948 onwards, so I have limited the scope of my discussion to that taking place when I had, as it were, a ringside seat, with occasional minor sorties into the arena. If there is a general theme, it is that, contrary to popular opinion of the LSE, the economists' approach to policy questions was conducted at arm's length from the political scene, though informal contacts with members of successive governments were certainly not unknown. The days of the assignment of members of staff to the Government Economic Service or to posts as policy advisers were yet to come. At most, senior members of staff might find themselves members of ad hoc *Commissions or Committees of Enquiry or of Research Committees.)*

I. INTRODUCTION

The Second World War led to the most complete mobilization of resources which the UK has ever experienced in order to 'produce' defence of the realm. The process of mobilization of economists to help run the war economy began slowly with the recruitment of an unpaid adviser to the Treasury by the name of J.M. Keynes, the author of a pamphlet on anti-inflation policy entitled *How to Pay for the War* (1940).

By the time the war ended, many well-known economists had made names for themselves in the upper echelons of government. They were involved in financial policy at the highest level, in the devising of rationing schemes for food and raw materials, and in the preparation of plans for post- war reconstruction both nationally, as in the famous Full Employment White Paper (1944), and internationally, as in the crucial negotiations led by Keynes at Bretton Woods which in turn led to the creation of the IMF. This was also a period when national income accounting was turned into an essential tool of economic policy.

The war had a profound effect on the study of economics. During the war itself, the learned scholastic debates which dominated much pre-war discussion had to be set aside. Lionel Robbins sums up the experience of many who were in government then or, like myself, have subsequently spent lengthy periods in Whitehall. Contact is inevitably lost with the fast-developing technicalities of the subject but

> in every other respect, the experience was gain. It lifted me out of the rather narrow academic atmosphere in which I had hitherto been moving with such absorbed concentration. It gave me the opportunity of rethinking the fundamentals of my subject in a *milieu* radically different from anything with which I had previously been confronted. It gave me inside acquaintance with the machinery of government and technique of administration ... and by putting me to work side by side with officials and professional colleagues whose background and outlook differed from my own, it enlarged the scope of my sympathies and understanding.[1]

The economic organization required by total war had much wider effects than enlarging the experience of economists. It seemed to provide a concrete case for the longer-term introduction of economic planning on collectivist lines. This was fastened on by a large number of writers who were enemies of the market economy and who were already friendly to Soviet Russia, though woefully ignorant of its economy, and deeply impressed by its response to total war, conveniently forgetting, perhaps, that Stalin had made a sordid bargain with the Nazis prior to the 1939 carving-up of Poland. Their number included prominent natural scientists, historians, philosophers, and literary men, such as Cyril Connolly and Kenneth Clark who saw the bombing of London as a symbol of the death of capitalism.

But even those not committed to wholesale collectivism, such as Lord Beveridge (of the famous Report on Social Insurance) and many democratic socialists, thought that the unity of purpose created by the war, coupled with the implicit 'social contract' between the government and the community that the unemployment of the 1930s must never be repeated, presaged radical changes in social policy which a capitalist economy could not countenance. In any case, after wartime shortages had been made good, the return to an underemployed economy – the natural concomitant to market capitalism – could only be avoided by fiscal stimulants to private and public investment.

What is striking about the LSE writing on post-war economic policy is that those who participated in the running of the war economy were at one with those who did not participate in seeing their task as that of destroying illusions about the attractiveness of collectivism and dispelling myths surrounding the historical record of capitalism and its alleged 'lackeys' – the Classical economists. I shall not attempt to measure the influence of their view; sufficient to say that collectivist views are today widely rejected, and if this is so, it is at least partly the result of their writings in the period from the late 1940s to the mid 1950s.

II. COLLECTIVISM: DIFFICULTIES AND DANGERS

The attack on the collectivist position was conducted in both positive and normative terms. In the spring of 1947, Lionel Robbins was invited to give the Marshall Lectures at Cambridge – a not insignificant approach perhaps – and out of them came a remarkable *tour de force.*[2] I am concerned at this stage with only one feature of it – the economic lessons of the war economy.

Robbins makes his position plain. The 'ordinary apparatus of calculation' – the market – was inefficient in allocating resources for wartime purposes for the maximizing unit was bound to be a government faced with total war. Even then, uncertainty about the relative gains and losses of large-scale military operations limited rational action and often led to large-scale inefficiency in resource use. Above all, the acceptance of a totalitarian system rested on a profound unity of purpose among the electorate, for the consequences of losing a war at the time seemed too horrible to contemplate.

However, no such community of interests exists in peacetime and, having fought for freedom, survivors, determined to exercise it both in respect of choice of occupation and choice in spending, have very disparate ideas about how to satisfy these choices. 'If it gives you any satisfaction', argues Robbins,

> you can still provide a formal description of the ultimate goal which has unitary appearance. Nobody is likely to quarrel with the statement that the object of policy should be to maximize welfare over time. But this is to state the problem, not to solve it.

Now two teachers at the LSE, Abba Lerner and Evan Durbin, had developed, along with Oscar Lange, a theory of what is now termed 'market socialism' in which the essential feature of collectivism, socialization of investment, would be combined with market allocation of resources. Robbins treats their approach with considerable sympathy but argues, convincingly in my view, that the apparatus by which firms under collectivism would be given instructions would be in practice too cumbersome. Later, his pupil Jack Wiseman pointed out that the appropriate instructions would themselves be impossible to formulate satisfactorily,[3] and checks on firms' efficiency could only be made on plans actually chosen without regard to whether the plans were correct in the first place. In those days, no collectivist supporter went so far as to make a case for competition between firms under market socialism, so Robbins eventually threw out his colleagues' proposals on the grounds that suppression of competition – including a free field for new entrants – meant death to efficiency.[4]

At the time when Lionel Robbins, James Meade, Frank Paish, Richard Sayers, Ronnie Edwards, Ronald Coase, and Arnold Plant (all to return to the LSE) were helping to run the war economy, the LSE was evacuated to Cambridge and Fritz Hayek went with it. It is no reflection on Robbins's work, which contains a sparkling passage on personal liberty and collectivism,[5] that one turns to Hayek for the rejection on normative grounds of collectivism as a solution of post-war economic problems.

I hardly need to remind the reader of the theme of *The Road to Serfdom* which appeared in March 1944.[6] That collectivism is inefficient was a proposition which might be accepted or rejected on the basis of reasoned argument and empirical analysis, but that it was totally undesirable on moral grounds whether as Fascism, Nazism, or Socialism was a different order of argument. I shall only remind you of his theme by one quotation:

> The tragedy of collectivist thought is that while it starts out to make reason supreme, it ends by destroying reason because it misconceives the process on which the growth of reason depends.

In short, collectivism in the end cannot tolerate freedom of thought and the associated reconciliation of differences by compromise and toleration. Many who were shocked, startled and antagonized by Hayek's position then have now accepted its message, if only in the light of bitter experience. In the immediate post-war period, Hayek attempted to buttress his position by publicizing the work of the Freiburg School now noted for its influence on German post-war economic policy. However, its uncompromising but understandable anti-Keynesian position, coupled with the difficulties in understanding its German modes of thinking, established barriers of communication between it and impressionable younger economists at the LSE and elsewhere, which were not removed for many years.[7] Hayek's later work on the same theme emanated from Chicago and, on his retirement, from Austria and Germany.

III. THE REHABILITATION OF CAPITALISM AND ITS 'APOLOGISTS'

The case for collectivism has often been made on the unsteady foundation of a comparison of an imperfect capitalist world with some idealized collectivist alternative, a type of logical error not confined, of course, to collectivist thinkers! A prominent and influential 'vulgar socialist' (to paraphrase Marx) position of the time compared the horrors of the industrial revolution laid at the door of capitalism with the delights of a disciplined, consciously planned society in which these horrors could never recur. An accusing finger was also pointed towards the Classical economists who were allegedly apologists for the capitalist system.

We cannot really blame the 'vulgar socialists' for accepting what was a common view of nineteenth century economic history, presented by respected social historians such as the Webbs and the Hammonds. The blanket statements about the immiserization of the proletariat in nineteenth-century Britain were tested and found completely wanting by a small, spare, bespectacled Lancastrian economist called T.S. Ashton who came to the LSE in 1947 as Professor of Economic History, and Hayek recruited him to spearhead an attack on the myths they had created.[8]

Ashton's position was that the statistical evidence concerning standards of living, particularly during the crucial period 1790–1830, offered no evidence to support the popular myth. Moreover, the implicit comparison between a past 'golden age' of agricultural society and the horrors of urban life associated with industrialism was totally misleading. Whatever one thinks about Ashton's work and those of his many followers, he certainly stirred the pot of controversy. At the very least, he showed that the facts of economic history presented a much more complicated picture than incautious social historians had painted, and forced those who had been reluctant to accept an alternative view to base their case against capitalism by reference to factors other than economic welfare, such as 'worker alienation' associated with factory organization.[9]

While unfamiliarity with economic measurement may have been a reasonable excuse for those who perpetuated the myths about the condition of working people during the Industrial Revolution, there is nothing in economic writings of any substance to support the view that the Classical economic tradition rested on subservience to capitalism. It would take an enormous distortion of Keynes's *General Theory* to read such a view into the book, though Keynes is attributed with the sullying of the Classical economists' reputation.

As Robbins noted, the break with the tradition that the Classical economists were not only outstanding analysts but men of honour and integrity was sufficient for him to write an entire book on Classical economic policy to counteract the view that they were to be ignored as misguided and dishonest apologists.[10] His book has spawned a whole series of treatises on a similar theme, and from individuals of very different political persuasion, most of whom have supported his position that the Classical economists were no respecters of persons when it came, for example, to the attack on monopoly and, following Adam Smith, were vitally concerned about the improvement of the economic condition of the working classes.

IV. THE DIMENSIONS OF POST-WAR ECONOMIC POLICY

So far, I have stressed the negative side of the debate on economic policy – the clear advice by major economists about what not to do. There is much to be said for negative advice, and more particular examples of it abound in the spate of LSE writings from the pens of others who had served in government. These range from attacks on post-war financial policy, by Frank Paish, to revelations about the 'brutal tyranny of monopoly' within the public sector, by Ronald Coase, and the follies of resale price maintenance, by Basil Yamey.

There were others, such as Jack Wiseman and myself, who attacked the inefficiency and arbitrariness emanating from a social policy based on public provision of social services at zero cost, instead of extending the range of transfer payments along with pricing of welfare services.[11] However, let me concentrate on what I shall call the 'grand design' policies associated with the control of the macroeconomy.

It is here that it is a pleasure to hark back to the days when James Meade came to the LSE hotfoot from advising the early post-war government. His book, *Planning and the Price Mechanism,*[12] is one of the most striking and important tracts of the times, and is significantly sub-titled 'The Liberal-Socialist Solution'.

Meade's basic problem was how to reconcile the economic freedom and efficiency associated with the international market economy with the equally important objectives (for him) of maintaining economic stability in an open economy and the pursuit of a more radical policy of social justice requiring a more equal distribution of income and wealth. This reconciliation depended on his view of how the economy worked – he adopted an essentially Keynesian position but one which recognizes that the economy may be prone to overheating as well as to underemployment, a position accepted by Keynes in his later utterances.[13]

Reconciliation also depended on the view taken of the effectiveness of alternative policy instruments in a world in which decision by government and individuals among trading partners would vitally affect our fortunes. I cannot go deeply into his analysis, but the gist is as follows: Keynesian stabilization measures were essential, but only in rare circumstances should these be supported by mercantilist policies which distorted the pattern of international trade. A vigorous social policy would be necessary, requiring the establishment of a national minimum and the promotion of redistribution of capital, but the methods of achieving these aims should be designed to interfere as little as possible in consumer choice and with the preservation of economic incentives.

The instruments for achieving these aims were carefully assessed. For example, Meade was one of the first writers to explore the possibilities of introducing a negative income tax scheme as an alternative to subsidizing food, rent, and welfare services. The international dimension to stabilization policy is thoroughly explored with a view to minimizing the need to interfere with trade flows in the name of domestic stabilization.

Economists are better at describing policy goals than the paths toward them. In contrast, his book takes full account of the need for gradual dismantling of wartime controls, particularly price controls, and faces up to such difficult issues as the extent to which efficient operation of the labour market required the curbing of trade union powers and/or the introduction of state intervention in the fixing of wage rates. James Meade may not have solved all the problems posed by the postwar economic situation but he faced up to them, and, as we know from his later writings, has devoted a large part of his writing to improving and refining his approach to economic policy in the light of the changing international economic situation and the developments in economic analysis.

We all know of his outstanding analytical ability and his original contributions in many branches of economic theory, but what he taught myself and many others is that it is also the duty of economists to try to invent workable institutional devices which will improve the operation of economic policy.

In the historical context of this paper, a rider is in order which stresses the point that what may be called the Keynesian predispositions of Meade were widely shared by Meade's colleagues at the LSE, including Lionel Robbins, whose contribution to the argument in *Planning and the Price Mechanism* is acknowledged in the Preface to the work. On the other hand, its liberal position on pricing did not appeal to a large section of the Labour Party brought up on the view that market forces were there to be suppressed at the earliest opportunity.[14]

Liberal Keynesianism certainly permeated the work of Richard Sayers – later a member of the famous Radcliffe Committee on the workings of the monetary system – and Henry Phelps Brown. So far as macroeconomic questions were concerned, LSE could no longer be accused of being a 'suburb of Vienna' – it was never really that – but clearly conformed to the much older Classical Economics tradition in which analysis was closely wedded to the pressing problems of the day.

V. CONCLUDING REMARKS

I have dealt with only a brief period in the intellectual history of only part of the LSE – roughly 1943 to 1953 – and have already stated that I shall not attempt to measure the influence of its economists on post-war policy. Nor have I considered the considerable international impact of LSE economic thinking through the frequent travels of its stars and the influence of its graduate students who flocked to it from all parts of the world. However, I am tempted to make a few personal observations based on my experience as one caught up in the post-war economic discussion, for I was a member of the LSE staff from 1948 to 1956.

My first comment concerns the organization of these intellectual efforts to define the scope and content of economic policy. There was none. There never was a concerted attempt by anyone at the LSE to promote a 'party line' on policy matters. There was not even a seminar at which the exclusive or main topic was current economic policy. At most, colleagues at LSE paid each other the compliment of offering their unpublished thoughts for comment and criticism.

I can illustrate this by a personal experience. Brought up in a more hierarchical system, I submitted the syllabus of my first course of lectures at LSE to Lionel Robbins for approval. He reproved me very gently, remarking that he was always willing to give advice but that he would never act as a censor.

My second comment concerns the balance of intellectual interests of economists during the period. I have been describing what many of my contemporaries at the LSE would have regarded as a peripheral activity. Lionel Robbins's view[15] that disinterested discussion of the leading questions of the day was a public responsibility of economists was respected, but it was not necessarily complied with. Plumbing the depths of 'the stream of esoteric truth' was more congenial, more intellectually rewarding, possibly perceived as more useful for professional advancement than keeping one's eye on the passing show of politics.

Personal involvement in politics, such as my own along with Frank Paish in helping to devise an economic policy for the Liberal Party, was regarded as questionable though generally it was accepted with amused tolerance. Possibly the reason lay in the lack of attention paid to economic analysis in the devising of policy. Things became radically different at the LSE, as elsewhere, once the government established a separate Government Economic Service and employed outside economic consultants in increasing numbers.

Finally, one might wonder what remained of the tradition of the Webbs and Beveridge who were more wedded to 'positive planning', when such influential figures produced such formidable arguments against it. The answer is that it was stronger than ever, and firmly embedded in the departments of Social Administration and Public Administration. Curiously enough, this did not turn the LSE into an intellectual battleground. The departments referred to simply ignored the outpourings of the economists and invented or imported economic analysis more congenial to their ideas about how governments should act.

Personal relations, on the whole, between the non-warring but rival intellectual groups were remarkably cordial.[16]

In a later period, the full force of the deep commitment of Richard Titmuss to social reform, coupled with his mammoth propaganda campaign against economics, were to have a more tangible if questionable influence on government policy than that of the economist. But that is another story and the economists' response to this revival of collectivist influence would take us far beyond the confines of the LSE.

NOTES

The subject-matter precludes consideration of important contributions to economic analysis (as opposed to economic policy) during the period in question made by LSE economists for whose work I have a profound respect.

1. Lord Robbins, *Autobiography of an Economist*, Macmillan, 1971, p. 185.
2. Lionel Robbins, *The Economic Problem in Peace and War*, Macmillan, 1947.
3. See J. Wiseman, 'Uncertainty, Costs and Collective Economic Planning', *Economica*, May 1953.
4. He wryly remarks: 'I confess that I find it more than a little paradoxical that at the present day we are continually told that in order to attain American standards of efficiency we must go over to wholesale collectivism' (*op. cit.*, p. 80).
5. The passage, incidentally, calls on Keynes's support for his panegyric of individualism, quoting the passage (often overlooked) on p. 380 of the *General Theory*, first edition.
6. F.A. Hayek, *The Road to Serfdom*, George Routledge and Sons, London, 1944.
7. In March 1950, the 'doyen' of the Freiburg School, the anti-Nazi Walter Eucken, unfortunately died in London in the middle of giving five lectures in English on the bitter lessons derived from Nazi economic policies. See his *Unser Zeitalter der Misserfolge*, J.C.B. Mohr (Paul Siebeck), Tübingen 1951, translated as *The Unsuccessful Age* (with introduction by John Jewkes), William Hodge, London, 1952.
8. See the essays by Ashton in F.A. Hayek (ed.), *Capitalism and the Historians*, Routledge and Kegan Paul Ltd, London, 1954; also T.S. Ashton, *The Industrial Revolution*, Oxford University Press, 1948.
9. The kind of factory organization associated with industrial production is not confined to capitalist society!
10. See L. Robbins, *The Theory of Economic Policy in English Classical Political Economy*, Macmillan, London, 1952. Lord Lindsay of Birker, Master of Balliol at the time, is given his come-uppance in (for Robbins) some unusually strong language. Cf. *op. cit.*, pp. 68–9.
11. F.W. Paish, *The Post-War Financial Problem and Other Essays*, Macmillan and Co. Ltd, London, 1950 (this book also includes two important essays on 'Economic Incentive in War-Time' and 'The Economics of Rent Restriction'); Ronald Coase, *British Broadcasting: A Study in Monopoly*, Bell, London, 1950; Basil Yamey, *Economics of Resale Price Maintenance*, Pitman, London, 1954; Alan Peacock, *Economics of National Insurance*, Hodge, London, 1952; Jack Wiseman, 'The Economics of Education', *Scottish Journal of Political Economy*, February 1959.
12. Published by George Allen and Unwin, 1948. A fascinating comparison can be made between this work and his more recent work, *The Intelligent Radical's Guide to Economic Policy*, Allen and Unwin, London, 1975.
13. Curiously enough, Keynes, whom Meade greatly admires, is not mentioned once in his book – perhaps an unconscious tribute to his influence.

14. On the other hand, there is a story illustrating the tolerance of his position among senior Labour politicians. When Meade presented his views to a policy committee of the Labour Party, he concluded by asking, 'Am I still a member of the Labour Party?' The ex-Chancellor of the Exchequer, Hugh Dalton (formerly Reader in Public Finance at the LSE) replied: 'James, have you paid your subscription?'
15. See Lionel Robbins, *The Economist in the Twentieth Century,* Macmillan, London, 1954, Chapter 1.
16. I enjoyed co-operating with David Glass and Lance Beales, well-known demographer and social historian respectively, in producing *An Introduction to Malthus* (ed. Glass), Watts, London, 1953, but it is quite clear that their distaste for Malthus and Malthusianism contrasts markedly with my attempts to view the Malthusian position on economic development as dispassionately as possible.

PART II

Analysis

10. The justification for progressive taxation

(In the autumn of 1994 I was invited by the Institut für Weltwirtschaft (Institute for World Economics) at Kiel to prepare a short monograph on this theme. It was to be aimed at an audience of business and professional persons who, even if conversant with economic issues and perhaps armed with a basic economics training, would not be familiar with recent fiscal theory. The Institute specified the questions that they discerned as being of interest to German readers, but the questions themselves concern a much wider audience. I was also obliged to minimize the mathematical content of the analysis and this has required me in some places to over-simplify the presentation of economic ideas. I believe that I have not misled readers by doing so, and those familiar with the issues raised in this contribution may nevertheless be interested in the general approach I have adopted. It will come as no surprise that I have concluded my exposition with a critique of tax theory from a contractarian standpoint. If this introduces a bias in my philosophy of taxation, it does not imply that I would wish to misrepresent competing philosophies of taxation, nor to underestimate the important contributions that they have inspired of an empirical character to which I refer.

Readers preferring a mathematical presentation of tax theory will find one in the discussion of the Laffer model in the next chapter.)

I. THE TERMS OF REFERENCE

This chapter concerns certain features of the personal tax system which are of contemporary importance in Western mature economies. I was asked to consider five questions:

1. Can progressive taxation of income be justified on economic grounds?
2. Is there a 'trade-off' between equity objectives promoted by tax progression and efficiency and growth objectives?
3. How far is the case for progression modified if consumption expenditure is taken as the progressive tax base and households rather than individuals are liable for payment?

4. Does it make sense to offset the degree of tax progression by making other taxes regressive?
5. How far are the aims served by progressive taxation compatible with those emanating from the political process? In particular, how far does the political process produce a situation where the minority of top income earners are subjected to ever-increasing degrees of tax progression by a political majority of lower income earners?

Before these questions can be considered, the major characteristics of a progressive income tax system must be outlined.

II. PRELIMINARIES

A tax base consists of an aggregation of identifiable economic units, in this case income, which attracts a liability to transfer resources to government. As income is normally unequally distributed as between individuals or households, an issue arises concerning the distribution of the burden of the tax. A progressive income tax follows a formula by which the higher up the income scale, the greater the proportion of income that is liable to tax. In other words, the relatively rich are expected to pay more per unit of income than the relatively poor.

For any such progressive tax formula to work, the following conditions must be fulfilled:

(i) The tax base must be clearly defined. In principle, presumably the tax base should be synonymous with national income, as manifested in the national accounts, what has been described in the famous words of Henry Simons as the 'annual increase in economic power'. This implies that the tax base includes not only money income, but non-money income of which the obvious items are production of goods for own consumption by farming households and housewives' services. Consistency demands that imputed income from ownership of consumer durables should be included, notably the annual value of home ownership. In mature economies in which ownership of business is divorced from control, two further major items for inclusion are capital gains from financial assets and undistributed corporate profits.

(ii) The constituents of the tax base must be consistently valued. This does not appear to be a problem in the case of money income, though that assumes that the tax base takes no account of lifetime income expectancy which would be necessary if a longer time horizon than a year were considered desirable. When there is no market transaction within the time period, then attribution of a money value will cause difficulties. This is nowhere better demonstrated than in the case of leisure. It might be claimed under (i) above that leisure is a vital component of 'real' income, though not included in national accounts, but a valuation would presumably require information on the opportunity cost of leisure to every individual whose income is included in the tax base.

Two important consequences for later analysis follow from these conditions. The first is that the definition and identification of the tax base leaves room for considerable disagreement about how the tax law should be formulated and whether it can be formulated with any precision. Unless draconian and arbitrary powers are assigned to the tax authorities, which would be repeatedly challenged in mature democracies, compliance of taxpayers with the law must entail some degree of negotiation. This is particularly necessary where the major source of information on income sources has to be derived from the individual taxpayer herself. The Classical economists, notably Adam Smith, were well aware of the need to minimize costs of compliance so as to reduce resistance to the 'onerous' nature of taxes. The tendency, therefore, in much tax theory to regard the taxpayer purely as a passive adjuster to an imposed tax regime may not even be a useful first approximation.

The second consequence is the attention drawn to a corollary of any principle such as 'the rich should pay a greater proportion of their income in tax than the poor'. This is that if 'unequals are to be treated unequally', then 'equals should be treated equally'. However, this assumes that difficulties of identification and valuation are equally distributed amongst taxpayers, which is hardly likely to be the case. Someone whose income is easy to detect and value, such as a professional employee in government, may be at a disadvantage compared with a counterpart in the private sector who derives her income from less easily detectable sources involving valuation difficulties as well. The practical result of 'unequal treatment of equals' may be political action by the aggrieved to protect their interests and recourse to tax avoidance and evasion. It is only fairly recently that modelling of tax systems has systematically examined such reactions to tax regimes.

(iii) Constructing a progressive tax system does not necessarily entail using income as the sole tax base. Indeed, the very difficulties associated with the identification and valuation of income may direct attention towards taxing what income receivers buy rather than what they earn. Prominent tax theorists have emphasized a point of principle, namely that taxation of expenditure may be more in keeping with the equity principle embedded in progressive taxation. This is because an income base takes no account of fluctuations in income receipts and in spending 'obligations' associated, for example, with changes in the pattern of family expenditure through time.

This is not to say that taxes on expenditure are not beset by similar deficiencies already noted in the case of the income tax base. This is a matter for later consideration. A corollary of this position is that progressivity could be achieved by a combination of proportional income taxation and a variety of taxes on consumption and property which, taken together, introduce the desired progressive element.

However, a word of caution is necessary in considering the design of a multi-tax regime. It has to be established that we know what the final incidence of the taxes will be. Reactions of taxpayers to the payment of any tax may make it possible for them to shift it to others. Some attention must therefore be paid to the vexed question as to whether those who pay the tax actually bear its burden.

(iv) The progression formula must be clearly defined. It is not possible to define the formula without reference to the particular principle of equity in operation. Again, we must store this point up for future reference in attempting to answer the first question in Section I above. At this stage it is useful to note the distinction made between the average and marginal rate of tax. At first sight progression would seem to mean that the increment of tax paid on any unit of income would rise as the number of units increases. In other words, a condition for implementing a progressive tax rate is that the marginal rate of tax rises as income rises. However, while this may be a sufficient condition for progressivity it is not a necessary one. A progressive tax system can be achieved by fixing an income expenditure limit below which no tax is payable, and then to tax incomes above that level at a proportional rate, that is a fixed marginal tax rate and not one which increases with income. Assume that the exemption limit is 100 income units and the proportional tax rate is 20 per cent. Compare the tax burden of A = 100 income units, B = 200 and C = 300. A pays no tax, B 20 units and C 40 units. The average tax burdens are A = 0 per cent, B 10 per cent and C 13.3 per cent. Thus the marginal tax rate (20 per cent) is constant, but the *average* tax rate rises with income thus producing progressivity. The association of progression with a constant marginal rate of tax as low as 20 per cent is not a random choice. In modern explorations of combining the objectives of 'fairness' with 'efficiency', it has been claimed that the 'optimal tax structure' should approximate to this kind of tax regime; but this once again is to anticipate later discussion.

III. 'ECONOMIC' JUSTIFICATIONS FOR PROGRESSIVE TAXATION

The term 'economic justification' implies that the tax system must take into account the material circumstances of the taxpayer, which, if widely accepted today, represented a radical part of the Classical economic programme at a time (the eighteenth century) when tax systems frequently exempted the privileged nobility. The material circumstances of each individual would be affected by the government budget in two ways: (i) through the benefits accruing from government services, notably defence and law and order; and (ii) through the taxes deducted from his income in order to finance these services. A 'just' system of taxation, therefore, had to resolve the problem of reconciling 'benefit' with some concept of 'ability to pay' for benefit received.

A historical 'tour d'horizon' is an instructive way of showing why progressive taxation is such a hot issue today. Broadly speaking, the problem of tax justice was resolved by Classical economists in the following way. First it was assumed that benefits received were roughly proportional with 'means' or income, with the cost of protecting property being proportional to its size. That being assumed, then each should pay according to benefit received, implying a proportional tax structure – but with one important proviso. There was no point in taxing those on subsistence wages, for this would, in the long run, reduce the ability of the poor to raise children and consequently diminish the supply of labour. In other words, a tax on subsistence wages would be shifted to other, richer, taxpayers. This offered a good *practical* reason for exempting subsistence wages, and supported precisely the progression formula given in II (iv) above. Thus were 'benefit' and 'ability to pay' 'principles' reconciled.

It is important to realize that there were two major assumptions in this approach. The first was that the 'sacrifice' anyone made in order to pay for government services was directly proportional to income. The second was that there were strict limits to the size of the government sector relative to the annual output of resources. The erosion of these assumptions offers us the clue to the evolution of intellectual support for both more progressive tax schedules and heavier average burdens while, at the same time, raising the further question of the side effects of taxation on the efficiency and growth of the economy itself.

Consider now the first of these assumptions. An alternative 'reasonable' assumption could be that as one moves up the income scale, the loss or 'sacrifice' would diminish with each additional segment of income – the loss of DM500 to a relatively rich person with annual income of DM300,000 would be less than to a relatively poor person with one of DM30,000. Thus is stated the 'law of the diminishing utility of income', which implied that proportionality in 'sacrifice' required that the *marginal* rate of tax should rise as income rises. The simple formula of a proportional tax rate plus a subsistence minimum would no longer be applicable. It is also to be noted that if those with the same level of income were to be treated similarly, then the important assumption was being made that those at the same income level would experience the same level of utility and, further, that the utility of different persons could be *compared*.

This form of reasoning associated with *utilitarian* thinking was adopted by fiscal theorists who still accepted the second assumption, namely that there were limits to the proportion of the tax 'take' to national income. It may strike the reader as odd that a hundred years ago, there was a consensus of view that the 'limits of taxable capacity' were fixed at somewhere around 10–12 per cent of national income. This rough-and-ready rule took account of two major concerns. The first was the desire to keep government expenditure under control in the face of possible bureaucratic 'waste' and the second was the adverse reactions of taxpayers to rising taxes which might lead them to reduce their work effort or seek ways of evading tax. Fifty years later, Keynes, supporting empirical estimates by Colin Clark, fixed on a figure of 25 per cent. Today, a figure of 35 per cent would be considered exceptionally low! This remarkable change clearly requires explanation.

One part of the explanation lies in the parallel change advocated in the functions of government associated with argument concerning the role of government in influencing the distribution of income. Should not the government act not only as a producer of services that could not otherwise be undertaken by the private sector but also act as a transfer system designed to achieve 'optimal' distribution of income? A particular version of the utilitarian argument has played a crucial role in answering this question. Why stop at 'proportionality of sacrifice' as the principle of taxation, why not minimise the *total* sacrifice?

Consider the following highly simplified example of a community of three individuals A, B, and C (a proxy for three income groups) with income levels of 100, 200 and 300 income units respectively. Assume as before that utility of individuals can be compared and that utility is somehow measurable. We shall call the units of utility 'utiles'. Therefore, as income increases, the 'utile value' of each unit of income decreases. Although we might expect that there would be a smooth and continuous decline in the increase of utile value as we move up the income scale, let it be further assumed that the utile value moves in discrete 'jumps' as follows:

First 100 income units = 100 utiles/100 = 1.0
Second 100 income units = 70 utiles/100 = 0.7
Third 100 income units = 30 utiles/100 = 0.3.

As we can compare the utility of individuals, then we can calculate the total utility derived from income for A, B, and C as follows:

A's total utility $= 100 \times 1.0 = 100$
B's total utility $= 100 \times 1.0 + 100 \times 0.7 = 170$
C's total utility $= 100 \times 1.0 + 100 \times 0.7 + 100 \times 0.3 = 200$

Now assume that the government wishes to raise 100 currency units in taxation. The 'Classical Progression' (CL) rule requires that A is exempt and B and C pay a proportional amount; the 'Proportional Sacrifice' (PS) rule means that A is exempt but B and C are taxed in proportion to their 'utile' count; the 'Least Aggregate Sacrifice' (LAS) rule results in C shouldering the entire tax burden (Table 10.1).

Table 10.1 Tax progression and utility

			Distribution of Tax		
Income Class	Income	Utiles	CL	PS	LAS
'Poor'	100	100	–	–	–
'Middle'	200	170	40	30	–
'Rich'	300	200	60	70	100
Total	600	470	100	100	100

CL = 'Classical Progression'
PS = Proportional Sacrifice
LAS = 'Least Aggregate Sacrifice'

It can now be shown that the LAS rule produces the least loss of utility of the three systems:

$$\text{CL loss} = 40 \times 0.7 + 60 \times 0.3 = 48$$
$$\text{PR loss} = 30 \times 0.7 + 70 \times 0.3 = 42$$
$$\text{LAS loss} = 100 \times 0.3 = 30$$

However, the formulator of the LAS rule, the British economist Francis Edgeworth, discovered something else from his analysis which shocked him greatly. This was that maximizing the utility of the community entailed an equal income distribution! A simple way of demonstrating this is to assume that the 100 units of tax raised from C is redistributed to A so that the post-tax income distribution is 200 income units for A, B and C. The total utility (measured in utiles) of the community rises from 470 to 510! This was the logical consequence of assuming the operation of the law of diminishing utility of income and that persons at the same income level experienced the same level of utility. Edgeworth felt obliged to point out that it was hardly likely that his principle would have any operational significance, for the very process of redistribution could reduce the total amount of income to be redistributed. Incentives to work and to save would be drastically reduced, not to speak of the possibility that the rich might emigrate to countries with more congenial tax regimes. The importance of Edgeworth's analysis is that it sets the stage for the discussion of the 'trade-off' between equity and efficiency that dominates contemporary fiscal theory (see Section IV below).

It will be observed that gradually the justification for progressive taxation has become associated with the much wider question of its use not solely as a method of resolving the problem of financing government services but as an instrument for achieving some 'just' distribution of income. This special status attached to distribution is nowhere better demonstrated than in the influential work of the contemporary US philosopher, John Rawls. Rawls bases his argument on two 'appeals to reason'. The first is that nobody can seriously believe that our 'just deserts' are reflected in our social and economic circumstances. Therefore, an unequal income distribution cannot be justified by a claim that we are entitled to what we earn or possess. Second, while we may all want to do the best for ourselves, there is always the risk and associated worry that we may land up at the bottom of the income pile. Therefore, the welfare of the poorest should take absolute priority over the welfare of others. There is a presumption that these two propositions justify equal income distribution and that the tax system should reflect this. However, for the same reasons that Edgeworth rejected equal income distribution, the Rawlsian position takes account of the effect of an equal income distribution on incentives to work and to save so that aggregate income would be diminished. Inequality of income distribution could therefore be justified, but only if this would improve the lot of those at the bottom of the income scale.

The implication for tax policy is that tax rates on all but the lowest income groups should be designed to maximize tax revenue for redistribution to the poorest. This does not necessarily mean that marginal tax rates should be very high, because this would depend on the point at which taxed individuals would substitute leisure for income. It would hardly improve the lot of the disadvantaged if those in higher income groups reduced their supply of effort! Therefore, the Rawlsian position differs markedly from both the Classical and Utilitarian positions. In the Classical view, tax progression has the practical justification of reconciling taxation according to 'ability' and 'benefit'. In the Utilitarian case, progression is justified as a way of maximizing aggregate utility. The Rawlsian position is derived directly from a pre-ordained principle of justice.

Up to this point, the justification for progressive taxation has been based on abstract, exogenous principles, without regard to their acceptability by taxpayers. It is only fair to Rawls and to latter-day Utilitarians to mention that they are sensitive to the need to square their principles of tax justice with their acceptance of democratic principles of government. Therefore, an important element in their argument is represented by the need to establish some 'consensus of fairness' which accords with their principles. This matter requires further discussion (see Section VII below). At this stage, however, we need to address the first question about the justification for progressive taxation.

One thing should be clear from the above analysis which is that the justification for progressive taxation must rest on an initial value judgment or set of such judgments of 'fairness' or 'equity'. It cannot rest on economic analysis which tries to generalize about the state of the world as it is and not as it ought to be. Of course, the policy interest in a particular view of the 'ideal' progressive tax system may be enhanced if there is a consensus of view of the kind sought by Rawls and others. Such a consensus, if it exists, does not raise the scientific status of the system but represents purely a coincidence of value judgments. This point requires particular emphasis because some economists in the post-Rawlsian discussion have tried to persuade us to accept that a special status attaches to an income distribution that takes into account the varying contributions to output by those with differing skills. While, as we shall see later, a consistent tax policy may require that the tax system should be modified to take account of individuals' varying ability to contribute to income, one does not have to accept that such a system is 'fairer' than any other. One need only pose the question – is it fairer that those with superior skills (and probably the more interesting jobs) should be afforded some special treatment? Nor need the reader be impressed by the fact that the pursuit of these ideas is carried out in recondite mathematical form, but one hopes not with the intention of 'blinding us with science'.

Nevertheless, the fiscal economist has an important part to play in showing how the public budget has to be designed to reflect any particular view of 'fairness' or 'justice'. Furthermore, the articulation of the fiscal regime implied by any such views draws attention to economic and social consequences in their implementation that may not be immediately apparent.

IV. THE TRADE-OFF BETWEEN EQUITY AND EFFICIENCY

It can be stated categorically that a trade-off between equity and efficiency objectives is recognised as a necessary restriction on the achievement of the goals of any group (e.g. political party, philosophical movement) with an interest in policy implementation through government action. However, this is a statement without much content until the term 'trade-off' is more precisely defined.

'Trade-off' means that the optimal policy from the point of view of any group is represented by the combination of equity (as measured by the desired income distribution) and efficiency (as measured by the annual output of resources) which is preferred above all other combinations.

'Trade-off' also implies that not all preferred choices are feasible. The 'feasibility' frontier will depend on the effect which a policy of redistribution will have on the production of the income that is available for distribution. The 'most-preferred' combination cannot now lie outside that frontier.

A simple numerical demonstration of the trade-off problem may help to elucidate these points and later discussion of them. Suppose that there are two individuals A and B. the former in a high earning category and the latter in a low earning category. (It simplifies the exposition to assume that B has zero income.) An income tax is imposed on A only and the proceeds transferred to B. As the tax rate rises, A's net wage rate is reduced and B's income is increased. A may respond initially by working harder but as the rate increases, the value of leisure rises and she begins to work less. It should be noted however that, in this simple exposition, the reduction in labour supply does not affect the wage rate. Revenue still rises for a time but then begins to decline, plausibly even before the 50 per cent tax rate is reached. In the extreme case of a 100 per cent tax, both A and B have zero income (Table 10.2).

Table 10.2 Trade-off of equity and efficiency

	Tax rate (%)	A's hours worked	A's daily income (DM)	Tax revenue	A's post-tax income	B's income
(1)	0	6.0	120.0	0	120.0	0
(2)	15	7.0	140.0	21.0	119.0	21.0
(3)	30	5.0	100.0	30.0	70.0	30.0
(4)	50	2.5	50.0	25.0	25.0	25.0
(5)	80	1.0	20.0	16.0	4.0	16.0
(6)	100	0	0	0	0	0

Table 10.2 can be used first of all to demonstrate, but only in a crude way, that the 'most-preferred' combination of equity and efficiency depends on an initial value judgment which defines the 'terms of exchange' between efficiency and equity and the feasibility frontier. We can identify four well-known philosophical positions by reference to the various tax rates:

(i) Egalitarianism. This position would be represented by Row (4) with a tax rate of 50 per cent. It is to be noted that this position is not synonymous with 'least aggregate sacrifice'. This would only be true if A continued to work the same number of hours per day with a 50 per cent rate as for a 0 per cent rate.

(ii) Rawlsianism. The 'least advantaged' person, B. obtains the maximum income with Row 3, emphasizing the fact that this position does not support pure egalitarianism, as A works less as the tax rate rises. If A worked the same number of hours per day with a 30 per cent rate as for a 0 per cent rate, then B's income would be maximized by equal income distribution, i.e. a rate of 50 per cent.

(iii) 'Sozialemarktwirtschaft'. It is not possible to define in such a precise way, the position of those who support the 'Sozialemarktwirtschaft' (Social Market Economy). Some have expressed support for a Rawlsian position; others would veer more towards a libertarian position. But we could specify their position as somewhere above Row (4) and below Row (1). This would depend on how far its supporters were committed to some form of social security system with a redistributory content.

(iv) 'Libertarianism'. The libertarian position would conform to Row (1), but not because of a desire to reduce anyone to total penury. The question in the libertarian mind is whether the provision of more than a subsistence minimum for those who cannot work requires state action at all, given the alternative of voluntary redistribution from those better-off to those worse-off. If state action is required, for example to prevent anyone falling into poverty, then the libertarian position would gravitate to somewhere between Rows (1) and (2).

This analysis imposes too many restraints on argument to be more than a starting point for consideration of a whole range of issues. One of prime importance is its static, short-term nature. Any redistribution policy has first of all to examine closely the characteristics of the 'poor'. A fair proportion of members of the lowest income category may remain permanently poor, notably the mentally and physically disabled, but there will be another group who are at the start of their careers who may reasonably expect to move up the income scale. (In the UK, a considerable percentage of those categorized as low income earners represent partners in newly-formed small firms.) Logically, this points towards a definition of income distribution which takes into account earnings over the life-cycle of income receivers. Opponents of utilitarianism also deny that interpersonal comparisons of utility (i.p.c.u.) are meaningful. Someone at a given income level may claim to be 'happier' or 'more unhappy' than some with the same income level or that at different points in time, at the same income level, they enjoy different levels of satisfaction. Therefore postulating that there is a firm functional relationship between income and utility is at best a convenient fiction. A refusal to accept that policy-makers should act *as if* i.p.c.u. are possible illustrates once again the limitations of economic analysis as a guide to what is the 'correct' degree of progression.

If economic analysis is limited in its discussion of optimal tax progression to examining the implications of different philosophical standpoints, in principle it should be able to determine the 'feasibility frontier'. The position of the frontier depends on the relationship between taxation and the supply of effort which is a central part of analysis of economic behaviour. The example in Table 10.2 is a useful point of departure of our discussion. It postulates a particular relationship between hours worked and tax rates by which, after a certain point, hours worked fall as the income tax rate rises. The 'feasibility frontier' can be plotted in simple diagrammatic form (Figure 10.1), and it will be noted that the rates of change between tax rates and hours worked vary. What we want to know about the feasibility frontier is how far its position and shape are affected by tax progression. This should then show the limits imposed in the trade-off between 'equity' and 'efficiency', which is fashionably symbolised in the so-called 'Laffer Curve' (see Quadrant 1 of Figure 10.1) depicting the functional relationship between the tax rate and the tax yield.

Our previous analysis suggests that we have to be able to calculate the relationship between the supply of hours worked and the tax rate. In theory, there appear to be two contradictory forces at work. If the tax rate is increased, then there is an income effect which may induce someone to work longer hours

Figure 10.1 Tax yield and tax rate

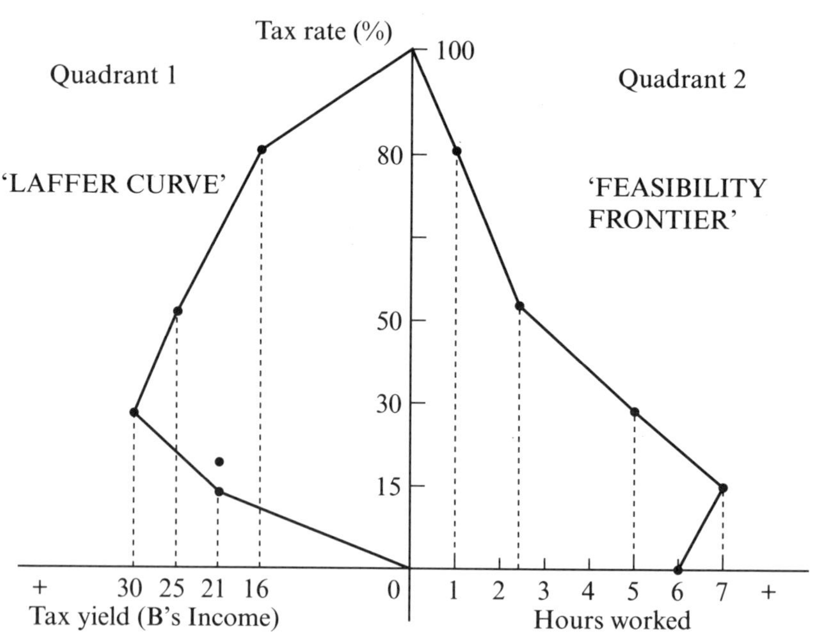

to make up the income difference. At the same time, there is a 'substitution effect', for the 'price' of leisure is reduced. Which effect is the stronger is not self-evident for it will depend on the preference system of the individual. A major complication in employing economic analysis is the possibility noted earlier that individuals may seek to minimize any rise in the tax rates not only by altering hours of work but by avoiding or evading income tax. Of course, if they follow this line of action, they must consider the costs incurred in exploiting tax loopholes, including in the case of evasion, the risk of legal penalties if discovered.

A great deal of empirical work has been undertaken in order to ascertain taxpayers' reactions to rate changes. This is a formidable undertaking if the results are meant to apply to the economy as a whole, embracing taxpayers in different social circumstances as well as in different income groups. The methodological limitations imposed on the investigator are obvious. An econometric investigation which tries to obtain some quantitative relationship of the kind shown in Table 10.2 and in Quadrant 2 of Figure 10.1 may find some correlation between historical time series of income tax rates and hours worked, but this hardly allows us to infer anything which would enable us to make a statement which would guide policy-makers. In the course of time, there are too many other forces at work that are likely to affect incentives, such as changes in the civil condition of income receivers, the effect of the pattern of government expenditure, notably the social security system, on the real income of taxpayers, and changes in the tax laws which may affect the choice of occupation. Likewise, direct interviewing of taxpayers, as well as running into standard difficulties associated with sampling, does not preclude the strong possibility that taxpayers will offer 'strategic' answers, particularly if they believe that the enquiry may influence the fiscal authorities. In particular, taxpayers may be reluctant to offer personal information on tax planning activities designed to minimize compliance costs.

It would be foolhardy to offer firm conclusions about the delineation of the 'feasibility frontier'. However, what may be said is that there is little evidence that the elasticity of labour supply, i.e. the percentage change in labour supply divided by the percentage change in wage, is sufficiently high (say > 1) to produce Laffer-type results of the kind found in our example. Probably the distorting effect of progressive taxation is more marked in regard to the incentive it gives to seek employments which are untaxed or difficult to tax, given the legal and administrative difficulties of devising a 'perfect' progressive system. When this happens, it militates against the movement of factors into employments which reflect their comparative advantage. It also engenders dissatisfaction and therefore lowers the 'Steuermoral' amongst those who lack the opportunities to exploit loopholes in the tax system.

V. MODIFICATIONS TO THE CASE FOR PROGRESSION

A. The Tax Base

The ensuing analysis could proceed on the assumption that the objectives of tax policy remain as before, the aim being to reconcile given principles of equity with efficiency. One could then consider whether an alternative tax regime, namely taxing expenditure, would better fulfil the given objectives. Before proceeding along these lines, it is necessary to take account of the fact that the taxing of consumption is associated with a quite separate principle of 'fairness' which is at least as old as Thomas Hobbes and received strong support from J.S. Mill in the nineteenth century and from Nicholas Kaldor in the twentieth century. The principle is that we should be taxed according to what we take out of the 'pool of resources' available and not according to the amount that we contribute to the pool. This is to say that, on equity grounds only, exempting saving from taxation has some special ethical significance. Certainly, an income tax would not be a suitable way of fulfilling this principle. It taxes saving twice, first as part of income as it accrues and as the return on saving invested. It also exempts dissaving out of accumulated capital resources. It is difficult to understand why any special significance should be attached to the activity of saving on ethical grounds. For most people, saving is an act designed to allocate their claims on resources through time in accordance with their own preferences. It is not some selfless act that ought to command special respect. Indeed, it could be claimed that it is particularly unfair if the weight of taxation should be a function of the distribution of one's expenditure obligations through time, thereby hitting those with young families before reaching their peak earning capacity and retired persons who no longer earn. Having made this point, the analysis confines itself to taxing consumption as an alternative means for promoting the previously identified propositions concerning equity and efficiency. At the same time, one must be aware that the rationale of the expenditure tax extends to the influence of a higher level of saving on the rate of economic growth.

The arguments supporting the case for using consumption rather than income as a tax base concern the practical implementation of the tax regimes compatible with equity and efficiency. Defining and valuing income is difficult under any circumstances and the inevitably arbitrary nature of decisions by the fiscal authorities may lead to anomalies of treatment leading to charges of both 'vertical' and 'horizontal' inequity. These difficulties are compounded, the greater the degree of progressivity of the tax system. In fact, much of the contemporary support for taxes on consumption has arisen from the recognition of the brutal fact that if the rule of law is to operate in tax matters, then the fiscal authorities cannot be endowed with the draconian powers that would be necessary to ensure that the income tax followed any radical principle of tax equity. At the same time, if taxpayers have both the incentive and the legal entitlement to negotiate their tax burdens with the fiscal authorities, there is a greater likelihood of the tax base becoming eroded. Thus much of the professional literature on the case for a general expenditure tax as an alternative to the personal income tax is accompanied by a litany of the dubious legal devices used by taxpayers in the endeavour to minimize their tax burdens.

Space does not permit a full examination of the merits of taxing consumption as an alternative to income, without a change in the range of equity proposals. The less ambitious proposals fasten on a reform of the Value Added Tax which would require it to reflect the degree of progressivity contained in any one of the equity proposals. It must be obvious that a multi-rate VAT structure designed to discriminate against better-off persons would be a virtual impossibility, if it is to reflect the sensitivity of a progressive income tax schedule. The implied substitution of a multi-rate VAT for a progressive income tax system would also be accompanied by very complicated effects on the structure of prices of final goods and services, with major difficulties encountered in measuring the final incidence of the tax changes. The much more radical proposal of instituting a universal expenditure tax (UET) would solve the problem of maintaining progressive rates of tax because the tax would be collected directly from the individual taxpayer and not through producers subject to VAT. However, if taxpayers are expected to keep a record of total consumption, it is difficult to see how this could be done without simultaneously introducing self assessment of tax. Furthermore, an annual progressive UET would create a major equity problem caused by the 'lumpiness' of purchases. The purchase of durable consumption goods, such as cars and houses, often undertaken during years of relatively low earning power, would put relatively poor persons into higher tax brackets. Some form of averaging device would have to be introduced which would be complicated by the problems associated with the choice of forms of consumption that are to be exempt.

The discussion of the substitution of a UET for the progressive income tax well illustrates the dangers of the methodology of tax analysis. One must be wary of comparing an actual, inevitably imperfect, tax system with some idealized hypothetical alternative! Thus, while it is easy to understand the intellectual attractions of a UET, it is difficult to believe that it would not be beset by administrative problems that would make it difficult if not impossible to preserve at least the semblance of equity that a personal income tax seems to provide.

B. The Tax Unit

Consider the following four cases of couples with different income characteristics and civil condition:

A. Unmarried couple, each with similar income level.
B. Married couple, each with similar income level.
C. Married couple, with husband's income much greater than the wife's income.
D. Married couple, husband being the only income receiver.

The tax regime is one where the first DM10,000 is exempt from tax, the next DM50,000 is taxed at 25 per cent and remaining income at 50 per cent. We wish to compare the tax obligations in each case, firstly when incomes are taxed separately and secondly when husband and wife (forming a household) are taxed jointly. The total income in each case is the same. The exemption limit is 'transferable' when incomes are combined for tax purposes in cases A, B and C and the husband received an equivalent allowance for his non-earning wife in the case of D.

Table 10.3 Tax treatment of tax units

		1 Income	2 Separate Taxation		3 Household Taxation
A.	M.	80,000	22,500	45,000	(45,000)
	F.	80,000	22,500		
B.	M.	80,000	22,500	45,000	57,500
	F.	80,000	22,500		
C.	M.	140,000	52,500	55,000	57,500
	F.	20,000	2,500		
D.	M.	160,000	57,500	57,500	57,500
	F.	–	–		

Table 10.3 is a record of tax obligations in each case. Its striking feature is that couples with the same *aggregate* income face very different tax bills according to whether they are taxed separately or taxed together. In both cases, couple A, who are co-habiting, but legally remain as separate tax units, pay considerably less than the other couples. In the case of a change in the system from separate taxation to combined taxation, the more equal the income of both man and wife, the greater their tax bill relative to cases C and D. If couple A were to contemplate getting married and in the hope of remaining married for, say, thirty years and with the same income expectations and tax regime, they would clearly suffer a considerable monetary loss equivalent to the (discounted) value of DM30,000 × 30 under combined taxation. On the other hand, if couple C were unmarried and taxed as separate households, their monetary gains on

marriage, becoming one household, would be, by the same token, quite considerable.

We have observed that the principles behind progressive taxation state that those in similar circumstances should be treated similarly. Assuming that the family circumstances in each case are the same – two persons living together – then this principle of horizontal equity would require that each couple should pay the same taxes. The situation depicted in Table 10.3, Column 3, which is our main concern, clearly violates this principle. However, the equity principle would suggest investigation of what is meant by 'similar circumstances'. Firstly, it could be argued that 'two can live more cheaply than one' meaning that there are economies of scale in co-habitation. This benefit, if taken into account, would imply that co-habiting couples, whether married or not, should together pay more tax than they would if they were living as separate households. Secondly, a family with only one earner or two earners, one with a relatively small income (Couples C and D) receive a real income bonus if the non-earning spouse provides domestic services that are not taxed. In principle, therefore, either non-earning spouses' services should be taxed as income or working couples should be allowed a tax deduction for purchase of similar services. The necessity for this kind of adjustment is more obvious when the household includes children.

Whatever equity principles suggest by way of modification of income liabilities in the light of the civil condition of couples, which would enable household taxation to conform to them, a change from separate taxation to household taxation also has efficiency implications. If we take couple C, the marginal tax rate for the secondary earner is higher under household than under separate taxation. Thus if the secondary earner sought to increase earnings by DM1,000 then his/her tax obligations under separate taxation would increase by 25 per cent of DM1,000, that is, DM250, whereas under household taxation, additional earnings of DM1,000 would attract a tax obligation of 50 per cent of DM1,000, that is, DM500. This offers a pronounced disincentive effect, usually to female participation in the labour force, so it is not surprising that the labour supply studies usually conclude that their labour supply is elastic with respect to the wage rate (net of tax). Hence the common conclusion of fiscal experts that separate taxation produces a smaller efficiency loss than household taxation.

However, the very pursuit of the implications for equity and efficiency presented by family circumstances shows how narrow is the compass of values normally considered in fiscal theory and of the content of individual utility functions. In particular, attitudes to the importance of family life must colour any final verdict on the choice of tax unit. A tax regime that encourages more female participation in the labour force is claimed to have an adverse effect on the personal development and contentment of children, while at the same time a system which penalises female participation may be regarded as an unacceptable form of gender discrimination. If real income is to be added to the tax base, then should the psychic satisfaction of having children and any future economic benefits that children may bestow on parents when they cease to earn be taken into account before regarding family size as a factor in determining family tax obligations? One needs to be aware of such issues, even though they cannot be pursued here. The important conclusion emerges that the problem of differential treatment according to civil condition would disappear if 'Classical' tax progression were adopted, that is to say, there would be an exemption limit combined with a fixed marginal rate of tax (Section II above). Taking the data in Table 10.3 with a DM10,000 exemption limit and an equivalent allowance for a non-earning partner, assume a fixed 25 per cent marginal rate of tax. Then the tax paid by couples would be the same whether they are taxed separately or together, even when the individual incomes differ greatly. For example in the case of Couple C, M would be taxed at 25 per cent of (140,000 – 10,000), that is, 32,500, and F would be taxed at 25 per cent of 10,000, that is, 2,500, so their total tax burden is 35,000. This is exactly the same amount as they would have to pay if they were taxed as one unit, since 25 per cent of (140,000 + 20,000) – (20,000) is 35,000.

The one exception to this proposition is when one of the earners has an income below the exemption limit of DM10,000, in which case a 'tax credit' to make up the difference would be necessary. If we extend this case to one where both earners have incomes below the exemption limit, or their combined incomes are below the exemption limit, a logical argument is presented for 'negative' income taxation at the bottom end of the income scale.

While these propositions are well-established in the fiscal literature, there still remains the question of the size of the tax take and what the marginal rate of tax would be. A relatively high fixed marginal rate is likely to have adverse efficiency effects already examined (Section IV above) and other forms of discrimination incompatible with equity considerations, particularly at the lower of the income scale between those just below and just above the exemption limit.

VI. OFFSETTING THE DEGREE OF PROGRESSION

Presumably the purpose of any modification of the degree of progression by using other taxes is to give effect to a change which is more in keeping with the chosen objectives of the tax system. Following the reasoning of the earlier analysis, the perceived optimal trade-off between equity and efficiency, subject to a resource constraint, is not being achieved. If, therefore, it is proposed to reduce the degree of progression, there is a presumption that it is hoped to achieve a preferred distribution while simultaneously improving efficiency or certainly without reducing efficiency.

There is an implicit assumption in the question before us that any change in the tax system is subject to the constraint of a *fixed yield*. It is also a convenient assumption because it removes the necessity for reviewing what could be a whole range of alternative budgetary situations involving use of other policy instruments such as government expenditure changes. An answer to the question would also require us to specify in detail the precise changes in the degree of progression which would depend on the implicit ideological shift governing the proposed change in the pattern of taxes. This problem is circumvented by assuming that no ideological shift would entail scrapping an exemption limit, and that lowering the yield of the personal income tax is achieved by reducing a fixed marginal tax rate. In other words we are considering the reduction in average tax rate progression. Of course, this is only one of a number of alternatives, but it is a useful one for examining the consequences of the change in tax policy. 'Laffer effects' are ruled out so that a reduction in average rate progression results in a fall in personal income tax yield.

If there were no inhibitions about increasing the degree of regressivity of other taxes in order to retain the tax yield, then one could concentrate on increases in taxes which minimized the effects on incentives to work. The most extreme tax change suggested by this requirement is to use a poll tax or to increase the rate of such a tax if it is already in existence, for its yield is independent of work effort. However, the regressive effect is so marked as to be unacceptable except in a situation where pre-tax income distribution were equal. In any case, exemptions would have to be made to compensate those who qualify for personal tax exemption. (It is widely believed that Mrs Thatcher's attempt to substitute a poll tax for a property tax in order to finance British local governments was a major cause of her political downfall!) At most, the poll tax is useful as a benchmark for it emphasizes that we are seeking tax changes which possess something of its qualities by minimizing effects on work incentives.

Economic analysis would suggest that we should be looking for a tax change which, as well as compensating for the fall in the yield of income tax, minimizes disincentives to work. Goods which are complements to leisure could be taxed more heavily, anything from golf clubs to ocean-going yachts. Apart from the administrative complexity associated with any form of differential commodity taxation, discrimination between different taxpayers according to their work/leisure preferences raises the same kind of issues as those associated with preserving 'horizontal equity' in income taxation. There is also the problem that, as it may not be certain whether any increase in 'leisure taxation' could be shifted forward to consumers, producers of 'leisure goods' may complain, not without reason, that they are being unfairly treated vis-à-vis other producers.

This mixture of practical issues and perceived inequities suggests that, *so long as there is a personal income tax in place which conforms to some given equity criterion*, then it is probably both desirable, in the light of the trade-off between equity and efficiency, and feasible to make up the loss in tax yield by spreading the burden evenly, e.g. by an increase in the VAT rate. There would still be the problem of how to prevent such an increase from eroding the value of the personal income tax exemption, but some countries already exempt food and other 'necessities' from commodity taxation. Such a proposal must be regarded as rather tentative, at least in the light of British experience. A recent attempt by the Chancellor of the Exchequer to avoid an increase in direct taxes by raising indirect taxes took the form of taxing domestic fuel, previously taxed at a reduced VAT rate, at the standard rate of 17.5 per cent, with a compensating increase in the size of benefits paid to those entitled to social assistance. The measure was defeated by the defection of some members of his own party when a vote was taken. Mr Clarke reacted by raising the tax on beer and spirits instead!

VII. PROGRESSIVE TAXATION AND THE DEMOCRATIC PROCESS

The devising of a tax system based on 'exogenous' principles of equity and efficiency begs the question as to whether such principles conform with the preferences of those who are expected to pay taxes. It is also to be noted that the policy prescriptions emerging from exogenously-derived principles assume that a quite separate analysis should govern what the total revenue raised should be, apart from revenue to finance transfers (negative taxes). As I have often argued, it is both ethically objectionable and politically unrealistic to treat the taxpayer as a Pavlovian dog reacting to stimuli administered by some 'ethical observer'. This suggests an alternative approach to the problem of justifying progressive income taxation, namely that it should emerge from the democratic process in which the consent of the governed, conventionally awarded equal voting rights, is paramount. The governed decide on the amount of tax to be raised, how it is to be spent, and what amount of tax each should pay. One can, as an individual political economist, argue that democratic decisions may result in 'unfortunate results' in terms of both the amount of revenue raised and who pays taxes, but that is not to support measures by which one's own views would be imposed on others.

The equal distribution of such an important property right as voting invites the speculation that the vote will be used by the majority of voters in order to increase their real incomes at the expense of the minority at the top end of the income scale. Again, reference to the history of fiscal thought has a bearing on present concerns. The Classical economists, notably David Ricardo and James Mill, contended that extension of the political franchise should only take place gradually along with economic growth, otherwise there would be an 'unwarranted' expansion in taxes, borne by the relatively rich and productive, in order to finance governments noted for their lack of attention to careful spending. Only when the working classes had a property stake would they be fully aware of the unwelcome consequences of combining redistribution with an expansion of the public sector. Slightly later, Alexis de Tocqueville argued that the expansion of the public sector in a form designed to benefit lower income groups would be a positive function of the extension of the franchise and the inequality of income distribution. He offered as empirical evidence the fact that the greater equality of pre-tax income distribution in the United States in the early nineteenth century had offset the extension of the franchise and had resulted in a much slower growth of the public sector than would be expected with the extension of the franchise in countries such as France and Britain.

De Tocqueville has been 'rediscovered' and public choice theorists have developed formal models of his propositions that have been subject to empirical testing.

In more modern guise, and accepting that the franchise is virtually co-terminous with the size of the adult population in Western countries, it is easy to imagine situations where there is a 'built-in demand for redistribution'. Assuming that all voters maximize their utility by maximizing their income, taking account of taxes and both money transfers from government and government services which can benefit them, with simple majority rule, the distribution and size of the tax burden will depend on the 'median voter' who has the decisive voice. Voters are then partitioned between those with incomes below the median level who choose candidates for the legislature who favour redistribution in their favour, whereas voters with incomes above the median level will prefer lower taxes and less redistribution. If the income distribution is 'skewed', which is commonly the case, then median income is below average income and there will be a majority of taxpayers who, potentially at least, can benefit from redistribution. It is this situation that gives rise to the fear that the political process produces an inherent tendency towards 'exploitation of the rich' through higher tax burdens that must involve an increase in average tax progression coupled with a growth in the size of the public sector relative to the growth in the economy as a whole.

Of course, there must be a limit to this process, as the analysis in Section IV makes clear. As post-tax incomes become more equally distributed through the combination of higher average rate progression and bias in government spending towards lower income groups, a stage must come where the finance of a growing public sector impinges on the majority of taxpayers. However, this extreme stage is unlikely to be reached at least in countries in which there is freedom of job choice, labour input, and the right to emigrate, as well as the right to vote and to lobby governments, and for the following reasons:

(i) As the average and/or marginal rate progression increases, those in higher income groups will have an incentive to seek untaxed or lower-taxed employments at home or abroad or prefer leisure not only through reduction in hours worked but also through earlier retirement. It becomes progressively more difficult to finance government expenditure, at least through taxation.

(ii) Voters now in the lowest income quartile may have expectations of moving up the income scale as they gain in skill and experience. Trading off present post-tax income against future post-tax income may indicate to them that the discounted value of their incomes aggregated through time would be higher if they did not vote in favour of taxing the relatively rich.

The reference to the dynamics of income distribution raises an awkward question that must be introduced as a caveat to the above analysis. There is one set of taxpayers who are *ipso facto* disenfranchised, and they are future generations. This may tempt present generations of voters to finance the growth in government spending through borrowing rather than through taxes, or to award themselves future claims against the government in the form of retirement pensions representing claims to future consumption that future generations of voters will have to forgo. The problem is exacerbated if a country approaches a situation where the adult population is static and ageing, as a result of the increase in life expectation, for the claims may be held in place by the concomitant ageing of the voting population. The older the median voter becomes, the stronger will be the demand for increasing the social security budget in favour of the aged, or for discriminatory tax exemptions for older income receivers. This potential intergenerational conflict has been a matter for concern among economists interested in the economics of public choice, but empirical testing has so far not produced concrete evidence of its existence. (The author recalls a conversation many years ago with the famous British Socialist Chancellor of the Exchequer, Hugh Dalton, himself a pioneer in the development of the utilitarian theory of taxation, in which he expressed concern at the growing fiscal power of the old – like himself! His 'solution' was either to disenfranchise those over the age of 65 or to 'enfranchise' future generations by giving parents extra votes according to the number of children in the family!)

VIII. CONCLUSION: THE 'UNEASY' CASE FOR PROGRESSIVE TAXATION

There is no doubt that those who favour tax theory based on utilitarian principles continue to press their case for influence over the tax structures of Western industrial economies, though in the 'modern' versions which take full account of effects on incentives to work and save. However, anyone of a 'liberal' disposition must be extremely wary about deriving support for progression from such principles, for the following reasons:

(i) The empirical foundations are questionable. 'Satisfaction' or 'happiness' must be difficult to measure and income and wealth are poor proxies. It may be accepted that, at the very lowest income levels, there is a positive relation between satisfaction or 'well-being' and income, but this functional relationship may differ markedly as between individuals as we proceed up the income scale. *A fortiori,* the propositions that there is equality of satisfaction between individuals similarly situated income-wise and that their satisfactions are comparable are equally suspect.

(ii) Even if utilitarian propositions seem to offer a useful working hypothesis, taking into account 'trade-offs' which constrain the degree of progression because of its effects on incentives, the ethical foundations are open to serious question. A full answer to this assertion would require one to enter the difficult area of moral philosophy. However, the basic ethical difficulty can be explained very easily. There is the hidden implication that society is better-off if the government can and does implement these principles, and is endowed with both the power and knowledge to do so. However, even those formulating these principles may shrink at the prospect that tax principles would justify some kind of dictatorship, however benevolent, and once this is admitted then appeal is being made to some other set of rules governing the structure of the fiscal system. This is why the authors more sensitive to the claims of individuals to decide for themselves what is the nature of economic justice have sought 'clearance' for their tax principles from a consensus of view. These authors must then seek to persuade those who have a moral claim to make political decisions that these principles are just. As observed in the previous section, if that moral claim were embodied in a democratic system of government which accepted majority rule, there are conditions under which tax progression would be the outcome of the political process. However, this is to accept a very restricted definition of 'consensus' which could result in the tyranny of the majority. There is a long and respectable tradition in the principles of public finance, beginning with Wicksell, that decisions about the structure and the volume of taxation and of government expenditure require maximization of consent and the nearest result possible in any feasible political process to a unanimous decision. The point that needs emphasizing in this context is that this 'contractarian' approach puts primary emphasis on how the rules governing taxation are to be determined. The budget is the outcome of this consensus and does not entail a pre-commitment to a particular tax regime.

(iii) The derivation of a tax system from the consent of the governed draws attention to a missing element in the conventional approach to tax analysis. No guidance can be given about the *position* as distinct from the *slope* of any tax curve displaying the relation between the size of income and the appropriate tax payment based on the diminishing marginal utility of income. This is because nothing is said about the size of the 'tax take' necessary to finance government expenditure on goods and services, as distinct from transfers of income between rich and poor. The size of the tax take is simply taken as given, implicitly assuming that 'government' decides. In contrast, if taxation is to be based on the consent of the governed, however that is defined, voters will have a distinct interest in the size of the tax take and how taxes are allocated to the financing of services provided by government. In both the old and 'new' Utilitarian approaches to justifying progressive taxation, citizens are given no encouragement to understand the implications of the tax burdens which they passively accept. In contrast, the contractarian approach emphasizes the importance of giving voters the opportunity of making rational choices about how taxes are to be allocated, which gives them a role distinctly more in keeping with their legitimate aspirations.

(iv) All tax systems designed to raise revenue forming a large proportion of total incomes must run into administrative problems. Taxpayers faced with non-negligible tax obligations and being the main source of information about their economic circumstances available to tax authorities, as we have seen, have a strong incentive to negotiate with the fiscal authorities. There is a reasonable presumption that costs of compliance with the fiscal law rise as the tax take rises. However, progressive taxation adds an extra dimension to the administrative burden, particularly if rates rise steeply with income. This is particularly true if incomes fluctuate from one year to another, intensifying bargaining between the tax authorities and taxpayers about the time allocation of income or requiring complicated rules for averaging incomes. Other complications associated with the determination of the family unit have already been noted.

It is not surprising that the image of progressive taxation as the hallmark of a 'good' tax system has become tarnished. As observed above, even those who build tax principles on utilitarian foundations conclude that the optimal system is approximated by a flat-rate proportional income tax with an exemption limit coupled with 'non-distortionary' taxes on goods and services. However, while this position is not so far removed from that of those who reject the utilitarian tax philosophy, there are two essential differences from the contractarian position. The presumption is in the latter case that proportionality in the tax system is an approximation to a 'pricing system' in which the benefits of government services are proportional to the taxes paid. Of course, it is a moot point whether this presumption would be justified by how voters or their representatives will behave in approving the government budget. The second difference follows from the first. If taxation reflects benefits, then voters cannot be indifferent to the quantum of government goods and services and therefore to the overall burden of taxation. Furthermore, if given the incentive and opportunity to participate in the process of government, contractarians believe that voters' status in determination of the size of the budget is properly restored, instead of being regarded merely as units in a tax equation. But whether this difference in treatment encourages voters to press for more accountability and efficiency in government, as contractarians would hope, is another matter.

APPENDIX: GUIDE TO READING

1. On the history of fiscal theory, see R.A. Musgrave, 'A Brief History of Fiscal Doctrine', in *Public Finance in a Democratic Society*, Volume II, Wheatsheaf Books, Brighton, UK, 1986, Chapter 23; and also Alan Peacock, *Public Choice Analysis in Historical Perspective* (Mattioli Lectures), Cambridge University Press, 1992.
2. Summaries and discussion of the theory of progressive taxation appear in all major textbooks on public finance. Amongst German contributions, see particularly: Norbert Andel, *Finanzwissenschaft*, 3. Auflage, J.C.B. Mohr (Paul Siebeck), Tübingen, 1992, Teil V; Charles Blankart, *Öffentliche Finanzen in der Demokratie*, 2. Auflage, Verlag Vahlen, München, 1994, Teil II; R.A. Musgrave, P.B. Musgrave and L. Kullmer, *Die öffentliche Finanzen in Theorie und Praxis*, Band 2, 5. Auflage, J.C.B. Mohr (Paul Siebeck), 1993.

   Notable accessible contributions in other languages are: Francesco Forte, *Principi di Economia Pubblica*, Terza Edizione, Giuffre Editore, Milano, 1993, Capitolo XVI; and Joseph Stiglitz, *Economics of the Public Sector*, second edition, W.W. Norton, New York and London, 1988, Part Four.
3. Concepts of equity in taxation concern not only economists but also lawyers and political philosophers. I have found the following to be useful and interesting: Francesco Guicciardini, 'Two Discourses on Progressive Taxation of Land Incomes, Sixteenth Century', English translation in *International Economic Papers*, Volume 9, pp. 7–19; Walter J. Blum and Harry Kalven Jr, *The Uneasy Case for Progressive Taxation*, The University of Chicago Press, Chicago, 1953; F.A. Hayek, *Law, Legislation and Liberty*, Volume 3, Routledge and Kegan Paul, London, 1979, Chapters 12 and 13; Dieter Bös and Bernhard Felderer (eds), *The Political Economy of Progressive Taxation*, Springer Verlag, Berlin, 1989, particularly the contribution by Bös and Tillman and those by Gray and Peacock; Allan Maslove (ed.), *Fairness in Taxation: Exploring the Principles*, University of Toronto Press, Toronto, 1993, particularly the extensive review by John G. Head, 'Tax Fairness Principles: A Conceptual, Historical and Practice Review'.
4. 'Optimal' taxation is discussed in the texts mentioned in 2. above. Policy implications are summarized efficiently in Christopher Heady, 'Optimal Taxation as a Guide to Tax Policy: A Survey', *Fiscal Studies*, Volume 14, No. 1, February 1993, pp. 15–41.

   For a formidable critique of optimal tax theory as applied to income taxation, see Martin Ricketts, 'Tax Theory and Tax Policy', in *Political Economy of Taxation*, ed. Alan Peacock and Francesco Forte, Basil Blackwell, Oxford, 1981, pp. 29–46.
5. For a useful non-technical outline of the Contractarian approach to tax theory and policy, see James M. Buchanan, 'The Political Efficiency of General Taxation', *National Tax Journal*, Vol. XLVI, No. 4, 1993, pp. 401–10.

   The author has dealt more specifically with the interaction between voter preferences and the growth and distribution of taxation in Alan Peacock, 'Staatsfinanzen und Staatsbürger', in Horst Zimmerman (ed.), *Die Zukunft der Staatsfinanzierung*, Wissenschaftliche Verlagsgesellschaft GmbH, Stuttgart, 1988.

11. The rise and fall of the Laffer curve

(The history of fiscal theory is punctuated with attempts to define and sometimes to measure the 'limits of taxation'. In general, the policy interest has centred in the possible connection between exceeding this limit and economic instability resulting from government attempts to meet any revenue shortfall by inflationary methods of finance. The most recent concentration of interest in the concept has been associated with the effects of a growing burden of taxation, measured by the ratio of taxes to some national income concept, on the supply of effort. Hence the considerable intellectual investment in the study of the Laffer curve, which purports to show how, in certain circumstances, governments can obtain the same level of tax revenue by lowering tax rates. Clearly, such an effect must be popular with those who regard the growth of the public sector as inimical to economic freedom. I was asked to explore Laffer's proposition in a contribution to a symposium on The Political Economy of Progressive Taxation organised by the Liberty Fund and held in Vienna in 1987. The logic of the Laffer position is not in question, but the basic proposition can only be true if one adopts implausible assumptions about the working of the economy and assumes that tax changes have no impact on the rest of the public budget. In particular, the analysis abstracts from reactions to tax changes which increase evasion and avoidance of taxes. As in all the essays concerning taxation in this volume, I regard the taxpayer as playing a positive role in dealing with the tax authorities and not as a passive reactor to stimuli offered by an omnipotent government.)

I. INTRODUCTION

The history of fiscal doctrine is strewn with statements concerning the critical point at which taxes will become 'dangerous' to the economy, by which is meant that the economy has to endure efficiency losses and even social disturbances which could undermine good government.[1] The Laffer curve is therefore at the end of a long line of such statements, but it is one which, in the course of professional discussion, has been given much more precision than previous ones. The incentive for doing so has been provided not merely by mathematical economists in search of a model to refine which contains some semblance of reality, but also by the intense interest displayed by policy-makers in search of an economic justification for lowering the average burden of taxes combined with reduction in tax progressivity.[2] The attraction is obvious when one considers the basic features of the curve itself. The demonstration of its existence, whether observable or not, is based on the mathematical truism that if tax rates levied on a given tax base, say income, are zero, then the revenue yield is zero and if they are 100 per cent, the yield will also be zero, it being assumed that the tax base will disappear.[3] There is a presumption, therefore, that, as tax rates move from zero to 100 percent, the tax yield will rise, reach a maximum and then fall. It follows that there could be circumstances where a government could reduce tax rates, with associated improvements in the supply of effort, and yet still maintain the revenue yield.

The author believes that a study of the controversy surrounding the realism and relevance of the Laffer analysis is instructive for those of us whose value judgments lead us to conclude that the case for progressive and 'heavy' taxation is, in the famous word of Blum and Kalven (1953), an 'uneasy' one. Even though he claims to demonstrate that the Laffer analysis does not offer the support for tax reform for which it was intended, the investigation of its properties does draw attention to other ways in which a large and growing public sector may be detrimental to the aspirations of a free society.

The study begins with a simple exposition of the Laffer analysis (Section II). It then presents and comments upon the critical literature which the analysis has spawned (Section III and IV). Most of that literature accepts the underlying thesis that taxpayers are passive reactors to stimuli offered by the fiscal authorities. The author then considers the implication for the analysis of adopting a 'public choice' approach to the Laffer 'paradox' and produces a rather different scenario describing the relation between the rise in tax rates and tax revenue (Section V). A final section (VI) offers some conclusions.

II. THE LAFFER MODEL

There are several mathematical versions of the Laffer model, which use different assumptions. The version used here is based on an amalgam of the Blinder (1981) and Fullerton (1982) models but these accord with the Laffer original as developed by Canto, Joines and Laffer (1981). For simplicity, following Fullerton, I assume that all income is labour income.

By definition:

$$Y = \overline{w}H \tag{11.1}$$

where $\overline{w}$ is some weighted average gross wage rate and H is the total hours worked in the economy.

The tax yield will depend firstly on the tax regime. A progressive income tax system is introduced in a very simple fashion by assuming a fixed exemption limit, *E,* and a linear tax system, so that

$$T = t(\overline{w}H) - \overline{E} \tag{11.2}$$

where t is the tax rate and T is the tax yield.

Now if $\overline{w}$ and H are positive constants, then

$$\frac{dT}{dt} > 0.$$

If this were so, then the yield of tax would go on growing even if $t > 1$, i.e. exceeds 100 per cent. Workers would go on working even if their income after tax were negative! This implausible situation is recognized by introducing a functional relationship between H and t. Following Fullerton (1982) a constant elasticity of supply of labour with respect to the wage rate after tax, $\overline{w}(1 - t)$, is used such that

$$H_s = B[\overline{w}(1 - t)]^{\in} \text{ , } \in > 0, B > 0 \,. \tag{11.3}$$

Whereas the supply of labour is assumed to depend on the after-tax wage rate, the demand for labour is assumed to depend on the gross wage. Using a constant elasticity of demand function, we can write:

$$H_d = A \cdot \overline{w}^{\eta} \text{ , } \eta < 0 \,. \tag{11.4}$$

Assuming that the labour market clears so that $H_s = H_d = H$, when we can express $\overline{w}$ as a function of t.

Therefore equation (11.2) is re-written as

$$T = t(\overline{w}(t) \,.\, H(t)) - \overline{E} \,. \tag{11.5}$$

By total differentiation

$$\frac{dT}{dt} = \overline{w}H\left[1 + \frac{\partial H}{\partial t} \cdot \frac{t}{H} + \frac{\partial \overline{w}}{\partial t} \cdot \frac{t}{\overline{w}}\right]. \tag{11.6}$$

Equation (11.6) tells us that whereas an increase in t will have a positive effect, *ceteris paribus*, the effect of such an increase in t could produce a fall in hours worked and thus in the tax base. We can no longer be sure that $dT/dt > 0$. Before we can determine whether the relationship between T and t traces out a Laffer curve, it must be remembered that the number of hours worked, and therefore the tax base, will depend on the demand for labour.

We are now able to solve for t and to determine, by setting (11.6) equal to zero, whether there is a maximum value for t. After some very tedious algebra, the interesting result is obtained that a maximum value for T is obtained when

$$t = \frac{\eta - \varepsilon}{\eta(1+\varepsilon)}. \tag{11.7}$$

Before exploring the properties of equation (11.7), let us proceed quickly to an illustration of the claimed policy significance of the Laffer curve.

Using the familiar technique of a four-quadrant diagram in which all axes arc positive, a simple shorthand method may be used to demonstrate the curve's fiscal implications. Taking the origin of the four-quadrant diagram (Figure 11.1) at 0, then the right-hand bottom quadrant displays the Laffer curve. It shows the relationship, therefore, between t and T. For simplicity, the curve is given as a triangle with the apex at Z. In the left hand bottom quadrant the relationship between GDP and t is shown. Again for simplicity it is assumed that GDP is independent of the tax rate, t, if $t < t^*$. When the tax rate rises above $0D$, hours of work fall in response to the further fall in the net wage, and when the tax rate is 100 percent, hours of work fall to zero. The distance $0A$ on the abscissa represented the GDP available for distribution between private and government goods. In the left-hand upper quadrant the opportunity slope is drawn depicting the exchange rate between private goods and government goods and, again, for simplicity's sake, the slope is assumed to be linear throughout its length. In the right-hand upper quadrant the relationship between total tax revenue and the supply of government goods is shown. It is assumed that the government is constrained by total revenue in the amount of goods it can purchase. Again for simplicity it is assumed that the government goods 'sanctioned' by the available revenue rise in proportion to total revenue available. In short, the prices of government goods are fixed.

Consider an economy which is 'over the Laffer Hill' where the tax rate is $0D^0$. The associated level of Y is $0M^0$, and the tax revenue T is $0C^0$. Given the price of government goods, this enables the government to 'buy' $0B^0$ level of such goods, leaving $0A^0$ of private goods.

The government could be just as 'well-off', in the crude sense of being able to buy the same level of government goods, if the tax rate were reduced to $0D'$, where the lower tax rate produces the same total tax revenue. However, this is because H increases in response to the fall in t, and, with given $\overline{w}$, Y increases to $0M'$. The private sector is 'better off', as a result. All is for the better in the best of Lafferian worlds. Taxes are lower, output is higher and so the opportunity slope showing the trade-off between private and government goods shifts upwards from M^0L^0 to $M'L'$.[4]

Figure 11.1

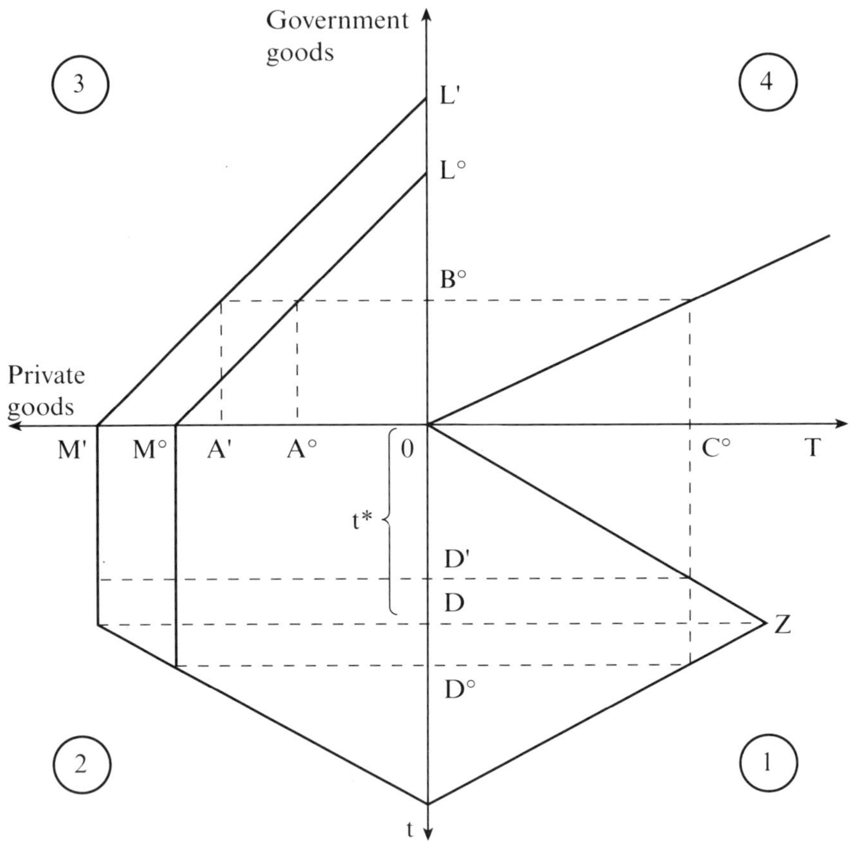

III. A CONFUSION OF CURVES

I have cheated in presenting the model in a form which dramatizes its policy content, for a number of important assumptions have been omitted, some of which are recognised by its author. These assumptions do not question the basic character of the relationship between the government and the taxpayer but they relate to any idea that there is a Laffer curve which is unique and immutable. These are now considered seriatim.

A. The Tax Base

We have to be clear whether broad-based or narrow-based taxes are being considered. Imagine a government which places a tax on tartan rugs. It is obvious that the cross-elasticity of demand for tartan compared with other rug material is so high that raising the tax rate on the area of tartan used would produce negative marginal revenue even in Scotland. Broader-based commodity taxes might also display Laffer-like properties. As David Hume (1752) remarked, 'a duty upon commodities checks itself; and a prince will soon find that an encrease of the impost is no encrease of his revenue'. He adds, characteristically, that 'It is not easy, therefore, for a people to be altogether ruined by such taxes'. These cases are obvious enough, but more graphic examples may be found in countries where local governments have taxing powers but know that they are constrained in raising rates by the possibility that their marginal revenue receipts will diminish if their inhabitants buy goods in neighbouring jurisdictions.

These homely examples indicate that the Laffer effect very much depends on high elasticities of demand in the case of commodities and, where the tax base is some form of factor income, on high elasticities of supply. However, presumably if we are concerned primarily with macroeconomic effects, the analysis is meant to apply to tax regimes where the taxes are broad-based. The question that this gives rise to is whether such taxes will be associated with high elasticities. I shall return to this question at a later stage.

B. The Tax Regime

Consider a government which wishes to raise a large proportion of its revenue (say 30 per cent) from a tax on persons and has a fixed revenue yield in mind. The observed elasticity of supply of labour will depend on whether the tax varies and how much it varies with personal income. In theory at least, the use of a poll tax would avoid a tax on margins and would have less disincentive effects than a progressive personal income tax. A change in the tax regime from the former to the latter would presumably mean that although the revenue yield would be the same, the Laffer curve would have shifted. This is, of course, an extreme example but it serves to underline the point made by Hemming and Kay (1980) that a Laffer curve can only be defined by reference to one particular point in time and must refer to a particular tax regime and a particular distribution of skills.

C. The Pattern of Expenditure

Unless we are looking at some set of mini Laffer curves associated with narrow-based taxes, which is surely not the case to which the Laffer analysis has been meant to apply, then one is faced with the further question of what to assume about the use of the proceeds of the taxes raised using different tax rates. This is the familiar problem of 'balanced-budget incidence' as it was christened by Richard Musgrave (1959).

An obvious ploy to remove this awkward problem is to try to assume an expenditure pattern which eliminates any effects on labour supply caused by government expenditure. Thus in the Canto, Joines and Laffer (1981) model, it is assumed 'for simplicity' that (a) government expenditure takes the form of transfer payments to individuals, receipt of which is unrelated to factor supply; (b) there is no waste or inefficiency on the part of the government; and (c) taxes and transfers are costless to collect and distribute, respectively. These conditions, as they claim, would eliminate any net income effects, leaving it possible to confine the analysis to the change in the relative prices of work and leisure resulting from the tax regime(s). Clearly, this can be no more than a subterfuge, and underlines once again the problem of how to devise a suitable empirical test when now the pattern of government expenditure as well as the pattern of taxes and the distribution of skills are changing through time.

There is a further problem which offers a pre-echo of our later analysis when taxpayers' perceptions of budgetary impacts are considered in more detail. Taxes are frequently earmarked to finance specific items of government expenditure, a state social security system being a prime example. In this case, the effects on incentives to work can be very complicated because the taxes and benefits received occur in different periods. Neo-Classical models of individual behaviour might throw some light on how to formulate some suitable behavioural hypothesis. Lindbeck (1982), for example, in another context, considers a two-period model of household behaviour for a social security scheme in which it is assumed that social security taxes are paid in period 1, and benefits received in period 2. If the individual can borrow freely in a perfect capital market, and if the discounted capital value of expected benefits for working an extra hour is smaller (greater) than the capital value of the taxes on that extra hour, there is a negative (positive) substitution effect against work in general, and in both periods! Even more complicated effects can be imagined, for the individual might also reassign his work effort through time. Thus even the simplest example, which takes no account of the complicated rules in actual social security schemes, produces a hornet's nest of problems, remembering also that the fastest growing taxes on income in OECD countries over the last two decades have been social security taxes.

The study of expenditure effects and of earmarked taxes reinforces the earlier point that a Laffer curve cannot be identified by reference to plots of tax revenue against tax rates (quadrant 2) and tax rates against GDP (quadrant 3) derived from time series, unless the tax and expenditure regimes and the distribution of skills remain unaltered during the period under scrutiny. It follows that tests of the shape and height of the Laffer curve have to eschew the familiar time series analysis.[5] The crucial question as to whether economies are likely ever to be on the 'downside' of the Laffer curve has to be tackled by some other method. A last-ditch argument which might be employed is to argue that, despite the conscious efforts of governments to redistribute income by fiscal means, the empirical results suggest that little redistribution has taken place. That being so, could it not be the case that at least net income effects of fiscal action are negligible? This is implausible because, if we concede the point, the fact still remains that even small changes in the distribution impact can mask major changes in the composition of taxes and expenditures, changes which are bound to have different impacts on the supply of effort.

IV. CAN WE BE OVER THE HILL?

Returning to the original question raised by the Laffer curve analysis entails a demonstration as to whether or not it is likely that there will be circumstances in which a major economy would find itself in the position where a cut in the average (direct) tax burden would raise the total tax yield. Given the insuperable difficulties presented by time series analysis, recourse is had to the identification of a given Laffer curve and the derivation from it of the value of 'the' tax-rate (t) which would maximize total tax revenue (T). This particular value of t, call it t^*, is then compared with existing average tax rates in whichever country we have in mind.

The first stage in the investigation is to identify the characteristics of the economy which determine the shape and location of the Laffer curve itself. This means assuming

(i) a given tax regime. A simple way of introducing a progressive tax system would be, as in Section 2, by introducing an exemption limit;
(ii) no change in the income distribution so that the distribution of skills remains unaltered with any change in t, and no change takes place in relative net incomes so that everyone's income after tax is reduced in the same proportion. This means that if there is to be no change in the progressivity of the tax, then, when the marginal tax rate is increased, the exemption limit must be raised;
(iii) some functional relationship between levels of remuneration after tax and the supply of work effort which identifies both substitution elasticity and income elasticity effects, as in equation (11.5).

The next stage is to examine the relationship between the values of the elasticities and the tax rate t^*. Table 11.1 shows that the value of t^* falls as we move towards the right-hand bottom corner of the matrix.

Table 11.1 Matrix of values of t* *For given values of* ϵ *and* η

ε η	–0.5	–1	–2	–3	–4	–5	–∞
0.5	1.33	1.00	0.83	0.77	0.75	0.73	0.67
1	1.50	1.00	0.75	0.67	0.63	0.60	0.50
2	1.67	1.00	0.67	0.55	0.50	0.47	0.33
3	1.75	1.00	0.63	0.50	0.44	0.40	0.25
4	1.80	1.00	0.60	0.47	0.40	0.36	0.20
5	1.83	1.00	0.58	0.42	0.38	0.33	0.16
∞	2.00	1.00	0.50	0.33	0.25	0.20	0.00

The third stage considers the question – how do we choose particular values of ε and η which accord with what is known about these elasticities? It is at this stage that anti-Lafferites have deployed what appears to be a successful pincer movement against the existence of the curve. In order for the value of t^* to come within a plausible range, say *circa* 0.5, then the elasticities of supply of and demand for labour have to be fairly high, or, in Blinder's words, 'quite sizeable'. However, such evidence as has been produced to quantify the elasticity of supply of labour alone supports the opposite conclusion. Consequently, any value of η of –1 or more, whatever the value of ϵ, produces a value of t^* of 100 per cent or more (see Table 11.1)! Within the strict confines of the Laffer analysis, as depicted by a whole string of academic journals, one is bound to conclude that the Laffer curve is a highly suspect construction. If we are looking for arguments and evidence to support the reduction of tax progressivity and the lowering of tax rates generally, then we must look elsewhere.

V. THE STATE-TAXPAYER RELATIONSHIP RECONSIDERED

The Laffer analysis may have had an immediate appeal to those of us who have been concerned about the consequences of the growth of 'Leviathan', who also include many who have based their arguments in support of 'collective failure' on analysis of public choice. It is therefore somewhat paradoxical to find that the Laffer curve is based on a policy-making model, very similar to that used to explain how Keynesian fiscal policy is meant to operate, in which the taxpayer is subject to various stimuli and reacts rather like a Pavlovian dog. The only counter-action open to taxpayers faced with an increase in marginal tax rates is to fold their tents and to creep uncomplainingly into the pastures of leisure – already a strong assumption for it presupposes that the substitution effect dominates the income effect. As I have argued elsewhere (Peacock, 1979) firms and households are not passive adjusters to a change in their opportunity sets forced on them by government, except perhaps in the short run. It is worth parenthetic mention that Buchanan and Lee (1982) emphasize, rightly, that the distinction between the short and long perspective of taxpayers makes a great deal of difference to how we view the Laffer approach. They argue that those supply-side economists who argued in terms of Laffer curve effects were implicitly adopting a long-run perspective. While, therefore, it may be an open question whether taxpayers will form firm expectations about the permanency of any changes in tax rates introduced by government, labour supply elasticities might be very different in the longer run when taxpayers have time to consider any compensatory effects produced by tax changes, e.g. their effect on government services (already mentioned in Section III above). But what is interesting in this context is that in the longer run this kind of 'command model' used by Buchanan and Lee is suspect for the very reasons which Buchanan-type public choice theory has emphasized. Taxpayers adjust their behaviour not only through 'investment' in ways of minimizing the effects of tax measures where it is assumed that such measures are imperatives. They can try to remove the coercive element in government action by exercising their power as voters and by their bargaining skills in dealing with the tax authorities who require their co-operation.

It would be entirely legitimate to start from a position in which, instead of assuming that government has complete control over the rates if not the yields of taxes, an antithetic, voluntaristic position is taken. This would require us to believe that in Western democracies, the electorates' preference systems have required a relative increase in the resources transferred to government use as inputs for the production of publicly-provided services and that redistribution through the transfer system reflects the importance in individual utility functions of concern for the welfare of others.[6] This view has excited sufficient interest to stimulate empirical investigation, and it has been claimed that there is no reason to suppose that a growing average tax burden will be associated with growing voter alienation. The corollary of this position is that if voter preferences change and fewer public goods are demanded then the tax burden will be adjusted downwards. Consequently, it is unnecessary to rely on Lafferian legerdemain to move taxpayers to preferred positions. Of course, those holding such a view will admit that the political system only approximates to a competitive market. Governments are not simply passive adjusters to electoral demands any more than taxpayers passively react to government-imposed tax regimes. However, there is one clear piece of evidence that a voluntaristic position, even as a first approximation to a model government, is untenable. If it were broadly true, then how is it possible to explain the observed growth in tax avoidance and evasion which have accompanied if they have not been caused by the growth in the average tax burden?[7]

It so happens that the phenomenon of tax evasion and the associated growth in the black economy offer a further dimension to taxpayers' reactions to changes in tax rates and their effects on t^* and T. The tax base now becomes a function not only of changes in H, hours of work, but also in the extent to which income is under-reported. Not surprisingly, therefore, the effect of the 'propensity to evade' on the original Laffer model has excited some interest and has been deployed to rescue its policy conclusions (see, for example, Feige and McGee, 1983, and Waud, 1986; but criticism by Peacock, Chapter 12 in this volume).

The mathematical complications of embodying an evasion component, and even an avoidance component, into equation (11.5) are best left to the imagination, but fortunately the results obtained are intuitively obvious if we stick to the formulation of the Laffer curve used in this paper. Assuming that the elasticity of evasion with respect to t is positive, then at the very least we can establish that an evasion-adjusted Laffer curve will have a value of t^* which is lower than for the evasion-unadjusted curve, and that the value of T will also be lower. In a model which embodies both tax evasion and avoidance, Waud is able to show that a value of t^* as low as 0.33 can be obtained, even when the elasticity of demand for labour is < -1.

The problem with the extension of the model to cover evasion is that it has been done on the implicit assumption that the probabilities of achieving avoidance and/or evasion objectives by taxpayers are fixed. Tax authorities are not simply passive adjusters to taxpayers' actions and they are normally dedicated to the business of rigging the odds against the taxpayer so that any bargaining advantages achieved by tax avoiders and the cheating of evaders can be circumscribed. It is clearly very difficult to embody changes in 'tax collection technology' into a formal model and no attempt is made to do so. However, there is one obvious weapon which the tax authorities may use if evasion grows with the rise in the average rate of direct taxes, recalling that all the models we have examined concentrate on taxes on factor incomes. They may decide that the marginal revenue return from devoting resources to improving the yield of taxes on expenditure is higher than the marginal revenue return from reducing avoidance/evasion of direct taxes. As I shall demonstrate, it is not even necessary to assume that the tax rates on goods and services need be adjusted in order to show that losses of revenue from Laffer effects may be compensated, if not fully, so, by changes in the yield of other taxes.

Let us retrace our steps a short distance and consider the evasion-adjusted Laffer model somewhat more closely. The first point to be made about it is that it implicitly assumes that the possibility of evasion either has no effect on the demand for labour or that it reduces that demand. This is certainly not intuitively obvious. As Peacock and Shaw (1982) argue:

> There is a strong presumption that if evasion is possible then the GDP will be higher than in the non-evasion case. (Of course, it has to be accepted that those who work in an employed or self-employed capacity in the shadow economy may add a risk premium to their offer price, so that the gross wage would not be a function solely of the income tax rate.) Nevertheless, in the absence of evasion possibilities, GDP is likely to be lower because at the margin the demand for labour services will fall if higher wages have to be paid to cover tax obligations. Provided that the demand for labour reveals positive price elasticity, and this does not seem an unreasonable assumption, it is clearly incorrect to estimate the revenue due to evasion by applying some tax coefficient to productive activities that would not otherwise exist.

This argument has been considered a substantial one by the UK Board of Inland Revenue (1981; see Peacock and Shaw, 1982) who have described tax evasion as a 'random tax-subsidy towards price reduction', though they strongly condemn evasion for other reasons. The second point concerns the question of the interdependency of tax yields, taking on board but without being dogmatic about the direction of change in H as a result of changes in the degree of tax evasion. For simplicity, assume initially Y divided between two groups of earners, evaders and non-evaders. The proportion of income earned in each sector is determined by an evasion coefficient, a, such that aY represents the income of evaders and $(1 - a)Y$ the income of non-evaders. Y is initially independent of t and a.

As evaders pay no direct tax, then

$$T = tY(1 - a)\,. \qquad (11.2a)$$

However, if they buy goods and services, evaders of direct taxes will pay taxes on expenditure embodied in the price of goods and services. Assuming a uniform consumption tax T_i with rate t_i

$$T_i = t_iC = t_i[b_1Y(1 - a)(1 - t) + b_2aY] \qquad (11.8)$$

where b_1 is the proportion of income spent on goods and services by non-evaders and b_2 the proportion by evaders.

From (11.2a)

$$dT/dt = Y[(1 - a) - t \cdot da/dt]\,. \qquad (11.5a)$$

We shall not attempt to find a general solution, but consider what would happen, using alternative assumptions if both the tax rate, t, and the evasion coefficient, *a*, increase. If Y is constant (denied by Laffer of course) then the sign of dT/dt is indeterminate. The increase in evasion will reduce the tax base, but the rise in the rate will increase the yield per unit of income. What is interesting is that whatever the sign of dT/dt, the yield of the tax on non-evaders' expenditure will fall because of the combined effect of t and a on the size of disposable income. On the other hand, the disposable income of evaders rises, and so will the yield of the tax on goods and services which evaders buy (cf. equation (11.8)). If we remove the assumption that Y is constant and adopt the Laffer assumption that a rise in t reduces hours of work of non-evaders, and a rise in the evasion coefficient, *a,* increases the hours of work in the evading sector, then it is possible to envisage a situation on the downside of the Laffer curve (defined in terms of the relation between direct rates and yields, as is normal), where a fall in the yield of direct taxes might be fully compensated by a rise in the yield of taxes on expenditure (cf. equation 11.5a).

The extension of the Laffer curve analysis in order to reflect a bargaining situation between taxpayers and the fisc, i.e. a minimum concession to realism, does nothing much to restore our confidence in its policy conclusions. The 'rescue operation' simply lands one in a minefield of further complications.

VI. CONCLUDING REMARKS

The purpose of this contribution was to examine how far the Laffer curve increased our understanding of the 'dangers' of high and progressive taxation. What conclusions do we reach?

(i) As an attempt to establish a generalization about the relation between the marginal rate of tax and the yield of tax garnished with empirical backing, the analysis does not seek to establish any particular set of tax principles. Such principles concerning the desirability or otherwise of progression, the degree of progression and the size as well as the distribution of the tax burden are matters for debate, even amongst those who share the same general economic philosophy. However, it is frequently the case that strong, attractive economic propositions are used to buttress widely different philosophical positions, and the Laffer curve is no exception. Nothing could be more attractive to those who prefer the public sector to remain large than a proposition that this can be done by cutting income taxes so that the budget can still remain balanced. Simultaneously, the curve demonstrates, as Figure 11.1 shows, that the fruits of tax reduction can be reaped in the form of a higher rate of growth of private real expenditure with the growth of the public sector kept in check. *A fortiori*, reducing the average direct tax burden by lowering marginal rates will be even more in keeping with this position. Laffer cannot be blamed if it is convenient to believe that he is correct. As Jonathan Swift put it:

All philosophers who find
Some favourite system to their mind
In every point to make it fit
Will force all nature to submit.

(For philosopher, perhaps one should rather substitute 'politician'. After all, philosopher means 'lover of wisdom'.)

(ii) It is comparatively easy to show that the Laffer analysis is based on a model which, in order to prove his basic proposition, adopts assumptions about elasticities of supply and demand for labour which seem implausible. Furthermore, it neglects important features of the working of government and the economy which insofar as they can be embodied in the model itself, do nothing to enhance its credibility.

(iii) An examination of the growth in the average tax burden in Western industrial countries brings out an important 'design fault' in the model, for it presupposes that throughout the period of growth, taxpayers have only one weapon against growing tax obligations – reducing their hours of work – or perceive that the marginal costs of tax avoidance or evasion exceed the benefits. Attempts to rescue the Laffer position by taking account of the phenomenon of 'tax bargaining' may improve our understanding of the implications of alternative assumptions of taxpayer behaviour, but that is not enough to restore one's faith in the presumed shape and location of the curve itself.

(iv) Nothing in what I have said is meant to suggest that the time and energy spent by economists crawling over the Laffer analysis and its assumptions represents some major malinvestment of intellectual resources. The question as to whether there are limits to the amount of taxation that can be raised is an important one for both the supporters and opponents of progressive taxation. Those who, following Rawls (1971), argue that society should choose that tax rate which maximizes the welfare of the worst-off individual are concerned about the determination of the point at which raising the tax rate further would mean lowering the standard of living of the least well-off if redistribution of income through budgetary action were to proceed further.[8] Those like the author who are of a more libertarian disposition, and who are therefore suspicious of large government, are anxious to know at what point the marginal benefit from extra public expenditure exceeds the marginal cost, but as perceived by the voter/taxpayer, and whether or not the implied average tax burden is above that rate. The fact that an answer is more difficult to find than Lafferian analysis has suggested is something which it has been worth finding out.

NOTES

The help of Oliver Heavens and Ron Edwards in checking through the mathematics of alternative versions of the Laffer curve is gratefully acknowledged.

1. For a useful survey and critique of the concept of an economic limit to taxation, see Shoup (1981).
2. The history of the Laffer curve in US policy discussion is described in fascinating detail in Roberts (1984).
3. The disappearance of the tax base is not a mathematical requirement. As Blinder (1981) points out, excise taxes have no such natural bound, and there are many examples of taxes on liquor, tobacco and petrol in which taxes have exceeded 100 per cent of the producer's price.
4. This illustration draws attention to the naivety of textbook presentation of alternative choices open to society between public and private goods. These presentations normally assume that the opportunity slope determining the limitations on choice is independent of the process of transfer of resources from the private to the public sector, For an important exception see the recent textbook by Stiglitz (1986).
5. For an interesting, but far from convincing, attempt to establish the shape and the position of a Laffer curve for the UK, see Beenstock (1979). For criticism of Beenstock's conclusions, see Hemming and Kay (1980).
6. For an authoritative review of these propositions, see Musgrave (1986).
7. I cannot embark on an analysis of the tricky question of how the extent of evasion and avoidance may be calculated. The David Hume Institute commissioned a study of the determinants and the magnitude of evasion which may be found useful. The study also includes a 60-item bibliography. See Pyle (1987).
8. For a formal demonstration of the proposition that, assuming that the Laffer curve is not devoid of realism, the sacrifice of private consumption in order to reduce inequality can result in taxes which are 'too high', see the intriguing article by Lambert (1986).

REFERENCES

Beenstock, M. (1979), 'Taxation and Incentives', *Lloyds Bank Review*, 134, 1–15.

Blinder, A. (1981), 'Thoughts on the Laffer Curve', in Laurence Meyer (ed.), *The Supply Side Effects* of *Economic Policy,* Boston: Kluwer Nijhoff Publishing.

Blum, W.J. and Kalven, H. Jr (1953), *The Uneasy Case for Progressive Taxation*, Chicago: The University of Chicago Press.

Buchanan, J.M. and Lee, D.R. (1982), 'Tax Rates and Tax Revenues in Political Equilibrium: Some Simple Analytics', *Economic Inquiry*, 20, 344–54.

Canto, V.A., Joines, D.H. and Laffer, A.B. (1981), 'Tax Rates, Factor Employment, and Market Production', in Laurence Meyer (ed.), *The Supply Side Effects of Economic Policy*, Boston: Kluwer Nijhoff Publishing.

Feige, E.L. and McGee, R.L. (1983), 'Sweden's Laffer Curve: Taxation and the Unobserved Economy', *Scandinavian Journal of Economics*, 85, 499–519.

Fullerton, D. (1982), 'On the Possibility of an Inverse Relationship between Tax Rates and Government Revenues', *Journal of Public Economics*, 19, 3–22.

Hemming, R. and Kay, J. (1980), 'The Laffer Curve', *Fiscal Studies*, 1, 83–90.

Hume, D. (1752), 'Of Taxes', in his *Political Discourses*, reprinted in David Hume, *Essays, Moral, Political and Literary*, edited by Eugene F. Miller, Indianapolis: Liberty Classics, 1985.

Lambert, P.J. (1986), 'Getting on the Wrong Side of the Laffer Curve', *European Journal of Political Economy*, 2, 193–202.

Lindbeck, A. (1982), 'Tax Effects Versus Budget Effects on Labor Supply', *Economic Inquiry*, 20, 473–89.

Musgrave, R.A. (1959), *The Theory of Public Finance*, London: McGraw Hill.

Musgrave, R.A. (1986), 'Leviathan Cometh – Or Does He?', in R.A. Musgrave, *Public Finance in a Democratic Society*, Volume II, Brighton: Wheatsheaf Books Ltd, Chapter 13.

Peacock, A.T. (1979), *The Economic Analysis of Government*, Oxford: Martin Robertson, Chapter 1.

Peacock, A.T., and Shaw, G.K. (1982), 'Tax Evasion and Tax Revenue Loss', *Public Finance*, 37, 269–78.

Pyle, D.J. (1987), *The Political Economy of Tax Evasion*, Hume Paper No. 6, Edinburgh: The David Hume Institute.

Rawls, J. (1971), *A Theory of Justice*, Cambridge, Mass.: Harvard University Press.

Roberts, P.C. (1984), *The Supply Side Revolution*, Cambridge, Mass.: Harvard University Press.

Shoup, C. (1981), 'Economic Limits to Taxation', *Atlantic Economic Journal*, 9, 9–23.

Stiglitz, J.E. (1986), *Economics of the Public Sector*, New York and London: W.W. Norton and Co.

Waud, R.N. (1986), 'The Tax Aversion and the Laffer Curve', *Scottish Journal of Political Economy*, 33, 212–27.

12. The disaffection of the taxpayer

(This chapter was given as the Presidential Address to the Atlantic Economic Society meeting held in Miami in October 1982. It was stimulated by a series of discussions with Francesco Forte leading to our edited work, The Political Economy of Taxation *(1981), and with my Buckingham colleagues, Keith Shaw and Martin Ricketts, both of whom contributed to it. As with the other chapters in this volume concerned with taxation, the analysis is influenced by the proposition that, convenient though it may be, it is misleading to regard taxpayers as passive reactors to tax measures. This is particularly true in the case when the tax system encourages taxpayers to evade or avoid tax. A middle section of this chapter is taken up with the problem of the interdependency of tax yields, which is exemplified in the possibility that if the proceeds of tax-evaded incomes are spent on taxed goods, then the conventional measures of tax evasion are likely to overestimate the amount of tax loss.*

The original presentation of this argument by Keith Shaw and myself, which is referred to below, has led, subsequent to its publication, to a cascade of articles which demonstrate what happens when our model is modified and extended. For an examination of this literature and special attention to dynamizing the model, see D.K. Bhattacharyya, 'Tax Evasion and Tax Loss: A Further Examination', Public Finance, *Vol. 49, No. 2, 1994. The glosses on our work do not affect the argument in this chapter, but would have to be taken into account in reaching any policy conclusions. Indeed, I have only modified the text very slightly in order to give further emphasis to this point, which was made in the original.)*

I. INTRODUCTION

In much of the modelling of economic policy, economists have regarded their role as that of identifying appropriate instruments for the government to employ in maximizing its welfare function. It has largely been accepted, at least as a first approximation, that instrumental variables appear as exogenous terms in the welfare functions of private firms, households and lower layers of government. The efficiency of the instruments, it is true, depends on how the reactions of economic actors in the private sector are gauged, but, on the whole, these actors are regarded as passive adjusters to changes in the values of the instrumental variables.

It is understandable if economists cling tightly to this familiar paradigm which presents the problem of policy implementation as essentially one of creating conditions analogous to those facing the control engineer. The introduction of 'feedback' effects through, for example, the exploitation by households, who are also taxpayers and voters as well as consumers, of their political power and their constitutional rights, introduces immense complications both in structure or policy models and in the appraisal of the efficiency process and a completely new perspective on the way the economy works. This is particularly true when, as in so many countries today, the dimensions of the public sector are such that the points of entry for negotiating with those who control policy instruments are numerous, and are not simply confined, as many 'feedback models' would have it, to the power to elect governments and to demand referenda.

My illustrious Presidential predecessors, Abba Lerner and James Meade, would adopt the stance, I suppose, that the challenge presented by feedback effects can be met by paying careful attention to the design of policy instruments. I yield to no one in my admiration of their unique combination of analytical skills and inventive capabilities in trying to minimize feedback effects in the design of anti-inflationary measures (Lerner, 1979; Meade, 1979). I am sure that they would be the first to admit that there can be no guarantee that in re-designing the rules of the game in the labour market the players will perceive that there will be prizes for all and that the 'referee', the arbitration authorities, will be immune from the pressures of organized groups of the players. They would be far from alone in thinking, and perhaps justifiably so, that these are problems which economists had better leave for others to solve.

Here I wish to open up debate in a completely different area of confrontation between the citizen and the state, that of the growth in tax burdens which is regarded as the necessary cost of implementing the major policy aims of Western democratic governments. As we all know, the feedback effect of the growth of the public sector made possible by the expansion in tax resources has manifested itself in some interesting political developments such as the organization of tax revolts, the formation of anti-tax political parties, and the formulation of proposals for constitutional limitations on the size and growth of tax revenues.

While I am interested in reviewing the weaponry employed by the 'disaffected taxpayer', as I shall label him, I should like to concentrate attention less on the group organization of tax resistance and more on tax avoidance and evasion as modes of action open to the individual taxpayer. I thus consider the confrontation of the taxpayer with the bureaucracy – the fiscal authorities – rather than with the legislature – the politicians concerned with the ultimate approval of tax legislation.

I choose this area not only because I think that it is an interesting and important one for economic policy, but because I believe that too little attention has been paid by economists to the private firm or citizen/bureaucratic interface, other than in the field of government regulation of business, in contrast to the interface between voters and politicians (as in the theory of public choice) and between politicians and bureaucrats (as in the economic theory of bureaucracy).

While using the dynamics of tax planning as an example of a fresh dimension in the interface between government and citizens, I not only wish to exemplify the use of economic analysis in the examination of policy feedback, but also to relate what I have to say to some much-discussed contemporary policy problems. I have in mind such matters as estimating the dimensions and exploring the welfare and policy implications of tax evasion, and I hope to throw some light on the recent discussion of the Laffer Curve as a point of departure for tax policy.

I am conscious that I am entering a murky area of applied economics similar to crime and prostitution, where the subject-matter have little if any incentive to reveal the facts of their economic life, but if I have any personal ambition as an economist it is to pioneer consideration of the use of economic analysis in unfamiliar but potentially important areas. I must leave it to you to decide how far I have succeeded.

II. DYNAMICS OF TAX PLANNING

In much of the economic analysis of the reaction of persons and firms, the range of possibilities open to the individual in minimizing the loss of utility resulting from tax measures is restricted to the choice between work, saving, and leisure. The analysis is often highly sophisticated – compare, for example, the excellent advanced text by Atkinson and Stiglitz (1980) on public economics – and important policy conclusions have been drawn from it. Thus, those economists who have revived the utilitarian theory of taxation and have redesigned tax objectives to include the effect of taxation incentives have argued strongly for much milder rates of progression than those advocated by their forebears. The famous 'Laffer Curve' which purports to show the relation between tax rates, Gross Domestic Product, and tax yields clearly depends on the disincentive effects on work resulting from growing tax burdens.

The reactions of taxpayers as depicted in such models are purely passive and are modelled on the implicit assumptions, firstly, that tax obligations are certain and, secondly, that the costs of compliance are zero or at least can be ignored. However, in the complicated tax regimes which characterize modern industrial society, there is little evidence that Adam Smith's maxims, that taxes should be certain in payment and convenient for the taxpayer to pay, are being followed. Consequently, taxpayers have reacted, as Adam Smith said they would, by comparing the benefits of evasion and avoidance with the penalties of detection and the risks of losing actions in the courts. In short, in designing tax systems which, among other things, are required to divert a large part of the gross incomes of individuals to the use of government, we cannot use a model in which the taxpayer is treated as if he were one of Pavlov's dogs. The dogs snarl and sometimes they bite (cf. Forte and Peacock, 1981).

Consider, for example, the 'taste for evasion'. What sort of individuals or firms evade and why? So far as individuals are concerned, one might hypothesize as follows. Assuming that the individual wants to achieve some 'target' real income (excluding leisure), then he can choose to minimize the difference between his gross and disposable income either by avoidance or evasion techniques. Different individuals and interest groups will face differential costs and benefits and this will determine their strategies.

Cross and Shaw (1982), using a probabilistic approach, have recently suggested that the individual taxpayer is in the same choice situation as that faced by a dual product firm whereby both 'products' offer gains in the form of reduction in tax obligations and carry production costs such as the penalties imposed on evaders and the costs of resources, such as legal and accounting services, employed in avoidance.

Broadly speaking, their analysis lends credence to the view that 'the rich avoid and the poor evade', at least in a progressive tax regime. This is because the initial cost of employing avoidance services may be high but the marginal cost will fall per pound or dollar of tax 'retrieved' up to the point where tax avoidance measures may demand highly specialized knowledge and encounter rising information costs. Therefore, at the lower end of the income scale, workers with a comparative advantage in a certain skill may be more likely to seek additional earnings, not in the form of taxed overtime nor in the form of leisure activities, but in the form of 'moonlighting' in exchange for unrecorded cash payments or payments in kind.

This analysis has been extended to consider what the reaction of taxpayers is likely to be if tax rates are increased. There appears to be some empirical evidence for the common supposition that a rise in direct tax rates will increase the degree of evasion, and will stimulate the development of sophisticated avoidance techniques. However, such a supposition must be qualified by the institutional assumptions which are built into the analysis. The degree of evasion and avoidance and the evasion/avoidance choice will be a function of the powers of investigation and resources available in exercising them of the revenue authorities, as well as the penalties which these authorities are able to impose.

If revenue authorities operate in a high-handed or arbitrary manner, subjecting taxpayers to what Adam Smith called 'odious examination' (Smith, 1976), then there may be a political backlash which will place limits on the resources and powers which tax authorities are allowed to possess. Likewise, the costs of compliance with the tax law may vary with the amount and the composition of the taxes raised. It is argued by small firms' associations in Britain, for example, that the requirements of company legislation, particularly in regard to accounting conventions, are so onerous for small firms that the incentive to comply is adversely affected.

Nevertheless, the basic proposition that evasion is the weapon of the 'small man' is certainly accepted by the British tax authorities, who have devoted a great deal of effort to preventing firms from hiring workers as 'self-employed' persons giving false names, to close examination on a sampling basis of the books of small firms alleged to be hiding the bulk of their transactions, and to the tracking down of 'moonlighters' who are registered as employed persons (or even as unemployed) but spend their 'leisure' exploiting their skills in the black economy. Judging by the activities of our tax authorities, the universally accepted proposition that the British workman is lazy is strongly suspect. To quote Adam Smith, he wishes 'to better his condition' – but by working if possible for himself.

III. THE MACROECONOMICS OF TAX EVASION

I have only been able to convey to you the flavour of the micro-analytics of tax planning with special reference to the evasion/avoidance choice. What is fairly certain is that there must be some connection between the growth in tax burdens, the associated costs of compliance, the complementary growth in the complexity of the tax system, the growth in the extent of tax evasion, and the growing sophistication of avoidance practices.

Let me describe for you the usual approach to the marshalling of evidence on this subject, concentrating on evasion. The extent of evasion is generally gauged from the measurement of the size of the 'informal' or 'black' economy.

There is considerable argument about the appropriate methods of measurement and wide variations are recorded in the resultant calculations. For example, one estimate for the UK put the percentage of GDP represented by the shadow economy as high as 15 per cent, representing £28 billion in 1980 (Feige, 1981), though this estimate has been questioned by other writers and is certainly regarded as far too high by Her Majesty's Inland Revenue Service which believes the percentage to be somewhere between 6.0 and 8.0. US percentage estimates have varied from as low as 3 per cent to as high as 27 per cent. Although I once undertook the unlikely task of calculating the GDP of a less-developed country and managed to treble the per capita income overnight by adding many non-monetary transactions to previous crude estimates, I would hesitate to make any judgment about the estimating methods used and the results that they produce. (For a most useful discussion of estimating methods, see Tanzi, 1980.)

However, I think that one would be safe in assuming two things about the shadow economy. The first is that it has grown in size over the last twenty years, possibly doubling in size in percentage GDP terms in several important industrialised countries. The second is that in a number of such countries, the size is now in excess of or is approaching 10 per cent of the GDP. I am more concerned with the statements which have been made about the magnitude of the tax 'losses' as a result of the growth of the shadow economy, which have been claimed to be large enough to be of considerable policy significance.

A common method of calculation, which seems at first sight to be self-evident (Feige, 1981), is to estimate the magnitude of the black economy income which would come within the definition of income for tax purposes. As it is virtually impossible to allocate this untaxed income to appropriate income groups in order to arrive at the total tax liability, some 'effective' rate of tax is used which takes into account in a rough-and-ready way the likely incidence of exemptions and allowances which might otherwise be claimed if the income were declared for tax. So, if the untaxed income in the UK, for example, is calculated at £28 billion and the effective rate of tax is 30 per cent, then the tax loss through evasion would be estimated as £8.4 billion. Thus, in simple algebra, the conventional view of revenue loss maintains that

$$T = t(Y - aY) \tag{12.1}$$

or

$$dT/da = -tY, \tag{12.1a}$$

where

T = the total yield;
t = the 'effective' tax rate;
a = the evasion coefficient;
Y = money income; and

$$0 < a, t < 1.$$

There are four difficulties about this calculation:

(i) It encounters a major problem often found in tax analysis – it compares an actual with a hypothetical situation. The calculation assumes that the only hypothetical alternative is one where the widening of the tax base through the removal of evasion will not affect the tax regime. However, what that tax regime will be will depend on how it fits with overall government policy. Thus, a government may prefer to counterbalance the widening of the tax base by a reduction in tax rates and raising of exemption levels, rather than simply increasing tax yields. Indeed, the erstwhile General Secretary of the Inland Revenue Staff Federation in the UK has argued very strongly that one of the benefits that its members could confer by being given greater powers to catch evaders would be the possibility open to the government of reducing tax rates (Christopher, 1979).

(ii) It is assumed that the level of the Gross Domestic Product would be unaffected by the elimination of evasion activity. There is a presumption that as evasion makes possible labour services which would not otherwise be offered, then its elimination might reduce GDP, and, therefore, the estimated tax base.

(iii) The estimates of income tax revenue loss overlook the fact that the proceeds of tax-evaded income are likely to be spent on taxed goods.

(iv) One man's expenditure is another man's income. Expenditure by evaders which is not siphoned off to the tax authorities will augment money incomes elsewhere in the economy. To the extent that these incomes accrue to non-evaders, to that extent income tax revenue will be increased.

These obvious points can be incorporated in a macroeconomic model of compelling simplicity in order to demonstrate just how far from the mark the conventional approach might land us. (The analysis which follows is a variant on that used by Peacock and Shaw, 1982.)

Assume a simple, closed economy such that

$$Y = C + A$$

where Y is the GDP and is decomposed into $a.Y$, the proportion of GDP evading tax and $(1 - a).Y$, the residual GDP, which is subject to a proportional income tax, t. Consumption is a function of disposable income so that

$$C = b_1 Y(1 - a)(1 - t) + b_2 aY$$

where b_1 and b_2 are the consumption coefficients in the non-evading and evading sectors, respectively. Given $A = \bar{A}$, i.e., all other expenditures (on investment goods and government expenditure on goods and services) are autonomously determined, then:

$$Y = \frac{A}{1 - b_1(1 - a)(1 - t) - b_2 a} \qquad (12.2)$$

The tax yield is now:

$$T = tY(1-a) = \frac{t\bar{A}(1-a)}{[1-b_1(1-a)(1-t)-b_2 a]} \tag{12.3}$$

A number of propositions can be derived from this simple model:

(i) $\partial T/\partial t > 0$, i.e., a rise in the tax rate always has a positive effect on tax revenue in money terms.

(ii) $\partial T/\partial a < 0$, i.e., a rise in the evasion coefficient has a negative effect on tax revenue in money terms, but the loss of revenue is less than that identified in the conventional model (see equation 12.1a). This is because the rise in a, as well as reducing the proportion of income subject to tax, increases the value of the multiplier and, therefore, produces a countervailing increase in Y.

(iii) $\left.\frac{\partial T}{\partial t}\right|_{a=0} = \left.\frac{\partial T}{\partial t}\right|_{b_2=1} > 0;$

This is probably the most interesting result for it is counterintuitive. It states that the change in money tax yield will be identical, for any given change in the tax rate, in the case where there is no evasion and in the case where there is evasion, *provided that* evaders, at the margin, do not save any part of their non-taxed income. It follows that, for any *given* tax yield, and given the same assumptions, the tax yield is unaffected by the value of a, that is, by the extent of evasion, provided that $0 < a < 1$. This is demonstrated in proposition (iv).

(iv) From (12.3), given $a = 0$

$$T = \frac{t\bar{A}}{1-b_1(1-t)}. \tag{12.4}$$

From (12.3), given $b_2 = 1$

$$T = \frac{t\bar{A}(1-a)}{[1-b_1(1-a)(1-t)-a]}$$

$$= \frac{t\bar{A}}{[1-b_1(1-t)]} \qquad \textit{Q.E.D.}$$

It seems to me that the assumption of a marginal propensity to consume out of tax-evading income of unity or thereabouts is not implausible, given the previous argument about the composition of the evading population. If that is so, then explanation of this counterintuitive result is all the more necessary. Briefly, the result comes about because the act of evasion implies a decrease in the *aggregate* savings ratio, but the induced additional saving in the non-evading sector, as a result of the expansion in Y, compensates for this reduction regardless of the marginal consumption propensity.

Of course, I cannot emphasize too strongly that I am only using this simple model in order to point us in the direction of further analysis. If one were looking for policy conclusions, one would have to construct a computable macroeconomic model embodying a foreign trade sector, taxes which also affect prices (such as VAT), a capital and money market, as well as a goods market; and so on. In the spirit of my original approach, one would have to be able to simulate possible behavioural reactions of policy-makers and how these in turn affect the behaviour of taxpayers.

These desiderata indicate that the model must embody a lagged structure. In this context, I should like to single out only one matter for further discussion before considering how the introduction of evasion affects one's view of the relevance of other analyses concerned with the influence of taxpayer behaviour on the total tax yield, particularly analysis based on the Laffer Curve, which has excited much interest.

The results presented do not explicitly tell us anything about the real value of tax revenues. If real output ($\bar{Y}$) were fixed in supply and the money supply passively adjusted to accommodate increases in national expenditure, then an increase in $a.$ which left money tax yields constant would simply mean that the real value of tax revenues had fallen. This would follow because the result of a rise in nominal Y would result in a proportional increase in the general price level.

On the other hand, if it is postulated that a rise in evasion is associated with the increase in employment of otherwise idle resources attracted into the black economy, then the multiplier effect resulting from an increase in $a.$ will result in higher real output.

In the extreme case, where there was no rise in prices as a result of the increase in expenditure produced by an increase in $a.$, then a rise in evasion would result in a constant real tax yield. It follows that a sufficiently strong positive relation between real output and tax evasion might even produce a rise in the real tax yield.

IV. THE 'WELFARE' EFFECTS OF TAX PLANNING

Being somewhat sceptical of approaches to policy which attempt to identify some grandiose social welfare function which is completely divorced from individual choice (cf. Rowley and Peacock, 1975), I propose to indicate the welfare effects of the disaffection of the taxpayer in an indirect way. I shall consider the effects of evasion and avoidance on the macroeconomic stance of the budget, on the design of tax systems, and on the structure of production. I shall leave the reader to decide how these effects are to be appraised.

Consider first of all the problem of the overall budgetary position. The worries about the revenue loss from evasion have been associated with the loss of control over revenue sources, which would reduce the ability of the government to use fiscal policy as an instrument to achieve the conventional range of macroeconomic objectives. For example, if it is believed that welfare improves as the rate of inflation falls, and that this rate depends on the ability of the government to control the growth in public debt, then any perceived loss of revenue as a result of evasion will be regarded as a hindrance to the pursuit of anti-inflation policy.

One's view of the effects of evasion and avoidance depends to some extent on whether one adopts a Monetarist or Keynesian stance to fiscal and monetary policy. A Monetarist stance fastens attention primarily on the size of the government borrowing requirement. Fears that evasion and avoidance will have a demonstrably unfavourable effect on this borrowing requirement are only justified if there is no pronounced interdependence in tax yields of the kind described.

A Keynesian stance requires that the budget becomes an instrument in which reliance is placed upon its built-in stability and on 'fine-tuning' possibilities if stabilization objectives are to be achieved. The interdependence of tax yields postulated in the simple model suggests that any 'first round' adverse effects of evasion and avoidance, which means that the fiscal authorities lose control over direct tax revenue, may be offset at least partially by the increase in the yields of taxes on expenditure as well as the taxable incomes of those whose goods and services are bought with the extra disposable incomes of avoiders and evaders. However, there is an obvious additional problem encountered by 'fine-tuning' requirements for, as well as the usual forecasting difficulties encountered in measuring the effect of tax changes, the fiscal authorities may have little direct information on the reaction of evaders and avoiders to 'fine-tuning' adjustments in tax rates.

The design of tax systems is usually associated with attempts to formulate some principle of income distribution which can be translated into instructions to the fiscal authorities regarding the rate schedules and their consistent application. In short, taxes are meant to conform with some principle covering both vertical and horizontal equity. I leave aside the vexed question as to whether such a principle ought to command the consensus of taxpayers and how that consensus is to be ascertained – by some technique of preference revelation or by some appropriate voting mechanism.

It is bound to be extremely difficult to ascertain the impact, shifting, and incidence of the tax changes resulting from evasion or avoidance. Let us assume that through some miracle of administration and of political consensus, an initial position is reached in which acceptable canons of vertical and horizontal equity are fulfilled. Now imagine that some innovation in evasion techniques – perhaps some computerized device which makes it possible to marry barter transactions in a highly efficient manner – takes place. It would be extremely difficult to ascertain how the relative positions of taxpayers might be changed, both in respect of 'unequals' and 'equals'. It does seem highly unlikely, nevertheless, that the final incidence of taxes, taking account of the interdependencies in tax yields already examined, would be such as to accord with the prevailing canons of equity

If this is so, not only does the onset of evasion cause difficulties in determining the extent to which the *status quo ante* has been disturbed, it may make it difficult to restore. If evasion is perceived to 'pay', then taxpayers may be encouraged to invest in finding out whether they should follow suit. On the other hand, taxpayers might be encouraged to invest in other forms of tax resistance, such as delays in tax payment, or tax revolts, which may force the tax authorities to divert more resources to catching evaders rather than to checking whether those easier to catch comply strictly with the letter of the law.

One final point might be made about the distributional effects of tax evasion. Evasion may itself be a result of inequities in the tax system and not only a cause. Take the example of a worker who can exercise the choice to work overtime as an employee or work on his own account. If he chooses the latter method of supplementing his income, then he may face much heavier compliance costs. His overtime earnings can be taxed at source, whereas determining the taxable income earned independently may require him to incur legal and accounting costs which, even if deductible against tax, may be onerous. Supporters of the proposition that long-term growth of GDP depends on encouraging the growth of small business maintain that the differential costs of compliance help either to stifle entrepreneurship at birth or force it to wear the badge of illegitimacy.

Finally, under the heading of welfare effects, consider the incentives associated with the productive potential of the economy. One of the most influential policy propositions in major industrial countries such as the USA and the UK is that a cut in high tax rates and reduction in the degree of progression is necessary to restore the incentives to work, save, and invest in the private sector, in which it is believed that productivity gains are much more likely to be realized than in the public sector. Furthermore, it is held that cutting tax rates does not necessarily result in a fall in revenue in the longer run, for the resultant growth in the economy by itself will help to generate revenue

This proposition is closely related to the so-called Laffer Curve analysis. The *simpliste* version of this analysis states that at a zero tax rate tax yield will be zero, and likewise at a 100 per cent tax rate tax yield will be zero since no one would have any incentive to produce taxable income. The continuous function relating tax yield to 'the' tax rate takes the form of an inverse parabola which shows that a tax rate between 0 and 100 per cent will maximize revenue yield and, also, that any given tax yield other than the maximum will be compatible with two tax rates.

This result rests on the assumption that as the tax rate rises, the level of GDP will fall, and it is this fall in GDP which produces the fall in tax yield. In short, the Laffer analysis accepts the conventional view which postulates that rising tax rates lower the price of leisure. No account is taken, therefore, of the reactions of taxpayers in the form of avoidance and evasion, and the consequential effects of avoidance and evasion on tax yields.

Now it is not disputed that high *effective* tax rates may have adverse supply-side effects, though I agree entirely with Carl Shoup (1981) that translating such analytical conclusions into specific propositions about the limits to taxation along Lafferian lines is a dangerous pastime. My contribution to this debate is a modest one. Consider what happens if evasion and avoidance are both positive functions of upward movements in the average direct tax burden. The Laffer-type analysis assumes that a rise in the average tax burden results in a shrinkage in the tax base or in its rate of increase through the decline in GDP or in GDP growth. However, as I have shown, if evasion and avoidance are widespread, GDP may not necessarily decline below what it would otherwise be, even in real terms, and in consequence the simple relation postulated in the parabolic Laffer curve cannot be sustained.

It is not suggested that adverse supply-side effects would be eliminated by the growth of evasion and avoidance, but that these effects are likely to be much more complicated than the Laffer-type analysis indicates. For example, adverse effects might very well occur in the longer run, particularly if tax evaders would otherwise be found in lower tax brackets and if maintaining direct tax yields called for higher rates of tax to be imposed on upper income echelons. (Note that this example illustrates clearly my previous proposition about being clear on the budgetary stance taken by the government – in this case maintaining a given revenue yield is assumed.)

Another example is to be found in the proposition that tax evasion may reduce the gains from specialization. It may encourage individuals with particular aptitudes and acquired skills, more appropriately exercised as an employee in industry, to enter forms of employment (including self-employment) that are difficult to tax but in which they are less skilled and not so well trained.

V. CONCLUSION

The general point I have made here is that when the public sector becomes large in relation to the rest of the economy, the simple models of economic policy which postulate omnipotent government maximizing some collective utility function and in which citizens are regarded as passive adjusters to government measures are no longer applicable. Moreover, even if public choice models emphasize that citizens are not maximizing their utility subject to binding constraints imposed by government but are striking bargains with politicians who supply services to them, such models have to be extended to cover the interface between citizens and the administration, for explicit account has to be taken of the fact that whatever the intentions of the legislature, complex modern legislation leaves immense discretion to government officials.

In maximizing their own utility functions, such officials cannot expect that if they act in an arbitrary manner their decisions will go unchallenged, and that is particularly true in cases where the individual citizen, in weighing the costs and benefits, allowing for uncertainty, of challenging such decisions, finds it is in his interests, either acting alone or in concert with others, to seek to have the law interpreted in his favour or to ignore the law altogether.

The interface between the tax authorities and the citizen offers a striking example of the growing importance of bargaining which results from the growth in government. Economists have traditionally deplored the diversion of human energies which is a consequence of bargaining situations. Fiscal economists have expressed disdain for the ingenious devices used by taxpayers in order to minimize tax burdens and, equally, are fearful of the consequences of seeking to destroy such devices by giving tax authorities more extended powers of investigation and wide discretion in the interpretation of legislation of growing complexity. Furthermore, the fact that even the country location of firms and individuals crucially depends on differences in the tax law between countries presages further development in an international monitoring system requiring exchange of information between national tax authorities, which infringe further on personal liberty.

One is entitled to believe that this diversion of professional resources into tax bargaining is worth the benefits which it produces in the form of the transfer of resources to public use, but one is equally entitled to believe that the cost is too great and that the only solution lies in reducing the overall burden of taxation and in simplifying the tax system. Either way, in appraising what the consequences of any change in policy is likely to be, no economic analyst can afford to employ models which underestimate the foresight, the intelligence, and the sensibilities of the individual taxpayer of today.

REFERENCES

Atkinson A. B. and Stiglitz, J. E. (1980), *Public Economics*, London: McGraw Hill.

Christopher, Anthony (1979), 'The Law is the Law is the Law ...', in *Tax Avoision,* Institute of Economic Affairs Readings No. 18, London: IEA.

Cross, R. and Shaw, G. K. (1982), 'The Economics of Tax Aversion', *Public Finance*, No. 1.

Feige, Edgar (1981), 'The UK's Unobserved Economy', *Journal of Economic Affairs*, July.

Forte, Francesco and Peacock, Alan (1981), 'Tax Planning, Tax Analysis and Tax Policy', in Alan Peacock and Francesco Forte (eds), *The Political Economy of Taxation*, Oxford: Blackwell.

Lerner, Abba P. (1979), 'MAP, The Market Mechanism Cure for Stagflation', *Atlantic Economic Journal*, Vol. 7, March, 12–19.

Meade, James (1979), 'Stagflation in the United Kingdom', *Atlantic Economic Journal*, Vol. 7, December.

Peacock, Alan (1979), *The Economic Analysis of Government*, Oxford: Martin Robertson, Chapter 1.

Peacock, Alan and Shaw, G. K. (1982), 'Tax Evasion and Tax Revenue Loss', *Public Finance*, No. 3.

Rowley, Charles and Peacock, Alan (1975), *Welfare Economics: A Liberal Restatement*, London: Martin Robertson.

Shoup, Carl (1981), 'Economic Limits to Taxation', *Atlantic Economic Journal*, Vol. IX, No. 1, March, 9–23.

Smith, Adam (1976), *An Inquiry into the Nature and Causes of the Wealth of Nations*, edited by R. H. Campbell and A. S. Skinner, Oxford: Clarendon Press, Book V, Chapter 2.

Tanzi, Vito (1980), 'The Underground Economy in the United States: Estimates and Implications', *Banco Nazionale del Lavoro Quarterly Review*, December.

13. Economic analysis of problems of government selective aid

(with Martin Ricketts)

(Although in recent years selective aid to industry has diminished in importance in EC countries, it is still used by member governments to support firms that are perceived to play an important part in regional or sectoral policies. At the same time, selective aid is clearly a method of support that goes counter to the promotion of the single market, so that if the EC Commission allows selective aid there is bound to be controversy about the decision. This chapter does not consider the international dimensions of selective aid policies, important though these are, but concentrates on the prior question of the role of selective aid as one amongst several policy measures that can be used to influence growth and employment, which must include doing nothing! The striking feature of selective aid as a policy is how often expectations regarding its results remain unfulfilled, yet, despite this, it remains in the government armoury. This chapter offers an economic explanation as to why this is so, using the principal and agent approach, now much in vogue. It was first presented to the 43rd Congress of the International Institute of Finance at its Paris meeting in 1987. The authors express their gratitude to the discussant of the paper, Professor Henri Vertainen, Helsinki, for his comments and criticisms.)

I. BACKGROUND

Governments of major industrial countries use selective aid, i.e. explicit subsidies to particular companies, as an instrument for promoting regional, sectoral and even macroeconomic policies, notably in order to improve or to sustain economic growth and to enhance employment prospects. (For an illuminating critique of subsidy policy, see Wiseman, 1981.) The general view of economists seems to be that selective aid is a relatively expensive way of achieving such policies, in comparison with alternatives, such as competition policy, privatization and de-regulation and more general macroeconomic budgetary measures, at least in mixed or market economies (for evidence, see Burton, 1983). 'Expensive' usually means that selective aid policy achieves less growth and employment per pound spent out of a given segment of the budget devoted to direct subsidies to companies, than would alternative policies. The budget constraint is taken to reflect the trade-off between growth and employment policies against attempts to control the rate of inflation. One of the principal reasons given for the 'expensive' character of selective aid measures is that they frequently require more funding than the budgetary authorities expect, or are prepared to admit *ex ante*, a characteristic which is shared by government contracts for the purchase of inputs used to produce government services such as defence and health. Each of us has their favourite tale to tell of public sector disasters, and the UK offers some classic examples ranging from the subsidies to produce Concorde to the Invergordon Aluminium Smelter case and the famous De Lorean scandal.

Our purpose here is not to pass judgment on selective aid programmes in some magisterial way but to investigate how far economic analysis can throw light on the question why selective aid policies so frequently turn out to be disastrous.

The approach we shall use is derived from so-called principal-agent analysis which is much in vogue (for a diagrammatical exposition, which is later applied in this contribution, see Ricketts, 1986). It seems sensible to consider a state-subsidized company as an agent of the government, the principal, which enters into a contract to carry out certain tasks in exchange for some reward. As we shall see, principal-agent analysis is certainly an improvement on conventional price theory in depicting the environment in which contracts between government and companies are formed. We must be frank and admit that we initially believed that this analysis would take us much further along the road of interpreting public sector 'horror stories'. That things turned out otherwise was a mildly chastening experience, but perhaps it will interest and possibly amuse readers to see how we wriggle out of our self-made difficulties.

II. CONVENTIONAL MODELS OF SELECTIVE AID AND THEIR DEFECTS

Conventional economic analysis can be used to introduce the problem. We shall take the example of a subsidy to the current operations of an already existing firm, rather than exploring the case where a subsidy is granted to affect the level of a firm's investment, which would require us to consider investment decisions. This enables us to use a simple one-period partial analysis which is perfectly adequate for our purposes. We imagine that the policy problem at hand is how to minimize the amount of subsidy given to a firm in order to produce some desired change in its level of output, where the latter can also be regarded as an indicator of employment objectives. The exposition is based on Peacock, 1984.

Consider Figure 13.1. The expected domestic demand for some industrial produce (say metal strip) is represented in conventional fashion by DD_1, i.e. the quantity demanded for the product increases as its price decreases. It is assumed that the product is traded internationally and suppliers of the product are 'price-takers'. The world price is initially expected to be P_w. The planned marginal cost curve (*MC*) of the only domestic firm supplying the product is upward-sloping and, as the firm cannot influence price, profits are maximized at $MC = P_w$, with sales equal to $0Q_d$. As $0Q_d < 0Q$, $0Q$ being the quantity demanded by domestic purchasers at the expected world price, the difference is expected to be made up by imports represented by Q_dQ(= *CP*).

Assume that the economic adviser to a government department believes that there is a high probability that the expected and actual outcome in this market for an industrial input will be the same. He presents this information (though

Figure 13.1

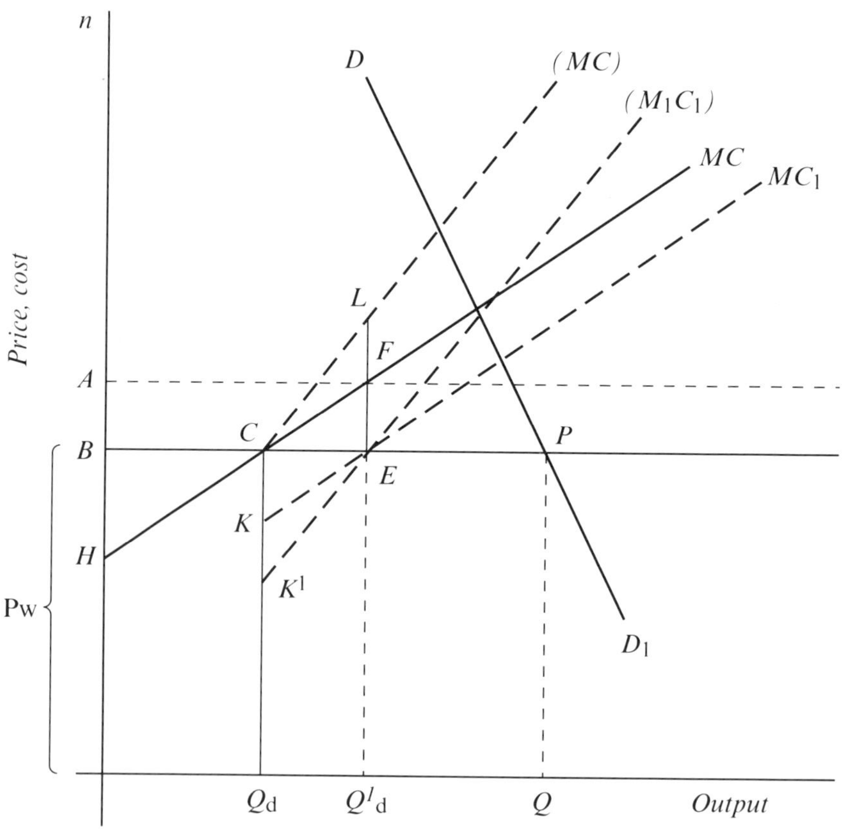

it is doubtful if he would have recourse to diagrams) to his Minister who has been given the responsibility for industrial policy. The Minister might decide that it would be in the government's interest to expand the output of the industry. There are several reasons which might lead him to conclude this – improvement of employment prospects in the region(s) where the domestic supplier is located; worries about the 'lack of availability' in the longer run of supplies from abroad; concern for the amount of foreign exchange required to finance imports of the product. Whether these reasons add up to a cogent and sensible economic policy is not explored, but certainly the list is a familiar one.

The textbook answer which our diagram suggests as the instrument for achieving the minister's objective is to offer an 'explicit payment' in the form of a 'direct', 'narrow-based', marginal output subsidy to the domestic producer. The amount of the subsidy will be a function of the amount of extra output required to generate the required increase in employment and/or import-saving. If we assume that the output 'target' is $0Q_d^1$, then the subsidy required must shift the *MC* curve downwards so that the subsidy-adjusted *MC* curve is M_1C_1. In exchange for the extra costs of production incurred *less* extra receipts received in order to produce the extra output (represented by triangle *CEF*) the domestic producer has to be 'bribed' by a subsidy represented by the area *CKEF*. Other things being equal, the domestic producer's surplus would be expected to rise from *BCH* (the difference between his marginal costs of production and his receipts when producing output $0Q_d$) to an area represented by the larger area *BCH* + *CKE*. It is assumed that the authorities would not be able to operate a subsidy system in which the amount paid would vary with each increment of output so that the producer only received just enough subsidy to induce him to produce the extra marginal output.

In a formal sense, it is possible to view this case as an example of principal-agent relationship, the principal being obviously the government which has entered into an agreement with the firm, the agent, whom it will recompense for carrying out certain agreed courses of action. Given the information presented in our illustration, there is nothing presaging disaster. The analysis assumes that the relationship between the input of aid and the required output of the firm can be precisely known in advance and no difficulties in drawing up a contract are revealed.

However, our example, which follows closely the textbook kind of formulation of problems of this kind, assumes away two important problems. The first is that it is based on the assumption that the agent's activities are perfectly observable so that the principal could detect if there is any departure from the contract, and this is unlikely to be the case. The second is that there may be considerable uncertainty in respect of both cost and demand conditions, that is to say the configuration of events shown in Figure 13.1 is a statement of the firm's plans which are based on firm forecasts of cost and demand conditions.

The first gives rise to a problem of moral hazard arising from the fact that the agent is the sole source of information about his costs. Assume that the firm inflates its estimates of marginal costs above those which are the 'true' estimates, as depicted by the hatched *MC* line passing through *C* and *L*. It then contracts for a subsidy per unit of *EL* instead of *EF*. The principal, if aware of the moral hazard problem, will institute some mode of enquiry into the 'reasonableness' of cost estimates by sending in accountants to check and/or by cost comparisons from precedents or comparable costs. Here we have the first glimmering of a difficulty which points the way towards problems of financial control, though hardly suggesting that disaster is round the corner. However the principal acts, resource costs have to be incurred, including time. Whether or not the principal has access to such resources is a moot point, recalling that resources have an opportunity cost.[1]

The second problem concerns uncertainty about cost and demand conditions. Even if the agent has a strong incentive to minimize cost, which would be present in circumstances we later describe, he will, depending on his attitude to risk, have a strong incentive to negotiate a contract which embodies protection against unknown exogenous shocks. Risk sharing with the principal is one obvious possibility. With the principal presumably subject to a budget constraint, though with some freedom in negotiating with the firm, the model of principal/agent relationship takes on the appearance of a bargaining situation rather than one of constrained maximization by the firm, passively adjusting to some exogenously-determined rate of subsidy.

A conventional microeconomic presentation offers a mechanistic view of the policy problem, making it look easy to execute a project once the objectives have been specifically determined. There is scarcely a hint of the 'overrun' problem which haunts government-industry interface. This is what has led us to look at the new-style principal-agent analysis which is now much in vogue.

III THE PRINCIPAL-AGENT FRAMEWORK

It is possible to illustrate the main features of the standard approach to the principal-agent relationship in a simple diagram. Consider the case in which some activity on the part of a firm will result in a changed probability distribution of 'social benefits'. Suppose, for example, that two social outcomes are possible, a relatively 'good' outcome measured by the horizontal dimension of the box in Figure 13.2 and a relatively 'poor' outcome measured by the vertical dimension. Profit to the firm (agent) is measured with respect to the origin O_F and the return to the government (Principal) is measured with respect to the origin O_G. Any point within the box represents a 'contract' between government and firm. At point *a* along the firm's certainty line, the firm receives the same payment

Figure 13.2

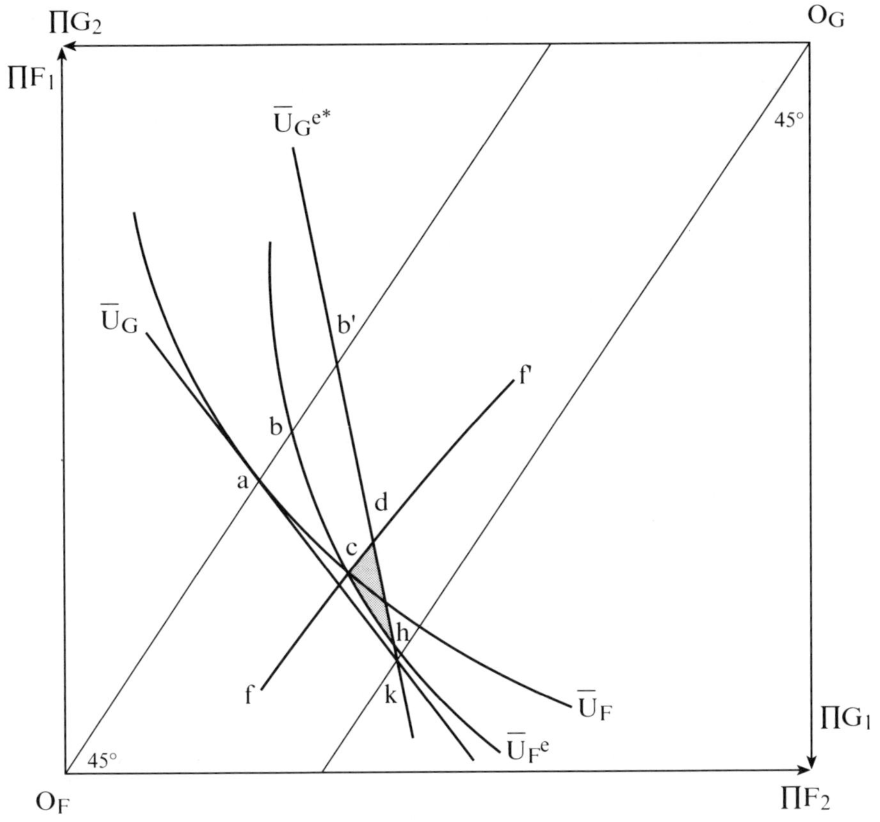

irrespective of the social outcome and the government bears the entire risk. Let the firm and the government be expected utility maximizers, and let the firm be risk-averse and the government risk-neutral. The firm's constant expected utility indifference curve through *a* is $\bar{U}_F$ and the government's indifference curve is $\bar{U}_G$. For the sake of argument, assume that $\bar{U}_F$ defines the minimum level of utility required to induce the firm to enter into any contractual arrangement with the government. At point *a* the government is maximizing utility subject to the constraint that $U_F \geq \bar{U}_F$. Risk is shared efficiently at *a* with the slopes of $\bar{U}_F$ and $\bar{U}_G$ both equal to the ratio of the probabilities of the two outcomes ($P_g/1 - P_g$) where P_g and $1 - P_g$ are the probabilities of the 'good' and 'bad' outcome respectively.

We now introduce explicitly the assumption that the government cannot observe the effort of the firm. The firm, however, by exerting a given level of 'effort' (e) can increase the probability of the 'good' social outcome to $P'_g > P_g$. 'Effort' in this context might take the form of expenditure on monitoring, management training, the employment of skilled personnel and so forth. Contracts yielding the firm an expected utility level $\bar{U}$, after exerting effort e, are delineated by the curve $\bar{U}^e_F$. the distance ab is the cost of effort to the firm and the slope of $\bar{U}^e_F$ at b is now $P'_g/1 - P'_g$. A contract at c, the point of intersection between $\bar{U}_F$ and $\bar{U}^e_F$, will just leave the firm indifferent between exerting and not exerting effort e. Indeed, all contracts to the right of *ff*', loci representing all points of intersection between 'with effort' and 'without effort' indifference curves having the same utility index, will induce the firm to exert effort. The greater probability of a 'good' outcome following the firm's effort will also affect the government's indifference curve through a which will now swivel around point k on the government's certainty line to $\bar{U}^e_G$.

Contracts represented by the shaded set of points *cdh* are therefore Pareto improvements on the contract at a. Any contract between c and d along the boundary *ff*' will make both the government and firm better off than at a. Risk is not shared efficiently however, as risk-sharing benefits have been sacrificed in the interests of producing effort incentives. If $\bar{U}_F$ and $\bar{U}_G$ are the minimum utility levels necessary to induce firm and government to participate in some agreement, the set of contracts *cdh* will represent the potential outcomes over which bargaining will take place. Perfect information about the firm's effort would, in principle, enable a contract to be struck between b and b' on the firm's certainty line. It would thus permit efficient risk sharing. Clearly, information costs will determine whether such a contract would be preferable to a contract between c and d.

Although highly simplified, Figure 13.2 and the explanatory paragraphs above illustrate the basic principles of the standard approach to the principal-agent problem (for further analysis see Ricketts, 1986). The efficient contract will depend upon the costs of obtaining information, the riskiness of the project to be undertaken, the degree of risk aversion of principal and agent, and the efficiency of effort on the part of the agent. The theory may be regarded normatively as a means of identifying efficient contracts (e.g. Laffont, 1987), or as a means of explaining and predicting the types of contractual arrangements which are likely to emerge in specified circumstances (e.g. Stiglitz, 1975). Where the agent is risk-neutral, a standard result is that the moral hazard problem may be simply overcome by a contract along the principal's certainty line. A contract at a point such as k in Figure 13.2, for example, would imply that the agent was bearing the entire risk and that all gains from extra effort would accrue to the agent. Point k could be interpreted as a 'fixed-price' contract by which the government pays a given sum for a specified result. We might imagine that the dimensions of the box vary entirely because of variations in the costs of meeting some objective, and that a contract at k implies that cost overruns are borne by the firm or agent. In contrast, a contract at *a* represents a 'cost plus' arrangement by which the firm receives a given payoff and cost overruns are borne by the government.

IV. THE APPLICABILITY OF PRINCIPAL-AGENT THEORY TO SELECTIVE AID

When governments attempt to implement selective aid policies, the problems they face, as we have argued earlier, are very similar in type to the problems confronted when a principal deals with an agent. The government will often be dealing with a particular firm in special circumstances; it will be attempting to persuade the firm to undertake activities which otherwise would not be undertaken or which would be undertaken in different ways; conditions will usually be uncertain; the firm will be costly to monitor; and the moral hazard problem is unavoidable.

Clearly, such an abstract approach, used either to identify 'good' or at least 'consistent' policies or to improve our understanding of the problems besetting existing policies, can only be a starting point. In matching this approach with the complex situations accompanying government intervention the conceptual apparatus may seem too frail to bear the weight of reality. In particular, it is a curious paradox that, although the theory of principal/agent is rooted in the recognition of information problems, the specification of either an optimal contract or an actual contract likely to be arrived at requires, indeed, a great deal of information, as we shall soon discover. The best case we can make for the principal-agent approach is that, in examining its assumptions, we are presented with a useful agenda for studying the possible dimensions of 'disaster'.

A. The Identification of Outcomes

In the first place it is necessary to identify and value possible 'outcomes'. Our simple presentation in Section III involved only two possible outcomes whereas most practical situations will involve an enormous range of possibilities. Objectives may be complex. In the case of employment creation for example, will skilled jobs be treated as equally desirable to unskilled jobs? Will jobs for local residents be considered equivalent to jobs for immigrant workers? Will jobs in the construction phase of a project be of equal weight to jobs created later on? Placing a social valuation on all the feasible outcomes allowing for such factors is a daunting task for any government. The employment consequences of selective aid may also represent only one element in the package of possible benefits of a scheme. Among the list of benefits associated with the Invergordon Aluminium Smelter project in the UK (cf. Scott and Cuthbert, 1985) were import savings, strategic defence considerations, preventing regional decline and making more efficient use of the social overhead capital of the area. Sufficient information is unlikely to be available to permit the aggregation of such diverse benefits and to attach probability values to the various possible combinations of outcomes. The very definition of a possible outcome is likely to be politically sensitive with politicians unwilling to attach any firm probability to certain events. Objectives may also be unstable over time. A common complaint of defence contractors is that performance objectives are changed continuously (an example was the publicly-expressed annoyance of General Electric (GEC) at changes in the performance specification for the British early warning radar system NIMROD).

B. The Efficiency of Effort

Second, the responsiveness of the probability distribution of 'outcomes' to the agent's 'effort' will be a contentious matter. Calculating the 'efficiency of effort' implies a great deal of knowledge about production technology. Precisely *how* are the social outcomes identified by government to he produced, and precisely what additional inputs will make these outcomes more likely and by how much? Neither party may be sure of these points, and subjective assessments may differ considerably. In the extreme case where the agent is assumed to know the cost characteristics which he faces and the principal does not, the classic adverse selection problem arises in addition to the moral hazard problem highlighted in section II. Even our analysis in Section II shows that the government has to rely upon information on all costs supplied by the firm. Yet the firm may have little incentive to communicate what knowledge it possesses accurately to the government. Any final 'contract' must address both adverse selection and moral hazard problems.

If it is assumed that the government is negotiating with a single firm, a 'cost plus' contract will give an incentive to the firm to *underestimate* the costs of meeting the government's objectives (exaggerating the efficiency of effort) in order to entice the government into a contractual relationship. This would explain the systematic underestimation of the costs of selective aid projects in the UK. Examples include the De Lorean fiasco and the Invergordon Aluminium Smelter already mentioned. Scott and Cuthbert (1985) calculate that the budgetary cost per direct job year created by the Aluminium Smelter project was £35,000. Budgetary cost per total job year (i.e. including indirect employment creation) they estimate at £26,500 or over two and a half times the GDP per head of the working population in 1981, the year the smelter closed. Yet the whole project was 'advertised' as one which would impose no costs on the taxpayer!

A 'fixed price' contract in which all cost overruns were borne by the firm would solve the moral hazard problem as we observed in section III, but only if the firm were risk neutral would this involve the efficient sharing of risk. Further, it would now give the firm an incentive to *exaggerate* the costs of its activities and *underestimate* the efficiency of effort in order to obtain the best terms from the ill-informed government. This redistribution between government and firm might be seen as of little consequence. All contracts between points *c* and *d* in Figure 13.2, for example, are efficient. However, the raising of funds by the government through the tax system or bond issues involves efficiency losses elsewhere and rents achieved by the firm at the expense of the government are not socially costless. This leaves open the question how far the incentive to exaggerate costs will be taken into account in devising an appropriate contractual environment.

C. The 'Observability' of Outcomes

As presented in Section III, the standard approach to the principal-agent problem assumes that outcomes are 'observable' by both parties. We have already drawn attention to the complexity of potential outcomes in most practical cases, but it is also true that the *ex post* observability is in some doubt. Costs, for example, are far from being objectively measurable and it will often be in the interests of firms, or governments, to indulge in 'creative accounting' in order to present results in the most favourable light. This lack of transparent observability of 'outcomes' may explain the apparent willingness of politicians to accept optimistic cost estimates uncritically. Governments will be interested not only in what is observable by ministers and civil servants, but also in what is observable by the public at large and the electorate. If the latter are well informed about outcomes, the government may perceive itself as the principal in a relationship not unlike that described in our simple earlier exposition. If electors are poorly informed or if illusion can be fostered, for example, by overstating benefits and underestimating costs and by 'covering up' notable failures, the relationship between firms and governments will be altered. The relationship becomes more of an alliance in which the government promotes its political influence and the firm pursues profits by exploiting *an information asymmetry not between government and firm but between an alliance of the two and the general population.*[2] An analysis of selective aid on these lines would then come to resemble the 'capture' theory of regulation rather than the principal-agent paradigm.

Some outcomes are by definition 'unobservable'. Take, for example, the assistance provided by the British Government under Section 8 of the Industrial Development Act 1982. An important criterion for eligibility is 'additionality'. A project is 'additional' if it would not proceed without assistance, 'or not on substantially the same scale, or not with substantially the same nature, or not in substantially the same timescale' (National Audit Office report, 1987, p. 15).

The government hopes that it is buying with its grants certain desirable social changes. But such changes are never directly 'observed'. Since there is no way of knowing what would have happened in the absence of a grant the 'outcome' is always a matter of subjective assessment – a guess about the way things might have looked if no grant had been given. The NAO report notes this problem explicitly: 'Decisions on additionality inevitably require largely subjective judgments sometimes between conflicting factors and the NAO noted cases where Department of Trade and Industry officials had had doubts as to additionality' (p. 15).

D. Risk Aversion

In the normative analysis of optimal contracting the degree of risk aversion of principal and agent will affect the optimal contract. Information on risk preferences is not public however, and it is not clear what part this is likely to play in any bargaining process. Pure economic theory might furnish us with plausible arguments based upon classical statistical theory and expected utility analysis for risk neutrality on the part of government (e.g. Arrow and Lind, 1970). But it is equally plausible in practice that individual bureaucrats or politicians responsible for policy formulation and implementation will be risk-averse.

A typical 'scenario' for a risk-averse bureaucrat in charge of negotiating selective aid projects might look something like this. The arguments in his utility function are wealth and 'reputation with his peers'. His risk-averseness is manifested in the choice of permanent pensionable employment and in his desire to protect his personal reputation. In our simple model in section II, the bureaucrat's reputation and promotion prospects, on which his future wealth depends, might be measured in terms of the minimization of the budget necessary to obtain the desired level of output and employment based on some *ex ante* and *ex post* comparison of outcomes. This would not suit the risk-averse bureaucrat at all. He obtains no direct financial advantages from minimization, and the high probability of mistakes in estimation would do his professional reputation no good.

What strategies does he then adopt? In the planning phase, he might endeavour to obtain control over the estimation procedures and decisions concerning the amount of subsidy. This might be followed up by an attempt to make the subsidies 'open-ended' or by some method which does not specify exactly in the contract what the precise subsidy will be. Another strategy might be to collude with subsidized firms to underestimate costs as a device to facilitate acceptance by sceptical officials of the Ministry of Finance, relying on the high 'exit costs' to government of discontinuing support, if the subsidy proves too low for the desired result. A common strategy is to seek a risk-sharing arrangement with other branches of government by canvassing support within government for commitment to the policy. Trading risk-sharing arrangements is a common bureaucratic strategy.

Risk-averse strategies extend to the process of monitoring results. Bureaucrats can make it difficult for outsiders, e.g. Parliamentary Committees and public critics, to find out what precisely has gone wrong. As is clear from the Scott/Cuthbert study, an immense amount of detective work and 'digging' was necessary before concrete results could be mustered. A common method of inhibiting enquiry may be to insist on secrecy because revelation of activities of the agent could benefit rival concerns. The important thing in the risk-averse strategy is to buy time. This facilitates preparation of *ex-post* justification of the 'disaster' by reference to intangible benefits (e.g. technological spin-offs) which have been agreed with other 'risk-sharers' as important. The more delay in full scrutiny, the less likelihood that politicians and the public will be interested in past failure and the more difficult it will be to trace who precisely was responsible.

Similarly, on the firm's side arguments for risk neutrality based upon the supposed efficiency of capital markets in spreading risks are unlikely to weigh heavily with managers whose reputations and jobs may be at stake. Bargaining will therefore proceed with both sides entertaining mere conjectures about the risk preferences of the other, and misleading information may play a part in establishing a final agreement. Whether, for example, a particular contract provides the firm with some minimum 'reservation level' of expected utility or a substantial rent in excess of this, will depend on attitudes to risk. The firm will always have an interest in persuading government negotiators that they are driving a hard bargain, and feigning a heightened degree of risk aversion could play a part in such a strategy.

E. Contract Complexity and the Passage of Time

The theoretical apparatus of section III was static and did not consider the passage of time. Because 'outcomes' are not necessarily observed at a given point in time but involve a set of events occurring continuously over time, a single contract would be impossibly complex to devise. 'Bounded rationality' in other words inevitably implies that the relationship between government and firm will not be explicitly defined in every detail in a state contingent contract. There will be 'implicit' elements and loose 'understandings' which will depend upon the generation of trust.

In some circumstances, where contracts with the same firm are continuously in operation over time, the 'discipline of continuous dealings' may be effective in establishing trust, and a strategy of 'take the money and run' may not be optimal for the firm. Where the relationship is sporadic or new, greater problems arise. Further, in some areas, the accumulation by the agent of transaction-specific know-how may make 'hold up' possible and the 'contract' may become subject to continual renegotiation over time. A government, for example, attempting to assist in the development of particular high-technology areas could become 'locked into' a firm whose 'know-how' cannot at sufficiently low cost be transferred to other potential suppliers.

V. CONCLUDING NOTE

In the course of writing this paper, one of the authors (Alan Peacock) became a member of the Arts Council of Great Britain and Chairman of the Scottish Arts Council and thus one of those responsible for the distribution of public monies to performing and creative arts organisations. By this appointment he became part of his own subject-matter! The reader will have to take it on trust that he found ample confirmation of the usefulness of the principal-agent analysis at least as a framework for the analysis of the outcomes of negotiating with a wide range of arts organisations. (For further discussion see Peacock, 1993, Chapter 7.) A general point worth making is that a fine line has to be drawn between engendering a degree of trust between the parties to the negotiation so that each realizes the constraints which bind the other, and preventing cordial relationships that may reduce the time costs of negotiation but which become too cosy. Direct subsidies confer particular advantages on incumbent companies who 'know the ropes', but those who supply them must always be thinking of the inventory of new ventures that offer a challenge to the accepted way of doing things and whose sponsors are seeking an opportunity for proving themselves. An apology is offered to the reader for this question-begging addendum to the above analysis, for it presupposes that direct subsidies not only can achieve their ends but are the most efficient way to promote the ends themselves. Nothing in the above analysis supports that proposition.

NOTES

1. As Vertiainen (1987) points out, the argument may need modification if the government is called upon to prevent a fall in output rather than to promote a rise. Assuming that the object is to retain the level of output at Q_d (see Figure 13.1), there is less room for overstating costs, as the cost structure is defined by the original point C, which presumably has to be made known to the government.
2. Vertiainen (1987) queries whether this information asymmetry would be possible to maintain in a democracy, and thus whether the 'unholy alliance' could be stable. We reply that even in democracies less obsessed with secrecy in government than the UK, secrecy might be 'justified' by the claim that the subsidized companies might be at a commercial disadvantage if their detailed affairs become public knowledge.

REFERENCES

Arrow, K. and Lind, R.C. (1970), 'Uncertainty and the Evaluation of Public Investment Decisions', *American Economic Review*, Vol. 60, June.

Burton, John (1983), *Picking Losers ...? The Political Economy of Industrial Policy*, Hobart Paper No. 99, London: Institute of Economic Affairs.

Laffont, J-J. (1987), 'Toward a Normative Theory of Incentive Contracts between Government and Private Firms', *Supplement to the Economic Journal*, Vol. 97.

National Audit Office Report by the Comptroller and Auditor General (1987), 'Department of Trade and Industry: Assistance to Industry under Section 8 of the Industrial Development Act 1982', HMSO, 24 April.

Peacock, Alan (1984), 'The Political Economy of Strukturpolitik', *Zeitschrift für die Gesamte Staatswissenschaft*, 140 (2).

Peacock, Alan (1993), *Paying the Piper: Culture, Music and Money*, Edinburgh: Edinburgh University Press.

Peacock, Alan, with Grant, Rob, Ricketts, Martin, Shaw, G.K. and Wagner, Elaine (1980), *Structural Economic Policies in West Germany and the United Kingdom*, London: Anglo-German Foundation.

Ricketts, Martin (1986), 'The Geometry of Principal and Agent: Yet Another Use for the Edgeworth Box', *Scottish Journal of Political Economy*, Vol. 33, No. 3, August.

Scott, Alex and Cuthbert, Margaret (1985), *Reviewing Industrial Aid Programmes: (I) The Invergordon Smelter Case*, Hume Paper No. 2, Edinburgh: The David Hume Institute.

Stiglitz, J.E. (1975), 'Incentives, Risk and Information: Note towards a Theory of Hierarchy', *Bell Journal of Economics*, Autumn.

Vertiainen, Henry J. (1987), 'Search for Cooperative Solutions', comments on this chapter presented at the 43rd Congress of the International Institute of Public Finance, Paris, 25–28 August.

Wiseman, Jack (1981), 'Is There a Logic of Industrial Subsidisation?', in Karl Haüser (ed.), *Subsidies, Taxes and Prices*, Paris: Editions Cujas.

14. Bargaining and the regulatory system (with Martin Ricketts)

(Although most of my academic writing has been devoted to the study of government expenditure and taxation, anyone serving in government or running a university would be bound to be aware of the all-pervasive nature of government regulation of the economy. In the early 1980s, whilst I was at the University of Buckingham, an attempt was made to combine the interests of lawyers and economists in the regulation field by a study of the economic impact of health and safety regulation comparing German and British experience. The study was sponsored by the Anglo-German Foundation and the results published in 1984 – see note 4. One outcome of the study is this attempt by Martin Ricketts and myself to explain how the regulatory system, as a bargaining process, is compatible with a model in which both regulators and firms strive to find benefits from investment in information and then bargain over the distribution of rewards. The circumstances which give rise to these phenomena suggest that 'capture theory', associated particularly with George Stigler, the Nobel Laureate, must envisage a very different set of circumstances than those that concern us. Nevertheless, both approaches criticise models of economic behaviour that represent entrepreneurs as 'constrained maximizers' reacting passively to regulatory regimes in which the law is always certain and administrators are endowed with perfect information.)

1. INTRODUCTION

The growth of selective intervention by government in the economy has required a sea change in the choice of analytical models derived from economics and used to explain what the effects of various forms of intervention might be. Traditionally models embodying some form of government measure designed to induce firms or individuals to conform to policy have assumed that these economic actors will adjust passively to the measure and in a predictable and hopefully testable way. Furthermore, applied welfare economics has to be based on the supposition that those having to apply the measure are in possession of full information on the economic circumstances of those subjected to regulation, are totally committed to the measure's application, and that the results of the measure are completely known.

If this were the case, then it would be difficult to explain many facets of the relations between those who execute policy and those who are the instruments of its fulfilment. Important examples are the widespread existence of negotiation over tax compliance by firms and individuals with tax authorities,[1] the surprise and disappointment experienced by governments at the failure of selective aid policies to industry to achieve expected results,[2] and the scepticism at the social benefits achievable through the regulation of public utilities.[3] Yet, the use of economic analysis in order to explore the dimensions of 'collective failure' resulting from attempts to eliminate 'market failure', perhaps because it savours of self-criticism, is relatively rare.

The authors of this chapter have been engaged with others in the study of government regulation designed to induce firms in West Germany and the UK to meet official standards of safety, health and pollution control.[4] This earlier work has stimulated them to explore further the analysis of what may be termed 'workable regulation' achieved through the process of 'negotiated compliance'.[5]

The problem with all regulatory systems is that of formulating rules which minimize the necessity for deriving information from the regulated about their production activities and whose effect on those activities is clearly discernible to the regulated. If the costs of acquiring this information are high, officials, inevitably subject to budget constraints, may have to temporize over the full and consistent application of the law. Likewise, the regulated, though aware of the costs incurred if they defy the law, such as shutdown in the extreme case, may be able to negotiate with officials about even the *definition* as well as the extent of compliance, particularly if they are the sole source of information that determines whether or not compliance will occur or has occurred. The stage is clearly set for bargaining between regulators and the regulated, for both have a mutual interest in reaching agreement.

In this contribution, we shall elaborate on the contents of the last paragraph by examining the following propositions:

1. Current modelling of the regulatory process concentrates on extreme cases which are not likely to be typical.
2. The appropriate model for examining regulatory activity in important areas such as safety, health and environmental damage would appear to be one which considers the regulated firms as being the 'agent' of the regulator rather than the 'exploited' or 'slave'.
3. Following a suggestion of Shavell[6] the managers of a firm may have a definite interest in establishing certain legal conventions. In particular, they will prefer a system based upon regulatory compliance by which liability to penalties only arises if regulations are contravened, rather than a system of strict liability

by which the occurrence of an event is sufficient to result in penalties being incurred.

4. The interests of bureaucrats and intermediaries will coincide with those of firm managers with respect to the legal framework.
5. For the preferred system to be workable, information about firm compliance must somehow be revealed and the problem of 'unobservability' or 'asymmetric information' overcome.
6. Many observed characteristics of the regulatory process in the UK are consistent with attempts on the part of the interested parties to solve this information problem.

II. THE STYLIZED FACTS

Before considering how to model the regulatory system, it is necessary to make some reference to the background of the 'information problem' and especially to the way regulations are drawn up and applied. The facts concerning health, safety, and environmental pollution regulation in the UK and West Germany are available[7] and a relevant summary of them would read as follows:

1. Statute law is often very vague in its assignment of responsibilities and duties to firms.[8] The 1974 Act in the UK covering health and safety at work is extremely complex and lays down five specific duties for employers covering provision of safe plant, provision of protective clothing and equipment to reduce the risks to health in connection with transport and handling of articles and substances, provision for training and supervision of employees in health and safety requirements, safety precautions to ensure access to and exit from plant, and commensurate welfare arrangements. But all these duties are to be carried out 'so far as is reasonably practicable'. Similarly in West Germany, both Federal and State Law concerning emission safeguards require that firms need a licence to operate for new plant or new forms of discharge of effluent, must take corrective action to abate existing pollution and be subject to close monitoring by the regulatory authorities. While the authorities have endeavoured to translate these instructions into technical standards, it is impossible to give precision in individual cases to 'best available technology' to be used in plant and, even it this were possible, authorities simply do not have the research facilities to check on whether the firm's assessment of that technology is 'reasonable'.
2. The more it seems possible to prescribe in detail the content of regulation, the more burdensome becomes the process of monitoring as well as the process of implementation. The British Factories Act of 1961, for example, lays down quite explicit provisions concerning cleanliness, overcrowding, temperature,

ventilation, lighting, draining of floors, sanitary conveniences, medical examinations and medical supervision. In the case of cleanliness it even specifies how often surfaces must be washed and painted and how. In West Germany, it has been estimated that there are over 100 bodies concerned with the formulation of 'technical rules' designed to be applied in factories.

3. The complexity of the regulatory detail combined with the idiosyncratic nature of each firm's production process must mean that regulators are forced to negotiate with firms over compliance with regulations. Whereas regulators have knowledge of detailed provisions in the regulations, they have to rely on the knowledge of firms of their production process in order to achieve compliance. This asymmetry in the information available to each party has important consequences which are considered in greater detail in Section IV below.
4. Negotiation is facilitated if technical agreement is obtained about the relation between regulatory measures and changes in the degree of safety, health and pollution levels. Firms have an incentive, and in some instances are obliged, to appoint officers technically qualified to monitor regulations and to apply them on lines negotiated with regulators. As in the case of negotiation over the tax laws, the sharing of technical expertise between regulatory bodies and regulators leads to 'gamekeepers turning poachers' and vice versa. (The last health and safety officer visiting our university expressed an interest in obtaining a post as a safety officer in a university institution!)
5. It becomes in the interests of regulators and regulated to avoid 'extreme action', notably recourse to prosecution and fines on one side, and legal action contesting regulatory decisions on the other. For example, in West Germany, of the 450,000 firms inspected under factory legislation in 1978, only 3 per cent were ordered to meet compliance conditions; UK experience in 1980 was similar.
6. Firms seek to make a virtue out of necessity by reducing the costs to them of obtaining technical information from regulation staff which may help them make design improvements which both aid compliance and also improve production efficiency. There is a parallel here with small firms who have induced the tax authorities in the UK concerned with the Value Added Tax to provide accounting expertise virtually free of charge in exchange for compliance with tax law.

In the sections which follow we attempt to explain these characteristics of the regulatory environment. We begin as indicated by general consideration of the difference between our approach and others, before turning to an examination of the use of the 'principal-agent' paradigm as the main framework of analysis.

III. A SIMPLE MODEL OF NEGOTIATION

Consider a profit-maximizing firm faced with costs of compliance with safety regulations. It has two weapons that encourage it to incur costs of bargaining with the regulatory authorities. The first is the fact that it is the sole source of information about the production conditions which will govern the detailed application of regulations, regulations which themselves are difficult to formulate precisely. The second is that the *gross* costs of compliance may be greater than the *net* costs firstly because the profit of the firm may be increased by the voluntary introduction of safety measures, and secondly, depending on market conditions, because the firm may be able to pass these costs forwards to consumers or backwards to factors of production.

Clearly, the optimal position for the firm would be one where compliance costs were zero, that is to say where the firm would incur the costs in any case, the resultant safety provisions voluntarily incurred met the regulatory requirements, and these requirements could be unequivocally specified without major costs of inspection and monitoring. For the regulator, the optimal position would be one where, within the budget constraint imposed on the regulatory bureau, the desired technical standards, assuming that these could be clearly specified, would be completely fulfilled. A further constraint would require that these standards did not put the firm out of business which, although not a defence in law in the UK, would not enhance the employment opportunities of regulators!

As we have argued, the fact that negotiation over regulation is intense and continuous indicates that neither firms nor regulators are likely to be able to achieve their optimal position.

A simplified example may explain how bargaining originates. Consider a profit maximizing firm which produces its optimal output *OB* as depicted in Figure 14.1. The firm is complying with whatever government regulations are currently in force in regard to safety measures. An innovation in accident prevention takes place and the regulatory authorities, following the doctrine in West Germany that innovation occasions the need to review 'best available technology', decides that this innovation requires more tightly drawn safety regulations whose implementation depends on information supplied by the firm. It is at least conceivable that the firm itself perceives that, under certain conditions, this innovation might improve its profit prospects, but this will depend on its effect on the shape and position of its total cost curve. We shall assume that this is so.

In Figure 14.1 the introduction of the innovation results in a shift in both the shape and position of the total cost curve of the firm as depicted by a change in the amount of fixed costs and the variable costs. For example, a new protective device for machinery requires some investment which adds to fixed costs. This might increase labour productivity by making it possible to increase the throughput of the. machinery, but as the numbers employed increase, the costs

Figure 14.1

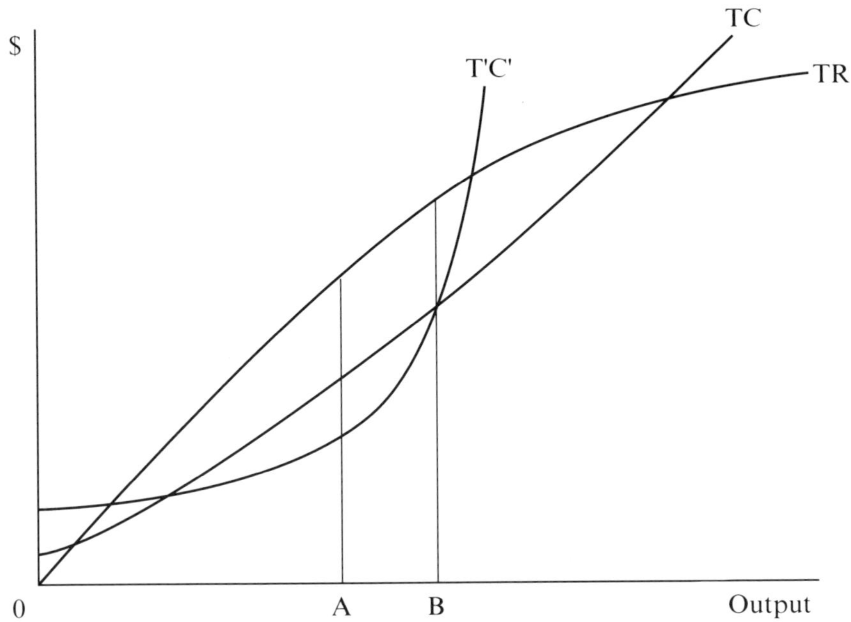

of monitoring the operation of the device may rise more steeply than would be the case if the accident prevention device were not introduced. It is assumed in this example that the firm has an incentive to introduce the device voluntarily because it is discovered that it will increase profit. This is depicted by the shift in the TC curve to T'C', with profits increasing and output falling from *OB* to *OA*.

However, it is not likely that the redefined optimal position for the firm will accord with the regulators' wishes. Let us assume that their conception of the required investment indicates that the expenditure of the firm is likely to be considered as too low. The firm knows this and can estimate the relationship between its profits and the cost of the investment, as in Figure 14.2, where Curve *AB* depicts the relationship between profit (π) and investment in the new safety device (*S*), with S^* as the optimal investment from the firm's point of view corresponding to output level *OA* in Figure 14.1. The further to the right of this position initially proposed by the regulatory authorities, the greater the incentive of the firm to exploit whatever bargaining power it may have acquired through its monopoly of information about its own activities and the limitation on the resources available to regulators for monitoring purposes.

Let us postulate that the initial level of investment proposed by the regulatory authorities is S' as shown in Figure 14.2, then if the firm passively accepts this proposal its profit level at output *OA* will be π', which is obviously less than π^*.

Figure 14.2

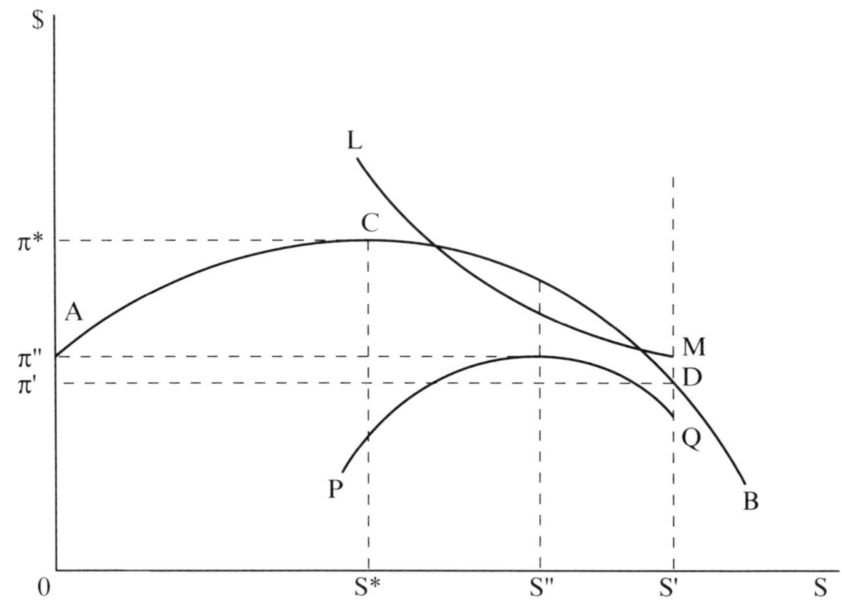

However, the firm is willing to incur bargaining costs provided that it can obtain an increase in profit above π' by inducing the regulatory authorities to reduce the investment in additional accident prevention to as near the level S^* as possible. It is likely that the more it attempts to reduce the costs of compliance, the more resistance it will encounter from the authorities and the greater the bargaining costs per unit of reduction in the additional accident prevention investment. The condition necessary to induce the firm to resist the authorities' initial proposal is that the bargaining cost curve (*LM*) drawn with respect to an 'origin' at *D* includes a portion which falls below the segment *CD* of the profit curve. Distance *MD* represents 'fixed' bargaining costs. If the curve took the form depicted in Figure 14.2 then the firm would expect to be able to settle for a level of additional accident prevention investment of S'' where the profit *additional* to π' would be maximized, as shown by the curve *PQ*. This yields a profit level of π'' ($> \pi'$, $< \pi^*$).

We shall explore the implications of 'negotiated compliance' in a somewhat different way shortly, allowing particularly for uncertainty, but our preliminary analysis does point towards important differences between our approach and that adopted in the US literature. In the first place, it shows that 'capture' theory envisages a very different set of circumstances than we have described. Capture theory implies that firms are willing to accept whatever regulation government has in mind to impose on firms, but in the expectation that the regulatory authority will supply gross benefits *in excess of the costs of regulation imposed on firms* which *firms* enjoy. These benefits consist of government measures which are designed to restrict entry into the regulated sector thus raising the likelihood that firms will make extra monopoly profits which exceed the extra costs derived from compliance with regulation. It is conceivable that one by-product of negotiated compliance might be a level of compliance costs which would restrict freedom of entry into regulated sectors, but we have no evidence to suggest that firms negotiating over compliance costs regard this as important. In any case, as Peltzman[9] has argued, it is not conceivable that those denied freedom of entry or harmed in other ways by 'capture' would remain inactive so that any regulatory system will be affected by the way the various groups successfully seek to attain their ends.

Further, our recognition of the fact that firms may benefit from the technical advice emanating from the regulatory process and may also be able to shift compliance costs to factors or to consumers calls into question attempts to measure the 'burden' on industry emanating both from the spending of regulatory agencies and the gross costs of compliance which are usually calculated by applying some 'multiplier' to regulatory spending.[10]

We question not so much the statistical methods used, though there are doubts about these, but the inferences drawn from them, at least as they apply to the major areas of regulation under scrutiny here.

IV. THE PRINCIPAL-AGENT PARADIGM

The approach of Section III is useful in drawing attention to the idea that firms do not passively accept regulatory edicts but invest resources in changing and adapting them. Nevertheless this way of looking at things is still somewhat 'deterministic'. Firms invest resources in bargaining or 'regulatory pressure' and this results in predictable 'returns' in the form of regulatory amendments conducive to a higher level of profitability. Profit-maximizing bargaining expenditures occur where marginal bargaining costs equal marginal benefits from bargaining.

There is, however, a 'co-operative' element to the relationship between regulator and regulated, at least in certain fields, which the above approach does not explain. In Sections IV and V, therefore, we indicate how some of the characteristics of the behaviour of firms and regulators may be seen as an attempt, beneficial to both parties, to overcome the information problem. We start with an extreme case in which the regulators have no means of verifying whether the firm's behaviour satisfies regulatory standards, although outcomes (e.g., the number and severity of accidents) are observable.

Consider a firm which is an expected utility maximizer and is risk-averse. The firm attempts to maximize:

$$E[U(\pi)] = pU(\pi_1) + (1-p)U(\pi_2) \tag{14.1}$$

where π_1 and π_2 are profits in states of the world 1 and 2, respectively and p, $(1-p)$ are the probabilities attached to these states. Plotting outcomes in the two states of the world along the axes we can then represent the firm's objective function in the usual way by tracing curves of constant expected utility. These curves will be downward-sloping and (in the case of risk aversion) convex to the origin.

Suppose that the two states of the world may be labelled 'accident does occur' and 'accident does not occur' respectively. A typical indifference curve might then be U_1^p in Figure 14.3. The superscript p indicates that the indifference curve relates to a situation in which the probability of an accident is p.

Totally differentiating expression (14.1) with respect to π_1 and π_2 and setting the result equal to zero yields an expression for the slope of an indifference curve. This will measure the firm's valuation of an extra pound of profits contingent upon a safe result, in terms of its willingness to sacrifice profits contingent upon an 'unsafe' result.

$$\frac{\partial \pi_1}{\partial \pi_2} = \frac{-(1-p)}{p} \cdot \frac{U'(\pi_2)}{U'(\pi_1)} \tag{14.2}$$

Where $\pi_1 = \pi_2$, the slope of the indifference curve will simply be $-(1-p)/p$. Thus, in Figure 14.3 the slope of all indifference curves with the same 'p' superscript will be the same along the 45° line labelled OA.

Now consider the problem of a regulator who wishes to improve the probability that the environment will be safe. Suppose that the safety of the environment is to some extent under the control of the firm. By investing a sum, S, the firm can increase the probability of a safe outcome from $(1-p)$ to $(1-p')$ where $p' < p$ (i.e., the firm can reduce the probability of an accident). Assume however, that because of extreme information asymmetries, the regulator is quite incapable of determining whether the firm has invested the sum S or not. In these circumstances, the firm is an agent of the regulator, and the problem becomes one of determining the nature of the 'contract' between them which will give the firm an incentive to invest the necessary resources and comply with the desires of the principal.

Since the actual *behaviour* of the firm is, by hypothesis, unobserved, any contract must depend merely on the outcomes which actually occur. In Figure 14.3 for example, we might imagine the firm at point a. At this point it is a matter of indifference to the firm whether or not an accident occurs. Profits are the

Figure 14.3

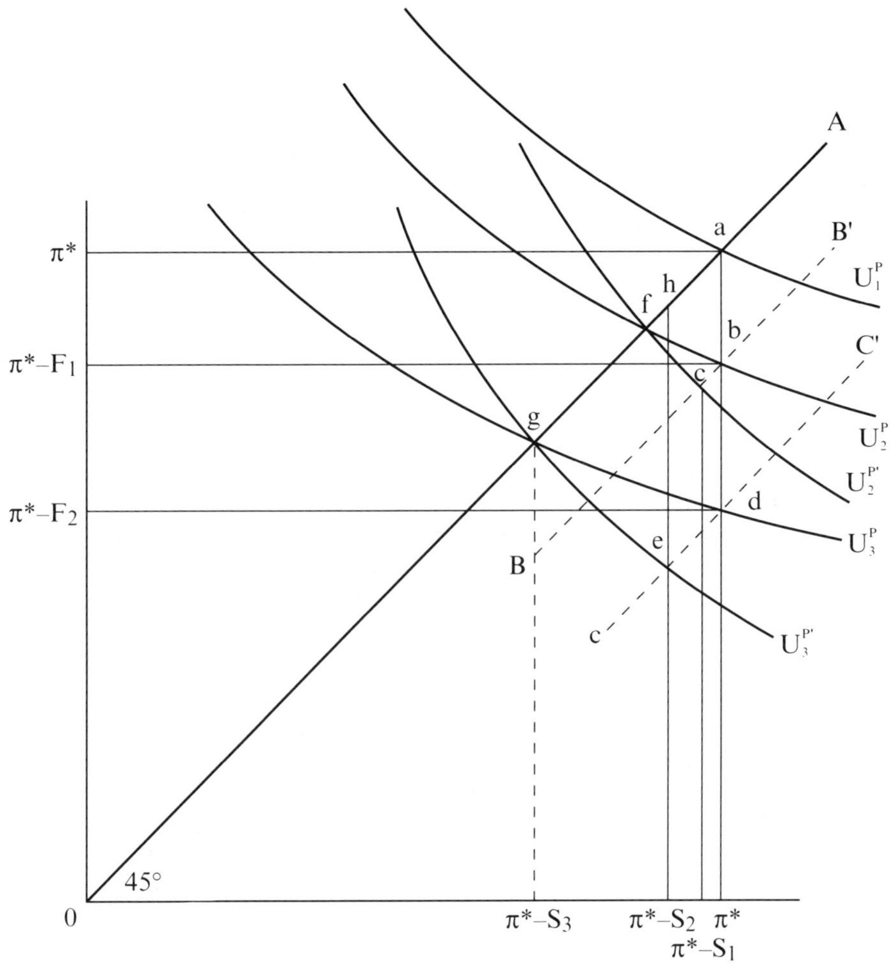

same (π^*) in either case. Now let the regulator propose the following 'contract'. 'If an accident does not occur you can keep your profits, but if an accident occurs you will be fined a sum, F_1.' The firm moves to point *b* in Figure 14.3. If the firm does nothing to change the probability of an accident occurring it will attain utility index $U_2^p < U_1^p$.

But we have argued that an investment in safety will change the ratio of state probabilities, How much would the firm be prepared to invest to achieve this result? If the probability of an accident were $p' < p$, the slope of the firm's indifference curves along *OA* would now be $-(1 - p')/p'$. The slope of the indifference curves with superscript p' will be greater than that of the curves with superscript p along OA. But at any particular point (say f) along OA, the expected utility to the firm will be the same irrespective of the ratio of state probabilities prevailing. Thus, both indifference curves through f have the same utility number attached (U_2).

Using Figure 14.3 and the above interpretation it is possible to see that in the presence of a fine F_1 the firm will have some incentive to invest resources in achieving a safer environment. In particular, the firm will be indifferent between point c on $U_2^{p'}$ and point b on U_2^{p}. Thus, the maximum the firm will be prepared to invest to change the probability of an accident from p to p' will be S_1. If this is insufficient to change the probabilities in the way described, the investment will not be undertaken. Supposing that the sum S_1 were insufficient and the regulator insisted that the improved safety must be forthcoming, a larger fine F_2 might be tried. The firm moves to point d in Figure 14.3 on indifference curve U_3^{p}. Indifference curve U_3^{p} cuts OA at g. Thus, the indifference curve with superscript p' through g will have the same utility index attached as U_3^{p}. This implies that the firm's utility at e in the 'safer' environment will be the same as utility at d in the 'unsafe' environment. Hence the firm will be prepared now to invest up to $S_2 > S_1$ in achieving the safety improvement.

Let S_2 be just sufficient to achieve the required improvement in safety. A fine of F_2 will be the minimum required to induce the firm to undertake the investment. (In fact, the firm will be just indifferent as between improving safety and not improving it.) Thus, a 'contract' between firm and regulator involving a fine F_2 will be established. In order to give the firm an incentive to undertake safety improvements, the firm must be given a stake in a safer environment. The fine of F_2 accomplishes this end.

It should be emphasized that the firm may itself have good reason to operate a reasonably safe environment for its workforce and we are not assuming that the firm will ignore safety entirely in the absence of the regulator. At point a, for example, the firm may already be investing resources in safety. Further investment, however, requires the regulator's intervention since it involves a greater than utility-maximizing concern for safety. We are, however, ruling out paternalistic motives for safety provision on the part of the firm.

V. THE VALUE OF INFORMATION

Consideration of point e in Figure 14.3 reveals that firms will have powerful reasons to try and change the regulatory environment. For given a level of safety investment, S_2, the firm is achieving a utility index of only U_3 when at a point such as 'h' it might achieve a utility index greater than U_2. At point 'h' the firm would undertake the safety investment, but would *not* have to pay a fine in the event of an accident.

Alternatively, from the regulator's point of view, it might be argued that point *g* would be desirable, since at *g* the firm is no worse off but the level of safety investment has increased yet further to S_3. Indeed, if regulators get no utility from fines and are interested only in safety investment, anywhere on the locus *gh* would be preferred by both firms and regulators.

The reason that such points are not achievable, however, is the information problem with which we started. Where the regulator cannot actually *observe* the firm's investment effort, any fine less than F_2 will give the firm an incentive to cheat on its promise to invest S_2. Suppose, for example, that the regulator withdrew all penalties and simply asked the firm to invest S_2. If the firm complied it would achieve point *h*. But if it cheats and does not invest, it achieves U_1^p at *a*.

Points on or near the locus *gh*, therefore, require 'observability' or at the very least considerable trust. Because of the benefits to be derived from achieving such points from the perspective of the firm, we might expect some ingenuity to be exercised in thinking of institutional devices which permit monitoring or observability or even trust where none existed before.

VI. INSURANCE CONTRACTS

In the interests of simplicity the role of insurance contracts has so far been ignored. The evidence suggests, however, that these contracts play an important part in the regulatory process. To facilitate the analysis and to develop further the approach of Sections III–V, consider a world in which the unobservability of safety-related activity was complete. We might imagine that a level of fines or penalties had been set at F_1 (Figure 14.4) and that at this level the firm is just willing to undertake S_1 of safety provision. An insurance company now approaches the firm with an offer to provide insurance coverage in case of the occurrence of an accident and hence a fine.[11] Clearly, the insurance company cannot observe the firm's safety activity any more satisfactorily than can the regulators and it will prudently assume that, with insurance coverage, the firm will abandon its safety expenditures. Thus, the terms suggested by the insurers will be based on the state probabilities which are expected to prevail in the absence of extra safety provisions. Assuming, however, that the insurance company offers actuarially 'fair' or only slightly 'unfair' terms on the basis of these probabilities, the firm will accept the insurance rather than undertake the investment S_1.

The situation is illustrated in Figure 14.4. At point *e* the firm is investing S_1 in safety projects and achieves utility index U_3^p. After the offer of insurance the

Figure 14.4

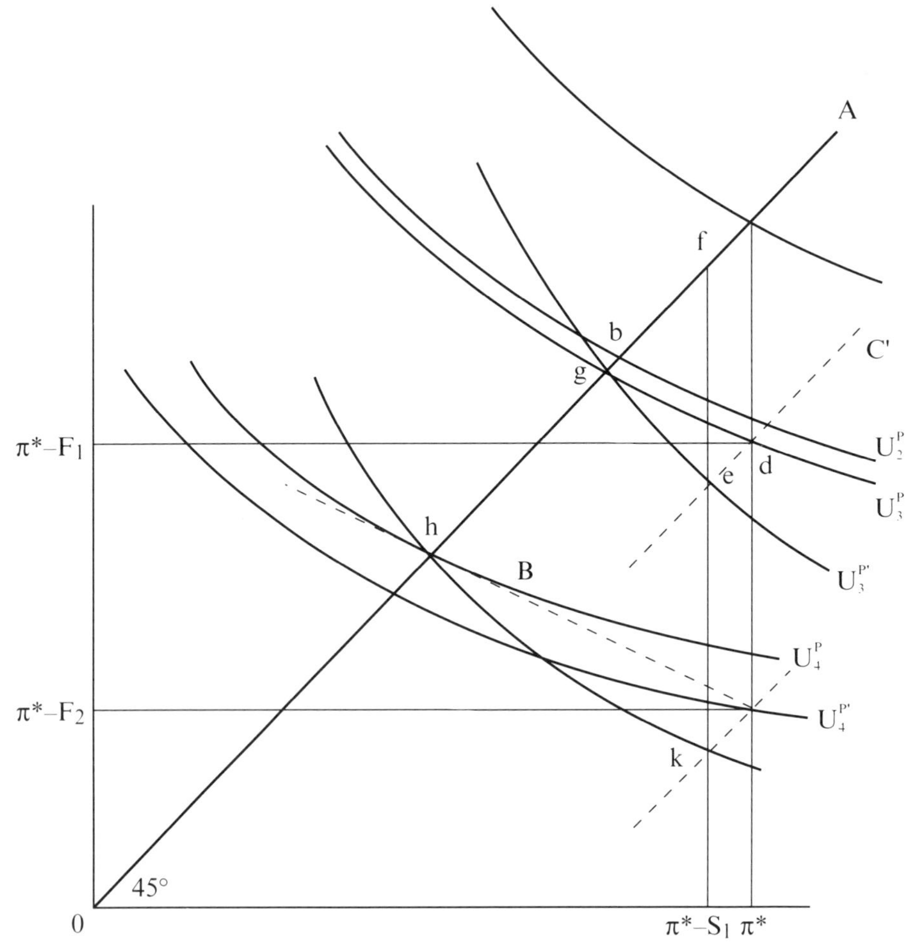

firm attains a point such as *b* on U_2^P. The firm operates at point *d* and then exchanges 'state contingent claims' with the insurance company so as to reach *b*. Clearly *b* is preferred to *d* providing that the 'top managers' are risk-averse.

This possibility that firms may buy insurance against the occurrence of accidents has an important implication. If regulators want to achieve a level of safety expenditures S_1, the fines and penalties they levy in the event of accidents will have to be even bigger. Suppose, for example, that they raise the fine to F_2 in Figure 14.4. At this level of penalty the firm is just indifferent between buying insurance and achieving point *h* on U_4^P, or investing the desired S_1 and achieving point *k* on $U_4^{p'}$. Investment in safety by the firm favourably affects the ratio of state probabilities, but it still leaves the outcome uncertain. The purchase of insurance does nothing to change the probability distribution of outcomes, but it completely relieves the firm of risk-bearing costs (at least from this source). Thus, the more risk-averse the managers, the more inclined they will be to purchase insurance, and the higher the fines will have to be to persuade them to forgo risk-sharing benefits in favour of investments which only improve the expected outcome.

Introducing the possibility of insurance into the analysis thus reinforces the conclusions of Sections IV and V. The prospect of overcoming the problems of 'unobservability' will appear even more attractive to the participants. Assuming once more that the level of fines or penalties does not enter the regulator's utility function and that these are regarded merely as policy instruments on their part, any points between *h* and *f* on *OA* will represent points of gain to both firms and regulators.

VII. INTERESTS AND INFORMATION ASYMMETRIES

Thus far in the analysis we have not considered the interests of the parties concerned with regulation in detail. The 'firm' was assumed in Sections IV and V to be an expected utility-maximizer, and 'regulators' were assumed to be interested merely in the level of safety achieved. This formulation skirted round a number of significant issues.

A. The Regulators

Even if regulators were primarily interested in improving safety, there would still remain the problem, within the principal-agent framework, that 'safety' is not observable. If a firm's investment, *S*, cannot be monitored, how are the regulators to know whether their level of fines is appropriate? Over time, it may be argued, the probability distribution of states of the world can be inferred from experience, and penalties adjusted accordingly (rather as it has been suggested that pollution taxes might be adjusted when knowledge of abatement techniques is scanty). The regulator would adjust the penalty over time and observe the effect on the probability of accidents until some politically 'acceptable' if not 'optimum' provision of safety is achieved.

Such a role is unlikely to appeal to the regulator, however. Accepting now the more modern view that bureaucrats will have interests in other factors than the general good of all, and that amongst these objectives will be budget size or size of establishment, a system based on sanctions and penalties will be much less favoured than a system based on continual monitoring and the negotiation of standards. Providing that the actual outcome (accident or non-accident) is cheap to observe and difficult for the firm to conceal, a system based on penalties requires far fewer administrative resources than a system based upon the implementation of regulatory standards. The former requires a fine-collecting service and a mechanism to adjudicate in cases of disputed outcomes. The latter requires resources to draw up regulations and monitor their actual implementation, an administratively far more demanding task. Regulators will therefore have an interest in constructing a system which revolves around the monitoring of standards and they will seek ways of making regulations enforceable and the behaviour of firms observable.

As we have argued in Section V, the regulator's interest in a system based upon observing and monitoring is not completely at odds with the 'public interest' view. Information, even if obtained by costly methods, may permit the achievement of greater safety provision at no utility cost to the firm. Thus, regulator-firm relations may not be accurately considered as a form of zero-sum game, with greater compliance a loss to the firm and an equal gain to the regulator. Rather, our observation of the regulatory process may be more akin to a co-operative game of *positive sum* in which regulator and regulated haggle over the distribution of the rewards and strive to make the result enforceable.

B. The Firms

In Sections IV and V we merely assumed a well-defined (and conventional) objective function for the firm. A firm is, however, a coalition of individuals and it is not clear that all individuals in this group would have identical objectives. It is convenient, therefore, to distinguish the top 'controlling' managers from other members of the firm, and argue that our function $U(\pi)$ applies to them. These managers then consider ways of overcoming the 'agency problem' which confronts them in the sphere of safety.

Any solution to this problem must do one of two things. Either it must remove the conflict of interest between principal and agent, or it must make the agent's (i.e., the firm's) behaviour observable. As long as the hypothesized objectives of managers and regulators remain unchanged a conflict of interest must continue. 'Observability', however, may not be such a lost cause. By appointing safety managers the firm is effectively introducing specialist monitors who have an interest in promoting safety. The variable S might now represent the budget of this particular manager's department, with $V'(S) > 0$, where V is the safety manager's utility function. Good relations between regulators and safety managers may then be seen as a mechanism for improving 'observability'. The same point may be highlighted by observing that at point e in Figure 14.3, the 'top managers' would be prepared to sacrifice up to $S_3 - S_2$ of resources in order to persuade regulators to join the firm, acquire any specialized information that was previously unavailable to them, and undertake the safety expenditure S_2 themselves. The benefit would be an end to the agency problem and an environment of monitored regulatory standards rather than high penalties in the event of accidents. From this perspective nothing could be more appropriate than that safety officers are ex-regulators.

Safety officers, however, are not current regulators, and it would perhaps be too extreme to assume that the interests of these groups always precisely coincide. Trust, reputation and goodwill are important to the establishment of contracts where information is asymmetrically distributed[12] and from this point of view as well, the use of ex-regulators as safety or environmental managers is significant.

Other gains to the top managers may occur from the appointment of safety managers. If regulatory intervention now takes the form of highly specific safety requirements, it is desirable from the top managers' point of view that these should reflect the special circumstances of the firm as far as possible. The appointment of specialists who have an interest in safety provision enables more trustworthy information to be communicated to regulators and a more cost-effective set of requirements to be enforced.

VIII. SUMMARY AND CONCLUSIONS

Observers of the regulatory process in the UK have drawn attention to the importance of negotiation and bargaining in the implementation of policy, the low incidence of prosecutions and heavy fines, and the problems faced by both regulators and regulated in the collection of relevant information. We have discussed the implications of these empirical observations for the theory of regulation. To this end we have focused primarily on the problem of monitoring, and have argued that much observed behaviour is compatible with a model in which both firms and regulators strive to achieve benefits from better information provision, and bargain over the distribution of the potential rewards.

NOTES

1. F. Forte and A.T. Peacock, 'Tax Planning, Tax Analysis and Tax Policy', in A.T. Peacock and F. Forte (eds), *The Political Economy of Taxation*, Basil Blackwell, Oxford, 1981.
2. J. Redwood, *Going for Broke: Gambling with Taxpayers' Money*, Basil Blackwell, Oxford, 1984.
3. G.J. Stigler, *The Citizen and the State: Essays on Regulation*, University of Chicago Press, 1975.

4. A.T. Peacock (ed.), *The Regulation Game: How British and West German Companies Bargain with Government*, Basil Blackwell, Oxford, 1984.
5. See especially C.G. Veljanovski, 'Regulatory Enforcement: An Economic Study of the British Factory Inspectorate', *Law and Policy Quarterly*, 5 (1983), 75.
6. S. Shavell, 'Risk Sharing and Incentives in the Principal and Agent Relationship', *Bell Journal of Economics and Management Science*, 10 (1979), 55.
7. Peacock, 1984 (see note 4).
8. For legal background see C.D. Drake and F.B. Wright, *Law of Health and Safety at Work*, Sweet and Maxwell, London, 1983.
9. S. Peltzman, 'Towards a More General Theory of Regulation', *The Journal of Law and Economics*, 19 (1976), 211.
10. M. Weidenbaum and R. De Fina, 'The Cost of Federal Regulation of Economic Activity', American Enterprise Institute, Reprint series, No. 88 (1978).
11. It is recognised that insurance against the legal consequences of a criminal act is not permitted. However, as we have set up the model, a firm pays a 'fine' if there is an accident and there is absolutely no implication that any criminal intent was involved. The firm *may* have undertaken all the requisite safety investment required of it, but by hypothesis no one can prove this or disprove it. Thus the 'fine' is simply an 'accident tax', and insurance a method by which risk-averse firms attempt to reduce the costs associated with its uncertain impact. Were insurance against such an accident tax illegal, however, the justification could be found in the following paragraphs of Section VI.
12. G.A. Akerlof, 'The Market for "Lemons": Quality Uncertainty and the Market Mechanism', *Quarterly Journal of Economics*, 84 (1970), 488–500.

15. Public X-inefficiency: informational and institutional constraints

(This chapter was custom-built for a conference on efficiency (or rather, inefficiency) in government organised by Horst Hanusch, the well-known German expert on public finance. I, like other conference-going economists, have sometimes tried to bargain my way towards a title more to my liking, but I am grateful to Horst for insisting that I not only provided an economic analysis of bureaucracy but also provided a framework for discussion of how bureaucracy could be controlled, which, after all, was one of the main themes of the conference. His firmness of purpose offered me the opportunity to systematize impressions gained from my three years in government to which I have already referred. I believe that this contribution adds something to the study of bureaucratic motivation and the difficulties encountered both in formulating a methodology of bureaucratic control and how to apply it . Since this chapter first appeared, the 'new' institutional economics has given further impetus to the study of bureaucracy as one example of the 'agency problem', which besets not only governments but all large enterprises. The UK government has led the way in offering private enterprises the opportunity to compete in the provision of public services and to an extent that I had not envisaged possible. I consider some of the issues raised by these developments elsewhere in this volume. So far as bureaucracy is concerned, I have moved back in time, and, as I expected, found most of my suppositions about bureaucratic behaviour embedded in the work of David Hume and Adam Smith! See Alan Peacock, Public Choice Analysis in Historical Perspective *(Mattioli Lectures), Cambridge University Press, 1992, Lecture 3.)*

I. INTRODUCTION

The subject allotted to me seems to indicate the following agenda:

(1) Present a model which indicates how X-inefficiency can arise in public bureaucracy;
(2) Outline the stages of investigation designed to determine its extent; and
(3) Consider how far there are built-in incentives to remove it.

In approaching this rather formidable subject my comparative advantage probably lies in having had three years' experience as a senior bureaucrat of a rather specialized kind, as Chief Economic Adviser to the Departments of Trade, Industry and Prices and Consumer Protection, UK Government, 1973–1976. I have also drawn on this experience, not only in order to try to throw light on the practical aspects of control of bureaucratic activities but also to suggest some modifications to the standard economic analysis of bureaucracy. I am aware that generalizing from one's own experience is suspect but even anecdotal evidence may be worth retailing if only because accounts of actual bureaucratic behaviour and its consequences are sometimes hard to find. As McFadden (1976) has pointed out, the assessment of bureaucratic performance should be a major area of application of 'process analysis' of the kind associated with Simon and others for there is a good prima facie case for supposing that the command and information structure may not only govern the constraints on bureaucratic action but also affect bureaucratic motivation as reflected in the objective function of bureau chiefs. The recourse to the study of bureaucratic performance by analysis of published information on the outcomes of bureaucratic decisions – the revealed preference approach – arises in part from the fact that bureaucracies use secrecy as a tool of the trade. Not only that, those who like myself have left the hallowed halls of Whitehall are frequently reminded that they have signed a document subscribing to the conditions laid down in an Official Secrets Act which make it wise to 'clear' anything subsequently written about one's period of service. Consequently, a process analysis is not considered a viable alternative or supplement to the analysis of implicit choice criteria employing econometric analysis.

However, subject to the traditional constraints on revealing trade secrets, perhaps at least a commentary on contemporary economics literature relevant to the main theme by someone who has been intensively engaged in the process of government may have more than a purely anthropological interest.

II. CONTEMPORARY MODELS OF BUREAUCRATIC BEHAVIOUR EMBODYING X-INEFFICIENCY

The originator of the term 'X-inefficiency' has recently redefined it as 'the excess of actual over minimum cost for a given output' (see Leibenstein, 1978). In identifying this phenomenon in public services, it is normally assumed that at a minimum the following circumstances will be encountered in public service organizations:

(1) A single decision-maker (bureau chief) who maximizes his utility;

(2) A utility function in which arguments can be clearly defined and the signs of the partial differentials of the arguments with respect to the utility of the decision-maker can be determined;
(3) A production function specifying a relation between inputs and output(s), with inputs and output(s) clearly definable and quantifiable;
(4) The opportunity for the bureau chief to indulge in discretionary action allowing him to choose non-cost-minimizing positions in the process of utility maximizing.

Orzechowski (1977) has provided a very useful simple model which predicts how X-inefficiency will arise. It entails modifying the Niskanen model by adding labour input as a preference variable alongside the output of the bureau, and by introducing a homogeneous production function with labour and capital as inputs. Two predictions follow from the working through of the model. The first is that labour and capital will be used in inefficient combinations compared with both the standard Niskanen model of bureaucratic behaviour and the competitive firm model in the standard textbook. X-inefficiency can easily be demonstrated to be a consequence of this prediction. Secondly, not only will the bureau operate at higher cost per unit, but it will have a larger labour/capital ratio than for the other institutional forms already mentioned. The empirical evidence reviewed by Orzechowski appears to offer considerable support for his conclusions.

I find this model to be a distinct improvement on those that represent bureaucratic behaviour as a form of frenetic activity designed to maximize either the absolute or relative (to the total public budget) size of the bureau. However, it fails to encapsulate two widely recognized features of bureaucratic leadership – caution and laziness. Remarks on this feature are not the monopoly of popular authors such as Dickens, Gogol and Trollope who lampooned bureaucrats as indolent wastrels. There are frequent references in the Classical economists and their followers to the 'delay, hesitancy and immobility' (to quote only Pigou (1952)) of those running government offices. It would be odd if economists, who have widely recognized leisure as an important argument in the individual welfare function, were not to at least consider why, in circumstances where discretionary behaviour is allowed, it is absent from the welfare function of the utility-maximizing bureaucrat It will be recalled that in an early article Hicks saw the discretionary behaviour open to monopolists as affording them the opportunity to 'maximize a quiet life'.

It might be argued that the taste for leisure of bureaucrats is captured in labour input as a preference variable, reflecting, perhaps, the greater opportunities for delegation of duties This has not been advanced as a reason for including the labour preference variable in the bureau chief's welfare function, for the usual argument rests on the importance of 'over-staffing' as an indicator of power and prestige or as a means of increasing the voting population with bureaucratic interest. In any case, the enlargement of staff, bringing with it the associated increase in managerial and administrative responsibilities would seem, if anything, to militate against maximizing a quiet life. Some other way must be found to incorporate leisure in the bureau chief's welfare function.

One possible reason for the neglect of leisure preference in the economic analysis of bureaucracy may arise from a major difference between US-type and European-type bureaucracies, namely the greater degree of job security of senior officials in the latter. Paradoxically, providing job security – but only for an elite who had undergone a rigorous selection process and been enjoined to maintain the highest standard of conduct and esprit de corps – was regarded as the reward for devotion to duty and the necessary defence against corruption. However, job security coupled with the normal expectations of promotion at least to some 'career' grade obviously allow more play for the long-term maximization of a utility function in which one of the arguments is a taste for leisure. Senior officials responsible for the overall control of bureaucracy seem well aware of the problem of the resolution of the opposing forces of devotion to the job and indolence which security engenders and, as I shall indicate, act accordingly.

With these reflections, I am emboldened to explore the properties of a modified model of bureaucratic behaviour, which might be awarded comparable status to those currently in vogue. My purpose is not to influence anyone's choice of models, but to try to indicate how far the problem of reducing X-inefficiency depends on that choice.

The Utility Function

The model developed below concerns a decision-maker (DM) at the 'policy execution level' of government who has security of tenure and who, though employed in a senior position, does not normally expect further promotion.[1] The decision-maker's utility function is specified as follows:

$$U = U\,[N, L, S], \quad (U_n, U_l, U_s > 0). \tag{15.1}$$

Thus our DM derives positive utility from the number of administrative grade officials (N) under his command, that is officials 'of his own kind' rather than simply every Tom, Dick and Harry. Those 'of his own kind' are officials who are potentially promotable to at least the DM's own level of operation. In other words, the normal assumption that the DM derives power and prestige from the numbers in his bureau needs to be modified to take account of the grade or status of those employed.

The next argument (L) represents what I have described elsewhere (Peacock, 1979) as 'on-the-job leisure'. It is easier to describe than to measure exactly. As a minimum constraint, bureaucracies lay down with some precision hours of work and leave conditions. For a DM, there is an 'option demand' on his time within (and sometimes outside of) business hours exercised by his superiors but, within working hours, this leaves considerable scope for leisure which may be rationalized as purposeful pursuit in the interests of the government. The experienced and skilful DM moves down the learning curve very quickly to the stage where he can delegate executive functions without losing overall control of the actions of subordinates upon which his credibility depends. Examples of 'on-the-job leisure' are attendance at official lunches, prestigious conferences in delectable locations (preferably in another country), receiving overseas delegations, visits as a VIP to concerns in receipt of government funds, and so on. Khrushchev had a splendid term to describe the more extreme devotees of on-the-job leisure. He called them 'busy loafers' (see Jacoby, 1973)![2]

The third argument (S) represents the 'surplus' over and above the wages and other emoluments payable to administrative grade staff. The higher the surplus, the easier the management of the bureau through the availability to the DM and his subordinates of the perquisites of office – renting better buildings, better office facilities and secretarial help. This argument is a variant of the familiar 'maximizing the budget of the bureau' though it does not carry the implication that this is done by maximizing bureau output.

The Constraints

It is obvious that if the 'mean sensual bureaucrat' can reasonably be depicted by the above utility function, then the negative externalities resulting from the DM's behaviour will produce a call for constraints from somewhere within the economy. For the moment, let us view the process of the development of constraints as a reaction to the strategic plan of the DM, who is constrained initially only on the input side by both 'objective' and 'subjective' factors. This has expositional advantages.

Let us assume that the DM is responsible for putting forward budget proposals and, following the conventional economic theory of bureaucracy, he is assumed to have a monopoly of supply of information concerning the relation between input and 'output' in his bureau and is a monopoly supplier of the service. The budget constraint may then be depicted as

$$B = \bar{\mathbf{w}} \cdot \bar{\mathbf{N}} + S \qquad (15.2)$$

where B is the expected budget, $\bar{\mathbf{w}}$ is a vector of fixed salary rates corresponding to each administrative class grade and $\bar{\mathbf{N}}$ a vector of employment according to grade. S is the surplus, as previously described. S could be envisaged as a 'mark-up' on the total wage bill, but is easier to manipulate if written as a constant. The important objective constraint, therefore, is the inability of the DM to fix salary rates, possibly because they are nationally negotiated between public service unions and some central government negotiating body. For simplicity, it will be assumed that all administrators are the same grade and receive the same annual salary:

$$B = \bar{\mathbf{w}} \cdot \mathbf{N} + S \tag{15.2a}$$

A second constraint is represented by the relation between the taste for 'on-the-job leisure' (L). It is assumed that

$$L = L(\mathbf{N}) \quad \text{with } L_{\mathbf{n}} < 0 \quad \text{and } L_{\mathbf{nn}} < 0 \tag{15.3}$$

An increase in administrative class numbers increases utility, but at the cost of L. More **N** means an increase in the time costs of supervision, giving of advice, assessment for promotion, etc. This is partly a subjective constraint reflecting the shape of the utility function and partly an objective one, time being limited.

The Model

Form the Lagrangian:

$$\mathbf{W} = U(\mathbf{N}, L, S) + \lambda_1 [L - L(\mathbf{N})] + \lambda_2 [B - \bar{\mathbf{w}}\mathbf{N} - S] \tag{15.4}$$

The first-order conditions are then:

$$\begin{aligned} U_{\mathbf{n}} - \lambda_1 L_{\mathbf{n}} - \lambda_2 \bar{\mathbf{w}} &= 0 \\ U_1 + \lambda_1 &= 0 \\ U_s + \lambda_2 &= 0 \end{aligned}$$

Simplify to:

$$U_{\mathbf{n}} + U_1 \cdot L_{\mathbf{n}} = U_s \cdot \bar{\mathbf{w}} \tag{15.5}$$

The conclusion of the model is that the DM maximizes utility when the marginal utility derived from increasing administrative manpower (**N**) is equated to the marginal utility derived from using the wages of marginal increases in **N** for 'surplus' (S) activities. It will be noted that, once **N** is determined, then the amount of on-the-job leisure (L) is determined. That this is a stable short-run equilibrium position may be demonstrated diagrammatically (Figure 15.1), always provided that the expectations of the DM are fulfilled.

The properties of the model will not be explored in full, though they will be partly investigated in examining methods of exposing X-inefficiency. Here, attention is concentrated on the different result obtained as compared with other models. Adopt the common assumption that output (Q) of the bureau is a function of variable cost, and the only variable cost is labour (L). For simplicity assume constant per unit costs of production. In the case of the Orzechowski model, the bias in favour of staff (for labour is a preference variable) produces the result that per unit costs are higher than minimum cost. However, once the cost of labour input is given, then the limitation on the demand for labour is determined solely by the maximum size of the budget. In the model I have presented, the increase in the utility of administration labour (N), as N increases,

Figure 15.1

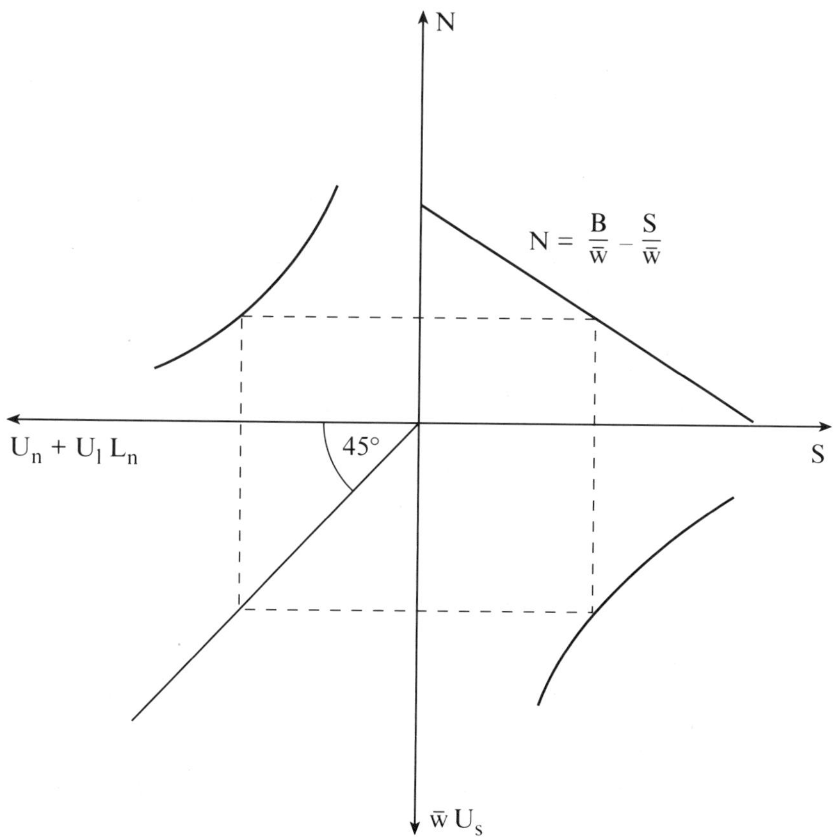

is offset by the decreasing utility from the reduction in on-the job leisure (L) resulting from the increase in N. This places an upper limit on the expansion of output which, given the first-order conditions in the utility function, make it possible for the output level to be below the output produced by the profit-maximizing firm producing under conditions of pure competition. In contrast, in both the Niskanen and Orzechowski models, the DM 'over-produces'.

III. IDENTIFYING X-INEFFICIENCY IN THE PUBLIC SECTOR

Assuming that there are built-in incentives that produce a demand for the elimination or control of X-inefficiency in the public sector, there is a presumption that an investigatory body of some sort must seek to identify its location and magnitude. Perhaps a useful parallel can be drawn here with anti-monopoly investigation designed to trace X-inefficiency, among other things, in the private sector.

The first stage in, say, some investigation into restrictive practices which could lead to the promotion of X-inefficiency in the private sector is to seek prima facie evidence of the existence and extent of monopoly power. This usually takes the form of identifying the 'market' and the division of market shares among suppliers in this market. The amount produced and sold by a particular supplier is only a preliminary piece of information to be obtained, for suppliers may be members of production cartels which lay down the division of output by supplier in formal or informal agreements.

Identifying the 'market' for bureaucratic services and the associated incidence of market power is clearly even more difficult than it is in the case of the familiar anti-monopoly investigations. In the latter, much depends on whether studies of market share throw much light on market power, given that the physical characteristics of a product are not necessarily a clear guide to the dimensions of the market. There are parallels in the public sector. Different bureaucratic agencies may have very different perceptions of their role in government, and outwardly give the impression of carrying out distinct and separate tasks, but in fact they may be offering services which are substitutes for one another. At the most general level, maximizing non-interference in domestic affairs by outside powers is the monopoly neither of the military and defence nor of the diplomatic arms of the bureaucracy. At a more mundane level, different economic agencies of government may be competitors in devising methods for protecting particular industries from foreign competition, depending on the policy instruments used, e.g. production subsidies or tariffs. In my experience, though the government in power, through the Cabinet, may have the final say, a good deal of time of senior bureaucrats is spent on regulating 'markets' in which they are potential competitors. This is not to say that each agency is anxious to negotiate for as large a market share as it can get, as would be predicted from more traditional models of bureaucracy. Once a policy strategy has been devised, agencies may resist being 'landed' with the more unfamiliar tasks or the ones which expose them to relatively greater risks of 'failure', as perceived by politicians and the public.[3]

The second stage in an anti-monopoly or restrictive practices 'probe' is to seek evidence that monopoly power operates against the public interest. I shall avoid obvious difficulties by stipulating that we all think it useful to investigate how far such power leads to a deviation from the competitive optimum, for, after all, it is on such deviations that the economic analysis of bureaucracy, following traditional welfare economics, has concentrated. Providing a check-list of indicators suggesting deviation is not difficult – look at barriers to entry, both technical and institutional, into the 'industry'; study the productivity in the industry; examine the history of innovations and the associated use or lack of use of patents; consider its lobbying activities with respect to government policy; scrutinize profit rates; and so on. Providing acceptable measures of these activities and how they are reflected in the industry's price and output policies is quite another matter.

Again there are parallels and contrasts to be drawn with any similar investigation of government bureaux. In reviewing methods used, the literature has concentrated, rightly so if our models of bureaucracy make sense, on identifying production functions, and on comparing public with private productive efficiency where it is possible to identify a similar product in each sector (for a most useful review of evidence, see Blankart, 1980). In contrast with private monopoly investigations where there may be strong incentives to seek agreement on questions of fact, if only because of the costs of answering them, any body investigating bureaucratic efficiency may face long arguments about such questions as the definition of output and the attribution of costs. The nature of the argument will vary depending on the 'degree of monopoly' vested in the bureau. Where, as is normally assumed in the standard economic models of bureaucracy, bureaux are sole suppliers of a non-marketed product, then the cost of extracting relevant information may be high. My own experience suggests, however, that bureaux are always on the lookout for potential competition from 'internal' (other bureaux) and 'external' (private operators) sources. With such a perception of their market position, even if the market can be partially regulated, they have an incentive to differentiate their product. Instead of withholding information, they respond to the pressures to reveal it, but are careful to 'massage' it for their own purposes. The use of information by bureaux has many facets but for the moment discussion is confined to its employment in negotiations with an investigatory body.

One of my duties in government was to attend a Top Management Group meeting which reviewed the activities of some twenty major divisions, each headed by an Under-Secretary, in some considerable detail. Four things struck me about their submissions and subsequent defence of them. Firstly, practically without exception they started by maintaining that there was little point in trying to define, far less measure, their 'output'. (Clearly, they had learnt just enough from their economics colleagues to be able to exploit public goods theory!) Secondly, if they were willing, if only for the sake of argument, to agree to the use of output indicators of some kind, they would insist that such indicators would not pick up the 'quality' of the product. A variant of this argument emphasized the difficulty of separating input and output. Thus what appeared to be 'on-the-job leisure', as I have termed it, was being confused with promotional efforts to improve acceptance of policies that the divisions were enjoined to execute. Thirdly, much was made of the argument that minimization of costs was constrained in so many ways by exogenous influences, e.g. collective bargaining agreements between employees and the government over pay and conditions over which the division had no control, though little attention was paid to the counter-argument that 'rival producers' might encounter similar problems. Finally, heads of divisions seemed to expect that final judgment of their activities depended as much on the skill and the elegance of presentation of their case as on the robustness of the arguments mustered in their own defence. Bureaucratic politics becomes frequently 'the art of the plausible'.

IV. THE CONSTRAINTS ON ELIMINATING X-INEFFICIENCY

The previous section offered some observations on the barriers encountered in identifying X-inefficiency. Identification is difficult enough but elimination runs up against a variety of obstacles. Following the analogy with elimination of X-inefficiency in the private sector, reducing average costs must be made 'worthwhile' to the producer and this will be made so by competitive pressure. The general problem of this approach is that, whereas strong lobbies may be built up within the economic system, e.g. through consumer organizations, against monopoly in the private sector, this is much less likely to happen in the public sector, once bureaucracy has become firmly entrenched.

The problem is best studied with a framework which displays the interdependencies between 'bargaining groups' within the economy rather than by confining attention to the legislator-bureaucrat confrontation suggested by the partial equilibrium approach in the conventional economic analysis of bureaucracy (see Fiorina and Noll, 1978a and 1978b, and Peacock, 1979). No single bargaining group, though aware of the cumulative effect of X-inefficiency on the growth in tax burdens, has an interest in curbing the growth of bureaucracy. As voters do not pay directly for government services and their contributions in the form of tax payments can therefore bear little relationship to the benefits which they derive from these services, they have a strong incentive to vote for politicians who will maximize their gains from government services and minimize their tax burdens. Likewise, firms, though not having votes, may be vitally affected by the way in which bureaucrats exercise their discretion in the award of contracts and subsidies, and may devote a considerable proportion of their time to maximizing their profits through the organization of lobbying activities as an alternative to profit-seeking in competitive markets for their goods and services. Under these pressures, legislators are forced to offer 'facilitation services' (to use Fiorina's and Noll's term) to consumers and firms, particularly those in their respective constituencies. Instead of becoming the enemies or critics of bureaucrats, they may therefore become their natural allies. By facilitating access to bureaucratic services and engendering support for popular programmes, particularly in the welfare field, they retain their political position more readily, given the existence of political competition between parties and politicians and the uncertainties attached to running for election on a 'cut spending' programme whose incidence may be less transparent and less attractive to voters.

Nothing in the previous paragraph is unfamiliar; nor does the argument necessarily point towards anything more than expansion of public goods production as distinct from the efficiency of provision. It is quite possible that legislators may even improve their image with the electorate by simultaneously supporting expansion of government and the tightening up of controls over efficiency in their provision. However, if we accept that the bureaucratic welfare function takes the form that I have assumed in section II above, then the chances of combining expansion of public services with the elimination of X-inefficiency seem remote. Moreover, if the 'Baumol effect' is at work, then public sector expansion implies a concomitant increase in labour input. A larger proportion of the working population acquire a vested interest in government employment and form an increasing proportion of voters. Bureau chiefs, at a minimum, must acquiesce in the lobbying activities of employees to promote improvements in their conditions of work, not solely as members of unions but also as voters capable of influencing the median voter position in respect of demands for public services and for their own employment.[4] Even if the process seems to be self-defeating, in the sense that voters as a whole must face a growth in the average tax burden, one cannot envisage that process coming to a smooth and gradual halt.

Notwithstanding the lack of incentives to promote efficiency in government services within the political process, Western governments have been sufficiently worried about the long-term consequences of government sector growth to build in to the expenditure control system procedures for making government departments cost-conscious. This task is frequently assigned to a 'watchdog' branch within the Ministry of Finance, which is placed in a strategic position both to persuade departments to mend their ways and, if they do not, to report and to recommend to those concerned, ultimately the Cabinet, that they should be made to do so. Not surprisingly, in view of the discussion in section III above, attempts to improve efficiency 'from within' encounter major difficulties (cf. Chapman, 1979; Heclo and Wildavsky, 1974; Meyes, 1979).

Once again, the analogy with anti-monopoly investigation may help us to understand how these difficulties arise. One of the problems of anti-monopoly investigation is seeking to establish which cases to pursue given scarce investigatory resources. In the UK the procedure has been to concentrate on a particular restrictive practice, e.g. fixing of the scales of charges by professional associations, identifying the 'species' known to support such a practice, and then to pick on one of the species to use as a test case. If the case goes against the defendant, a precedent may be set which could be sufficient to induce other members of the species to abandon the practice – or so it is hoped. Whether such a precedent will be set will depend on what is at stake for those who have been following the practice. Other members of the species will presumably conduct their own cost-benefit analyses, pitting the cost of fighting cases through the courts and of lobbying members of the legislature and bureaucracy against the likelihood of success in being able to continue the practice.

A government investigatory body, even one given full powers to detect X-inefficiency, is in a very different and more sensitive position vis-à-vis the investigated. In the private sector, the presumption is that the restrictive practices are themselves illegal and the problem is to establish their existence. It is normally assumed that if these practices are abandoned, then more competition will prevail, resulting in a diminution of allocative and X-inefficiency. In the public sector, however, it is reasonable to make the initial assumption that the budget of the bureau has legislative approval and that accounting and audit requirements are being complied with, i.e. the bureau works within the law. Inefficiency in a different sense may be revealed in faulty budgeting, but there is no necessary connection between errors in forecasting expenditures and X-inefficiency. Any rooting-out of X-inefficiency must depend firstly on some fundamental political change which would mean the 'death' of the bureau, either because its service is scrapped or because it is 'taken over' or absorbed in some other government organization in order to exercise control over the appointment of more efficient bureau heads. Such a change is not likely to be made solely as the result of any recommendations of an investigatory body. Secondly, removing X-inefficiency could be instituted through 'self-discipline' exercised by the bureau itself induced by its estimate of the influence of the findings of the investigatory body on those responsible for approving its budget. It follows that the 'domino effect' made possible by establishing that the law is being broken by one firm or professional body and could be being broken by others, as found in private investigation backed by the threat of prosecution, is unlikely to operate in the public sector. The most that an investigatory body in the public sector might be able to do to produce anything like a 'domino effect' is to be empowered to operate in a manner similar to tax authorities in a tax regime characterized by self-assessment. Self-discipline could be reinforced by the power of the investigators to decide without prior notice on whom they would pounce.

Accounts of investigations by 'watchdogs' hardly support the contention that self-discipline could be enforced in the way just described. If limited resources prevent investigation of bureaux simultaneously, some order of priority in investigations is implied. However, once this issue of orders of priority arises, the powers of the watchdog are likely to be called in question. The selection of 'suitable cases for treatment' may become a high-level political issue which it may not be possible to resolve except at Cabinet level. The final order of priority may be entirely uncorrelated with the expected prevalence of X-inefficiency, for Ministerial assent to an investigation will depend on what other policies are being traded at Cabinet level, on the bargaining skill of the Minister and the position he/she holds in the political hierarchy. It is assumed, of course, that Ministers derive a negative utility from investigations into the efficiency of their own bureaux, possibly because investigations will employ the resources of the bureau originally designated for more 'useful' purposes and possibly because of the effect of the announcement of such investigations on the Minister's party and public image.

These difficulties clearly increase the power of the bureau faced with investigation. It is true that anti-monopoly investigations of private concerns must require co-operation of the concerns themselves in the provision of information but this can be backed by legal powers which facilitate the revelation of their activities. The problem is writ much larger in the public sector, for the procedural hurdles improve the chances of the investigated bureau for resisting disclosure of information and for employing delaying tactics. Furthermore, insofar as the bureau does co-operate in the investigation and even accepts its conclusions, its consent may only be 'bought' at a price, such as a recommendation that a change in procedures to reduce X-inefficiency in one programme will be counterbalanced by the promise of support for the expansion of another.

Many of these problems are illustrated by the attempt in the UK to develop what became known as the PAR system (Programme Analysis Review) in 1970, supplementing the macroeconomic public expenditure survey committee (PESC). The Treasury were allotted the task of reviewing departmental programmes, broadly speaking with a view to 'selling' ideas originating in programme budgeting to government and bureaux alike. It was soon found that running a number of PARs simultaneously ran up against resource constraints – the skilled manpower was not available. The Treasury, already requiring departmental co-operation over other major matters of policy, was unwilling to institute a PAR solely on the grounds that it improved control at the centre and in any case needed to rely on departments to conduct a large part of any enquiry using its own resources. The individual departments had therefore to be convinced that there was something in it for them and were in a strong position to influence the form of the exercise and its time-scale. I was involved in one PAR exercise in which the interval between the first meeting with the Treasury at which terms of reference were considered and a second at which they were reconsidered was no less than one year! In the end the exercise was virtually abandoned. The overriding consideration throughout the exercise was the avoidance of any actions which might give offence, and this is entirely understandable in a bureaucracy in which a zealous investigator might find himself at some later stage in his career serving one of those who had been investigated. As one departmental Under-Secretary put it, 'Socrates was the first person to do a PAR. He did it on Athens, going around asking fundamental questions. Athens put him to death. That's why I don't want any more PARS' (Heclo and Wildavsky, 1974, p. 288).[5]

SUMMARY AND CONCLUSION

In this chapter I have attempted to develop a variant of the economic analysis of bureaucracy which can serve as a suitable framework of analysis for the procedures associated with attempts to remove X-inefficiency. In placing emphasis on what has been called the 'entrenched lethargy' (Chapman) of bureaucrats, the analysis embodies characteristic of such beings by the Classical economists and their descendants. It is believed that the additional dimension to the analysis directs attention towards a neglected feature of bureaucratic supply, namely regulation of the 'market' between bureaux. Both the identification of X-inefficiency and the prospects for its removal are analysed by a comparison between anti-monopoly investigation in the private as contrasted with the public sector.

An 'inside' view of bureaucracy which I have tried to give may promote a greater awareness of the magnitude of the problem of removing X-inefficiency. It does not engender any new proposals for its removal and, it must be admitted, it merely confirms what we already know – how difficult its removal can be!

NOTES

I gladly acknowledge my indebtedness to my colleague Martin Ricketts, particularly in respect of the formulation of the model in section II of this chapter.

1. In the UK his grade would correspond to that of an Under-Secretary.
2. This is to be compared with the acid description by a retired senior civil servant, Leslie Chapman, of his fellows:

> These are the men who are able to turn out a well-written memorandum or make well-phrased contribution to a discussion, both so shot through with provisions and hedged about with reservations that they can never be wrong. They are great people for committees and in this business they excel. Whenever anything new is proposed they see the possibility of complications and find it necessary to consult numbers of other people of their own kind. Their attitude to all things, especially to proposals for change and, most of all, to proposals for increasing efficiency, is one of mildly amused unconcern. Enthusiasm is vulgar. Certainty about anything is probably irresponsible. (Chapman, 1979)

3. For a discussion of bureaucrats and attitudes to risk, see the interesting article by Forte and di Pierro (1980).
4. For a full discussion of the growing literature on this subject, see Courant *et al.* (1979).
5. The urgent need to control government expenditure growth in the mid-1970s led to the introduction of the system of departmental 'cash limits'. This virtually killed off the PAR system and certainly no further exercises of this kind are at present contemplated.

REFERENCES

Blankart, C.B. (1980), 'Bureaucratic Problems in Public Choice: Why Do Public Goods Still Remain Public?', in: K.W. Roskamp (ed.), *Public Choice and Public Finance*, Proceedings of the 34th Congress of the International Institute of Public Finance 1978 in Hamburg, Paris: Editions Cujas, 155–67.

Chapman, L. (1979), *Your Disobedient Servant*, Harmondsworth, Middlesex: Penguin Books.

Courant, P.N., Gramlich, E.M. and Rubinfeld, D.L. (1979), 'Public Employee Market Power and the Level of Government Spending', *American Economic Review*, 69, 806–17.

Fiorina, M.F. and Noll, R.G. (1978a), 'Voters, Legislators and Bureaucracy: Institutional Design in the Public Sector', *American Economic Review*, 68 (Papers and Proceedings), 256–60.

Fiorina, M.F. and Noll, R.G. (1978b), 'Voters, Bureaucrats and Legislators', *Journal of Public Economics*, 9, 239–54.

Forte, F. and di Pierro, A. (1980), 'A Pure Model of Public Bureaucracy', *Public Finance*, 35 (no. 1, Festschrift: Paul Senf), 91–100.

Heclo, H. and Wildavsky, A. (1974), *The Private Government of Public Money*, London: Macmillan.

Jacoby, H. (1973), *The Bureaucratization of the World*, Berkeley, Los Angeles: University of California Press.

Leibenstein, H. (1978), 'On the Basic Proposition of X-Inefficiency Theory', *American Economic Review*, 68 (Papers and Proceedings), 328–32.

McFadden, D. (1976), 'The Revealed Preferences of a Government Bureaucracy: Empirical Evidence', *Bell Journal of Economics*, 7, 55–72.

Meyes, T.A.J. (1979), 'Some Experience with the Control of the Growth of Public Expenditure in the Netherlands', IEA Conference on The Grants Economy and Collective Consumption, Cambridge (unpublished).

Orzechowski, W. (1977), 'Economic Models of Bureaucracy: Survey Extensions and Evidence', in T.E. Borcherding (ed.), *Budgets and Bureaucrats*, Durham, N.C.: Duke University Press, pp. 229–59.

Peacock, A.T. (1979), *The Economic Analysis of Government and Related Themes*, Oxford: Martin Robertson.

Pigou, A.C. (1952), *Economics of Welfare*, 4th ed., London: Macmillan.

16. Government debt and growth in public spending

(with Ilde Rizzo)

(I have written several articles, alone or in collaboration, on the growth of public spending which followed on from my joint work with Jack Wiseman on The Growth of Public Expenditure in the United Kingdom *(National Bureau of Economic Research, 1961). None of these publications have specifically considered the proposition that the growth in public debt could be a determinant of the growth in public spending, a proposition considered as long ago as 1903 by the Italian fiscal writer Amilcare Puviani. Modern investigation of the government debt/spending relationship is associated with the public choice approach to public finance, notably in the work of its doyen, James Buchanan, who has done much to establish the importance of the Italian contribution to fiscal theory.*

Two circumstances account for the writing of this chapter. I was forced to give further consideration to public debt problems during the deliberations of the Fowler Committee (see Chapter 22 below) in which calculations were made of the 'unfunded' obligations arising from the UK state pensions system. As chance would have it, one of my colleagues at Buckingham, Ilde Rizzo, was writing a thesis on public debt problems using a public choice approach, now available in her very well received book, The Hidden Debt *(Kluwer, 1990). The results of our discussions led to this review of the thesis that there is a 'debt illusion' which conditions the growth in public spending, methods of testing the thesis itself, and how far unfunded obligations add a further dimension to the hypothesis which places more emphasis on the growth of future as distinct from present government spending. The relevance of this chapter to the theme of this volume is, obviously, worries about the lack of transparency in the system of public finance which may encourage governments to take advantage of taxpayer/voter ignorance of the full implications of the funding of government debt. I have considered this matter further in Peacock, 1986.)*

I. INTRODUCTION

Throughout many generations, economic pundits have argued that governments have a unique opportunity for behaving 'irresponsibly', usually in the sense of being able to inflate their budgets, through their power to issue debt. At the same time, whether their motives will match their opportunities, so that this power will be exercised, will clearly depend on the advantages to be gained by doing so. It therefore comes as no surprise that the public choice approach to the understanding of the operation of the public sector has paid particular attention to the question as to whether the growth in public spending is a positive function of the public debt / public revenue ratio. This is because public choice theory has concentrated on a close examination of the welfare functions of the actors on the political scene – voters, politicians and bureaucrats – whose actions determine the growth and form of the public sector (for a useful survey, see Frey, 1983).

This article re-states the hypothesis put forward by Buchanan and Wagner (1977) that debt is a major cause of public expenditure growth though in a wider context than in the original formulation (Section II). It then evaluates recent attempts to test their hypothesis by Niskanen (1978) and Shibata and Kimura (1986) (Section III). We then endeavour to show that the approach to this important question of the 'debt-propelled public sector' is radically altered if we adopt a wider concept of public debt.

II. FISCAL ILLUSION AND DEBT NON-NEUTRALITY

Before examining the Buchanan-Wagner (B-W) thesis, it is important to realize that much attention has been devoted in recent economic analysis to the proposition that the issue of debt has similar, possibly identical, effects to the raising of tax revenue. If this so-called 'debt-neutrality thesis' were accepted, it would clearly rule out of consideration any thesis based on the existence of fiscal illusion, which is the basis of the 'debt-propelled public sector' argument. It is therefore appropriate to consider the debt-neutrality hypothesis in advance of discussion of the B-W thesis.

The hypothesis is basically very simple and is attributed to Ricardo, though Ricardo himself hedged his own propositions about with various important reservations (see Ricardo (Sraffa edition), 1951). When a government issues debt finance instead of tax finance, individuals must perceive that additional future taxes will have to be raised in order to pay the debt interest. The future taxes discounted at the debt interest rate have an equal present value with taxes which might have been used to finance current expenditure so that the timing of tax liabilities has a neutral effect on the wealth of the taxpayer (for a modern exposition, see Barro, 1974).

Although the theory of debt neutrality is in keeping with the general emphasis placed in public choice theory on the key role played by the perceptions of the individual taxpayer as a consumer of public policies, it is precisely from proponents of public choice theory that major criticism of the debt-neutrality thesis has emanated. Thus some writers have emphasized that neutrality rests on perfect foresight and complete information which no taxpayer can reasonably possess and, even if he could forecast accurately the timing of debt interest changes resulting from debt issue now in place of taxes, his wealth position might be altered if the tax system embodied distributional elements (see Carmichael, 1982). The argument cannot be easily resolved, but clearly resolution will depend upon empirical investigation. Much of this investigation, however, is concerned with the effect of the debt/tax mix on aggregate demand (see, for example, Feldstein, 1982), whereas our interest lies in the effect of the debt/tax mix on public spending. It is nevertheless interesting to note that while the empirical evidence for non-neutrality may not be conclusive, the hypothesis of debt-neutrality is called very much into question and that, therefore, investigating the public choice dimension of the debt neutrality debate may provide a fruitful line of enquiry.

The public choice argument for debt non-neutrality emanates from the concept of fiscal illusion, and the effect which illusion will have on the way that the taxpayer perceives his economic position. In the recent literature of public choice, fiscal illusion is considered to depend mainly upon the cost of obtaining accurate information on the individual fiscal burden and it is claimed that these costs are likely to vary according to the different kinds of public revenue and the structure of the revenue system. Thus the institutional manner in which citizens are made to pay for government services can affect taxpayers' perceptions of the price of these services and this in turn will affect the demand for them. Therefore, a common explanation for the differential growth of public spending follows the line of argument that the differential depends on the degree of elasticity of the tax structure (see Craig and Heins, 1980). In other words, there is less resistance to spending when yields of tax can increase without alteration in rates of tax. Another line of argument stresses that information costs vary with the complexity of the tax structure. Individuals perceive the costs of government services to be lower under a system relying on many tax sources than under a system depending heavily on a single source of revenue (cf., for example, Pommerehne and Schneider (1978), who state and test this hypothesis). A natural extension of the fiscal illusion approach beyond tax revenue must be the debt/tax mix. Hence the B-W hypothesis which states that the replacement of current tax financing by government borrowing has the effect of reducing the perceived price of government goods and services because taxpayers do not fully anticipate the future tax liability implied by borrowing. Accordingly, taxpayers underestimate the 'price' of publicly-provided goods and the demand for them is therefore increased.

While this version of the fiscal illusion argument has the subtlety associated with the public choice theorists, there does not seem to be any a *priori* reason why debt-propelled public spending should be a permanent phenomenon with voters consistently misperceiving both the total and marginal costs of taxes imposed on them (cf., for example, Gandenberger, 1986). Yet this permanent state of illusion is important if the level of public spending, far less its growth, is to be significantly affected. Nevertheless, at this stage of the argument, we shall stifle any doubts about the B-W thesis and consider some of the attempts made at empirical investigation of debt illusion.

III. EMPIRICAL INVESTIGATIONS OF THE DEBT-ILLUSION HYPOTHESIS

Niskanen (1978)[1] produces empirical support for the B-W thesis in the following manner:

(a) A demand function for government services is specified in which total real federal expenditures are expressed as a function of real national product per adult (which picks up 'income effects'), the real annual hourly earnings in the private sector (which picks up 'cost effects' on federal spending), the total US population over 21 (which picks up 'scale effects'), and, of most importance to this analysis, the ratio of total federal tax revenues (R) over total federal expenditures (X) (which picks up the 'price effect'). Allowance is made for 'autonomous' demand factors, such as the impact on spending of the Korean and Vietnam wars.

(b) Using ordinary least squares to estimate the associated 'test equation', the perceived tax-price elasticity, using R/X as the price variable, is calculated at –0.6, a figure which is very little altered if first differences are used, that is to say the relation between the change in federal spending and the change in R/X makes little difference to the elasticity calculation.

Niskanen concludes: 'Federal deficits, thus, significantly increase total (real) federal spending. And the increasing proportionate deficits during the last decade have significantly increased the rate of growth of real federal spending.'

Niskanen's methodology can be questioned on two grounds. Our own objections to his approach have their origins in the previous discussion of fiscal illusion. The fact that a negatively elastic demand is identified does not necessarily imply that the variations in the dependent variables (total real federal expenditures) which are not explained by the tax-price are to be explained solely by the debt component. As pointed out in Section II above, many sources of fiscal illusion exist – the degree of complexity of the tax system, the degree of elasticity and the composition of the tax system – and any variation in the value of these variables will affect the explanatory power of the estimated equation, without necessarily including the debt component as an independent variable. This points towards a major weakness of the Niskanen test. Instead of establishing a direct relationship between public spending and public deficits, he estimates an equation where it is only indirectly expressed, i.e., through the *tax*-expenditure link, but he does not explore other possible factors, other than the debt component, affecting the equation itself. Our objection does not weaken the B-W thesis, but does cast doubt on the test performed and also the difficulties which must be encountered if their thesis can be satisfactorily tested.

Whereas our objection is to the logic of the Niskanen method of testing, Shibata and Kimura (1986) claim that the econometric method used is inappropriate. We cannot do justice to their useful discussion of the finer points of econometric testing, but their approach is clear enough. The ordinary least squares test employed is consistent with the contrary conclusion, viz. the rapid increase in US federal spending has contributed to high federal deficits. To attempt to find a causal and not simply a correlative relation between debt and public spending, they understandably employ an econometric method which recognizes the lagged relationship between cause (the change in the debt/revenue ratio) and the effect (increased public spending). Using time series methods they found that the causal link is not established in either the US or Japan. They proposed an alternative hypothesis, namely that a revenue increase and spending increase occur simultaneously, implying that an automatic revenue increase resulting from economic growth and inflation under a progressive tax structure will be the main factor governing public expenditure growth. The alternative hypothesis is consistent with Japanese but not with American data.

The first point to notice is that the alternative hypothesis put forward by Shibata and Kimura specifically rejects a public choice approach which assumes that voters' perceptions are a major influence on actual public spending. Effective budgetary choices are those of bureaucrats who can exploit automatic increases in revenue resulting from economic growth and inflation and who fix incremental revenue and expenditure changes simultaneously. However, the thesis that a major source of public expenditure growth is the automatic increase in taxes is also compatible with one of the fiscal illusion hypotheses, viz. that taxpayers are not aware of their potential loss of disposable income through the increase in taxation, provided, one might add, that their real disposable income continues to grow. Nor does it exclude the possibility that, simultaneously with an increase in tax yields and public expenditure, bureaucrats exploit fiscal illusion by other means such as the reduction in the perceived tax-price resulting from a reduction in the revenue/debt ratio. Yet

Shibata and Kimura have nothing to say about the effect of government expenditure growth on the *composition* of government revenue.

The second point to be made about the Shibata/Kimura analysis relates to their position about 'two-way' causality. While accepting that the B-W hypothesis should be tested by the use of a time series analysis, the fact remains that whereas the B-W hypothesis offers a specific reason why an increase in debt relative to other revenue will cause an increase in spending (through the fiscal illusion effect), the causal relation between an increase in spending and increase in the debt/revenue ratio makes no sense as a testable hypothesis unless an explanation is offered why the government would want to alter the debt/revenue mix simply because government spending shows an increasing trend.

We are bound to conclude – and that should come as no surprise – that the evidence for the debt illusion hypothesis is far from conclusive. On the one hand, Niskanen does not actually test the B-W thesis directly and his results do not provide empirical support. On the other hand, the rejection of the B-W thesis by Shibata and Kimura is itself not convincing. We appreciate that testing runs into difficulties of specification which are bound to be difficult to overcome[2] but even if they could be, there remains the fact, which Niskanen recognises, that public deficits are characteristically a small proportion of public spending and, consequently, any impact that a deficit may have on the level, if not the growth, of public spending cannot be large. This does not lead us either to reject the debt illusion hypothesis or to argue that the hypothesis, if true, could only point towards a minor influence on public spending. The reasons which lead us to reach this conclusion must now be explained.

IV. UNFUNDED OBLIGATIONS AND DEBT ILLUSION

There is another approach to the examination of the role of public debt as a causal factor in public expenditure growth which requires us to consider the part played by unfunded obligations of government. The most striking example of such obligations is to be found in future pension payments in state retirement schemes. The similarities and differences between funded and unfunded obligations have been explored in a separate paper by one of the authors (see Peacock, 1986), and certainly there are several difficulties encountered in trying to calculate the present value of such unfunded liabilities as are incurred through, say, a Pay As You Go pensions system. In this context there are two things to be said. The first is that there is considerable professional support for the inclusion of unfunded obligations or implicit liabilities of government in the public sector balance sheet (see, for example, Hills, 1984, and Buiter and Tobin, 1979) mainly because it is argued that such obligations are perceived to be accumulated assets by contributors to state pensions and therefore affect their economic behaviour in various ways, notably through their savings decisions. The second is that those who have attempted to make balance sheet estimates of such obligations have come up with staggering totals. Thus Boskin (1984) estimated that the deficit derived from unfunded pension obligations in real (1980) discounted dollars was twice the US federal debt, as conventionally measured, and likewise Hills (1984) for the UK estimates a figure which is three times the British national debt.

The adoption of a wider definition of public debt, and therefore the acceptance of the fact that its magnitude can be greatly increased, enhances interest in the B-W argument and more particularly that part of it which relies on government exploitation of fiscal illusion but, as we shall see, it offers also a different perspective on the issue of empirical testing. It is worth recalling that Puviani (1903), whose name is usually associated with the theory of tax illusion, suggested that illusion can also be exploited through the issue of public debt, for the 'visible' amount of public debt can be disguised by the complexity in its structure with different maturities, different types of securities and different yields. The addition of unfunded obligations widens the range of opportunity for governments to exploit debt illusion.

It has been argued in a previous paper (Peacock, 1986) that it may not be necessary for the government to rely on the techniques of the illusionist in order to exploit the technique of issuing unfunded obligations as a way of increasing future public spending. Individuals who are members of a compulsory state social security system may readily accept their obligations to pay contributions currently in the expectation that future generations of taxpayers (who have no current voting power) will 'pay for' their pensions and will support governments who promise 'jam tomorrow'. However, an important element of illusion may remain if, as seems likely, the taxpayer/contributor overestimates the 'rate of return' from his 'investment' in social security. Overestimation may arise from the 'illusion' that future generations will in fact be willing to bear the redistributory impact of a system of pension provision which makes them responsible for meeting obligations to which they were not a party.

The discussion of the concept of unfunded obligations seems to support the hypothesis that the growth of public spending in the long term can be markedly influenced by 'debt-propulsion'. It is to be noted, however, that the possibility of increasing unfunded obligations reduces the perceived price not of present but of *future* public expenditure.

We accept that there are other dimensions of this theory of debt illusion which would need to be explored before it could be regarded as entirely robust. For example, the extent to which present generation voters will seek to 'exploit' future generations must depend on how far voter utility functions embody arguments relating to the satisfaction that they may derive from bequests to their heirs. However, our present concern is with the problem of measurement and if it is reasonable to claim that the definition of public debt should embrace unfunded obligations, any attempt to test the hypothesis that the growth in public expenditure is a function of debt illusion cannot be carried out by standard techniques. The value of the dependent variable is recorded in estimates of future trends instead of in *ex post* calculations and therefore, *ex definitione,* neither the techniques used by Niskanen nor those used by Shibata and Kimura would be appropriate.

NOTES

1. Niskanen's model has been adopted by Provopoulos (1982) to test for the Greek case.
2. Testing Buchanan and Wagner's thesis encounters several problems of simultaneity and identification. The most straightforward way of representing the independent variable is the rate of change in public borrowing as share of GDP, or in per capita terms. However, this gives simultaneity problems: an increase in federal spending might be interpreted as the cause of an increase in the level of borrowing rather than the effect. These problems would be reduced by expressing borrowing as share of total revenue; such an indicator seems preferable to the Niskanen procedure because it is directly representative of the aggregate in which we are interested, whereas its inverse, i.e., the share of taxes as share of total revenue (or total spending), stresses only the negative effect of the tax-price and refers to debt only as one of several sources of revenue. Public borrowing, as a share of total revenue, might be considered as a suitable exogenous variable. Analogously, another indicator might be found by relating public borrowing only to the tax component of total revenue, in order to stress substitution between them. Moreover, such an indicator would allow for a more precise measure of the relative size of borrowing increases with respect to 'visible' taxation, given that the denominator would be net of such an increase. This indicator may be considered as a rudimentary way of expressing the rate of substitution existing for any given level of expenditure at any period of time. Changes in such a rate may be considered to be the result of political strategies aimed at gaining political support for increasing expenditure at the lowest political cost, where such cost is a function, for instance, of the degree of visibility of different sources of revenue. The argument for a two-way causality problem seems to be weak in this case. Indeed, the opponents of the fiscal illusion hypothesis might claim that increases in expenditure are determined by factors other than public deficits and that, as a consequence of these increases, government has to raise revenue, shifting from taxation towards debt only because the latter has less impact on the taxpayers' economic behaviour, such as the incentive to work and to save. Such an argument would simply recognise that tax liability relative to debt is differently perceived than other tax liabilities and this would provide a case against the debt-neutrality hypothesis.

REFERENCES

Barro, R.J. (1974), 'Are Government Bonds Net Wealth?', *Journal of Political Economy*, Vol. 82, No. 6.

Boskin, M.J. (1984), 'Federal Government Deficits: Some Myths and Realities', *American Economic Review*, Papers and Proceedings, 296–303.

Buchanan, J. and Wagner, R. (1977), *Democracy in Deficit: The Political Legacy of Lord Keynes*, London: Academic Press.

Buiter, W. and Tobin, J. (1979), 'Debt Neutrality: A Brief Review of Doctrine and Evidence', in G. von Furstenberg (ed.), *Social Security versus Private Saving*, Cambridge, Mass.: Bellinger.

Carmichael, J. (1982), 'On Barro's Theorem of Debt Neutrality: The Irrelevance of Net Wealth', *The American Economic Review*, Vol. 72.

Craig, E.D. and Heins, A.J. (1980), 'The Effects of Tax Elasticity on Government Spending', *Public Choice*, Vol. 35.

Feldstein, M. (1982), 'Government Deficits and Aggregate Demand', *Journal of Monetary Economics*, Vol. 9.

Frey, B. (1983), *Democratic Economic Policy: A Theoretical Introduction*, Oxford: Martin Robertson.

Gandenberger, O. (1986), 'On Government Borrowing and False Political Feedback', in Bernard P. Herber (ed.), *Public Finance and Public Debt*, Detroit: Wayne State University Press, pp. 205–16.

Hills, J. (1984), 'What Is the Public Sector Worth?', *Fiscal Studies*, Vol. 5, No. 1.

Niskanen, W.A. (1978), 'Deficits, Government Spending and Inflation', *Journal of Monetary Economics*, No. 4.

Peacock, A.T. (1986), 'Is There a Public Debt Problem in Developed Countries?', in Bernard P. Herber (ed.), *Public Finance and Public Debt*, Detroit: Wayne State University Press, pp. 29–41.

Pommerehne, W. and Schneider, F. (1978), 'Fiscal Illusion, Political Institutions and Local Public Spending', *Kyklos*, Vol. 31.

Provopoulos, G.A. (1982), 'Public Spending and Deficits: The Greek Experience', *Public Finance/Finances Publiques*, No. 3.

Puviani, A. (1903), *Teoria della illusione finanziaria*. Milano.

Ricardo, D. (1951), *The Works and Correspondence of David Ricardo* (ed. Piero Sraffa), Vol. IV, Pamphlets and Papers, Cambridge University Press, pp. 186–7.

Shibata, H. and Kimura, Y. (1986), 'Are Budget Deficits the Cause of Growth in Government Expenditures?', in Bernard P. Herber (ed.), *Public Finance and Public Debt*, Detroit: Wayne State University Press, pp. 229–42.

PART III

Policy and reform

17. Fiscal theory and the 'market' for tax reform

(My first practical involvement with tax problems arose from an assignment from the then UK Government Colonial Office in 1952 to prepare the first complete estimates of the National Income of Tanganyika (Tanzania), all on the strength of having written a joint textbook with Harold Edey on National Income and Social Accounting. Douglas Dosser, my very able associate in this enterprise, and I did a pretty thorough job, but in trebling the 'back of the envelope' estimates of income per capita, we implicitly questioned official views on the amount and composition of taxes. It was my first experience of being the messenger who would be shot at for bringing bad news, although we had tried to convey our message in polite language. Subsequently I worked for OECD on fiscal problems of southern European countries and was approached informally to head up the new Fiscal Affairs Department of the IMF though I suspect that I was too much of a loose cannon to have survived as an international bureaucrat. But my real blooding in tax reform problems came as a member of the Musgrave Commission on Tax Reform in Colombia. (The English version of this report was published as Tax Reform in Colombia *by R.A. Musgrave and Malcolm Gillis, Harvard International Tax Program, Cambridge, Mass., 1971.) Between 1968 and my temporary disappearance from academic life to go to Whitehall (1973-1976), Keith Shaw and I worked for OECD and for the Harvard Development Advisory Group in Indonesia on fiscal policy and employment, but I cannot commit him to a mode of discourse on tax reform which betrays my scepticism about the approaches to reform adopted by fiscal economists nor to my rather pessimistic view of the prowess of economists at reducing sales resistance to their reform proposals.*

This chapter is a distillation of my experience presented, broadly speaking, in the form of a public choice analysis. Since it was written, optimal tax theorists have addressed themselves to some of the problems raised by their previous neglect of the problems of implementation of their ideas on tax design and reform, particularly the agency problems arising in the relation between tax authorities and taxpayers. But it has taken them a long time. I am glad to see, however, that one of the star fiscal economists of today saves me the necessity of an examination of the later literature, and, gratifyingly, uses similar arguments to my own (see Joel B. Slemrod, 'Tax Analysis with a Human Face Closing the

Gap between Theory and Practice', in Public Finance and Irregular Activities *(Edited by Werner W. Pommerehne), Supplement to* Public Finance, *Volume 49, 1994). Several of the ideas in this and the following chapter owe much to discussions with Francesco Forte – see the references in Chapter 18.)*

I. INTRODUCTION

The research into the economic effects of different tax regimes or, more modestly, of particular taxes is undertaken, often with considerable financial support from state and private foundations, with a view to designing 'better' tax systems. Presumably those who transmute research findings into the design of these systems do so because they derive some reward or satisfaction from pursuing this activity to the exclusion of other activities. Likewise, those who 'buy' the proposals do so because the purchase of 'inputs' of tax reform provides a greater utility to them than the alternative uses of resources.

There are two definitional matters to be disposed of first of all. The term 'market' is used very loosely. I can identify neither a demand curve nor a supply curve for tax reform with some equilibrium 'price'. However, if one thinks of a market in a more traditional sense as a device for identifying buyers and sellers and for reducing the costs of potential exchange, it must be broadly true that there is a market in even such an isolated though important activity as making suggestions for altering the structure of taxes.

My purpose here is to investigate the characteristics of this 'market' or rather certain sectors of it. Such an investigation may have an intrinsic interest to fiscal economists and tax experts, but I would hope that it might also have a more practical purpose, that of stimulating others to make suggestions as to how the market might bring about a better coincidence of wants between buyers and sellers.

The second definitional matter concerns the meaning of the term 'tax reform'. I define the term as a set of proposals which entail either a major change in the yield of government revenue raised in the form of taxes in relation to the Gross Domestic Product or a major change in the prevailing methods of raising taxes, i.e. a major change in tax structure. I am aware that a distinction is now being made by optimal tax theorists between 'tax design' and 'tax reform'. Tax design specifies the composition and yield of taxes as they would be derived from fundamental principles. Tax reform, on the other hand, consists of proposals for the adaptation of the existing tax system so that the system moves towards whatever is regarded as the optimal tax structure. I do not find this a particularly useful distinction in what is meant to be a piece of positive analysis and shall not employ it.

Therefore, the 'product' tax reform which is considered here is one which is manifested in a proposed major change in either the yield of tax in relation to GDP or in the structure of the tax system or both.

The 'purchasers' of the product are taken to be governments in power or opposition parties who hope to replace the governments in power through an electoral process. The 'suppliers' of the product are independent fiscal economists who either offer gratuitous advice or are appointed *ad hoc* members of a fiscal commission or some such body either by government or opposition. An important role is also played in the 'market' for tax reform by bureaucrats, such as those in a Ministry of Finance or Ministry of Economics, who have an accumulated expertise in practical operation of tax matters and who have therefore a strong vested interest in monitoring tax reform proposals.

II. THE DEMAND FOR TAX REFORMS

Some years ago Suphan Andic and I (Andic and Peacock, 1966) argued that systems of tax reform presumably should be based on a close study of the general aims of economic policy, upon some technical view taken of the way the economy works, and of the relative efficiency of tax measures compared with other measures as policy instruments to achieve the specified aims. We criticized a number of schemes for tax reform on the grounds that they did not clearly specify aims, they used strong assumptions about the way the economy worked, and they frequently did not make sufficient use of a case for tax reform as compared with other possible instruments. Though this has been described as a 'purist view' (cf. Bird and Oldman, 1975) it has become quite generally accepted that the ends-constraints-means paradigm offers a useful framework for explaining the rationale of tax reform (cf. Oldman and Surrey, 1972, and Musgrave and Gillis, 1971). On reconsidering our position, I believe that it still represents a useful point of departure for explaining how demands for tax reform may be generated. The general reason for this is as follows: a demand for tax reform by a government or opposition party presumably arises because policy instruments are no longer co-ordinated with policy objectives. Tax reform may be considered to be the best means by which co-ordination may be re-established.

As I have argued elsewhere (Peacock, 1979), one initial source of demand may arise because a government or an opposition party decides that it wishes to alter its priorities in policy objectives. (In technical language, 'trade-offs' between arguments in the government or party welfare function have changed.) What causes such a change in priorities need not concern us at this stage, but it is easy to envisage a case where a power shift in a government, resulting in a greater demand for economic equality, engenders interest in the feasibility of a more radical tax programme including more progressive income taxes and the introduction of personal wealth taxation, perhaps coupled with an increase in the yield of taxes in order to finance more extensive social programmes. This example underlines the importance of the interdependence of tax reform with other associated budgetary changes.

However, even if aims and trade-offs do not alter there could be circumstances where the economic constraints on maximizing the government or party welfare function alter radically and call for budgetary adjustment. In the 1970s the prospect of having to face up to an era when energy prices relative to other material inputs would continue to rise offered a graphic illustration of such a situation. Its relevance for tax reform measures is soon apparent. In the short run, it had pronounced effects on the ability of Western industrial countries to meet their growth, stabilization and even equity objectives with growing demands for automatic indexing of the direct tax system and other major adjustments in the structure of both income taxes and taxes on expenditure. In the longer run, continuing energy shortage focused attention on the control of energy supply and demand through the use of taxes on energy (cf. Webb and Ricketts, 1980).

Finally, within the context of our constrained optimization approach, tax reform may be suggested by changes which have taken place in the relative efficiency of tax measures and possible innovations in tax collection. For example, extensions in progressive income taxation may reduce the opportunity cost of evasion and avoidance to taxpayers and, for a given target revenue yield, *might* improve the relative efficiency of some form of progressive expenditure tax. Further, development of data processing methods has been an obvious influence on the administrative feasibility of VAT. It is worth incidental mention that data processing developments played a major part in the improving of the transparency of tax reform measures by allowing computerized models of changes in tax structure and rates to be employed (Pechman, 1965).

A logical construct such as the theory of economic policy may help one to analyse the 'true' preferences of governments for tax reform which would offer clear instructions for drawing up terms of reference for those who supply them. However, the initial requirement for such clarity in instruction would be that the government were prepared to reveal a unique welfare function with clearly specified arguments and trade-offs, that officials who would ultimately be assigned to the task of carrying out tax reforms and those of them likely to be intimately affected by their implementation would be completely devoted to the pursuit of the government's aim and agreed with one another on the technical and administrative desiderata on which any reform would be based. It would require further that the government could ignore 'feedback' from the electorate concerning the choice of 'suppliers' of reform, their speculations on possible recommendations and their attitudes to any proposals which the government sought to implement. Such requirements would only obtain in a dictatorship.

In practice, in countries with elected governments the weights given to the arguments in government welfare functions are constantly shifting reflecting both the power and personality of its members and the need to 'trim' political ideals to the desire to maximize electoral support. Even if the balance of power is sufficiently stable to manifest itself in a clearly defined and stable welfare function, and a clear link can be established between that function and the need for some change in the policy instruments, the priority assigned to tax reform will entail argument between bureaucrats advising Ministers about the relative efficacy of tax as against other policy instruments. Such argument may reflect genuine differences of opinion on technical matters, based on widely differing experience in the administration of policy instruments, but regrettably also will be coloured by the vested interests of those involved. If the economic theory of bureaucracy tells us anything, it is that there is ample room in government departments for the exercise of discretionary behaviour, though inter-departmental rivalry and revelation of disagreement between departments on economic control, including tax matters, may weaken their position. (Sometimes there is an incentive for bureaucrats to resolve these disagreements, notably in the case where their preference systems reveal to each other that they are united in opposing the changes in the policy 'mix' which government aims imply!)[1]

The 'internal' constraints on political action arising from the need to maximize voter support and the difficulties of controlling the discretionary behaviour of bureaucrats clearly influence the formulation of requests for tax reform proposals but 'external' constraints are also of growing importance. Governments in industrialized countries – within, say, the OECD grouping – are increasingly concerned about the growing importance of international trade and payments on their individual growth performance. Devising rules for maximizing the benefits from international trade encompasses co-ordination of tax policies concerning the treatment of foreign nationals and firms, and the development, for example, of harmonization 'rules' for tax treatment of internationally traded goods. In addition where international co-operation to achieve this end takes the form of joint provision of public services – the EC is an obvious example – governments are forced to consider how equity can be achieved in their finance. The general nature of the 'external' constraint on tax policy depends, therefore, on the bargaining skill and power of individual governments which clearly means that negotiations over tax harmonization and tax sharing arrangements are coloured by other elements in the 'bargains', including agreements on tariffs, non-tariff barriers etc. which affect international trade flows.

It is difficult to discern exactly the kind of demands for tax innovations which will be generated by these relatively new phenomena. It is known that one of the prime concerns of countries increasingly dependent on international trade and investment flows is how to maintain revenue yields in the face of avoidance and evasion techniques of considerable sophistication used by both companies and individuals. Thus while countries will have a mutual interest in co-operating to reduce avoidance and evasion, at the same time, as in cartelization agreements between firms, they have an individual interest in maximizing their share of any revenue yield which might depend on international agreements. In the particular case where, as in the EC, the finance of a Community Budget may be increasingly dependent on the Community yield of VAT, individual countries will begin to take an even closer interest in each other's tax base, and therefore in the relative amount of avoidance and evasion. Probably what all these considerations amount to is an increasing emphasis on seeking innovations which reduce the costs of tax compliance, for it is extremely doubtful if public opinion will otherwise countenance the growth of an international bureaucracy devoted to tax auditing, fraud detection and covert consultation between national tax inspectorates as one of the costs of preserving international economic co-operation (cf. OECD Committee on Fiscal Affairs, 1978). The intellectual source of such innovations is unlikely to be found exclusively among economists interested in tax problems save in those rare cases where they actually interest themselves in devising institutional and administrative changes.

In short, the composition of demand for tax reforms is very varied, with orders of priority differing as between individual governments, bureaucrats, international agencies and the public at large. One should not be surprised, therefore, that in cases where a government feels impelled to mount a major investigation of its tax system the terms of reference have to be couched in the most general terms. Too close an identification of demands for tax reform with policy objectives and trade-offs may generate 'noise' within the business and private tax-paying community including foreign nationals. This may help to account for the popularity among governments in power for 'hiving off' the generation of tax proposals to commissions and committees of *éminences grises* who are given wide scope in interpreting their terms of reference, and full opportunity to examine the comments and complaints of interest groups. This gives a government ample opportunity for gearing acceptance or rejection of the final recommendations of such bodies to its current view of its objective function and how it may best be maximized without having to question their technical expertise.

III. THE SUPPLY OF TAX REFORMS

There has been a remarkable growth in the supply of schemes for tax reform of both a limited and 'root and branch' variety in recent years, if we are to judge from the content of the major professional journals. This phenomenon is the result of two factors. The first is that the growth of public intervention in the major economies offers a ready field for appraising the effects of fiscal measures which are associated with this growth and the extent to which they accord with traditional welfare criteria.

The second factor is the heavy subsidization of supply in the form of research grants from both private and public sources. A large part of this funding is unconditional, with the investigator left free to choose the area and even the duration of research. An investigator in this position who maximizes his utility will be influenced, not unreasonably, by the desire to improve his chances of tenure and promotion. This requires him to produce a measurable output but in the form of research papers which are accepted for publication in learned journals preferably of international repute. It is true that, in the case of fiscal theory, such output may form the 'intermediate input' which tax reformers may use in devising schemes which may command the attention of governments. It might also be claimed that fiscal theorists may derive more utility than other economic theorists from 'forward' integration into the practical reform 'business' by themselves trying to translate their theoretical constructs into feasible reform proposals. The fact still remains that this highly subsidized output does not even have to be sold in the market and those who base their schemes for reform on welfare economics criteria will no doubt feel impelled to justify what they do in terms of externality arguments. It comes as no surprise, therefore, to find that a coincidence of wants between 'sellers' and 'buyers' of tax reform proposals may not be easy to achieve. Indeed, schemes of tax reform are there for the taking virtually as 'free goods' – but are there any takers? I can think of good reasons why takers are likely to be few and far between, given the current dominance in tax theory of the neo-utilitarian approach, and these reasons have nothing to do with the obvious difficulties of transmuting highly abstract propositions into clearly defined tax proposals.

Consider, for example, the essential elements in optimal income tax theory. A utilitarian social welfare function is the criterion of social choice with interpersonal comparisons of utility considered acceptable, and utility cardinally measurable. Utility depends on the individual's consumption but, in contrast to the traditional Edgeworthian analysis, consumption includes leisure. Furthermore, aggregate income (or consumption) is no longer taken as given in the Edgeworthian model. The constraint on maximizing the social welfare function now becomes some production function in which it is commonly assumed that total product depends on the skill and time input of the community, the required government revenue and any restrictions placed on the form of the tax function (e.g. a linear income tax only). Variations on the theme of the basic model investigate such matters as the influence of different shapes of identical utility functions of individuals, non-identical utility functions, and the consequences of modifying the classical utilitarian maximand (maximize the sum of individual utilities), e.g. exploring the implications of the 'maximin' criterion of Rawls.

'Takers' may be repelled by several features of this intellectually influential approach to tax problems:

(i) It is not at all clear why 'takers' should be persuaded of the virtues of a utilitarian welfare function. In fairness, it must be stated that at least lip-service is paid to the idea that such a function may be arbitrary (cf. Feldstein, 1976a; Stern, 1976) but the concentration of optimal tax theorists on a utilitarian welfare function of one variant or another can only be interpreted as a commitment at least to the premise that equity and efficiency, *as they define them*, are the only relevant arguments in the welfare function. For example, the most frequently voiced criticism of the optimal tax literature is the neglect of the very concept which influences much practical discussion of tax reform – that of horizontal equity, though latterly some optimal tax theorists have begun to recognize its importance (Feldstein, 1976b).

(ii) Empirical backing for translating tax principles into a suitable tax structure with specific tax schedules is meagre. The recognition of the problem of identifying the relevant variables and of quantifying them is put forward in a revealing way by Atkinson and Stiglitz (1976):

> On the basis of certain ethical premises, *it is decided* that individuals with different characteristics should pay varying amounts of tax. If we could observe these characteristics *costlessly and perfectly*, that would be the end of the analysis: we would *simply impose* a lump sum tax on individuals, with the amount differing according to their characteristics. The theory of optimal taxation would then be concerned simply with deriving, on the basis of specified ethical premises, what the functional relationship between characteristics and taxes 'ought to be'. (Atkinson and Stiglitz, 1976, p. 56, italics mine)

Of course, this problem of identifying characteristics is common to all attempts to turn economic analysis into specific recommendations expressed in quantitative form but it is clearly particularly difficult to specify both the shape of individual utility functions and also differences between these functions. Even if one tests 'plausible' utility functions embodying the trade-off between income (consumption) and leisure, as a substitute for empirical evidence, the resultant optimal tax schedules (with no linear constraint) will be acutely sensitive to the shape of the welfare function, and to differences between individual welfare functions.

(iii) Even if the government in power, or the main opposition party which would form an alternative government, accepted a utilitarian-type welfare function and the estimation of the constraints in maximizing it, it must have strong residual doubts about both the technical and political feasibility of implementation. Much has been made by optimal tax theorists themselves of the limitation imposed on implementing their own proposals by administrative costs. However, the kind of advice proffered (see, for example, Heller and Shell, 1974) seems to presuppose that government has the power and will to act like Leviathan. Thus allowing for the introduction of the real resources used by government in administering alternative tax regimes, Heller and Shell envisage situations where it would be socially optimal to shut down one set of firms which, though more efficient than another set, are more costly to tax. This is certainly a logical consequence of introducing an administrative sector where the cost function is related to the type and amount of tax but only on the assumption that no additional 'policing' costs need be incurred by government from the necessity to eliminate any X-inefficiency resulting from reduction in competition as firms are eliminated.

However, where governments have to trade off their ideological position (including its position on optimal taxation) against the need to retain political support, i.e. they maximize length of political life, then they will be acutely sensitive to the gains and losses to taxpayers resulting from any attempt to maximize a utilitarian-type function. Taxpayers (who are also voters) who expect to suffer losses may exercise political muscle either to block reform or to seek compensation through some adjustment in the amount and/or composition of government expenditure. Even if these taxpayers/voters believe that their attempts to influence legislators are likely to fail, one cannot leave out of account their investment in other courses of action (having weighed expected gains and losses) such as tax avoidance, tax evasion, emigration to other tax jurisdictions, change of occupation, all viewed against the background of what may be achieved by longer-term political campaigning to change the tax laws. No doubt optimal tax theorists can bring compliance costs within the ambit of their models but, if compensation is necessarily ruled out in maximizing the welfare function, they must not be surprised to find themselves labelled either as extremely naive in rejecting the presence of any market between legislators and voters, or as advocates of dictatorship. Alternatively, they have a major investment to make in trying to make their particular welfare criteria persuasive to the electorate. Bradford and Rosen (1976) regard this as 'obviously a tall order'.

The well known alternative paradigm in modern tax theory is the 'exchange-contractarian' model devised by Wicksell and developed by Buchanan (1976) and others. It can, of course, be presented in equally abstract terms and consequently its operationality may seem just as questionable. However, it has one strong point in its favour once it is taken for granted that a major tax reform is not something which can be imposed on an unwilling electorate whose utility is measured simply in terms of their reactions to what they are forced to regard as some 'exogenous' influence on their economic position. The success or failure of a tax reform then ultimately has to rest on its compatibility with the democratic decision-making process. This fact has an immediate appeal on normative grounds to many of us who find it distasteful to rest a case for tax reform on a claim to know better what is in the interests of those who have to face its consequences, and this fact also presents a challenge to those who wish to persuade governments and through them the electorate that any particular change deserves their support.

The contrast between the two approaches is vividly demonstrated in attitudes to so-called tax loopholes. The 'erosion' of the income-tax base and emergence of what has been called, rather misleadingly, the 'tax-expenditures' phenomenon characterized by special exemptions and allowances is seen as a violation of the principle of horizontal equity, i.e. 'equal treatment of equals', with either income or utility as the measure, and of the principle of vertical equity insofar as tax exemptions appear to favour the rich. It is worth noting, *en passant,* that support for the principle of horizontal equity can only be derived from optimal income tax theory if it is assumed that individuals have identical tastes and differ only in their ability to earn income. It follows that any horizontal inequity which follows from special exemptions and allowances must reflect market imperfections which prevent individuals from taking advantage of tax concessions of this kind, having regard to their own tastes and preferences. As Feldstein (1976b) has argued, the fact that any such concessions are only worth pursuing by the rich is irrelevant. So long as the rich have equal access to the concession what is at issue is the reduction effected in the degree of tax progression and not the principle of horizontal equity. This kind of point is more likely to occur to those who support the contractarian approach, but it is not the gravamen of the case made by them against the utilitarian case concerning loopholes. As Buchanan (1976) and Weidenbaum (1978) have argued, if tax loopholes reflect the outcome of political bargaining process in which taxpayers/voters have been given full opportunity to consider alternatives, then present-day worries about tax erosion are of much less concern to contractarians. Even if it is conceded that taxpayer/voters are not aware of the full extent and implications of tax loopholes, this lack of awareness is likely to reflect the more general phenomenon of the costs of acquiring information about all aspects of a modern fiscal system of relevance to taxpayer decision-making.

IV. CONCLUSION

What I have tried to clarify in the above analysis is that the underlying behavioural characteristics of customers for and suppliers of tax reform measures seem to erect communication barriers between them which prevent the operation of an efficient market. I do not claim to know how such a market might be created and hope that others with more experience of such matters will be stimulated to make suggestions.

I have only one such suggestion of my own which arises from practical experience. Tax reform measures, as I initially defined them, are not something 'bought' by governments every day and there is understandable consumer and, let it be said, producer ignorance about what the precise effects of proposed tax changes will be on the welfare function of a government. There is a broad analogy with the architect-client relationship in putting up a new building, and the lesson which may be drawn from this relationship is the necessity for the 'architect' and the client to be in continuous contact throughout the whole of the operation. This was the method devised and operated by none other than Richard Musgrave as head of the Colombian Tax Commission of 1968 of which I was a member.

The agenda for reform was discussed in detail with President Lleras Restrepo and there was daily contact with government officials.[2] The members of the Commission were determined to translate first principles, on which their views differed considerably, into practical measures which would be widely acceptable, and this required concentrated, exhaustive (and exhausting) discussion backed by a mass of quickly produced and well-processed data on an enormous range of issues prepared by expert researchers. The final recommendations were prepared in the form of alternative packages and where disagreements were unresolved, though after determined attempts to resolve them, no watered-down compromises were insisted upon, but clear expressions of dissent were stated. It is a miracle that at the end of the operation everyone was still on speaking terms. (For further details see Oldman and Surrey, 1972.) And some of the major proposals were actually instituted! Remember the practical skills and persuasive powers of the doyen of our profession next time you grapple with the more recondite chapters of *The Theory of Public Finance*!

NOTES

1. In the author's experience, any tax change proposed by a government department concerned with economic matters which might reduce the revenue yield is resolutely opposed by the tax revenue departments who seem universally to regard revenue yield as an absolute constraint. This opposition can be interpreted in various ways. It may be regarded as a manifestation of fiscal rectitude or of the fear that in the long run the real costs to revenue administrators may increase if at a later date revenue yields have to be raised, requiring additional 'investment' in overcoming tax resistance.
2. The press, too, took a lively interest in the affairs of the Commission. In one daily paper a cartoon had a caption reading: 'Musgrave – Grava más'. (Musgrave turned round in Spanish means 'tax more'!)

REFERENCES

Andic, Suphan and Peacock, Alan (1966), 'Fiscal Surveys and Economic Development', *Kyklos.*

Atkinson, A.B. and Stiglitz, J.E. (1976), 'The Design of Tax Structure: Direct versus Indirect Taxation', *Journal of Public Economics*, July–August.

Bird, Richard M. and Oldman, Oliver (eds) (1975), 'Fiscal Policy and Economic Development', in their *Readings on Taxation in Developing Countries* (3rd edition), The Johns Hopkins Press.

Bradford, David F. and Rosen, Harvey S. (1976), 'The Optimal Taxation of Commodities and Income', *American Economic Review*, Papers and Proceedings of American Economic Association, May.

Buchanan, J.M. (1976), 'Taxation in Fiscal Exchange', *Journal of Public Economics,* July–August.

Feldstein, Martin (1976a), 'On the Theory of Tax Reform', *Journal of Public Economics,* July–August.

Feldstein, Martin (1976b), 'Compensation in Tax Reform', *National Tax Journal*, Vol. XXIX, No. 2, June.

Heller, Walter Perrin and Shell, Karl (1974), 'On Optimal Taxation with Costly Administration', *American Economic Review*, May.

Musgrave, Richard A. and Gillis, Malcolm (1971), *Fiscal Reform for Colombia: Final Report and Staff Papers of the Colombian Commission on Tax Reform,* Harvard Law School International Tax Program.

OECD Committee on Fiscal Affairs (1978), *Activities 1971–77 and Current Work Programme*, Organisation for Economic Co-operation and Development, Paris.

Oldman, Oliver and Surrey, Stanley (1972), 'Technical Assistance in Developing Countries', in Richard M. Bird and John G. Head (eds), *Modern Fiscal Issues: Essays in Honour of Carl Shoup*, Toronto University Press.

Peacock, Alan (1979), *Economic Analysis of Government and Related Themes*, Martin Robertson, Chapter 14.

Pechman, Joseph (1965), 'A New Tax Model for Revenue Estimating', in A.T. Peacock and G. Häuser (eds), *Government Finance and Economic Development*, OECD.

Stern, N.H. (1976), 'On the Specification of Models of Optimal Income Taxation', *Journal of Public Economics,* July–August.

Webb, Michael G. and Ricketts, Martin J. (1980), *The Economics of Energy*, London: Macmillan.

Weidenbaum, Murray (1978), 'The Case for Tax Loopholes', in Donald H. Skadden (ed.), *A New Tax Structure for the United States*, Bobbs-Merrill Educational Publishing.

18. Designing tax reform: identifying the problems

(Whereas the previous chapter adopted a positive approach to the problems of tax reform considered as a 'deal' between those who demand tax reform proposals – politicians and government administrations – and the fiscal economists who supply them, this chapter adopts a normative approach. I was one of a number of economists asked by OECD to give their views on the general design of tax reforms for Central and European countries undergoing the change from command to market economies. I naturally assumed that the most important single task of tax reform in these countries was to promote the efficient operation of the market economy, though recognizing that any economic improvements resulting from the changeover must embody a wide distribution of their benefits. I suggested that, inter alia, the precondition of any successful tax reform would have to be strict control over government spending and its growth. I was not entirely surprised to find that the officials of Western government tax offices assumed implicitly or explicitly that they should concentrate their advice on how 'new' market economies could increase *tax yields – cf. note 1 to Chapter 17 above. There was also a general unwillingness to recognise that tax reform measures, particularly in a market economy, have to be judged in terms of their relative efficacy alongside alternative policy instruments. Indeed, one of the main characteristics of 'mixed' economies with large public sectors is that the machinery of government becomes so complicated that government departments with a vested interest in the operation of a particular policy instrument, e.g. health and safety regulation, may be counteracting the thrust of tax measures. Perhaps Central and East European policy-makers have more to learn from us about the measures that are best avoided rather than from those that have some claim to be successful.*

My conclusions appear to be supported by the extensive survey of fiscal policy in these countries in the IMF's World Economic Outlook, *May 1996. Focus on Fiscal Policy, Chapter V, in which reference is made to the 'daunting fiscal challenges' (p. 77) that these countries still have to face.)*

I. INTRODUCTION

This chapter examines the underlying problems encountered in Western industrial countries in operating highly sophisticated and therefore complicated tax systems. It examines the underlying logic of these systems, and traces the connection between actual tax regimes and the philosophies which underpin them. This approach highlights the difficulties of policy implementation. It is accepted that nobody holds the extreme view that a Western-type tax system should be adopted in all its particularities by Central and Eastern European economies, but if that were the case, it would have to be assumed that policy objectives were becoming identical and trade-offs between them similar, that the structure of the Central and Eastern European economies would adapt quickly to those of Western economies, as would their tax administrations. It would also have to be assumed that Western tax systems were perfectly adjusted to conform to their own governments' individual and collective (EC) objectives, and easily adapted to meet any changes in the 'mix' of policies. That is far from being the case.

Some general problems of tax reform within the framework of two 'policy paradigms' are examined below. The first is the more familiar 'constrained maximization' model of government policy, including tax policy (Section II), and the second the 'public choice' model (Section III). In Section IV, a few ways are suggested in which some of the problems revealed by the policy paradigms might be dealt with in a system of tax reform of interest to Central and Eastern European countries.

II. POLICY PARADIGM (1): THE TRADITIONAL APPROACH

The policy paradigm which has had a marked influence on the examination of the role of the tax system is one which 'looks down from above' on taxpayers. It is assumed that there is a 'government in power', presumably commanding some general popular support. The government has objectives which can be translated into proximate aims of policy expressed in money values: rates of economic growth, allocation of resources between sectors which take account of external effects, and some optimal distribution of income measurable in, say, Lorenz curve form. The achievement of these objectives is constrained by the resources available or the 'productive potential' of the economy. These resources may be influenced in the direction indicated by policy aims by the use of 'tax handles'. The optimal tax regime is one which maximises the 'welfare function' of the 'government'.

Recent concentration on tax reform in Western countries has been influenced by a variant of this type of model which tries to offer quite specific guidance on the trade-off between improving productive potential and greater tax equity, both horizontal and vertical. These reforms have clearly been influenced by the neo-utilitarian school of public finance specialists who argue: (i) welfare of individuals rises with income but at a decreasing rate; (ii) individuals with the same income level have the same welfare level; and (iii) welfare of individuals can be compared. It can be shown that these three assumptions point towards pure egalitarianism but this did not please even the original formulators, who pointed out that in the process of redistribution to achieve the end, it clearly could not be assumed that the same level of income would be available for distribution. Latter-day theorists have taken account of the effects of taxes on incentives to work and on the distribution of skills in the population. The 'optimum' direct tax system is no longer egalitarian but postulates a quite modest degree of tax progression, but still rests on the assumption that 'income' can be precisely and clearly defined.

Both versions of what are called the conventional paradigm deny any role to the voter-cum-taxpayer (VCT) in the political decision-making process. For the neo-utilitarians, taxpayer co-operation is superfluous because the welfare of VCTs can be discerned without consulting them. There are two points to be made about this paradigmatic peculiarity. The first is that one may question whether, in a free society, taxpayers should have such a minor role to play. It is worth noting that in the important statement of 'Taxpayers' Rights and Obligations' prepared by the OECD Fiscal Affairs Secretariat, the derivation of these rights does not extend to any direct say in the formation of tax policy but only from the wholly commendable but limited proposition that taxpayers should feel fairly treated *once the tax law is decided.* I shall return to this matter in the list of recommendations.

Secondly, the rather mechanistic character of 'optimization' approaches to economic policy leads economists, at least, to make rather naive assumptions about taxpayer reactions to changes in tax structure. VCTs are regarded as maximizing their welfare, subject to the binding constraints of tax legislation. This assumes that they do not weigh the costs and benefits of seeking to modify these constraints by some form of individual or collective action. The combination of highly complex tax structures which affect individuals through the taxation of their wealth, income, or consumption and the problems of drafting tax codes offer many opportunities for bargaining with the tax authorities or for trying to evade tax obligations. Recognition of these uncomfortable facts means that a general equilibrium model of the economy upon which government is superimposed as a controller may be of limited use and some kind of multi-sector bargaining model may have to take its place. Tax administrators will accept the view set out above, but may argue that they take the awkward fact of life –

bargaining – into account. How they do so is an empirical matter, but their instincts may lead them to try to eliminate the bargaining element altogether if they possibly can and to harry evaders in the black economy. They are to be commended for doing their duty, but it is arguable whether their efficiency should be judged by the extra revenue they raise or the number of evaders they catch.[1]

The problem of 'tax bargaining' is closely related to a third matter which is barely touched on, viz., what is being assumed in the analysis of taxes and their economic effects about the *overall burden of taxation*? Consider this question in the context of a Western economy in which total government expenditure is assumed to grow in line with GDP. This country, in line with prevailing tax philosophy, decides to reform its income tax by lowering its whole schedule of tax rates and broadening its tax base. The growth in spending, ignoring the use of debt finance which can only be of limited significance, requires that the lowered rate of increase in income tax yield is compensated in some way, e.g. (i) by a large increase in real income of taxpayers as a result of improvement in work incentives; or (ii) by a yield increase as a result of broadening the tax base; or (iii) by an increase in the yields of 'unreformed' taxes; or by some combination of these methods.

The analysis of the economic effects depends crucially on the alternative assumptions regarding the tax regime, but also on the size and rate of growth in public expenditure. Pressure to improve services will call for concomitant increases in revenue. It is claimed that the growth in expenditure has had the effect of forcing tax authorities to reduce the transparency of taxes by some form of 'fiscal illusion'. As James Buchanan argued in the discussion of the recent United States move to reduce personal income tax rates but to compensate them by an extension of the corporation tax base: 'the major shift in taxation from the individual income tax to the corporate tax base will reduce, perhaps substantially, the individual voter's ability to perceive the cost of program benefits'.[2] One would have thought that, at the very least, the VCT has a right to know something about the distribution of benefits and tax burdens as a whole. We all know the fragility of such estimates because of the problem of identifying the 'counterfactual' position and deciding on the correct tax incidence assumptions. In the United Kingdom, our Central Statistical Office still produces ludicrous calculations because it leaves out those items on both sides of the account which it finds difficult to allocate!

The fourth and final matter to which the policy paradigm draws attention is *the assumption of effective policy co-ordination.* Taxation (including negative taxation) is only one of a number of instrument sets that governments may use in order to achieve the same ends. There are two major practical problems encountered in achieving policy co-ordination. The first is in deciding which one of a number of instruments is the most effective. For example, if the aim is to reduce the external diseconomies associated with pollution, is it more effective to tax the polluters, to subsidize them on condition that they forgo the use of pollution-creating inputs, or simply to restrict their activities by some form of regulation? The second is that the assignment of particular policy instruments to particular government departments creates a vested interest in the use of that instrument by the Minister in charge and his officials. Unfortunately, in my experience in government, ministers, anxious to dramatize their concern for the public weal, will not be impressed by arguments produced by their officials which demonstrate that the instrument controlled by some other department would be more effective! This point can be illustrated with reference to tax policy vis-à-vis other policies using several examples.

III POLICY PARADIGM (2): THE PUBLIC CHOICE APPROACH

The reason for considering this alternative paradigm lies in the contention of its authors that it is more in accord with the principles of the market economy. This is because public choice is designed to replicate the market system, so far as that is possible, in the relations between the government and voters.

The public choice approach to tax reform is therefore very different from that derived from traditional fiscal analysis:

(i) The tax system is a method for paying for services rendered – taxation according to benefit;
(ii) The 'optimal tax regime' is derived solely from the stated preferences of taxpayers (taxpayers 'look down from above' on governments!);
(iii) It follows that the system for stating these preferences must be able to reflect these preferences so far as that is possible;
(iv) Taxpayers must have the fullest information on the tax plans of the government and their effect on individual economic circumstances.

The public choice approach solves the problem of preserving the nexus between revenues and expenditure but clearly it involves some very radical proposals. First, the starting point of tax reform must be an examination of the decision-making process of government. This was the basic point made by Wicksell one hundred years ago and which led him to develop his theory of fiscal voting. Its counterpart in modern discussion is the attempt by Buchanan and others to devise ways in which the growth of the public sector can be controlled so as to anticipate the problems which arise in conflicts between voter interest groups. One cannot deny that such discussion runs into as formidable problems as those encountered by neo-utilitarian writers, e.g. in regard to the feasibility of tax or expenditure limitation proposals.

Second, the approach points towards the removal of 'tax illusion'. This harks back to the old classical ideas of making the system certain, convenient for the taxpayer as well as 'fair'. The transparency of the tax system is all-important.

The problem with this approach is translating it into a precise tax regime. It could be avoided by saying that this is unnecessary if the constitutional provisions are in place and 'tax illusion' can be eliminated. It is then unnecessary to specify 'global' government objectives at all, if the welfare function of the community is derived from individual choices! This could be regarded as a bit of a cheat.

The public choice approach may be translated into some actual tax proposals:

(i) The personal income tax should be based on self-assessment with the individual taxpayer responsible for the calculation of the tax due. This principle is designed to improve taxpayer understanding of the tax system as applied directly to him or her. I realise the practical objections to this proposal – the extra time and effort for the taxpayer, the problem of verification on a sampling basis and so on. However, one must set against this the need to encourage taxpayer involvement in the fiscal process as the badge of citizenship. Collection at source is more the badge of servitude. This approach contradicts that favoured by Leif Muten, who, in commenting on recent Swedish reforms, argued that 'we must assume that it is progress when the trouble of filling out the yearly tax return is taken away from the great number of taxpayers'.[3]

(ii) The greatest source of 'fiscal illusion' is the corporation tax. It has been effectively used by government to disguise the fact that its ultimate incidence must be on individuals. The public choice solution points to the abolition of the corporation tax altogether, and the assignment of dividend distributions and retained earnings of companies to individual taxpayers, subjecting them only to income tax. This should increase the transparency of the tax, which is all the more necessary in any country in which the proportion of the working population holding shares could increase with the growth in privatization. There are obvious objections. The corporation tax has been considered to be a regulatory instrument of importance designed to influence aggregate saving and investment behaviour, the Swedish investment deposit fund scheme being a famous example. This view emanates from an essentially Keynesian view on the way the economy works and how fluctuations and growth in incomes and employment may be controlled. I shall not enter into a discussion here on whether this is sufficient reason for retaining the tax. More practical reasons are that the corporation tax may be a useful bargaining weapon in international tax agreements and also is a convenient tax collection device. It may also persuade taxpayers that the rich will not escape their fiscal duties. However, these arguments may seem a little too convenient for the tax authorities.

(iii) 'Voter alienation' resulting from the necessity of having representative government as the practical method for giving voice to voter demands may be reduced by de-centralization of power. Therefore, public choice analysts frequently support federal forms of government with devolution of taxing powers.

The main criticism of the public choice approach is that it implicitly assumes that a 'just' distribution of income will emerge from the market system. However, if voters perceive that the income distribution is not 'just' then voters may adopt strategies designed to minimize their tax burden rather than to reflect their 'true' preferences for public services. Trying to make taxes their equivalent of 'prices' fails unless some 'pre-budget' or 'original' distribution of income is agreed as 'just'. What is 'just' is not itself agreed amongst public choice theorists themselves!

IV. SOME GENERAL RECOMMENDATIONS

I have concentrated on some of the problems encountered in highly complex tax systems in countries in which the public sector plays a large part in economic life. Ideally OECD countries should be making major changes in their tax systems before recommending that they should be adopted by others. In practice, Eastern European countries may not be able to contemplate changes which are completely independent of actual tax systems in OECD countries. In the case of the former GDR, for example, the tax policy options are limited by the short-term necessity of bringing its tax system into line with that of the FRG.[4] While that may be an extreme case, the desire of Eastern European countries to form close ties with the EC must require a fair measure of tax harmonization along EC lines. The acceptance of this limitation does, however, reduce the range of solutions the problems to which were discussed above.

This note is based upon the premise that the most important single task of tax reform in Eastern European countries is to promote the efficient operation of the market economy. This means paying particular attention to the impact of the tax system on private enterprise, which requires a number of preconditions.

The first precondition is that close control must be exercised over the growth in the public sector and therefore in the overall tax burden. It is accepted that sweeping generalizations about the 'limits of taxation' are often based on logical inconsistencies and vague rules of thumb. Nevertheless, it is well established that the growth in the public sector to the point where overall government expenditure exceeds 40 per cent of GDP is associated with a growing complexity in the relations between government and private enterprise.

Scarce entrepreneurial resources are inevitably diverted towards strategies designed to maximize profits (or minimize losses) from transactions with government rather than with final consumers. The point is recognised by OECD,[5] which noted that in recent years evidence has begun to accumulate that the economic costs of financing government spending are not as small as was once thought, a finding that is particularly strong at the margin; the costs of increasing the size of the public sector, as well as the gains from reducing it, are significantly larger than the average economic cost of public sector spending. However, OECD seems to put its faith in reducing these costs by moving towards consumption-based and away from income-based taxes. This line of argument would be more convincing if there were a clearer idea of the authors' assumptions about the *size* of the overall tax burden.

The second precondition is closely related to the first one. There have to be proper constitutional provisions in place which, at the very least, reveal government detailed plans for future tax and expenditure changes, and the purpose of such changes. These plans should also specify the contents of tax legislation, and should set in place accounting and audit systems designed to promote effective monitoring of the sources and destination of government finances. Such information would facilitate public discussion on the role of the public sector. These reflect the well-known traditional precepts of public finances which are designed to make public budgets and accounts as transparent as possible, a fundamental requirement in a democracy.[6] In this context, it is argued that transparency is an essential means for reducing, to use Marxian terminology, 'taxpayer alienation'. Taxpayers have the right to know not only how their tax bill is arrived at, but also how their taxes are being used. Of course, they may regard it as too much of a time investment to examine the vast number of public documents associated with the budgetary control, but their 'agents', their elected representatives, must have this information, to digest on their behalf. Furthermore, such constitutional provisions are meant to set a pattern for information supplied to the taxpayer in simpler form and at a more mundane level. In a democracy some such constitutional provisions and the information that they generate are regarded as a citizen's right. It may be a big step in the argument to suggest that more information to the taxpayer will suddenly produce a well-mannered dialogue between taxpayers and tax officials leading to better relations between the taxpayer and the tax authorities.

The final precondition rests on the proposition that the free market economy will only be perceived as the harbinger of economic and social improvement if its benefits are widely distributed and a large proportion of the working population have a stake in private enterprise. While 'tax neutrality' has been invoked by fiscal experts as the prime guide for a tax system designed to work with market forces, so that pressure from special interest groups can be more easily resisted, strictly applied it would act as a deterrent to the foundation and development of small enterprises and discourage investment in share capital by small savers. Many OECD countries retain 'intentional non-neutralities'[7] which favour small enterprises and small savers. It has been argued[8] that there are still several important anomalies in the treatment of small business by EC countries, notably in relation to VAT, the administration of which appears to place a differential burden in compliance costs on small as compared with large enterprises. However, rather than be drawn into argument about this question, the small firm problem can be seen as a classic case where lack of co-ordination in government policy (see above) leads to inconsistent use of policy instruments. Thus tax concessions to small business may pale into insignificance as an instrument to promote competitive enterprise alongside legislation on employment protection and social security, health and safety regulations, quite apart from industry-specific government measures. If, as seems the case, the differential burden on small firms of both regulation and taxation is substantial, then this will reduce their competitiveness.[9]

As an act of filial piety, let me close with a quotation from David Hume: 'we have, with regard to taxes, an instance of what frequently happens in political institutions, that the consequences of things are diametrically opposite to what we should expect on first appearance'.[10] Even if fiscal experts are fully conscious of the need to examine carefully whether or not a particular tax measure will achieve its intention, Hume's words comprise a sage warning!

NOTES

1. For further consideration see Alan Peacock and Francesco Forte, 'Tax Planning, Tax Analysis and Tax Policy', in Peacock and Forte (eds), *The Political Economy of Taxation*, Blackwell, Oxford, 1981.
2. J.M. Buchanan, 'Tax Reform as Public Choice', *Journal of Economic Perspectives*, Volume 1, No. 1, 1987.
3. See his 'Comment' in J. Pechman (Editor), *Tax Reform*, Brookings Institute, 1988.
4. See Bernd Genser, *Tax Policies for a United Germany,* IMF Fiscal Affairs Department Working Paper 90/89, October 1990.
5. See OECD, *Structural Adjustment and Economic Performance*, 1987, Chapter 10.
6. For a perceptive exposition and justification of these precepts, see F. Forte, *Il Bilancio nell'Economia Pubblica: Tomo I. Teoria generale del bilancio pubblico*, Giuffre Editore, Milano 1985, pp. 25–43.
7. See OECD, *Financing Public Expenditure: The Role of Tax Reform and Designing Tax System*, 1991.
8. See Graham Bannock, *Taxation in the European Community: The Small Business Perspective*, Paul Chapman Publishing, London, 1990.
9. See Graham Bannock and Alan Peacock, *Governments and Small Business*, Paul Chapman Publishing for The David Hume Institute, London, 1989.
10. David Hume, 'Of Taxes', in *Essays: Moral, Political, and Literary* (1748), edited by Eugene F. Miller, Liberty Classics, Indianapolis.

19. The political economy of devolution: the British case

(Anyone interested in the expansion of economic freedom has to consider how far the structure of government promotes that end. I found myself in this position as a member of the Royal Commission on the Constitution which I joined in 1971. The Commission reported at the end of 1973, but by that time I had become a senior civil servant and was therefore precluded from taking part in the ensuing debate until well after the crucial period.

This chapter was first published in 1976 and is in essence a defence of the position of the Memorandum of Dissent to the Majority Report of the Commission, which opposed partial devolution to Scotland and Wales and argued for general devolution, in fact for a variety of federalism for the UK. The bulk of the Memorandum was drafted by Norman (later Lord) Hunt who became the constitutional adviser to the Labour Government elected in 1974. My contribution concerned the working out of the financial implications of a devolved system of government. I also recorded differences between Norman and myself regarding both the planning functions of devolved governments and the use of a methodology which assumed that devolution simply meant re-allocating the existing functions of government without considering whether all these functions were necessary in the first place. This last point has played a major part in my present thinking on the devolution question, which I summarize at the end of this preface.

I decided to include this rather ancient piece as a small contribution to contemporary history. It may be interesting for three reasons. First, it demonstrates how constitutional problems which are left on one side simply do not go away. We are in the midst of a debate in which the same issues are raised and the same logic of analysis can be deployed, as I show later. Second, it demonstrates the dilemma facing Royal Commissions set up to pronounce on highly contentious issues. To produce firm, agreed conclusions would require sharing the same value judgments, but the conventional way for governments to choose members requires representation of diverse interests and expertise with the strong prospect that they will disagree.

The Chair of a Commission can adopt one of three positions in trying to resolve this dilemma. The first is to present alternative solutions derived from different sets of value judgements. Our original Chairman, Lord Crowther, considered the possibility of presenting the government with alternative 'models' of devolution reflecting different sets of objectives, but he died in office and the idea was dropped. In any case, the Chair then has to face the criticism that he/she has not tried hard enough to seek agreement, and a 'take your pick' result may be regarded as unhelpful. The second approach is to seek a consensus of view, but this may simply result in a watery compromise. Government officials may not object to this result because they may be in a better position to influence subsequent decisions by government if no firm line is taken by the Commission.

The last approach is to define a 'core' of agreement and to allow individual members, if they so wish, to dissent on particular issues. In our case the succeeding Chairman, Lord Kilbrandon, attempted to identify the 'core' by reference to the evidence received from the public about the changes that they considered desirable. However, Norman Hunt and I did not agree with the interpretation of the evidence and insisted on presenting what amounted to an alternative report.

The third and final reason for including this piece is that it records the uphill struggle that two social scientists had to face in trying to alter the traditional methods by which Commissions accumulate evidence. Relying on the presentation of memoranda by interested parties is an economical way of achieving this end, but hardly a reliable one. Norman and I sought to define the dimensions of the evidence that would be relevant and this not unnaturally led us to the conclusions that we should be sponsoring or conducting research of our own. This was all the more necessary because the Treasury and the Inland Revenue had a strong vested interest in preserving the status quo *and had presented some very negative observations on the prospects of devising a devolved system of government. Also, their statements had a suspicious* ex cathedra *quality about them and made no attempt at fiscal modelling. Reluctantly, the commission appointed a research officer, Dr David King, later to become well known as an expert on the fiscal aspects of devolved government, and also sponsored an attitude survey as we requested. This had an amusing consequence. When we decided to 'go it alone', we were informed that the administrative facilities of the Commission need no longer be put at our disposal. But Norman and I were the only members of the Commission capable of checking on the technical arguments on the fiscal and financial matters in the Majority Report! A bargain was struck with the officials and an appeal to the Chairman or beyond was avoided!*

The present debate (1996) concerns once again the advisability of partial devolution to Scotland and Wales, and I still hold that partial devolution is an essentially unstable position. It is difficult to believe that English regions would be content with a situation where there would be inequality of political rights. Even if some modus vivendi *were found which would reduce Scottish representation in Parliament, the very existence of a separate Scots government, albeit with limited powers, creates a power base which enhances its bargaining strength vis-à-vis central government, and this could not be countenanced for long by other parts of the UK.*

However, this is not to assume that I would attach any priority to overall devolution as a method for expanding economic freedom. In the interim between the 1970s debate on devolution and the present, a potentially more effective and more direct way of devolving power has been at work, namely privatization. This attempts to increase the power over economic decision-making, putting it firmly in the hands of the individual citizen, both through extension of capital ownership and by increasing the range of alternative sources of supply through competition. With political devolution, the individual citizen is still faced with a high opportunity cost in trying to influence legislators to provide services efficiently so that they conform to his perception of what he should be obliged to pay for them. I would be the first to agree, as I emphasize throughout this book, that the policy of assigning to individuals more responsibility for their own welfare presents formidable difficulties of implementation. However, having embarked on this policy, which has had widespread if reluctant acceptance, a concentration of effort on overcoming these difficulties, notably in the field of the regulation of industry and the professions, appears to me to have much higher priority than embarking on a constitutional change which has been made to look much easier to implement that in fact would be the case. In particular, it is extremely doubtful if any viable form of devolution could be instituted without a review of major elements in our constitution, including the powers of both the Lords and the Commons.

There is a further problem of equal importance. One would be embarking on a major constitutional change at a time when it is not clear whether the UK will support the transfer of economic powers to the EC which would require an additional tier of government with a European Parliament able to initiate legislation in a similar manner to a Federal Parliament. This raises the perplexing issue as to whether this would increase the overall size of the public sector, which would be inimical to the expansion of individual economic freedom. Even if it did not, it would mean a re-allocation of power which could affect all layers of government within the UK, including those of a devolved parliament. Either way, the co-ordination of policies is bound to result in a net expansion in the number of administrators and in the size of the judiciary, alongside an increase in the job prospects for politicians, particularly those with no alternative career prospects with comparable status and rewards, who support the introduction of both a new layer of government between local authorities and central government and our full participation in a Federal Europe.)

I. BACKGROUND

Worried by the growing support for the Scottish National Party (SNP) and for its Welsh counterpart Plaid Cymru (significantly known by its Welsh name), as instanced by the 1967 by-elections, Mr Wilson, the then Prime Minister, appointed a Royal Commission on the Constitution under the chairmanship of Lord Crowther, a time-honoured method used by British governments to buy time.[1] Though its terms of reference were very wide and could have been interpreted as covering the whole range of constitutional problems, it was clearly understood that the main question facing the commission was whether, how, and to what extent government should be further devolved within the United Kingdom.

The Commission was appointed in April 1969 but did not report until December 1973. By that time, its activities had been largely forgotten about, and when its 500-page report, together with a 200-page Memorandum of Dissent[2] and a considerable number of volumes of evidence and research reports, appeared, the editor of the well-known journal *Public Administration* was tempted to recall David Hume's acerbic remark on the appearance of his *Treatise of Human Nature,* which fell 'dead-born from the press'. However, the polite parliamentary gestures of approval for services rendered were in stark contrast to the close attention paid to various schemes of devolution based on the evidence and conclusions of the Commission, which at the end of 1974 were officially offered for discussion. By then the Labour government faced loss of support to Scottish and Welsh nationalists and to the Liberal Party, which had a strong commitment to transfer of power from the centre to the regions.

In essence the Labour government has accepted the principal recommendations of the majority of the commission's members and is committed to setting up separate directly elected assemblies in Scotland and Wales. These assemblies will be endowed with considerable control over expenditure functions at present undertaken by the Scottish and Welsh offices – the central government's executive 'arm' in these regions – but will have very little discretion over means of finance. Though all members of the commission opposed the setting up of a federal government structure in the United Kingdom and rejected the demand of nationalist parties for Scottish and Welsh independence, two members of the commission, Lord Crowther-Hunt and myself, preferred a form of devolution that offered the same opportunities for control of the executive by regional assemblies in the English regions as well as in Scotland and Wales.

I have chosen to avoid giving a detailed description of the various schemes of devolution proposed, for I believe that the value of the devolution debate for an international audience lies more in examining the intellectual process leading to devolution proposals and less in a detailed examination of their content, interesting and relevant though this could be to other countries.

In Section II below, I briefly review the place of the devolution debate within the framework of the recently developed economic theory of representative government. Having explained how a demand for devolution has arisen, I describe in Section III how the Kilbrandon Commission (hereafter referred to as KC) went about the task of measuring its intensity. In Section IV, I review the two main sets of devolution scheme proposed and speculate on their economic impact. In the final section, I endeavour to draw some lessons from the devolution debate in the United Kingdom.

II. MODELS OF CONSTITUTIONAL CHANGE

The model of constitutional change that one could employ to explain the demand for devolution would depend on the questions one seeks to answer. Latterly, economists who have made the running in this area have been interested in developing positive models in which individuals try to induce governments to do what they want, i.e., reduce their frustration with government policy, by a series of signalling actions within a given jurisdiction or by mobility or the threat of mobility to other jurisdictions within the nation-state (see Breton, 1974; Breton and Scott, 1978). The signalling actions can range from direct engagement in politics to adjustment of economic behaviour, but all these kinds of action – together with mobility – involve costs that have to be matched with benefits, and both the costs and benefits may be uncertain.

If Breton and others are right, the variance in the distribution of preferences of citizens for different types of services and their methods of finance will increase as the degree of centralization increases. By any standards, the United Kingdom has become a highly centralized state, as measured by the growth in the relative importance of central government finance not only of central but also of local government services. (I prefer this measure of the degree of centralization to the Breton/Scott use of the relative size of expenditure responsibilities at the centre.) Local governments are still immediately responsible for important social services, such as housing and education up to university level, but their standards of services are strongly influenced by central government both through legislation and by sources of finance. Local governments are 'creatures of the centre' in another fundamental sense, for they have no separate constitutional existence; their powers are determined by Acts of Parliament, i.e., legislation enacted by the central government. It follows that citizens with preference systems differing markedly from those reflected in public expenditure and taxation would derive only a restricted net benefit by movement from one jurisdiction to another. In a study of local government in urban areas in both the United States and the United Kingdom, for instance, it has been shown (see Aronson, 1974) that fiscal factors affected the distribution of population in both countries but that the percentage of correct predictions is lower in the UK case. Aronson explains this by the fact that fiscal differences between towns, as measured by the coefficient of variation for tax rates and per capita expenditure, are not as great in England as in the United States. This could be the result, as Aronson asserts, of more homogeneous individual preferences in England than in the United States, but I believe that his second reason is more important, namely, the effects of grants from the centre to local governments, which are based on an equalizing formula.

Because of the high proportion of total central and local current governmental services financed from the centre, roughly 84 per cent in 1974, the efforts to influence their amount and composition must be concentrated on the political signalling system, which could influence central-government decisions. However, this part of the signalling system is highly restricted, for policies are decided and implemented by a government formed by a majority party in a parliament which itself is elected by a system of simple majority voting. It is also restricted by complete immunity of the higher civil service from direct electoral pressures, for this highly paid bureaucracy is not voted into office but is recruited by competitive examination for administrative posts that carry security of tenure. It is no surprise, therefore, that pressure-group action designed to exercise a *continuing* influence over politicians and bureaucrats has become of growing importance in the United Kingdom, of which the best-known examples are the activities of the Confederation of British Industry and the Trades Union Congress, which have almost acquired the status of 'estates of the realm'.

The growing demand for devolution suggests that the traditional signalling systems are not working as well as they should and that the deviation of individual and group preferences from those reflected in the existing amount and pattern of government services has become more marked. Thus the interesting feature of the British situation is that it appears to have engendered demands for *changes in the signalling system itself*, as expressed in the demand for proportional representation in national elections and for some system of devolved government.

This is an unusual situation in the United Kingdom, though Home Rule for Scotland was a lively subject of debate after the First World War. A Royal Commission, therefore, would be bound to proceed rather warily. Though the terms of reference of the KC were wide enough to make it possible to recommend a fundamental constitutional reform, its members chose to assume that, broadly speaking, the existing functions of government and particularly the economic functions should be taken as data but that their division between layers of government was the matter at issue.[3] Recommendations for devolution would therefore have to depend on wider considerations than reducing the deviation between collective and individual preferences as depicted in individualistic approaches to the theory of government, though such models can be extended, e.g., through postulating interdependent preference functions, to take account of distributional growth and stabilization aims calling for collective action.

The KC, therefore, had to act in a similar fashion to a political philosopher deploying a normative rather than a positive theory of constitutional change. The analogue in economics used to depict this approach is a constrained maximization policy model in which an objective function embodying several arguments has to be maximized subject to resource and other constraints.[4] The commission simply interpolated an additional argument into the objective function or, more modestly, a political boundary condition, viz., alternative forms of devolved decision-making, and then in a not particularly rigorous way formed a judgment on its effect on social welfare.

III MEASURING THE DEMAND FOR DEVOLUTION

While a Royal Commission could in principle deliver its recommendations *ex cathedra* without reference to outside opinion on an issue such as constitutional reform, it would have to face strong criticism if it did not at least take evidence, as such commissions traditionally have done. The usual method is to issue an open invitation to the public to offer written evidence, though a commission may ask specific organisations and individuals to submit evidence and will reserve the right to decide whom to call to give oral evidence, particularly if it is believed that otherwise it would not obtain a reasonable cross-section of opinion. However, even if care is exercised, the taking of evidence is a very haphazard method of proceeding. Given equal individual interest in expressing views on devolution problems, the costs of doing so fall very unequally on different sections of the community. It comes as no surprise that most of the evidence was received from the literate middle classes, who bear lower costs in articulating their preferences and are able to go through various professional bodies ranging from local government officers' associations to churches that can have their expenses met by others, including the taxpayer or ratepayer. To some extent the KC reduced absolute, if not differential, individual costs by taking evidence in different parts of the country, but in practice this benefited Wales, Scotland, and Northern Ireland, where thirty meetings were held, in contrast to England, where only two meetings were held outside London. This clearly reflected the bias in membership towards the Celtic fringe, a bias reinforced by the appointment of Scottish, Welsh, and Northern Irish assistant commissioners but none from England.

After considerable argument, the commission agreed to supplement this traditional source of views by a detailed survey of attitudes toward devolution and other aspects of government (see Social and Community Planning Research, 1973). The difficulties in using such a method for eliciting opinions on specific kinds of devolution are immense. It would have required the Commission to prepare models of devolution in advance of the survey, which they were in no position to do. It would assume that these models and their implications for the respondent were fully articulated and understood, and even if these difficulties were overcome, and allowing for the risks of low response rates to complicated and difficult questions, there would be still left the problem of evaluating attitudes towards hypothetical alternative schemes. The attitudes survey, therefore, apart from probing general attitudes toward government, could trawl only opinions on devolution of the most general and abstract nature, such as eliciting reasons for wishing for devolution and for preference between devolution to a regional administration and devolution requiring elected bodies. An illustration of these difficulties is given later.

In evaluating the evidence, the MR (Majority Report) and MD (Memorandum of Dissent) agreed on three main points: (1) there had developed a growing lack of communication between central government and the electorate; (2) the political power of individuals and their elected representatives in parliament had declined, while that of the central administration and *ad hoc* bodies appointed on its recommendation had increased; and (3) in respect of (1) and (2) there was no marked difference of opinion on these matters between regions of the United Kingdom. But, on the vital question of remedies, the MR and MD disagreed on the interpretation of evidence.

The MR argued that the survey provided no substantial evidence in favour of a bigger share in political decision-making as distinct from bringing the administrative apparatus more directly in touch with the people. The problem, in their view, was one of 'a felt lack of communication' rather than 'a felt lack of participation'. Moreover, they believed that the survey pointed toward more 'spontaneous' interest in devolution in Scotland and Wales than in English regions. The MD, on the other hand, made two technical criticisms of the survey, perhaps with the benefit of hindsight. First, it could not elicit the difference between discontent with the government of the day and discontent with the system of government itself, and second, it was not asked to set its findings against comparable information on attitudes, notably by national opinion polls and Gallup polls covering similar problems. It found ample evidence in the survey itself for a demand for more individual participation in the political decision-making process and no evidence that this demand varied in intensity between the Celtic nations and the English regions.

As a signatory of the MD, I believe, of course, that its analysis of the evidence in the survey and of other evidence is much sounder than those of the survey investigators themselves and of the MR. However, this is neither to say that the survey was not competently carried out nor that its interpretation was easy. As an indication of the inherent problem of investigation and interpretation, let me take one striking example. It is obvious that whoever were to take the decisions in a devolved system, attitudes towards forms of devolution would depend on the costs and benefits attached to any particular scheme. The impact effect might be to produce recognizable benefits derived from greater power over the amount and mix of publicly provided services, but these might be offset by costs in the form of adverse real income changes. Thus, a relatively poor region with complete responsibility for running its own services would

Figure 19.1 Proportions wanting devolution if consequences economically bad for region

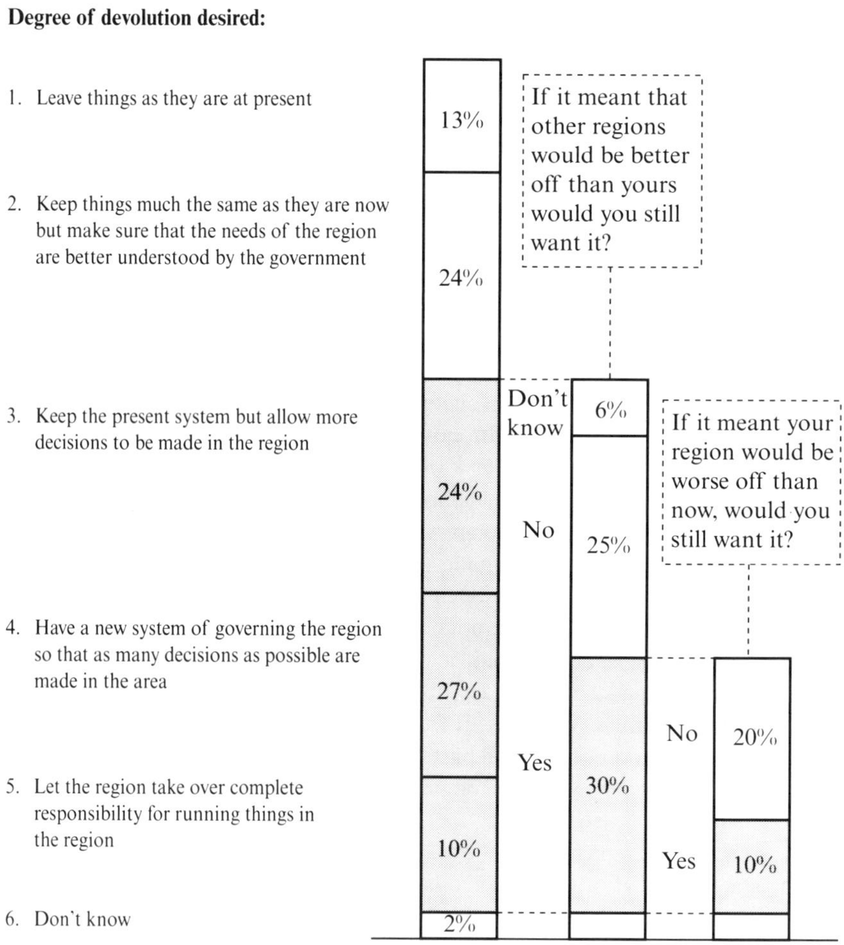

Source: Commission on the Constitution, Research Papers No. 7, Chart 2, p. 98. Reprinted with permission of the Controller of Her Majesty's Stationery Office, 1973.

pay the price in a fall in the positive 'fiscal residuum', to use Buchanan's term, which would initially reduce per capita real incomes, and, in addition, it is conceivable that individual regional government services might lose the cost advantages associated with the scale of central government operation. Even then, it would be difficult to translate these effects into a cost and benefit calculus for other than some mythical 'representative' individual, whereas any particular individual might be able to adjust his real income position *within* the new system through the new dimension introduced into the political signalling system, e.g., through the changing opportunities for tax avoidance or through political action with others to alter regional-government tax schedules. Further, the individual's judgment is not based solely on short-term considerations and therefore on the impact of the change in the governmental system within his own region. His judgment of the net present value of devolution will depend on whether, for example, other regions are endowed with comparable systems of government and how far the fiscal arrangements with the centre would affect regional incomes. These factors would affect his judgment, not only because his utility might depend on how others in other regions were treated, but also because it might depend on his view on the opportunities to improve his position through inter-regional migration.

When the survey was taken, the KC had not even got to the stage of listing any possible 'runners' for the devolution stakes. Even if it had, it would have been an impossible task to give respondents anything other than a very general idea of how they might be affected by any possible scheme. Furthermore, the costs to the individual of going through the process of cerebration that might have required him to undertake some rather sophisticated analysis would probably have reduced the response rate to a negligible percentage. Thus the attitudes survey could only offer general evidence on the *expectations* of respondents of devolution on themselves and others without being able to probe how these expectations were formed and how they might vary if individuals were offered a (hypothetical) choice of alternative schemes. I reproduce as Figure 19.1 one chart of the attitudes survey without comment in order to demonstrate these difficulties.

IV. THE DEVOLUTION SCHEMES

The final outcome of the commission's deliberations and of the government's proposals are only partly based on the evidence that we have examined, which is probably not surprising if only because of the inherent difficulties in basing proposals on attempts to reveal the electorate's preferences. I cannot possibly do more than summarize the main differences between, and the consequences of, two sets of proposals, those of the MR and those of the MD. And there is not space enough to comment on the intense speculation surrounding the constitutional aspects of these proposals. I shall concentrate exclusively on the possible economic effects of the alternative systems.

Table 19.1 summarizes the principal features of the various types of schemes, ignoring certain variations in them put forward by individual members and other constitutional matters (such as changes in House of Commons procedure and in relations between Westminster and the Channel Islands and the Isle of Man).

The MR proposals amount to saying this (see MR, 1973, Chapter 8):

> There is a general demand for a limited extension of the signalling system which indicates that the electorate could be predicted to support constitutional change. This demand varies according to region. Scotland and Wales prefer a change which requires a limited degree of *political* participation through regional legislatures which would give substantial freedom to vary the *composition* of social and environmental services but without requiring control over the total expenditure on these services or over the methods of their finance. English regions will be content with an improvement in communications between government departments, parliament, and their electorate. Devolved government only to Scotland and to Wales would have the following advantages:
>
> (a) It would reflect the electorate's preferences;
> (b) It would cause the minimum of administrative disruption, given that Scotland and Wales already have separate Government Departments responsible for a large part of their administration;
> (c) Effects on economic objectives other than improved allocation of resources would be minimized, for macroeconomic policy would be constrained only by more spending freedom for a very limited segment of total spending by public authorities. Distributional effects would similarly be minimized. In any case, central government would be left with sufficient instruments, other than composition of expenditure, to make any corrections necessary to offset the effects of devolution on growth, stability, and income distribution.

As the government's proposals follow these recommendations closely, they deserve particular attention. The general case made for partial devolution may be conceded, save for point (a) (see pp. 279–80), which I believe conflicts with the evidence, such as it is. However, there is a major unstated assumption, which is recognized in the government's statement (see Command Paper 6348 (1975)) that the position regarding the English regions must be considered separately, and this is the belief that a new political equilibrium will be established. There is a good case for believing that this assumption is untenable, and I shall now explain why.

Consider the 'representative' canny Scot or go-getting Welshman weighing the costs and benefits of new-found freedom. Through his regional politicians

Table 19.1 Principal features of devolution proposals

	Majority Report	*Memorandum of Dissent*	*Government Proposals*
1. *Extent of devolution*	Devolution to Scotland and Wales only.	Devolution to all regions.	Devolution to Scotland and Wales now. No decision on England.
2. *Rationale*	a. 'Historically identifiable' nations – Scotland, Wales. b. Existing administrative devolution to build on, i.e., Scottish and Welsh Offices. c. Demand 'stronger' in Scotland and Wales.	a. Principle of political equality. b. Demand equally distributed throughout United Kingdom. c. Improved division of labour between central and regional government.	a. Same as for MR, 2a. b. Same as for MR, 2b. c. Same as for MR, 2c.
3. *Political institutions*	a. Elected assemblies in Scotland and Wales by proportional representation. b. Executive authority vested in Ministers appointed from Assembly. c. Advisory councils for English regions. d. Representation in UK House of Commons for Scotland and Wales in proportion to population. e. Regional Committees in UK Parliament.	a. Elected assemblies in all regions by proportional representation. b. Executive authority in Assembly committees reflecting party composition. c. Representation in U.K. House of Commons for all regions on population basis. d. Possible reform of House of Lords to reflect regional representation.	a. Elected assemblies in Scotland and Wales by simple majority system. b. Scotland: executive authority vested in members of Assembly of the majority party. Wales: executive authority vested in Assembly committees reflecting party composition. c. No firm proposals at this stage. d. No change in representation of Scotland and Wales in House of Commons (central legislature).
4. *Financial powers*	a. Responsibility for expenditure on all main social and environmental services within total agreed with central government. b. Substantial freedom in expenditure allocation within agreed total. c. No firm views on central-regional revenue sources.	a. Same as for MR, 4a. b. Same as for MR, 4b. c. Devolution of some taxing powers in order to promote regional political participation.	a. Same as for MR, 4a. b. Same as for MR, 4b. c. No new sources of regional revenue other than power to precept on local government taxes (the local rate).

he may be able to alter the pattern of devolved government service in a way that moves constraints on his optimizing behaviour. However, the gain in movement to a more preferred position may be offset by a rise in the relative price of services, so increasing his budget constraint. This could happen in two ways: (1) from more 'X-inefficiency' arising from lack of regional experience in expenditure control and project appraisal and perhaps from discrimination in favour of own-region suppliers to government; and (2) from 'scale' effects produced by operating services at a regional rather than national level, which would result in higher marginal and average costs. It has been argued (King, 1973) that the most important case for consideration of scale effects would be hospitals, which in recent years have absorbed nearly 20 per cent of current and capital expenditure on 'devolvable' services. Since the devolved governments will not be responsible for finance of these services, the loss in real income to members of the 'Celtic fringe' would take the form of lower standards of service at the present level of finance available on a regional basis.

However, being no fool, our representative Scot or Welshman realizes that his devolved government has an important additional weapon that may yield a compensatory real income effect. His regional assembly, serviced by its bureaucracy, represents the creation of a new power base capable of exercising direct and continuous pressure on central government in a way denied other regions. Favourable bargains will be sought (1) in the financial allocation available to devolved governments and (2) in the way other policy instruments could be used to discriminate in favour of a particular region, e.g., siting of central-government defence establishments and purchasing policy. At the same time, pressure through regional representatives in the central legislature could be maintained, since regional representation is not to be reduced.

It is therefore difficult to believe that regions without the proposed Assemblies would not be concerned about a prospective political change that could put them at a relative disadvantage. Table 19.2 offers skeleton profiles of the regions of the United Kingdom which would bring the point home to them. Devolved government is being offered to two regions representing less than 15 per cent of the total population of the United Kingdom, with a low relative population density where, admittedly, GDP per head is relatively low and unemployment is relatively high, but where the degree of economic disadvantage is not much greater than in some other regions, notably less than in the North region. More telling still is the fact that devolvable government expenditure per head in Scotland and Wales is much higher than in all other regions, though it is difficult to establish whether this reflects a concomitant difference in standards of services on offer. Though there is little firm evidence for recent years, there is little doubt that after deduction of allocable taxes Scotland and Wales are net gainers from the financial operations of the central government. The conclusion, therefore, that other regions will press hard for equality of political rights and thus for comparable power bases seems irresistible.[5]

Therefore, though it has been rejected for the present, this conclusion offers point for further consideration of the MD, which starts from a fundamentally different position. Its argument might be summarized as follows: (see MD, 1973, Chapter 6)

> The demand for more political participation is widely distributed, contrary to the interpretation of evidence by the MR. Equality of political rights is equitable in principle and, for the reasons given, a reasonable prediction of what ultimately will be politically acceptable. Moreover, it leaves the legislature free to take a much more active interest in important national and international issues and therefore to exert more pressure on the executive, for regional assemblies can concentrate on the redress of local grievances. It follows not only that there should be elected assemblies in all regions but that they should have some devolved taxing powers as well as freedom in expenditure allocation, so that regional political participation is fostered. To reinforce contact between different layers of government and to reduce centralizing tendencies, local government would have no direct link with the central government but would be represented in the functional committees of the regional assembly. Likewise, a proportion of elected representatives of the regional assemblies would be members of the House of Lords (the British Upper House), which would both raise the prestige of regional assemblies and offer the House of Lords a more positive role in the process of government.

Space prevents a detailed examination of the problems facing such a radical change in the structure of British government. It is clear that the MD is written on the assumption that dissemination of political power is an important argument in the community's objective function that must be assigned a considerable weight. At the same time, though it spells out its proposals in detail, it leaves at least partly unsolved the extent to which particular financial arrangements designed to further the aim of dissemination of power (e.g., taxing powers) will affect the values of the other arguments, notably stabilization and distributional objectives. A good deal of the official evidence to the KC by the Treasury and Inland Revenue argues for nothing more than token devolution of taxing powers and complete control over the total regional assembly budget because of the fear of surrender of budgetary instruments important for stabilization. I have argued elsewhere (Peacock, 1973) that this evidence rests on a fairly simplistic model of the role of fiscal policy in controlling fluctuations in income and employment. What must be emphasized is that the MD argues that such important issues as these cannot be resolved without much further study and that any precise proposals would take a generation to work out. This view is in stark contrast with that of the present government, which hopes to begin the process of (limited) devolution within the lifetime of the present parliament.

Table 19.2 Regional economic profiles

Region	Population (in millions) (1973)	Population (% of UK) (1973)	Persons per sq. km (1973)	Rel. pop. density (1973)	GDP (factor cost) per head (1972)	Rel. GDP per head (1972)	Unemployment (% av.) (1973)	Devolvable per head (1969)	Rel. Devolvable Gov. expenditure[a]
England:									
North	3.3	5.9	170	74.1	819	85.0	4.7	128.5	116.6
Yorkshire/Humberside	4.8	8.6	340	148.5	903	93.7	2.9	98.0	88.9
East Midlands	3.4	6.1	283	123.6	928	96.3	2.1	90.4	82.0
East Anglia	1.7	3.1	138	60.3	919	95.4	1.9	94.4	85.7
South East	17.3	31.1	632	275.9	1,117	115.8	1.5	94.4	85.7
South West	3.8	6.8	164	71.6	932	96.7	2.4	93.3	84.7
West Midlands	5.1	9.2	397	173.4	984	102.0	2.2	91.7	83.2
North West	6.8	12.2	845	369.0	900	93.3	3.6	104.6	94.6
Scotland	5.2	9.4	66	28.8	880	91.3	3.5	144.1	130.8
Wales	2.7	4.9	132	57.6	843	87.4	4.6	233.0	211.4
Northern Ireland	1.5	2.7	110	48.0	678	70.3	6.0	–	–
United Kingdom	55.6	100.0	229	100.0	960	100.0	2.7	110.2[b]	100[b]

Sources: HMSO Abstract of Regional Statistics: 1974 for Cols. 1–7; King (1973) for Cols. 8 and 9.

[a] 'Devolvable' expenditure is total government expenditure *less* 'unallocable' expenditure (mainly defence).

[b] Great Britain only.

V. CONCLUSION

Faced with the far-reaching consequences of the oil crisis for the pursuit of the traditional objectives of maintaining a high level of employment and controlling inflation and with the need to improve the poor growth performance of the UK economy, embarking on a major constitutional reform could hardly have come at a more inopportune moment for the British government. However, as already indicated, its political survival and, indeed, that of any alternative government is estimated to depend upon making some concession to the demand for political and economic decentralization. At the same time, these concessions do not embody what would commonly be regarded as a major economic indicator of transfer of power, namely, the devolution of responsibility for financing a major part of decentralized expenditures, the main ground for rejection of transfer being the need to maintain centralized control of finance for economic stabilization purposes. As pointed out, this approach may be based on strong technical assumptions and a mistaken view of the strength of demand for devolution. It is arguable, first, whether or not devolution of financing power would make much difference to the central government's capability for preserving economic stability (see King, 1976). Second, it is questionable, as I have argued in Section IV, whether or not the political inequalities created by the proposed system would be tolerated by the 'losers' in the English regions.

The final paradox in the British situation is that the decision whether or not and how to devolve government seems certain to be taken in a way that could be regarded as contrary to the whole spirit of the growing demand for political participation. Such is the power of a British government in office and the strength of party discipline that an Act of Devolution can be passed in the central legislature by simple majority of members who themselves are elected by a simple majority system, and in a matter of months after a public statement of intention (such as a White Paper). No referendum, special majority provisions, presidential veto, or delays by an Upper House will stand in the way. If and when they finally come into being, the regional assemblies will be the creatures of parliament and will have no independently guaranteed constitutional rights. In the home country, the 'Mother of Parliaments' remains a matriarch.

NOTES

1. The original Chairman, Lord Crowther, better known as Geoffrey Crowther, died in 1972 and was succeeded by Lord Kilbrandon, a Lord of Appeal. This is why the Commission is known today as the Kilbrandon Commission. The present author replaced Professor Donald Robertson of Glasgow in November 1970, Professor Robertson having also died in the course of the commission's work.

2. The constitutional convention is that a substantial minority of members must dissent from the majority's findings before they can publish a minority report. There were only two signatories to the Memorandum of Dissent, Lord Crowther-Hunt (no relation of the original Chairman) and the author.
3. The author, in a prefatory note to the Memorandum of Dissent (MD), argued strongly that the problem of devolution embraced that of re-examining the allocation of functions between the public and private sector (see MD (1973), p. xi).
4. I am no authority on the latest developments in political philosophy. Surely someone has clothed political theories in this methodological garb. Thus Hobbes: objective function has one main argument – preservation of peace. Constraint – men are by nature querulous, therefore, in the absence of policy intervention, lawlessness and life 'nasty, brutish and short'. Appropriate policy instrument – firm dictatorial government.
5. At the time of writing, attempts are already being made to muster support for regional assemblies in England. For example, Members of Parliament with constituencies in the North of England are examining proposals for a regional assembly in the North. An attempt has also been made to revive the ancient Cornish Parliament.

REFERENCES

Aronson, R. (1974), 'Financing Public Goods and the Distribution of Population in Metropolitan Areas: An Analysis of Fiscal Migration in the United States and England', in A.J. Culyer (ed.), *Economic Policies and Social Goals,* York Studies in Economics, London: Martin Robertson.

Breton, A. (1974), *The Economic Theory of Representative Government,* Chicago: Aldine, Chapters 5 and 6.

Breton, A. and Scott, A. (1978), *The Economic Constitution of Federal States*, Toronto.

Command Paper 6348 (1975), *Our Changing Democracy: Devolution to Scotland and Wales*, London: Her Majesty's Stationery Office.

King, D. (1973), *Financial and Economic Aspects of Regionalism and Separatism*, Research paper No. 10, Commission on the Constitution, London: Her Majesty's Stationery Office.

King, D. (1976), 'The Fiscal Implications of Devolution', Lecture delivered to Institute for Fiscal Studies, London.

MD (1973), Memorandum of Dissent by Lord Crowther-Hunt and Professor Alan Peacock, Command Paper No. 5460–I, London: Her Majesty's Stationery Office.

MR (1973), *Report of the Royal Commission on the Constitution*, Command Paper No. 5460, London: Her Majesty's Stationery Office.

Peacock, A. (1973), 'Economic Policy and the Finance of Intermediate Levels of Government', Appendix A to MD (1973).

Social and Community Planning Research (1973), *Devolution and Other Aspects of Government: An Attitudes Survey*, Research Paper No. 7, Commission on the Constitution, London: Her Majesty's Stationery Office.

20. The 'politics' of investigating broadcasting finance

(The only time in my life that I found myself pursued by the media was when I was appointed to investigate broadcasting itself as Chairman of the Committee on the Financing of the BBC in March 1986. It was widely assumed that the Committee members were hired guns instructed to conclude that the BBC should cease to be publicly funded and should rely on advertising income, a view particularly associated with the then Prime Minister, Mrs Thatcher. Any hope that we would be allowed to get on with our investigations uninterrupted by media attention was soon dispelled, for too much appeared to be at stake if the government were to take our findings seriously. Various attempts were made to manufacture disagreement between our members, and I am told that a particular major consultancy employed someone to examine my career for flaws in my professional reputation and character that might be used to 'rubbish' our final Report! It followed that a strategy had to be developed which would create the conditions which would make it possible for the Committee to concentrate on the task before it. This involved negotiations with the government itself over terms of reference and resources available to conduct appropriate research, with the interest groups (including politicians) anxious to influence our findings, and with the public at large, whom the system is meant to benefit. As Chairman, therefore, I had to become a political animal, and it may be that my experiences may suggest that social scientists have much to learn by becoming, if only temporarily, part of their own subject-matter.)

INTRODUCTION

The Committee on Financing the BBC, of which I was Chairman, submitted its report in May 1986 and it was published in July of that year. Its recommendations received widespread publicity and produced a deluge of comment, particularly from those most likely to be affected by its conclusions – the broadcasting companies themselves. This article is not concerned in any detail with the Committee's analysis of the problem of financing television and radio and is certainly not a defence of the recommendations. It concentrates on a study of the process of carrying out an enquiry of this kind, in the belief that such a study may be both interesting and instructive. (The economic analysis underlying the Committee's work is presented in Peacock, 1986, Budd, 1986, and Brittan, 1987.) Nevertheless, it is worth a sentence or two to remind the reader of the main contents of the report. It describes the existing system of broadcasting finance and how it evolved, and draws attention to the phenomenon of the 'comfortable duopoly', in which the broadcasting market is carved up between the BBC, largely financed by a compulsory levy – the licence fee – and the ITV companies who are protected by a franchise arrangement which allows them to dominate access to broadcasting time 'slots' for advertising. The Committee argued that this system is inherently unstable and will in any case be challenged by technological changes, notably cable and satellite transmission, which will offer consumers more choice. Furthermore the major objection to a subscription system for broadcasting or to charging for particular programmes (Pay TV) no longer holds given the growing sophistication in methods of encoding broadcasting signals. Its recommendations were designed to prepare the way for the development of a 'consumer-driven' system of broadcasting in which the individual viewer and listener would express choices by payment, and in which more freedom of entry of independent producers would be encouraged, while at the same time protecting the public interest in supporting programmes of an informative and instructive nature which would not survive commercially (see the Report of the Committee on Financing the BBC, Cmnd 9824, 1986, particularly Chapter 12).

The Committee's approach to the financial problems of broadcasting and its far-reaching conclusions came as a surprise. It was supposed to have been appointed to reach foregone conclusions. This was not the case. It was widely expected to recommend that the BBC should take advertising. It did not so recommend. It was believed that the terms of reference would so confine its activities that it would not be able to consider the wider aspects of broadcasting resources and how they should be financed. In fact, it offered revolutionary proposals designed to alter the whole system of broadcasting finance. A running commentary by the press made much of wide differences of opinion among members of the Committee on essential matters, yet the Report was unanimous, with notes of reservation offered in only two cases. (In one of these the disagreement was not about aims but about means.) The longer-term scenarios for facilitating the introduction of a consumer-driven system of broadcasting were accepted by all members of the Committee. It was forecast that the Committee would not make its deadline of reporting within a year. It did. It was suggested that in the time available no empirical research worth the name could be provided. In fact, the commissioned research is generally recognized amongst experts as of very high standard. On its appearance, it was widely believed that the government would 'kick it into the long grass'. (Mr Robert Maxwell went so far as to warn me that the Committee had committed the terrible crime of having deprived the Prime Minister of an election issue!) It is early days yet to say how much attention the government will eventually pay to our findings. At the time of writing, it has set up a Cabinet Committee to consider its proposals in detail, chaired by the Prime Minister. In January 1987 two of the main short-term recommendations – no advertising on the BBC and indexing of the licence fee to the Retail Price Index – were accepted by the government. Those most affected by the proposals have declared their implacable opposition to the Report. That much is true but virtually no broadcasting pundit believes any more that the '*status quo*' remains an option. Some of them, such as Lord Thomson of Monifieth, Chairman of the IBA, have been gracious enough to state that the report provides the essential agenda for discussion of the future of broadcasting.

I cannot fully explain this remarkable disparity between the general expectations of those who take an interest in broadcasting – press, politicians and broadcasters themselves – and what our Committee has recommended, and the subsequent discussion of our findings. A partial explanation must lie in the intense emotions which the obtrusive medium of television seems to engender and the strong vested interests in its structure and mode of operation, both of which encourage rumour and speculation at the very mention of possible changes in the broadcasting system. Such an atmosphere, reminiscent of the soap operas which to many represent the very essence of television, hardly encourages the belief that a group of individuals with differing professional backgrounds and experience can sit down and agree on what the important issues are, and on what information and analysis will throw light on them. Indeed, those who created such an atmosphere, or some of them, clearly intended that the Committee should be prevented from conducting its operations in the cast of mind which would encourage the cool look at the task before it, from being able to collect its evidence unhampered by premature claims that we were selecting that evidence, and from being able to keep our counsel on matters of policy recommendations until we had carefully considered how far we could agree amongst ourselves.

This contribution is a personal account of how, as Chairman, I tried to fulfil the task set before the Committee. This is not an original idea. Lord Annan (1981), the Chairman of the previous enquiry into broadcasting, produced a most lucid and absorbing account of his experiences, which I cannot possibly emulate. I shall differentiate my product from his in a number of ways which are best explained by saying that I speak as an economist rather than, like Lord Annan, as a historian. But both accounts have this in common. The task of being Chairman of a Committee of Enquiry on a controversial issue has to be something more than that of producing answers to difficult questions in co-operation with colleagues. It must include the creation of the conditions which make it possible for the Committee to pursue its proper task. This involves the Chairman in activities which I shall broadly describe as political. I shall therefore concentrate on the negotiation and discussion with the outside world and not on the internal politics of the Committee, though clearly the internal and external politics will be inter-related. My aim is to describe and to analyse rather than to criticize the behaviour of those who took part in this political process.

INITIAL NEGOTIATIONS

The first area of negotiation concerned my own appointment, and what might be called the job specification.

Once having agreed in principle to be Chairman of a Committee, one might have expected that there could be an intense and concentrated period of negotiation between the Chairman, the relevant Secretary of State and his senior civil servants about the objects of the enquiry, the role of the Chairman and individual members, the choice of members themselves, and the resources to be provided and instructions on their use. Clearly a good deal could hang on such negotiations, including whether or not one should commit oneself finally to taking on the job.

I had no difficulty agreeing the terms of reference with Mr Leon Brittan, then Secretary of State for the Home Department, and this saved a lot of time because terms of reference are not negotiable, though a Secretary of State may be willing to discuss amendment and may even ask for advice (but not for a decision) on their scope. I was particularly pleased that the terms of reference covered a wide range of options for financing broadcasting, and that they recognized the close connections between the different parts of the broadcasting system and between that system and the Press. The one thing that I was concerned about was the question how far we should simply examine alternative systems of finance only or would be expected to make specific recommendations. There was a good chance that a Committee might agree on the effects of financial changes on the broadcasting system and on the welfare of viewers and listeners, but it seemed to me at the time that to go further might only offer us the opportunity of agreeing to disagree on the ranking of the options that we were to examine. I was assured that on this question the Committee could decide for itself. Subsequently, much was made of the narrowness of the terms of reference and a conspiratorial view was taken of them. Some very anxious TV personalities, for example, wrote to *The Times* complaining that our terms of reference did not permit us to discuss the merits of the *status quo*. My reply was the first of a continuous series of statements trying to reassure the public that the government was not committed to change, had said so, and that therefore the examination of the status quo as an option was essential, if only as a frame of reference which would facilitate comparison between alternative methods of financing broadcasting.

A remarkable feature of these initial negotiations with the Home Office was the lack of concern over what some would regard as important details in any job specification. Let me give a few examples. Firstly, I do not have in my possession an official letter of appointment, not because I have lost it but because such a letter does not exist! A parliamentary statement of my appointment was taken as sufficient. Secondly, I was given no advice or instructions on the Chairman's function or on the conduct of business. Although I have served on government committees and on a Royal Commission before, and could claim some knowledge of the inner workings of government, I was not aware of the so-called 'Balfour Rules'[1] on the conduct of committees, and these were certainly not drawn to my attention. It suited my temperament to be left to get on with things so I worked on the assumption that if I did anything totally outrageous or violated the Constitution, I would be duly admonished. A third example is more important. At no stage was any observation made or instruction offered by members of the government on what they would consider should be the Committee's conclusions. I made a particular point of finding out at an early stage what form official evidence would take. In the case of the Prime Minister's office, I was informed that no evidence would be offered. It was natural for the Home Office to provide us with what turned out to be an extremely useful survey of the broadcasting scene, but it contained no recommendations. We received much useful technical advice from other Departments, notably my old Department, Trade and Industry. We almost pleaded with some Departments, such as the Treasury, to give us their views, but they were not to be drawn.

I labour this last point because a deliberate attempt seems to have been made by politicians and others opposed to the Enquiry to claim that it was rigged in order to be sure that it would recommend that the BBC should be forced into the market-place. The kindest words that I can find about such allegations is that they were naive. If a government has made up its mind on a policy matter, then the obvious vehicle for the design of policy recommendations is an inter-departmental committee of officials with outsiders confined to the role of advisers, as with the recent committees set up to examine the future of the pensions system (on which I served). It hardly indicates confidence in a particular policy if an outside body has to be employed to whitewash it, and even if such a curious procedure were adopted, the government would have to choose a body of 'yes-men' ('yes-persons?') to apply the solution. Such a description certainly did not fit our Committee, as its list of members (see note below) makes clear.

Why, then, will a government give so much of a free hand to a committee both in respect of the interpretation of its terms of reference, and of its procedures and practices? The answer lies, I believe, in the fact that the government has no obligations towards such a committee. It could dissolve it at any time, as has happened with a change of government. It is not bound to publish its findings. No constitutional procedure requires that its contents need to be reviewed and commented on by any administrative or legislative committee, or be the subject of parliamentary debate. The financial risks are very limited.

Funds could be withdrawn at any time, and members are not normally remunerated, at least not in a form which could be the subject of a claim for redundancy payments.

NEGOTIATING RESOURCES

The second area of negotiation concerned resources and their deployment.

The first question which concerned me was the location of the secretariat. Living in Edinburgh as I do, it occurred to me that whatever might be the optimal location for Committee meetings and taking of evidence, valuable time might be saved all round and expenditure cut if the secretariat were centred in Auld Reekie. I lost this round with the Home Office who saw difficulties, as the sponsoring Department, in having staff of their own seconded to a 'foreign country' and beyond immediate face-to-face contact or, alternatively, in having to persuade the Scottish Office in Edinburgh to detach staff to serve us. Like all skilful negotiators, they offered me an option by asking me not to make up my mind until I had met the civil servant whom they wished to recommend as Secretary. I quickly realized that they were recommending an absolutely first class man, a highly trained physicist and OR expert for whom servicing the Committee, were he appointed its Secretary, would be his 'blooding' as an administrator. Bob Eagle might have to be anchored professionally and domestically in 'The Smoke', and had an understandable aversion to air travel, but he proved to have all the qualities necessary for a difficult assignment – quick on his feet, immense industry, unflappability and cheerfulness! The problem of running an office had no terrors for him and he sensed very quickly what would be the important 'inputs' which would require negotiation. An important example was his insistence that we had an in-office word processor with a full-time operator. The capital equipment presented no difficulty, but skilled operators are like gold. The effect of this on the productivity of draft preparation and revision was quite dramatic and made the time-scale look much less forbidding.

The second concern was the budget. Being difficult to cost, the total budget allocation had to be fairly flexible and negotiations were more concerned with authorizing forms of expenditure and the application of established civil service rules about making contracts, the scale of allowances to committee members and research staff and matters of this kind.

My previous experience on committees alerted me to the possibility that the Home Office might question the use of funds for research. Committees sometimes have access to research already undertaken in government departments, and in fact we were given full information on the present state of broadcasting technology and on the system of broadcasting regulation and useful impressions of broadcasting policy problems in other countries by the Foreign Office. Some Committees rely almost exclusively on those who present evidence to generate research, and certainly some of the evidence we received was backed by empirical research of high quality. However, I formed the impression very quickly that there could be no guarantee that the research already conducted or likely to be generated by the Committee's existence would necessarily address itself to the questions of direct interest to the Committee and, indeed, it would be difficult to forecast what some of those questions might be or where they might lead. We clearly needed a team of researchers offering tailor-made studies, who could turn their minds quickly to issues presented to them as we progressed and who could offer expert appraisal of statistical and economic evidence as it came before us. The Home Office raised no objection to this while rightly insisting that scales of remuneration had to be agreed with them and that outside contracts must follow their tendering rules. They also co-operated fully in achieving quick publication of the major research studies.

Committees of this kind, as I have indicated, are not remunerated, though I remember that Sir Roy Allen as Chairman of the Committee on the Impact of Rates some twenty-odd years ago, of which I was a member, insisted that we should be paid a fee per meeting attended. The allowances for Committees of this kind are traditionally less than generous, and my Committee was no exception. Two matters nearly resulted in revolution. When I was temporarily a Deputy Secretary in the DTI, I was obliged to take a taxi even for short distances if an official car was not available. As Chairman of the Committee I could not claim a taxi fare unless I signed a statement claiming that I had heavy baggage. (Shortly before becoming Chairman of the Committee I was approached about the possibility of becoming Chairman of a standing Advisory Committee for a Department of Government that I prefer not to name. The post was unpaid and the senior official who was asked to sound me out, when he heard that I was moving back to Scotland, actually had the temerity to observe that it might just be possible to pay my travel expenses to London meetings!) Gladstone said that the income tax had turned us into a nation of liars. That observation might well apply to expenses. There is a strong temptation to lie in order to be able to take the occasional taxi and I am fairly sure that had I claimed to be loaded to the gunwales with papers on coming to London my word would not have been questioned, though it might well have been doubted. The problem was solved and within the rules, by allowing me when under time pressure to hire a car from the government car pool and to charge it to our budget. The second matter concerned allowances when abroad. Four members of the Committee sat down for an evening meal in Rome – not a frugal but certainly a modest affair – and discovered on paying the bill that they had exhausted one whole day's allowance!

There is no satisfactory solution, I suspect, to this matter which must sound petty to some. There must be rules, and no one expects ever to be fully compensated for their expense in terms of both time and money. On the other hand, there is the lingering feeling that members of such Committees are being had for suckers and perceive their treatment as that of lesser beings than those of comparable experience and professional standing within the civil service.

NEGOTIATING WITH INTEREST GROUPS

It might be thought that a Committee appointed to consider a radical change in the structure of broadcasting finance would not need to apply itself to the task of generating evidence. Interested parties would flood it with memoranda, taking the opportunity simultaneously to make their views public in a way which might influence those in power in their attitude to the eventual conclusions that the Committee might reach. The supply of evidence and the offer to give oral evidence would far outstrip the demand in terms of the time available for the Committee to digest the evidence and to question those supplying it. It is certainly true that there was no lack of evidence submitted – 843 individuals or organizations made submissions. However, whatever the volume of supply of evidence we were particularly concerned that it was not dominated by the large producer interest groups who, very understandably, would not wish to encourage competitive evidence from those who wished to enter and to share their market or who might claim that they did not provide good service.

To this end, the Committee first of all went further than most, I suspect, in disseminating information to the public about its view of the issues which would have to be resolved. Invitations to address meetings were readily accepted and serious queries about our activities answered. We were responsible for an innovation in holding a one-day conference on 28 November 1985 in Church House, London. The idea was to have the main interest groups present their views in public and to discuss them in front of members of the public who were admitted on a first-come first-served basis. It was hoped that this public exposure would indicate that the issues that we were concerned with were not simply short-term ones but, given rapid changes in technology, concerned the whole future of broadcasting transmission and its effect on the ordinary household. I cannot claim that the meeting was a pronounced success. The actors in the public drama were not disposed to discuss with one another, but, by and large, further publicized their entrenched positions. The 'public' merely heard a repetition of what had become a dialogue of the deaf. Instead of acquiring a reputation for openness and receptivity, the Committee was attacked by those who had not been asked to present their views as having reduced them to the role of second class citizens. Members of the observing public present resented not being able to participate, and this fact was exploited by one politician present who, I believe, would be against the televising of parliament. The television interviewers were able to make mincemeat out of me, and I thoroughly deserved it, having obviously made a naive forecast of how the meeting would go. It was a political error, but, I hope, an understandable one

I shall not dwell long on the ways in which the Committee itself took a positive role in obtaining evidence, for the methods of doing so are familiar and do not enter into the realm of politics as I have defined it. I suppose it could be claimed that the Committee's wish to have independent sources of information and analysis was designed to strengthen its authority in later debate. Indeed, it was partly designed to steer the debate itself, and I believe it was a useful strategy to publish our research findings as far ahead of the main Report as possible, thus showing that the Committee would rest its conclusions on the weight of the evidence and not on *ex cathedra* utterances. Visits to television stations, meetings with the top brass of broadcasting authorities at home and abroad were clearly *de rigueur*. Each of us would have favourite stories to report of our travels. Those of us able to make it to Rome will remember for a long time the lunch given for us by the British Ambassador to Italy, Lord Bridges, at which he lectured us and his guests on the importance of maintaining broadcasting standards through public authorities, all in beautiful Italian! A more unusual feature of self-education was the video-cassette of 'prime time' programmes from several countries which included advertising which was a first introduction to some members into the mysteries of VCRs. I was supplied with a satellite dish to receive about eight European channels. This required me to obtain, with a little difficulty, a DTI licence and, with rather a long delay, planning permission from the Edinburgh District Council. This excited some press interest and my neighbours, far from objecting to a dish of 1.8 m diameter over the wall, asked to be cabled up to it. This news spurred the Director of the Cable Authority to write to me that cabling up my neighbours turned my house into a cable station. This would require two further licences, but, as the Edinburgh cable concession had already been allocated to another company, any application made by me would have to be refused! This was an interesting insight into the issues surrounding freedom of entry into the broadcasting business.

Negotiation in the assembly and hearing of evidence required me, advised by the Committee, to make sure that we had a clear understanding with the BBC about procedure. Before considering this aspect of politics, I should say something about the BBC's posture on matters of this kind. As we all know, it commands at home and abroad great respect as a pioneer of broadcasting, and its reputation within its peer group approaches the invincible when it comes to awards conferred by international broadcasters on one another. It is the owner of an enormous stock of programmes and archival material. It is justifiably proud of its innovations in transmission technology. It sponsors major research effort in listeners' and reviewers' reactions to programmes. It is a large music and book publishing house. Small wonder then that it impresses, indeed overawes, those who are appointed to investigate its functions. It is indeed a body 'on whom assurance sits as a silk hat on a Bradford millionaire'[2] and none the worse for that some might add.

In my first meeting with the Chairman of the BBC and senior executives something of this patrician stance was conveyed and I remember that this was symbolized in two towering figures with menacing scowls who looked down on this stocky figure like the giants Fasolt and Fafner on the dwarf Alberich in *Das Rheingold.* According to a report in *The Times* I caused consternation by answering the Question 'what can we tell you?' by replying 'nothing' and by requesting that their evidence should be with the Committee in two months. As it was agreed on this occasion that we would make more progress if we had informal confidential meetings, the BBC started one down with us by babbling to the press. But nothing was to be gained by sticking to these preliminary postures and Stuart Young and I were easily able to agree to have a schedule of meetings with full opportunity for the presentation of supplementary evidence. Once the BBC had realized that we knew what questions to ask, they seemed only too willing to act as our guide, philosopher and friend through the labyrinthine structure of broadcasting, even to the extent of arranging our visits abroad. This offer had to be politely refused. It would have been wrong to have proceeded on the assumption that the BBC knew all that was to be known about broadcasting even if it were true. Indeed some of us suspected, and it turned out to be the case, that they were unfamiliar with the economic analysis of broadcasting for the simple reason that they have never had to concern themselves with major economic issues.

Although it is not my purpose here to comment on the evidence presented in any detail, I feel bound to add that the BBC missed a crucial opportunity to display its command of broadcasting issues in its presentations. Instead of taking the lead in a full discussion of the financing options available and how these might relate to criteria for policy, the BBC brushed aside any suggestion that change was necessary, other than some minor adjustments in the methods for raising the licence fee which might make the fee more acceptable to the public. It relied on the weight of its authority and its past experiences and not on a properly structured economic analysis which considered how far past experience would remain relevant. The attacks on the Committee's views on Subscription and Pay-TV made in their name, once the report had appeared, were embarrassing in the crudity of their language and speciousness of economic arguments.

Naturally enough, professional politicians were monitoring our activities and some were anxious to influence our approach to financing problems. Some of them submitted evidence in an individual capacity, notably the former Home Secretary, Mr Merlyn Rees. After the initial reactions in parliament to the setting up of the Committee I had expected to be taking shelter from the flak rather than be entering into negotiation with sceptics. The most active group demanding clarification of our approach was the Conservative Party Media Committee in the House of Commons, several of whose members had been or still were TV personalities or had been closely concerned with the regulation and administration of broadcasting. They tried very hard to draw me on what our conclusions were likely to be and how they would view them, but there was a notable lack of unanimity of view on broadcasting finance amongst its experienced members. I dare say that this lack of unanimity also characterizes comparable opposition committees, but I was not asked to meet them. At his request, I willingly met Mr Clement Freud, the chairman of the Liberal Party committee, but hardly expected to be told in as many words that our journey through broadcasting finance was unnecessary and, even if a case for looking at broadcasting issues could be made, we were, he supposed, hired guns and therefore not to be trusted. As the Leader of his Party had publicly expressed confidence in my judgment, if also expressing doubt about my mission, and his predecessor, Lord Grimond, had agreed to chair our public meeting, I am afraid that I was unforgivably angry with and extremely rude to Mr Freud about this slur on our characters, all the more unforgivable because I rather enjoyed myself. Mr Freud was relieved, I believe, that he was not actually physically assaulted. Mr Norman Buchan of the Labour Party and I have come to know each other rather well as members of the travelling debating society created by the Committee's existence, so I was disappointed when he was not able to deliver his Labour comrades to me and me to them. Our easy passage, whilst in *situ,* with the professional politicians had probably nothing to do with skill in discussion and negotiations and is more likely to be a reflection of the opportunity cost of their time when issue after issue on which they are expected to pronounce is forced on their attention. Spasmodic eruption of interest in our doings is all that one should have expected and to have thought otherwise indicates how one can become obsessed with a public issue and greatly overestimate its importance and one's own.

DEFENDING OUR FINDINGS

I come to the final stage which is perhaps the most fascinating of all for the participants, all eager to know how their creation will be received.

There is first of all an important personal decision to be taken. Once a Committee Report is received by the relevant Department, that Department, as I have explained, has no further obligation to the Committee though good manners requires the Secretary of State to thank its members by letter. I have served on some five committees and in all but one the thank-you letter came from a different Minister than the one who had originally appointed the committee. Mr Hurd did more; he gave us an excellent dinner. It would be entirely understandable if committees returned to known fields and pastures old, thankful that it was all over and like Florestan in *Fidelio* consoling themselves with the words 'süsser Trost in meinem Herzen meine Pflicht hab' ich getan'.[3] The report could be left to make its own way into the world and obligations to it would be completed by good proofreading before publication.

Lord Annan stated in his splendid Ulster Television Lecture that he regarded it as his duty to expound and defend his Report and he clearly did so with great skill. I was less sure about where my duty lay but I was concerned about the lack of champions to defend the interests of those for whom we agreed that the whole system of broadcasting was designed – the viewers and listeners – as were other members of the Committee. Moreover, having made recommendations which would clearly affect powerful producer interest groups in ways which they would perceive as adverse to their interests, there was no guarantee that the forthcoming debate would be conducted on impartial lines.

I did not view this task with relish when the Report was about to appear. There had been a set of unfortunate leaks, unfortunate because they took particular recommendations, such as the rejection of advertising by the BBC, out of context. The press were also unanimous in their view that members of the Cabinet were reacting most unfavourably to what they had been told about the Report's contents. Our child would be strangled at birth. The producer groups most affected by our recommendations controlled not only the channels of communication with the public, but also the professional bodies who had the best facilities for organizing discussion and debate of broadcasting issues. They had immense resources for promoting and disseminating their views. The work of the Committee being over, I had no further claim on comparable facilities. I had my typewriter, access to typing and precious little else. What should be one's strategy?

I had little time to think out what to do before I was inundated with invitations to speak at conferences, write, lecture at home and abroad, take broadcast 'phone-ins' on radio and appear at short notice in television interviews. At least there was no difficulty about entry into the business of discussion, even though in some cases I was obviously being set up as a sitting target. I decided that at the outset I should accept as many invitations as possible in the early days in order to establish as clearly as possible what was correct and what was myth in the exposition and criticism of our findings and conclusions. I appeared on every kind of radio and television programme, ranging from a breakfast appearance to the late night news. I expounded our main thesis at all levels of discourse from the academic lecture to the popular newspaper article. I wrote at least six separate scripts adaptable for different occasions and which had to be kept in constant repair. I made appearances in places as distant from one another as Toronto and Stockholm, Edinburgh and Milan. I bombarded anyone who expressed interest in our work with manuscripts. I made contact with any public officials who showed the least inclination to listen to me. Following Lord Annan's precedent I shall keep this up for a year, subject to avoiding exhaustion and divorce.

I shall only make two observations drawn so far from this feverish activity. The first concerns relations with government after publication. I have had only two short official meetings, one with all Committee members, to discuss the report, though I have had some contact with Government bodies closely concerned with the technology of broadcasting and useful discussions with members of public corporations closely involved with broadcasting. While it has been made clear that the Report is being closely studied, these bodies know my thinking and that of other members of the Committee, but one rarely knows theirs. One hears about various branches of government instituting studies of various aspects of the report and commissioning work by outside experts, but one learns about these things by chance or by daily reading of the *Financial Times*. Much more attention is openly paid to one's professional advice by overseas governments faced with similar problems. I am not arguing that there is necessarily anything wrong with this situation, though there is an odd Kafkaesque feel about this sudden severing of the nexus between the government and its one-time advisers. An ongoing dialogue might have its uses such as the right of a rejoinder to criticisms made within government itself. This position is reinforced in the case of broadcasting where the interests of those whom broadcasting is meant to serve are clearly under-represented whereas the large broadcasting companies are in close and frequent contact with officialdom.

My second observation relates to the recent controversy about biased television reporting sparked off by Mr Tebbit. The acid test as to whether the BBC and ITN companies can claim to be unbiased reporters of current affairs is provided by their reactions to the Committee's findings. Its recommendations imply the break-up of the 'comfortable duopoly' which could be threatened in any case by the growth of cable and satellite delivery systems. It is too much to expect that the major terrestrial broadcasting companies in the UK could express pleasure at the Committee's conclusions. The reporting that I have monitored has been principally in the form of off-the-cuff remarks, largely by broadcasters, and at the time of writing no programme has appeared, so far as I am aware, where the issues raised by the Committee have been properly presented and discussed. It is not so much biased reporting as covert censorship. Now one must not get this matter out of focus for, alongside international events, the subject of the financing of broadcasting, which is hardly a glamorous one anyway, may seem small beer and lacking in immediate appeal. It is nevertheless important and affects us all. The tenets of 'public service broadcasting' which the BBC in particular claims to follow surely call for a more responsible approach to the study of the future of an industry in which the BBC perceives that it should have pride of place.

SUMMING UP

The inevitable question arises, was the effort put into negotiation and discussion worth it? I am too close to events to be able to offer an objective assessment. I cannot prove it but I believe that our Report benefited from our having to defend the very fact of our existence from the beginning. It enabled us, I believe, to anticipate objections that had not occurred to us and to obtain responses to the research that we had commissioned and to our ideas on procedure which sharpened up our arguments.

A related question is how one views the chances of the main recommendations being accepted, given the intense and vehement opposition to some of them. I suppose some would answer with the old adage that the better the report the less likely that it will be accepted. I am reminded of the delightful letter written by David Hume (1758) to Adam Smith on the appearance of the latter's first major work *The Theory of Moral Sentiments:*

> Show yourself a Philosopher in Practice as well as Profession. Think on the Emptiness, and Rashness, and Futility of the common Judgments of Men: How little they are regulated by Reason in any Subject …
>
> A wise man's Kingdom is his own Breast: or, if he ever looks farther, it will only be to the Judgment of a select few; who are free from Prejudices, and capable of examining his Work. Nothing can be a stronger Presumption of Falsehood than the Approbation of the Multitude; and Phocion, you know, always suspected himself of some Blunder, when he was attended with the Applauses of the Populace.

But then he adds the punch line:

> (I now) proceed to tell you the Melancholy news that your book has been very unfortunate: for the Public seem disposed to applaud it extremely …

I think that there is little likelihood that the public will be so disposed in our case but a little misfortune, in the Humeian sense, could very well befall us.

NOTES

This chapter is based on lectures given to the London School of Economics Society and to The David Hume Institute, Edinburgh. It should be obvious to the reader that I owe an immense debt to my fellow members of the committee on Financing the BBC – Mr Samuel Brittan, Ms Judith Chalmers, Mr Jeremy Hardie, Professor Alistair Hetherington, Lord Quinton and Sir Peter Reynolds. It will also be obvious that they had a great deal to put up with in their Chairman! I have deliberately refrained from considering the internal politics of the Committee's work, not only because this is a subject all on its own, but also because I feel strongly that our good relations assumed that we could express our views to one another in confidence.

1. They were derived from the Report of a Committee headed by Lord Balfour of Burleigh published in 1909 which considered how the business of Royal Commissions should be conducted.
2. See lines 233–4 in 'The Waste Land', Eliot (1940).
3. 'Sweet consolation in my heart – I have done my duty'.

REFERENCES

Annan, The Lord (1981), 'The Politics of a Broadcasting Enquiry', The 1981 Ulster Television Lecture, 29 May, Ulster Television Ltd.

Brittan, Samuel (1987), 'The Fight for Freedom in Broadcasting', *Political Quarterly*, January.

Budd, Alan (1986), 'The Peacock Committee and the BBC: Liberal Values versus Regulation', *Public Money*, Vol. 6, No. 3, December.

Eliot, T.S. (1940), *The Waste Land and Other Poems*, Faber and Faber.

Home Office (1986), *Report of the Committee on Financing the BBC (Peacock Report)*, Cm. 9824, London: HMSO, July.

Hume, David (1759), Letter to Adam Smith, 12 April 1759, reprinted in *The Correspondence of Adam Smith*, ed. E.C. Mossner and I.S. Ross, Oxford, at the Clarendon Press, 1977.

Peacock, Alan (1986), 'Making Sense of Broadcasting Finance', Robbins Lecture, University of Stirling, 9 October.

21. The political economy of public service broadcasting

(It can fairly be claimed that one of the results of the work of the Committee on the Financing of the BBC was that broadcasters, in Europe as well as the UK, could no longer assume that the broadcasting system could and should be producer-driven. If it is accepted that consumer preferences should be the dominating force in determining the scope and content of broadcasting services, then technological and institutional changes have now made this possible. The role of government then becomes that of giving effect to those consumer preferences that cannot be fulfilled in a commercial broadcasting market, notably demand for public service broadcasting (PSB). In this chapter I argue that while PSB requires public funding and regulation of broadcasting services, it does not require that a state broadcasting service should be the sole producer of PSB and the sole receiver of government financial support. Therefore, the justification for the continuation of state broadcasting services, the BBC being a notable example, invites critical assessment.

This chapter was originally written as an introduction to the political economy of broadcasting for broadcasters and those interested in broadcasting regulation. Economists will easily identify places where I have avoided some of the analytical refinements in the now extensive literature on the economics of broadcasting, but may be less familiar with its policy implications which are my main concern.)

I. INTRODUCTION: THE STORY OF MR MATON

This chapter is a discussion of the policy issues that arise in devising a system of broadcasting designed to maximize the satisfaction of those who listen to and watch broadcast programmes. These issues arose in the very early days of broadcasting and it serves my purpose well to begin by telling you the story of Mr Maton (see Coase, 1948).

Mr Maton owned an electrical shop in an English village called Hythe near Southampton and had built himself a radio receiver back in 1924 (two years after I was born). As an experiment he connected his set with a wire to a loudspeaker so that his wife could also listen to programmes in another part of the house. He was glad to find his experiment successful and he experimented further by wiring up his neighbours' speakers and eventually by 1926 secured 150 subscribers to his service, which required him to use 10 miles of wire. When officialdom in the form of the Post Office, the new British Broadcasting Corporation and government authorities got to know of his initiative, he was faced with considerable interference with his business. The Post Office insisted that he must have a special licence to run his relay system, and that all his subscribers should be obliged to have a receiving licence. The BBC managed to persuade the government that he and any imitators should be prevented from relaying any other programmes than those that it provided. Politicians were worried in case 'wire broadcasting' might lead to the transmission of 'unsuitable' programmes from foreign countries. The infant radio industry lent their weight to officialdom by supporting these restrictions, as they were worried about the effect of relaying on the demand for broadcasting sets.

Now, clearly, Mr Maton had offered a useful alternative to those who, for one reason or another, preferred not to buy a set of their own. The loudspeaker was easier to operate than a receiving set of that period, sets were not inexpensive and a weekly subscription to Mr Maton might compare favourably with buying a set on credit. In some areas, wire broadcasting provided better reception. As time went on, receiving sets improved and became cheaper relative to other household appliances, and, of course, eventually TV became an important competitor. Wire broadcasting, though a predecessor of cable transmission, effectively disappeared soon after the Second World War.

This is a true story and encapsulates a struggle between enterprise and officialdom that takes place nowadays on an infinitely wider stage than that occupied by the satisfied villagers of Hythe. As I soon discovered when I became Chairman of the Committee on the Financing of the BBC (CFB) in 1985, the very idea that the ultimate judge of a broadcasting system should be the consumer was even at that late date regarded as bizarre in the UK and, as I found, in other Western democracies. Even in the 1980s the Canadian broadcasting authorities tried to prevent lumberjacks in Northern Canada from rigging up dishes to receive programmes from the US which provided better picture quality and programmes more to their liking. Even as late as 1995 the Austrian broadcasting authorities had to accept that they could no longer monopolize domestic programmes, when faced with an appeal to the European Court of Human Rights that this violated the right of free speech.

In case there is any initial misunderstanding about the thrust of my argument, let me make it clear that I see an important role for government in regulating broadcasting but one which has to be judged in terms of the effects of government action on improving consumer satisfaction. However, before examining this role, let me explore in more detail what exactly maximizing the satisfaction of the consumer/viewer means and entails.

II. CONSUMER SOVEREIGNTY

In talking about maximizing the satisfaction of viewers and listeners, I am going much further than the proposition that any broadcasting system should operate in the interests of consumers; I am arguing that, by and large, consumers themselves are the best judges of those interests. This is a strong proposition based on a fairly commonly-held value judgment which economists, more than others, seem inclined to accept. Nobody is obliged to accept this value judgment, and a wide consensus amongst economists on its acceptability does not improve its status alongside other value judgments. However, an important point to make here is that other judgments of the function of a broadcasting system are likewise of a subjective character. I emphasize this because we are often led to believe that those who are expert in broadcasting and transmission are the best judges of the performance of the industry. We should always be somewhat suspicious of those who claim to be judge in their own case, particularly if they claim additionally that they are the guardians of the public interest.

The common mechanism which enables consumers to express their preferences is the market, which entails direct payment by consumers for desired amounts of the goods or services required and at the time when they are wanted. Satisfaction of wants depends also on how much consumers have to pay and full information on the alternatives available, so that they can strike the right balance between alternative uses of income. The market must be characterized by competition which ensures that there is an incentive to offer services at the lowest possible prices compatible with remaining in business and maintaining and improving quality. The market has to be or become a low-cost method of exchanging information between consumers and suppliers, and has to promote quick adjustment of prices, quality and the supply of new products to any changes in consumer preferences. The policy conclusions for broadcasting must be that viewers should have access to a large number of competing channels and should pay directly for the programmes that they wish to watch.

Even around 1970, when I was midway through my academic career as an economist, television was given as an example of a service which could not fulfil the technical conditions that make a market possible. There were two reasons given: (a) at that time electromagnetic spectrum permitted only a limited number of channels without inter-channel interference, though it could accommodate local channels in a limited number of locations; and (b) technical devices had not been developed which would have enabled programmes sent through terrestrial channels from being denied to non-payers for the service. When the CFB reported in 1986, we made much of the point that satellite broadcasting transformed the situation. It solved the problem of spectrum space, and it internationalized the market for it afforded access to world-wide transmission. Additional spectrum space also allowed wider band widths offering an improvement in transmission quality through stereo sound broadcasting and higher definition TV. However, the technical presuppositions in our report are already nearly ten years out of date. Although we showed awareness of the importance of cable delivery as a potentially economical way of delivering satellite transmission we barely touched on the question of 'broadcasting self-service' which offers a further dimension to the amazing range of products that will be available, not only through conventional forms of TV transmission and tele-recording by viewers, but through personal computers with access to the Internet.

Apart from the clear indication that this gives about the rapid development of a highly competitive market, these developments must profoundly affect the commercial strategies of the old-established terrestrial broadcasters. Given the world-wide prestige of the BBC, it is worth noting what that august body has to say in a recent apologia (BBC, 1995a). After projecting growth in the number of households in the UK owning a personal computer from 24 per cent in 1992 to 42 per cent by the year 2000, it offers this view of what will happen by this latter date:

> In the future people will be able to download a feature film and select from a range of endings. They will be able to watch a bespoke news bulletin constructed automatically by a computer program that knows which subjects interest them and which do not. They will be able to buy shares and order groceries, or learn a language or new skill in a wholly interactive way, or speak in sound and vision with a relative in another continent

adding as a trailer for the remainder of their subtly argued propagandistic report:

> Although these services will provide significant competition for terrestrial broadcasters they will not always be universally affordable, or even desirable. (p. 16)

There are two other aspects of this technical revolution that deserve mention. The first is that even the newer modes of delivery of conventional programmes and competing substitutes, notably cable, face considerable uncertainty if on-line services develop through a link-up with the conventional telephone system and home computers. Commercial companies face major decisions about lining up modes of delivery, including multi-media link-ups, in order to be sure that they are ahead in the technology game. The uncertainty about the costs and benefits of alternative technologies constantly subject to scientific improvement will lead companies to look closely at access to material for programmes and services, for ultimately consumer satisfaction and willingness to pay will depend on the quality of programme content. Second, putting any numbers to calculations of these costs and benefits is made even more difficult by further uncertainty about the nature of the product in the *consumer's* mind. It is one thing for commercial companies to take risks when the product and the market is well-defined, but quite another when the consumer has not only to acquire much more information about what services can be obtained from the new technologies but will also be expected to be willing to invest in equipment and know-how in increasing amounts.

Nevertheless, it seems safe to conclude that we have already entered an age in which governments will have to accept that the thrust of technology and the growing experience by viewers and listeners of its benefits to them will make it well nigh impossible to exercise the firm control over the broadcasting market which has been considered previously as desirable. But before elaborating this conclusion, I have to consider what forms of intervention by government appear to be necessary in the first place if consumer sovereignty is the aim.

III. CONSUMER CHOICE AND CONSUMER INTERESTS

It was quite clear in the early days of broadcasting in the UK and in other countries that both broadcasters and the governments who regulated their activities simply did not believe that, so far as choice of programmes was concerned, consumers would act in their own best interests. 'Give consumers what is good for them not what they want' paraphrases the severe judgment of the famous BBC chief, John Reith, and his immediate followers. While this view has lost its credibility, the patrician attitude towards viewers and listeners is still present amongst public service broadcasters, even if they have to be more sensitive in days of growing competition to audience reactions. The well-known British political commentator Matthew Parris complained *(The Times,* 24 July 1995) about the 'suppression of any reference to customer choice. Instead, terms like "ratings war", "squeeze on quality" and "competition for viewing figures" are employed. Always "viewing figures", never "viewers", you notice. We avoid mentioning that millions of people have indicated the balance they want in the media'.

What, then, is the measure of success that producers of programmes regard as important? In bald terms, it is the reputation that they have amongst their peer group – broadcasting should be judged by broadcasters. This is exemplified by the BBC's proud listing of major television and radio BAFTA and EMMY awards in its Annual Reports (e.g. BBC Report and Accounts 1994/95).

There is nothing bizarre or unusual about this approach to seeking indicators of performance quality, which is common amongst professional bodies, including those whose members are academic economists, such as myself. It can also be argued that accolades awarded by the industry to its own kind may convey useful information to consumers of the product anxious to develop an interest in programmes which test their intelligence and understanding. But this is no argument for forcing consumers to pay for programmes that they do not wish to watch, and is only one source of information about the potential value of programmes to viewers and listeners.

Now it is certainly true that consumers may be uncertain about the relation between what they buy and the satisfaction they hope to derive from purchase and may have to invest in information, preferably from non-biased sources. This is particularly true of once-and-for-all, expensive purchases such as buying a house, a life assurance policy or surgery. But surely this is not true of broadcasting programmes where viewing or listening is a continuous process and 'trial and error' as a method of obtaining information is inexpensive. As we move into an era in which broadcast services are largely priced and there is wide choice, the consumer can learn very quickly how to get the best value for money.

A more cogent argument for restricting or guiding choice concerns what economists term the 'externalities' of choices, which in broadcasting applies to the possible effects on others of the choices made by those who prefer to watch socially unacceptable programmes. There is no precise definition of what is 'socially unacceptable' but it is claimed that programmes containing violence, explicit sex and sadistic practices are the source of criminal impulses. A more subtle 'negative externality' concerns the effect of freedom of choice of programmes which promote an alien and unacceptable culture which is perceived as undermining attempts to preserve one's own or go even further and are propagandistic and even seditious. I recall that when I first had to present the Report of the CFB to the then Home Secretary, Douglas Hurd, I was very surprised to find that his overriding concern about our findings was that they appeared to support no control over programming, which was not the case (see Chapter 4 above).

Of course, viewers and listeners themselves will normally accept the necessity for control over the timing and content of programmes, if only to protect minors; in other words freedom of choice extends to perceiving benefits in having choices restricted. Different countries will have different views on the form and extent of such controls and the penalties of non-compliance such as loss of a broadcast licence. These will be expressed through the political process and in the consequential form of broadcasting regulation. However, the very fact of differences in national viewpoints poses a major regulatory problem. With international reception available, citizens of one country are able to watch programmes by overseas broadcasters which domestic broadcasters may be prevented from showing. Attempts to obtain international agreement on what is acceptable or not are difficult and any form of international regulation costly. The alternative of making it a criminal offence to watch overseas programmes with unsuitable content raises awkward problems about the liberty of the subject, quite apart from the difficulties of detection. When the attempt was made in Eastern Europe before the breakdown of Communist regimes to ban satellite reception by forbidding the import or unauthorized manufacture and distribution of satellite dishes, enterprising citizens risked prosecution and imprisonment by constructing dishes out of dustbin lids

So, while I accept the externalities argument and the case for regulation of programme content, I have no practical solution to offer. Nor do we seem to have progressed beyond the point where the dilemma is recognised. Two Scots lawyers, experts in the law of the 'electronic frontier', even go so far as to conclude that

> No national system of control can have more than a marginal effect. The urgent need is for a vastly increased degree of international consensus in all areas of the law. Like the corner shop faced with the competition of the superstore, the day of the national legal system may be approaching its end. (Lloyd and Simpson, 1994)

I leave the lawyers amongst you to ponder that statement!

IV. MARKET 'FAILURE'

A related though distinct issue raised by consumer sovereignty is whether it receives full expression in a competitive market. Individuals may derive a general satisfaction from the provision of broadcasting services to the community which is distinct, though difficult to distinguish, from their own immediate enjoyment of them. A useful term for this form of satisfaction is 'option demand' which is best illustrated by example. Thus I may not watch educational or cultural programmes but I may derive a satisfaction from their availability, perhaps because I might at some stage seek to understand and enjoy them or derive satisfaction from the fact that my children and friends do. I cannot necessarily assume, however, that those who seek to interest audiences in such programmes which may present new, unfamiliar, hopefully exciting ideas and situations will be willing to accept the commercial risks of production and transmission. At the same time, while I might be willing to pay for them, I am very unlikely to be willing to do so unless others who could benefit from these programmes are willing to do the same. The 'free-riding' problem is difficult to overcome through voluntary agreement when large numbers are involved, though there are many examples, particularly in the US, of broadcasting stations producing cultural programmes financed in part from voluntary subscriptions. Thus individual viewers and listeners may prefer some form of compulsory levy to finance such programmes rather than face high voluntary transaction costs and the risk of breakdown in voluntary negotiations. This, in general terms, is the case for public financing of some broadcasting services which are perceived as being of general benefit to the community. How this is to be translated into currency values and into programme content is a difficult matter. A reasonable consensus might be found for public financing of news and current affairs, documentaries, arts, cultural and educational programmes.

There are two important features of this view of public intervention that distinguish it from the 'public service broadcasting' concept as it is generally understood and promulgated by public broadcasting institutions. The first is that the 'remit' is much narrower. Insofar as it is possible to make sense of the term 'public service', it seems to mean to organisations such as the BBC, and those influenced by its traditions and expertise, anything that they wish to provide in the way of programmes, whether or not such programmes can be provided by commercial competitors. A little more precision can be afforded to the concept by the notion that the public have a right to expect 'good quality' and 'innovatory' productions of any sort irrespective of their degree of popularity. The argument then becomes centred in how this is to be achieved by public action. It is certainly argued by economists that commercial broadcasters will be unwilling to take the risks associated with innovations either in the nature of the product or in methods of production that would 'improve' quality, by resisting the tendency to continue with well-tried formulas of success which advertisers may prefer. This argument is similar to those used to justify public support to research and development in industry. It has less weight when competition prevails at all stages in the productive process, for competition is a spur to innovations which make companies technically more efficient and more responsive to audience pressure for new products.

Whether one adopts a narrow or wide definition of 'public service broadcasting' (PSB) the case has only been made so far for public *funding* of PSB, but not for public *provision* of PSB through a state monopoly financed in whole or in part by taxation or a licence fee. By way of background, consider the position in the UK, which is not dissimilar from the situation in some other Western countries. The BBC as a public corporation receives the bulk of its revenue from a compulsory levy on receivers in return for a 'guarantee' provided by its state-appointed Governors that it will provide PSB-type programmes and 'good quality' popular programmes. Commercial terrestrial channels are regulated by a separate body, the Independent Television Commission (ITC), and they, too, only receive licences on condition that they also produce programmes with PSB content, but they receive no government support for this purpose. This seems to be to offer the worst of both worlds. There is no competitive tendering for funding of PSB programmes and the BBC is given an unfair advantage. Furthermore, the commercial terrestrial channels are more directly faced with growing competition from satellite channels with no PSB obligations, offering a temptation to minimise the fulfilment of the latter.

The solution offered by the CFB is one which has excited more interest in countries other than the one for which it was designed, the UK. Granted the case for public funding, then the licence fee could be better justified as a levy for that purpose on viewers which could be used to finance bids for PSB contracts from all national broadcasting stations; and there could even be separate regional arrangements given effect by assigning a proportion of the regional contribution to the licence fee total to regional PSB programme makers. There would have to be a governmental funding agency with clear terms of reference who would decide on the general balance of PSB programming, perhaps sensitized by polling licence fee payers as to their preferences. The funding body would then accept tenders for contracts for specified periods of time to broadcasting companies with suitable guarantees of their fulfilment, e.g. through provision of performance bonds by the companies.

In case you regard this as merely some professorial fantasy, a proposal along these lines was seriously considered by the Singapore government based on a report by National Economic Research Associates (NERA) which I helped to prepare. The scheme was for the Singapore Broadcasting Corporation (SBC) to agree a contract with the government to provide PSB programmes in predetermined amounts. The contracts would be awarded based on the 'opportunity cost' of the programmes. The production cost of each programme would be agreed and a sum added to that representing the loss of revenue from not transmitting commercial programmes which would be replaced, i.e. advertising and sponsorship revenue less any such revenue earned from PSB programmes. The main difference with the scheme I outlined would be the absence of competitive tendering, and this would mean that PSB production costs would have to be subject to efficiency checks. It was suggested that contracts should run for three years and, once initial funding had been agreed, the remaining years' funding would be linked to some external price index which would remove the necessity for continuous negotiation on costs. I understand that the main features of this scheme are now being incorporated in the SBC system.

When I review schemes of this sort in the light of the future pattern of broadcasting, I am made more aware of the difficulties of reconciling them with consumer sovereignty as I have described it. We have to remember that expanding choice and 'self-service' broadcasting will not only present governments with a bewildering variety of possible outlets for PSB programmes, but also greater difficulty in ensuring that consumer preferences for PSB will be sustained. I am always a little unhappy about direct subsidies to industry as a means for lowering the price to consumers so as to induce them to consume more of a particular product, mainly because of the difficulty of ensuring that incentives to keep costs down remain in place. I have toyed with the idea of trying to subsidise the viewers and listeners directly, possibly by the issue of vouchers in the form of a card for insertion in a receiver which reduces the 'price' of viewing PSB programmes. This would only work for systems where consumers were charged for individual programmes rather than for the use of a channel, and could be expensive to administer. But if self-service broadcasting becomes a reality, what then? Could some scheme be devised so that self-service would ensure that PSB would be an integral feature? Perhaps a rebate could be given by the subsidizing authority on the presentation of the bills paid by consumers for broadcasting services, but this would require that bills are itemized so that PSB services are identified.

V. CONSUMER SOVEREIGNTY AND COMMERCIAL BROADCASTING

Our pioneering friend, Mr Maton, financed his operation by subscription, though his electrical business may have benefited in other respects through his initiative, but the history of commercial broadcasting, until recently, is the history of wooing advertisers rather than audiences to pay for transmission. Would consumers not benefit more from a system where no charges are levied for programmes and advertisers continued to finance commercial stations?

In evidence to government committees, like my own, advertisers produce two arguments to support an affirmative answer to this question – but both are suspect. The first is that the marginal cost to the listener and viewer is zero, i.e. once they have paid for their set and licence fee (where appropriate), programmes are ‘free’. In a restricted sense, this is true, but what the argument ignores is that the cost of advertising is embodied in the price of goods bought in the shops so that the listener/viewer as a buyer of these goods is likely to bear at least some of the cost.

The second argument is more subtle. Advertising goods in mass consumption increases demand for them and, through economies of scale, brings down their price to the final consumer. However the listener/viewer regards the programmes round which advertising is clustered, as a consumer of mass consumption goods he/she will benefit. This is a good example of what logicians call the ‘fallacy of composition’. An individual company may reduce its costs and pass this reduction forward to consumers as a result of increasing demand for its product through advertising, *provided* that rival sellers do not do so. However, unless there is an aggregate increase in the demand for the product, then the ‘scale effect’ will not operate when *all* competitors are advertising. Indeed, abstracting from the possibility that economies of scale are not necessarily present in all lines of production, it will follow that some part of the total advertising expenditure incurred by rival sellers must be ineffective. In the famous words of Lord Leverhulme, 50 per cent of all advertising is wasted, but the difficulty is discovering which 50 per cent!

Broadly speaking, economists who have analysed commercial broadcasting take the opposing view, namely that the interests of listeners and viewers do not correspond with those of advertisers. Briefly, their argument goes as follows: in an advertising-supported system of broadcasting, people express their preferences by watching or not watching particular programmes, but the value of alternative programmes to viewers depends on their willingness to pay which takes account of the intensity of their preferences. The commercial station's success in attracting advertising to place round programmes will be directly related to the size of the audience, and how much viewers/listeners wish to watch them is not a relevant factor. For example, a popular comedy programme might attract an audience of 10 million whereas a less popular documentary may attract only 6 million. Suppose viewer appreciation of comedy is fairly low so that the most any individual would be willing to pay for it is 5 pence and the average is 2 pence; suppose, in contrast, those keenest on a documentary might be willing to pay 10 pence and the average per viewer is 5 pence. Simple arithmetic shows that the 'willingness to pay' in aggregate terms for the documentary is much higher than for the comedy programme. A related proposition put forward by economists is that if we extend the analysis to cover two competing commercial channels, then competition for mass audiences will encourage companies to produce similar programmes and minority tastes will be ignored. (For a development of this argument, see Cave, 1989.)

When we extend the economic model to take account of a multi-channel system with subscription as an alternative source of revenue and of 'zapping' and of 'zipping' using a VCR, not to speak of hiring and buying video cassettes, then the analytical results can be very complicated. The central point remains that there cannot be a full identity of interests of advertisers and viewers, but, in a highly competitive system, advertisers clearly must be more sensitive to viewers' tastes and preferences.

A more obvious difficulty in seeking to establish and maintain consumer sovereignty is how far commercial broadcasting companies will try to exercise 'countervailing power' by mergers designed to exercise greater control over what is already an international market. This gives rise to the usual worries about the concentration of power in too few hands and the associated fear of reducing the competition in ideas and opinions. As I have already indicated, major players in the broadcasting game, given technological uncertainties and difficulties in forecasting the extent and composition of demand, are likely to ensure that they have acquired a balanced portfolio of both programme material and media outlets. It is no wonder, therefore, that national regulatory bodies for broadcasting are having to pay increasing attention to the problem of how to counter any restrictive practices in the international broadcasting market and to control cross-border programme content.

VI. THE FUTURE OF THE BBC 'MODEL'

The logical conclusion from my own analysis is that public financing of PSB should continue, but that there are no technical or economic reasons that require that programming, scheduling and transmission of broadcasts must be undertaken by a public corporation. So far as the UK is concerned, this would represent a major change in the structure of broadcasting, for it would remove the case for the BBC having to continue as a largely publicly-financed institution. This is true whether a narrow or broad definition of PSB is accepted. Given a narrow definition, BBC would continue to have a monopoly of funding of non-commercial broadcasting, thus perpetuating what economists call a 'principal-agent' problem. The 'principal', the funding authorities, would be faced as at present with 'one bidder' for public funding – its 'agent', the BBC. In such bi-lateral situations, the funding authorities, as principal, have great difficulty in assessing the efficiency of the 'agent' as a PSB supplier. The CFB offered a crude device for maintaining efficiency which was to tie the licence fee financing the BBC to the Retail Price Index, and the government has implemented this recommendation. At least this has made the BBC much more cost-conscious, but, in the longer run, this device becomes the focus for continuous argument, not only between the principal and agent but within the political arena. If a broad definition of PSB is accepted, and the licence fee is used by the BBC, as at present, to be all things to all listeners and viewers, then this amounts to supporting unfair competition between the BBC and commercial broadcasters whose franchises are only awarded if they produce programmes of comparable quality to the BBC.

When these thoughts are advanced in the current debate in the UK, it is generally assumed that privatizing the BBC would simply turn it into another commercial broadcasting station subject to the regulatory regime now applied to independent companies. This is not a necessary development. Even if that were the case, it would start with immense advantages in any competitive situation – international prestige, long experience and expertise in all forms of broadcasting, and archival material of enormous range and depth – though it could be argued that its archives should be in the public domain and open to exploitation by all broadcasters. However, it is possible to envisage the BBC becoming a non-profit-making corporation like our National Trust which is our biggest single enterprise in the field of presenting our national heritage. It could even command a considerable revenue in the form of voluntary subscriptions provided that the subscribers would have some part to play in its governance.

Whatever the logic of the case for a competitive broadcasting market, tempered by public funding of PSB and some regulation of content and quality of programmes, the UK government is clearly reluctant to privatize the BBC. The consultation process instituted by the UK government three years ago on the BBC's future is firmly based on the assumption that the BBC will continue in being as a public corporation (see Department of Heritage, Cm. 2098/1992, p. 5). Consultation with the public, with broadcasting pundits, with special interest groups and professional bodies is designed to gain an impression of ways in which its operations might be adjusted to take account of the impact of multi-channel broadcasting coupled with multi-media delivery of services which could once be provided only by terrestrial radio signals.

The question inevitably arises as to why a government which has given an enormous impetus to privatization of other public utilities in order to give consumers a better deal and which has been copied all over the world should not have included broadcasting on its list.

A preliminary answer may be derived from a study of those government services which the British government has left within the public sector. Notable amongst these are education and health where it has been claimed that to turn professional administrators, teachers and doctors into entrepreneurially minded leaders of privatized services would cause too great a culture shock. A smooth transition to consumer-directed services would require too much investment in retraining, quite apart from encountering strong resistance to the ethos of competition (see Peacock, 1984). In contrast, public corporations selling their services directly to the public, such as power and light and water, even if not profit maximizers, are wholly familiar with the market-place. Privatization accompanied by more freedom of entry to allow others to compete against them did not require some fundamental change in their mode of operation. However, broadcasting does not fit any more into the former pattern of a service like health or education. A large private sector already exists and there is considerable mobility of senior executives between the commercial sector and the BBC.

A second answer is derived from the pragmatic stance particularly associated with British legislators and politicians: 'if it works, leave it alone'. This is well expressed in the words of one of our Committee members, Samuel Brittan, who, although a strong advocate like myself of freedom in broadcasting, wrote subsequent to the CFB:

> To some, privatisation would then be the next logical step. But I would hesitate to comment myself. We are not establishing a broadcasting system in a new country. History and tradition do matter; and the continued public ownership of the BBC will do little harm so long as an eagle eye is kept open for privilege and favouritism. (Brittan, 1987)

A complementary argument is that we must not fall into the trap of comparing some existing, albeit imperfect, system with some hypothetical, untested alternative, of the kind that I have outlined above. However, this is a false contrast because the initial premise is open to question; it may 'work' now but how long will it 'work'? The crucial issue is the method of funding, as public broadcasters all over the world must know. If they wish to exercise the 'wider service' option of a broad range of programming in direct competition with private operators, they cannot sustain a growing claim on public financing, and must seek permission, where this is needed, to exploit other revenue sources. In other words, they become privatized in all but name, though retaining the privilege of some public funding for specified PSB, which, as I have argued, need not be undertaken by one broadcasting company. For example, even though it takes no advertising, in 1995 the BBC derived about 16 per cent of its income from commercial activities such as sale of programmes, publications and satellite income. (For further discussion, see Foster, 1992.)

A third answer is one which I find emanates frequently from broadcasting pundits outside the UK, namely the BBC's international reputation for quality of programmes and objectivity in presentation of current affairs and news bulletins. This has led the Chairman of its Governors to state with obvious pride that 'the BBC has been described to me as the greatest cultural organisation, not just in this country but in the world' (BBC, 1995b, p. 12). It is reasonable to argue that international prestige is something which is perceived as conferring unconvenanted benefits on the British populace, and that they should be willing to pay for these, as, in fact, they do through the grants in our Foreign and Diplomatic expenditure to support the BBC overseas service. I have no objection to this arrangement, and, indeed, admire greatly this aspect of the BBC's activities. However, this is hardly an argument for retaining the BBC as a public institution largely financed by a compulsory levy. Indeed, the BBC's exploitation of its overseas reputation has become the core of its growing commercial activities and there is no need to subsidize these.

I think that the most substantial argument is a more fundamental one, though I cannot fully accept it. Many television commentators claim that there must be a national television service, with reception for citizens in all part of the country, which acts as a focus for the preservation of national culture and therefore national unity, in the face of the cultural competition offered by access to the now bewildering variety of TV services supplied internationally. The argument is less about support for some chauvinistic perception of national culture and more about the quality of imported programmes. The comparison is often made between the ubiquitous 'fast food chains' which offer the young simple informal and cheap fare and their effect on traditional cuisine which requires care and attention to prepare; the US sitcoms are seen as the visual equivalent to this gastronomic revolution. They are regarded at best as 'enjoyable rubbish', to quote the felicitous phrase of Lord Quinton, a member of the CFB, but, more conspiratorially, as a major source of erosion of national cultural and even moral values. I am sure that this is an argument which has a wide appeal in Asian countries, notably Japan and Korea, as well as in English-speaking countries (see Kang and Morgan, 1987, and references therein). The BBC has placed growing emphasis on its role as a kind of unifying force in a world of rapid cultural change not only outside Britain but within, with a particular role as the presenter of programmes covering national events. Even economists have stressed this argument: 'There is little doubt that in today's society the viewing of television is part of what creates any sense of commonality that we have' and a BBC-type service would 'maintain a sense of national identity which transcends more local communal identifications and allows individuals to understand themselves as members of a particular nation' (see Graham and Davies, 1992).

One can agree with the sentiments expressed about the possible subversion of national culture by the all-pervasive nature of TV and this, taken together with the long-standing reputation of the BBC, seems to partly justify the present government's decision to renew the BBC Charter. However, this does not necessarily clinch the argument. The fostering of the qualities which forge a nation's character and influence and which are generally respected, such as enterprise, inventiveness, tolerance and justice, is hardly the function of the broadcasting system, rather it is the function of the educational system in the widest sense. The taste of viewers and listeners is a reflection of these qualities and at most broadcasting is one source of knowledge and should not be raised to the status of a Church, however broad and accommodating its presentation of moral and cultural values may be. Even if it is conceded that there is a public interest in raising the level of understanding of a nation's own cultural diversity and the threats it may face from cheap access to the trivialities of Tinseltown, this does not make the case for confining state financial support to a single, monolithic supplier of PSB. Here I must rest my case for a more critical stance towards the retention of public broadcasting outlets, but the debate will continue and I hope that I have made a sufficiently interesting, if not persuasive, case to invite further discussion.

CONCLUDING THOUGHTS

I began this chapter with the story of Mr Maton, who was clearly a lateral thinker whose efforts were not fully appreciated by officialdom. Let me end it with the story of Trevor Baylis, a former champion swimmer, one-time escapologist in a Berlin circus and a stunt man in films. He recently invented a radio which runs on clockwork and requires no mains electricity or batteries. It is the ideal receiver for poor Africans who find these sources of power unavailable or too expensive. It is now going into production in South Africa and will provide employment for 100 disabled workers. I am glad to admit that my initial source of knowledge of this discovery was a BBC programme! We come full circle back to the thinking individual who recognises a need and uses his ingenuity and skill to satisfy it, just like Mr Maton. Let us hope that Mr Baylis has an easier time than Mr Maton in convincing those with a vested if legitimate interest in broadcasting that the true object of a broadcasting system is to reflect the preferences of the listener and the viewer which can only be achieved by constant adaptation to changing economic and technological circumstances.

REFERENCES

British Broadcasting Corporation (1995a), *People and Programmes: BBC Radio and Television for an Age of Choice.*

British Broadcasting Corporation (1995b), *Report and Accounts, 1994/95.*

Brittan, Samuel (1987), 'The Fight for Freedom in Broadcasting', *Political Quarterly.*

Cave, Martin (1989), 'An Introduction to Television Economics', in G. Hughes and D. Vines (eds), *Deregulation and the Future of Commercial Television*, Aberdeen University Press for The David Hume Institute.

Coase, R.H. (1948), 'Wire Broadcasting in Great Britain', *Economica,* August.

Foster, Robin (1992), *Public Broadcasters: Accountability and Efficiency*, Hume Paper No. 18, Edinburgh University Press for The David Hume Institute.

Graham, Andrew and Davies, Gavyn (1992), 'The Public Funding of Broadcasting', in *Paying for Broadcasting: The Handbook*, Routledge (for the BBC).

Department of Heritage (1992), *The Future of the BBC: A Consultation Document*, Cm. 2098, London: HMSO, November.

Home Office (1986), *Report of the Committee on Financing the BBC (Peacock Report),* Cm. 9824, London: HMSO, July.

Kang, John Geun and Morgan, Michael (1987), 'Culture Clash: Impact of US Television in Korea', *Journalism Quarterly.*

Lloyd, Ian and Simpson, Moira (1994), *Law on the Electronic Frontier*, Hume Papers on Public Policy, Vol. 2, No. 4, Edinburgh University Press for The David Hume Institute.

Parris, Matthew (1995), *The Times*, Monday 24 July, p. 16.

Peacock, Alan (1984), 'Privatisation in Perspective', *Three Banks Review*, December.

Peacock, Alan (1989), 'The Future of Public Service Broadcasting', in Cento Veljanovski (ed.), *Freedom in Broadcasting*, London: Institute of Economic Affairs.

Peacock, Alan (1993), Evidence to the National Heritage Committee of the House of Commons, 25 May, House of Commons Paper 700 (i) 1993.

22. The credibility of economic advice to government

(Much writing by former economic advisers to governments takes narrative form, and there is much to be learnt from their accounts about the interplay between advice and political decision-making. These narratives, together with interviewing, have produced raw material for social scientists claiming objective status who have generalized about advice-giving activities, often concluding that advisers become the slaves of their political masters. I have tried to combine the two approaches by using my experience as an adviser to explain how the 'market' for advice works and the position in which advisers find themselves in seeking to establish their credibility. This chapter was written on the invitation of the Editors of The Economic Journal. *In it there are references to my previous attempts to analyse economic advice-giving as a member of the civil service. I follow up those earlier contributions by considering the role of the 'outside' adviser. In short, in this Chapter I attempt to defend the proposition that sensible and perceptive 'clients' within governments will respect totally independent advice and that advice-giving experience improves the analytical perspectives of the economics profession itself.)*

I. INTRODUCTION

In a challenging paper, Frey and Eichenberger (1992) have argued that

> economists react to relative prices in their capacity as scholars: the competitive American academic market drives them to specialise in publishing abstract papers in narrow neoclassics; the closed European markets induce economists to be theoretically broad and to specialise with respect to institutions. They engage more in advising and practical politics.

They contend that European economists have a 'proud performance with respect to practical policy-making'. More controversial is their prediction that the differences will narrow as a result of European integration, for that will increase the size of the academic market and increase competition between academics, and thereby make the evaluation of academic output in the form of published work a more important indicator of the quality of an economist's output.

The authors offer empirical support for their conclusions which I do not dispute, but while I believe their observations offer a useful point of departure for the discussion of the place of advice-giving in the composition of economists' output, there are two qualifications to it which strike me as important.

The first is that 'professional output' and 'advice output' display elements of complementarily. In my experience, much advice-giving requires not only a broad knowledge of economic analysis but often specialized knowledge in areas in which one may have made a contribution. Indeed, the very experience of advice-giving may improve economic analysis in ways which satisfy academic criteria. The economic analysis of government, and of bureaucracy in particular, is a case in point. Furthermore, economists are no exception in wishing to satisfy not only their 'customers' in either the private or public sector but also their peer group. As I have argued elsewhere (Peacock, 1991), advice-giving economists may attach importance to long-term income prospects and to public prestige, but self-respect and what Alfred Marshall called 'the desire for excellence' can be sufficiently important for them to wish to maintain their professional reputation. Of course, as they get older, they may no longer stalk the pages of the prestigious academic journals, but that 'fate' awaits most economists, academic or not!

My second observation emphasizes that 'the proud performance', as Frey and Eichenberger call it, of economists engaged in advice-giving is characterized by a continuous struggle to maintain and to improve the credibility of advice. Three problems face economists who are specifically asked to give advice to government, as distinct from those who offer it gratuitously through press articles, pamphlets and the like.

(i) The problem about which advice is sought may be complicated and difficult, and its economic dimension may be the subject of honest professional disagreement. It may be a sign of the maturity of economics that these disagreements have been revealed by them to the world in several studies, of which one of the most notable is that of Ricketts and Shoesmith (1990). This study attracted widespread press comment, repeating familiar jibes about 'two-handed economists' and 'five economists with six opinions, two of them Keynes's'. Economists usually take heart from the familiar fact that employment opportunities for economists in business and government do not seem to have been unduly affected by evidence of professional disagreement. George Stigler (1991) maintains that jibes about economists' differences of opinion are evidence of envy rather than contempt. Nevertheless, the practical result is that in any advice-giving context, the economist probably has to work his passage more than his natural science equivalent.

(ii) Government officials and politicians are not necessarily convinced that economists have an expertise in economic questions over and above their own. As I have remarked elsewhere, I have known senior government officials claim that only the doctrine of comparative advantage convinces them that they should stick to administrative questions and leave the economic advice to economists. There is a serious point to be considered here, because nowadays those encountered by economists in the course of advice-giving, more than in the past, frequently have an economics training of some sort. They may need convincing that the economist has something more than analytical skills to offer and will look for a track record of experience in examining public policy questions.

(iii) Even if the economic advice is recognized as authoritative, it may frequently be the case that it is unpalatable. I recall a particular occasion in 1974 when Mr Benn sought evidence that would support his policy of seeking planning agreements with major British companies. (Selective policies of this kind are still part of Labour economic philosophy.) It was important for him to establish that British manufacturers had somehow failed to improve their plant and that manufacturing investment displayed more instability than investment directly controlled by the government in nationalized industries, government departments and local authorities. As his erstwhile Chief Economic Adviser I was given two weeks to present the results of detailed researches undertaken by economists in the Department of Industry together with other research results for presentation to a formidable array of industry and trade ministers. The research results did not offer much support for Mr Benn's supposition and the meeting was hastily abandoned in midstream![1] It is a matter for debate whether in this kind of situation economists should be expected or obliged to exercise powers of advocacy and persuasion.

These observations are the point of departure for some thoughts on the credibility of economic advice to government policy-makers. I have discussed in some detail elsewhere the process of advice-giving within government (see Peacock, 1979, 1991). Here I look at advice given 'from outside'. The precise role of an 'outsider' will vary from case to case. The less interesting one is where he/she is asked to submit a technical report on some economic question and has no responsibility for what happens to it. The more interesting case is where he/she is expected to be associated with policy recommendations to be presented for public discussion. I shall take as my main illustration the question of the future of the retirement pension system, which has been a hot issue from the day that the British system became an earnings-related one in 1975.

II. THE CHOICE OF THE PENSIONS ISSUE

As an immediate beneficiary, I have a clear interest in the pensions issue, but there are substantial reasons why it should be chosen to illustrate my theme.

(1) Concern about the future of pensions continues to be expressed by all the major OECD countries. The reasons are well known. First, economic advance and change have raised fundamental questions about whether or not governments should intervene to the extent demonstrated by compulsory income-related contributions. Second, population ageing has drawn attention to a potential pensions 'burden' which highlights both equity and efficiency issues in deciding how that 'burden' is to be shouldered (see Holzmann, 1989).

(2) Supply-side policies emphasizing the encouragement of competition, notably through greater freedom of entry, raise questions about the desirability of state encouragement by fiscal and other means to occupational pension schemes which may be designed to restrict the mobility of labour.

(3) The professional literature on the economic analysis of social security has burgeoned with the recognition of the financing problem to which present pension systems give rise (see, for example, Musgrave, 1986; Rizzo, 1990).

(4) The reconsideration of our state pensions system was the occasion for what could be fairly described as a constitutional innovation. The official Enquiry into Retirement Provision set up in 1984 was chaired by the Secretary of State for Health and Social Security himself and contained as full members Ministers from his Department, Ministers of State from the Treasury and Department of Employment, the Director of the Prime Minister's Policy Unit, the Government Actuary and three independent 'outside' advisers (two actuaries and an economist [myself]). As well as written evidence, oral evidence was given in public sessions by interested parties and experts. The outside advisers took part in both the analysis of the issues and the formulation of policy recommendations but were not committed to any final proposals submitted by the Secretary of State to the Cabinet. At the same time, they were free to publish any reservations that they might have about proposals, once these were in the public domain.

In what follows, I can hardly offer a disquisition on every aspect of the pensions problem. It is only necessary for my theme to consider how the economist's approach to the problem is regarded by those who seek his/her advice.[2]

III. MODELLING

The Thatcher Government's interest in change in the pension system was sparked off, of course, by the emerging costs of a State Earnings Related Pension System (SERPS) combined with demographic change. At the time of the enquiry (1983), roughly 23 per cent of the adult population were pensioners and it was estimated that this percentage would reach 27 per cent in 2025/26. The Government Actuary's figures suggest that every 10 per cent fall in pensioners' mortality rates would raise annual pension costs by 5 per cent. Another way of looking at the problem is found in the growth of pension awards for men over the same period from 24.6 per cent of their average earnings to 39.5 per cent on earnings-linked upratings. Obviously, an economist would point out that the net cost would be lower because of the fall in the numbers of those receiving means-tested benefits and the extra tax revenue from increased pension levels. This was readily admitted. Such savings were reckoned (at then existing tax rates) to reduce the SERPS element in pension costs by about one-third.

Whatever the method of financing envisaged, the magnitude of such changes in pension payments could give rise to a severe transfer problem, in the sense that the growth in retired persons' consumption would be at the cost of alternative uses of resources. Transferring entitlements to retirement benefits to pensioners could entail a growing burden of taxation or some form of levy on the working population and this could materially affect incentives to work, to save and possibly to form families.

The problem is of sufficient interest internationally to have stimulated a number of long-term growth models in which the interaction between government financing and provision of pensions and saving and work propensities have been fully articulated (see Kauffman, 1992). These models can embody simulations to test their sensitivity to alternative values of their parameters. Whatever one thinks about the possibility of adapting such models to fit actual cases, the necessity to think along such lines in considering the magnitude of the transfer problem can hardly be disputed.

Not having command over the resources to explore the use of such models, my first problem was how to convince the committee and the government departments represented on it to undertake this task. I discovered that the only long-term economic model available was in the hands of the Government Actuary's Department. The Actuary's calculation of the pensions burden is simply a projection which embraces alternative assumptions about demographic trends, real income, and employment trends, but no attempt is made to test whether these assumptions are compatible with one another, as would emerge from a long-term growth model. I had some difficulty convincing the committee that it was indeed an odd situation if long-term economic forecasting was co-ordinated by the Government Actuary rather than the Treasury! I managed to persuade the committee that we should press the Treasury for some kind of view on the long-term economic situation which would offer a check on the Actuary's calculations. The Treasury obliged with perfectly sensible speculations on future trends, but nothing approaching the sophistication of models found in the social security literature was produced. Clearly, the opportunity cost of going any further was too high to the Treasury, whose main preoccupations are short-term. In addition, the Treasury was clearly sceptical of devoting resources to an enquiry which could have major implications for the growth and composition of government and for the tax system, especially if it was not 'in the lead'.

The lesson to be learnt by outside economic advisers is to be sure before you begin that research resources are available either inside or outside government commensurate with the task. (It is useful though not essential to get 'insiders' to conduct the research because then they are committed to the result!) This is a lesson that I should have learned as a member of the Allen Committee on the Impact of Rates (1965). Its chairman, the distinguished statistician Roy Allen, not only saw that the research resources were available. He produced, so far as I am aware, the first official report on fiscal matters which contained the results of multiple-regression analysis! Later as Chairman of the Committee on the Financing of the BBC I requested, and obtained, valuable research back-up.

IV. POLICY OBJECTIVES

While the point of departure of the pensions problem was the question of future cost, it is important to observe that the enquiry was not set up as a cost-cutting exercise, but was obliged to conduct a fundamental review of retirement provision beginning with an analysis of the objectives, considered as part of general government policy.

The conventional wisdom supports the view that economics is or should aspire to become a positive science. This would imply that one's position on a committee concerned with policy matters should be to consider the implications of objectives but take no part in their formulation. Many years ago in *The Economic Journal*, Ralph Turvey opined that in giving economic advice his 'personal feeling is that the value judgments made by economists are, by and large, better than those made by non-economists' (Turvey, 1963), and I was severely critical of his view at the time. I would never go as far as that, but I now concede to Turvey that economists who adopt a position of 'highbrow agnosticism' in formulating policies are not likely to be listened to. Thus, while the economist has certainly no special status in formulating principles governing policy, his/her training does lend itself to their clear articulation.

Outside members of the committee were in any case invited to list their criteria, and I had no difficulty in accepting the invitation. (I only list and elaborate on them to the extent necessary to aid discussion of the credibility issue – for further elaboration, see Peacock and Barry, 1986; Chapter 6 in this volume.)

(i) The overriding criterion, assuming broad agreement on the distribution of income and wealth, should be the sovereignty of the consumer.
(ii) The government should lay down a minimum provision standard for pensions, in accordance with the expectation that if this were not done, the community would be subject to the 'moral hazard' problem; an individual who makes no provision may assume that some provision will be made for him/her.
(iii) Individuals should be free, so far as is practicable, to meet the 'provision standard' by personal saving. (I did not oppose the identification of an individual 'retirement account' with some restriction on the composition of the portfolio.)
(iv) Individuals making pension provision should be able to obtain the service as cheaply as possible. (This would not preclude regulation of the pensions 'market'.)
(v) Pension provision should be so designed that, as far as possible, it does not work to the detriment of other important objectives of economic policy, notably encouragement of mobility of capital and labour. (Here I was obviously concerned about the growth of occupational pension schemes which discriminated in favour of 'stayers' and against 'leavers' and could have undue influence on the share market.)

When viewed against the state pension system of the time, this position would have radical consequences. It would mean a state commitment, however financed, to the provision of a basic pension only. Indeed, I argued that the basic pension was too low and ought to be raised – in that one matter I was on the side of Jack Jones. It would also mean the abolition of the State Earnings Related Pension System (SERPS). If saving for retirement on a voluntary basis was to be encouraged, it required the 'personalizing' of the pension system to a degree which would imply a radical change in the occupational pension structure, e.g. by allowing individual employees to contract out. If encouragement extended to providing tax relief for retirement saving, then this would mean major changes in the tax system.[3]

In fact, what I tried to do was to articulate value judgements and the policy consequences to which the government were not necessarily totally opposed, and some of which were later to be strongly supported by the chairman (Norman Fowler) at Cabinet level (see Fowler, 1991). This is not to say that they were immediately popular. Politicians are understandably wary about having their value judgments too precisely reflected in recommendations, particularly if these imply fiscal and legislative changes which are manifestly the concern of other government departments. It may tie their hands when it comes to seeking support from those who have a different view of policy priorities. Nor will politicians take it for granted that the economist's perception of what is in the interests of the consumer will conform with voters' perceptions of radical changes in the pensions system. Whatever the benefits arising to individuals from being able to choose their pension arrangements, some would gain and some would lose as a result of the changes necessary in the fiscal and regulatory regimes. The interest of those concerned with the implementation of change would also be affected. Administrative changes would alter the balance of interests within the bureaucracy, and encouragement of competition in the pension market would not exactly be welcomed by insurance companies designing and advising on occupational pension schemes.

An economist who did not expect this reaction to an exercise in economic logic of this kind would be extremely naive. The most that he/she can expect is to have it agreed that his/her talents lie in persuading politicians and civil servants to make clear exactly what their aims are, what the trade-offs are between them and how feasible it is to match aims with a coherent set of policies and, eventually, programmes. After all, economic advisers outside government bear no cost of change, other than the criticism they may have to endure from their fellow professionals. One cannot expect more than acceptance, somewhat reluctantly perhaps, of the fact that economists are rather good at establishing the logical connection between ends and means.

V. THE OUTCOME

It may be acknowledged that economists are good designers of policies which are consistent with stated objectives. They are generally less interested and often regarded as less competent in discourse on policy implementation. I have heard prominent economists argue not only that we should not get involved in devising ways of implementing policy, but that somehow or other we would sully our intellectual integrity by stooping to such a lowly task. The economist who wishes to maintain credibility with his clients will certainly not do so by refusing to engage in discussion on the practicability of alternative policy packages.

So far as objectives are concerned, I was not able to convince the committee that the state's sole responsibility would be to provide a minimum income during retirement and to leave to individuals the decision as to whether they should make arrangements to top up this minimum. Perhaps I did make some of them feel slightly uncomfortable by emphasizing that compulsory income-related pensions manifested a paternalistic approach which seemed out of keeping with other government programmes. As the Green Paper (1985) states: 'there is a danger that some employers and employees would take a short-term view, preferring more take-home pay to the possible distant prospect of security in retirement'. What we did agree on – and this proposal nearly obtained Cabinet approval – was that SERPS should be abolished and replaced by personal pensions or occupational pensions of a minimum standard. That was the next best thing to wholly voluntary provision encouraged by tax concessions.

Any 'objective function' would have to be maximized subject to constraints, the most obvious and important one being the budget constraint. It was never made clear in our discussions how binding such a constraint might be, although clearly the growing cost of pensions had to be borne in mind. If that were so, it could be argued that any short-term increase in expenditure resulting from my proposal that the basic pension rate should be increased would not come up against the financial constraint, provided that it could be counterbalanced by the reduction in future outlays as a result of the abolition of SERPS. A Treasury official confronted with this argument maintained that her department would not countenance any increase in expenditure now whatever the future savings would be – the latter would presumably be subject to an infinite rate of discount! I think I won the intellectual battle, but certainly did not help to win the war. Even hardened and experienced campaigners should know that the Treasury usually holds the trump cards, and are not against holding them close to their chest! Apart from my own lone attempt to have the basic pension raised, the Secretary of State was outmanoeuvred by the Treasury and, at the eleventh hour of Cabinet discussion, the Chancellor of the Exchequer opposed the abolition of SERPS. As so often happens, the Treasury had it both ways. They had no positive suggestion to make for the reform of the pensions system, yet claimed to be the only government department with a right to put forward changes in the finance of the National Insurance system (see Fowler, 1991). The 'mish-mash' result was the present modified SERPS system coupled with very complicated provisions covering the accessibility of personal pensions to those who contract out of occupational schemes. I am glad to leave the future professional monitoring of this situation to the Institute for Fiscal Studies (see, for example, Disney and Whitehouse, 1992 and references therein)!

There were other aspects of the discussion of implementation in which one sought to extend the horizons of Ministers and officials in their search for suitable policies, of which the most important was to remind them that the problem of the finance of retirement cannot be considered solely as one of pensions provision. Our discussions seemed to assume that throughout the time period for which policies were being designed, the distribution of income and wealth between the working and non-working (old) population would remain constant. A growing proportion of older persons were likely to be owning houses unencumbered by mortgage debt and without having to pay income tax on the imputed value of self-occupation. A growing proportion would retire, under present tax arrangements, with substantial tax-free lump sum payments. The retired, independent of means, were already receiving substantial benefits in kind from the NHS and were major users of subsidized central and local services, including arts and leisure facilities. The 'earnings limit' on pensioners who continue to work and earn has now been abolished.[4] Of course, as any public choice analyst will know, these government influences on the real income of the retired are a reflection not simply of the myopia of policy-makers but also of the substantial voting power of senior citizens.[5] It is easy to understand why such matters were left on one side, apart from the proposal that tax-free lump sum payments on retirement should be subject to an upper limit, which is now in operation. It would have involved the concerns and interests of an even wider range of government departments who would have had to be consulted, with the threat of much further delay and compromise. At least in raising such questions, those who had to formulate and implement policy were forewarned, even if they were to reserve judgment about whether they should be further pursued. I doubt whether any time would have been spent on even considering them if the economist had refused to be involved in discussing the policy path to follow and had merely pointed towards the goal to be reached.

VI. SOME CONCLUDING THOUGHTS

This example chosen from my own experience demonstrates that where economic advice has to be 'made to measure', economists who wish to be heard have to work their passage with (often) highly experienced and intelligent people who will not be impressed solely by the quality of the economic analysis. The customers are much more likely to be receptive to advice if its instigator understands, even articulates for them, their objectives and is prepared to enter into what may be a long and difficult dialogue on how objectives might be achieved, often requiring several different scenarios. There is nothing inherent in such collaboration which requires the economist to trim his analysis to suit the client; and a sensible and perceptive client will not be looking for a hired gun.

Is credibility of economic advice important to the economics profession? I sense that many academic economists, regarding themselves as pure scientists, would say 'no'. 'They might agree with the first Marquess of Halifax that 'The Government of the World is a great thing, but it is a very coarse one, too, compared with the fineness of speculative knowledge' (Halifax, ed. Kenyon, 1969), but that is as far as it goes. Sticking to model building and testing has much to be said for it, although nowadays awkward questions are asked about what 'performance indicators' should be used to measure the non-marketed output of pure research. Even academics who preach the virtues of the free market do not actively petition to be subject to the pressure of market forces while simultaneously arguing that alternative measures of performance are inadequate!

Finally, to elaborate a point already made, my experience suggests that the provision of resources to enable economists to undertake advanced teaching and research depends on the public's and government's perception of the value of economic advice to them. (The doctrine of consumer sovereignty trotted out by many of us not only takes it for granted that consumption is the sole aim of production but also that consumers know where their own interests lie!) Furthermore, the advice-givers perform an important service to their own profession by the identification of new areas of research emanating from the problems encountered by policy-makers; and their own experience may improve our analytical perspective on how politicians and public servants behave, and how to model their economic relations with other sectors of the economy.

NOTES

1. This incident escapes the attention of Mr Benn in his fascinatingly comprehensive account of his years in office. That I was clearly a disappointment to him is evident from reference to other close encounters (Benn, 1990, pp. 148, 152, 191).
2. A fuller account of my views can be found in Peacock and Barry (1986).
3. The principles that might be applied to the tax treatment of long-term saving in the British economy are admirably set out in Wiseman (1988).
4. I first campaigned for the abolition of the earnings limit forty years ago. It is somewhat ironic that abolition coincided with my reaching pensionable age!
5. For exploration of the use of public choice models to explain the influence of voting power on fiscal variables reflecting social security schemes, see further Rizzo (1990) and von Weizsacker (1990).

REFERENCES

Benn, T. (1990), *Against the Tide: Diaries 1973–79*, London: Arrow Books.

Disney, R. and Whitehouse, E. (1992), 'Personal Pensions and the Reviewing of Contracting-out Terms', *Fiscal Studies*, Vol. 13, No. 1, and references therein.

Fowler, N. (1991), *Ministers Decide: A Personal Memoir of the Thatcher Years*, London: Chapmans, Chapter 11.

Frey, B.S. and Eichenberger, R. (1992), 'Economics and Economists: A European Perspective', *American Economic Review*, Vol. 82, 211–20.

Halifax, Marquess of (1969), 'Moral Thoughts and Reflections', in *Halifax: Complete Works* (ed. J.P. Kenyon), London: Penguin Books, p. 216 (first published posthumously in 1750).

Holzmann, R. (1989), 'Pension policies in OECD Countries: Background, Trends and Implications', *Journal of Public Policy*, October–December, 467–91.

Kauffman, B. (1992), *Microeconomics of Saving*, Commission of the European Communities, Economic Paper, No. 89, and references therein.

Musgrave, R.A. (1986), 'A Reappraisal of Financing Social Security', in R.A. Musgrave (ed.), *Public Finance in a Democratic Society*, Vol. II, pp. 103–22, Brighton: Wheatsheaf.

Peacock, A.T. (1979), *The Economic Analysis of Government*, Oxford: Martin Robertson, Part IV.

Peacock, A.T. (1991), 'Economic Advice and Economic Policy', in D. Greenaway, M. Bleaney and I.M.T. Stewart (eds), *Companion to Contemporary Economic Thought*, London and New York: Routledge, Chapter 35.

Peacock, A.T. and Barry, N. (1986), *The Political Economy of Pension Provision*, Hume Occasional Paper No. 2, Edinburgh: The David Hume Institute.

Ricketts, M. and Shoesmith, E. (1990), *British Economic Opinion: A Survey of a Thousand Economists*, London: Institute of Economic Affairs.

Rizzo, I. (1990), *The Hidden Debt*, Dordrecht: Kluwer Academic.

Stigler, G. (1991), 'The Direction of Economic Research', in G.K. Shaw (ed.), *Economics, Culture and Education: Essays in Honour of Mark Blaug*, Aldershot: Edward Elgar.

The Reform of Social Security: Programme for Action (1985), Command Paper No. 9691, London: Her Majesty's Stationery Office.

Turvey, R. (1963), 'Present Value Versus Internal Rate of Return – An Essay in the Theory of the Third Best', *The Economic Journal*, Vol. 73, p. 93.

Weizsacker, R. von. (1990). 'Population Aging and Social Security: A Politico-Economic Model of State Pension Financing', *Public Finance*, No. 3, pp. 491–509.

Wiseman, J. (1988), *Long-Term Savings in an Enterprise Economy: A Case Study of the Principles and Practice of UK Economic Policy*, Hume Occasional Paper No. 10, Edinburgh: The David Hume Institute.

23. The utility-maximizing government economic adviser: a comment

(This 'parting shot' is an addendum to the previous chapter. Two colleagues whose professional contributions I much respect used a previous account of my advice-giving experience to claim that economists at the policy-making level in government are ultimately bound to trim their economic analysis to support their political position. I dispute this conclusion, arguing that if we regard economists as utility-maximizers like other human beings, then their interests are not served by trimming their advice. I would be the first to admit that this view is based on introspection and casual empiricism but I do not consider that my hypothesis is implausible. I would also be the first to admit to eccentricity, if my hypothesis were falsified by suitable testing devices, but at least I would then have encouraged the extension of our knowledge of the advice-giving process.)

I. INTRODUCTION

One of the striking contributions of public choice analysis has been the analytical transformation of the government bureaucrat from being a guardian of the public weal into a common-or-garden rent-seeker or, at least, a mean, sensual maximizer like everyone else. Economists are employed by governments in many different grades and capacities. They even run 'bureaux' – in my own case I was for three years joint head of the Economic and Statistical Divisions of the UK Department of Trade and Industry, which meant directing the work of over 50 economists and about double that number of statisticians. In the literature written by economists on the provision of economic advice to government, there is copious information supplied on the process of advice-giving but little mention is made of the motivation of those who give it. I have tried elsewhere, albeit tentatively, to fill this gap by raising the following question:

> If the economist firmly believes in the robustness of utility theory, then presumably he/she accepts that utility maximization is as much a characteristic of an economist as of other human beings. Why should economists analyse the behaviour of bureaucrats, often concluding that they are 'rent seekers' rather than dispassionate

guardians of the public interest, without recognising that the pot may be calling the kettle black? (Peacock, 1991)

My short answer, admittedly based on introspection and casual empiricism, is that economists are utility-maximizers like everyone else. Career prospects embodying long-term income opportunities are therefore an important argument in their utility functions. Like other professional cadres, they trade off material wealth against job satisfaction and reputation with their peer group. Of course, investment by an economist in reputation may not be at the cost of income if promotion prospects, as in reputable university institutions, are based on peer group assessment.

The position may be less clear-cut in the case of economists employed in government. Take the position, as in the UK, where there has been a career structure for an economist within government. In the more junior posts, technical competence is likely to be the most important criterion for promotion, and income improvement will depend on assessment carried out by senior economists. Hence the position may not be very different from that in universities. At more senior levels, however, where economists are directly involved in giving advice on the effects of policies and come into contact with senior administrators and with politicians who form the government in power, there are two differences. Communication and managerial skills as well as technical competence will be an important element in the job specification. Promotion will be governed by the decision of the most senior administrators endorsed by the political head of the relevant department; and posts may sometimes be filled by 'lateral' transfer from outside government, as in my own case. For posts with the equivalent of Permanent Secretary rank, the approval of the Prime Minister may be required. In short, any economist in the higher echelons faces important constraints if (s)he wishes to maximize professional reputation. The dilemma is similar to that faced by those attracted to become chairpersons of large economics departments or deans of social sciences faculties in universities, but who wish to continue contributing to major professional journals.

We all know what happens when academics taste power. Some succumb to its allure and desert their profession. In the case of the British civil service it is not uncommon nowadays for economists employed as professionals to seek transfer to the administrative class where there is the opportunity for greater advancement. This trend has been supported by the reduction in top posts in economic advice-giving as the result of the change in the thrust of economic policy during the Thatcher regime, which blocked promotion from the middle ranks. Nevertheless, economists have been considered as front-rank candidates for posts as regulators of privatized nationalized industries.

If employment opportunities in government depend on politicians in government and senior administrators, what choices are open to economists in government service who wish to retain their professional reputation? Before giving my own answer to that question, I must comment on a recent article in *Public Choice* by Philip Jones and John Cullis (1993), which offers an indirect but rather striking answer, particularly as it uses as evidence previous statements of mine about economic advice-giving (Peacock, 1977, 1988).

II. THE 'VULNERABILITY' OF ECONOMIC ADVICE

Jones and Cullis advance five propositions and I shall comment on each, and on two of them extensively.

Proposition 1: Results in social sciences research are far less certain than as perceived by those who are not involved in research.

Comment: Agreed.

Proposition 2: Political leaders will attempt to minimize any uncertainty in policy-making in order to make themselves attractive to the electorate.

Comment: Hardly a universal proposition. In my experience the opposite is more likely. Too strong an attempt at delineating exactly what a policy entails may be counter-productive if the results of that policy are going to be uncertain. I offer an alternative proposition which I have advanced and documented elsewhere (Peacock, 1977) which, in my view, would make the authors' point more forcefully and more accurately. Political leaders maximizing their reputation with the electorate and their party will seek to dramatize the importance of the instrument of policy which lies within *their* control. A Minister of Industry will listen more sympathetically to economic advice which demonstrates that subsidies to industry are a primary means for promoting a general political objective such as improving the economic growth rate.

Proposition 3: If policies must be consistent with a political ideology and also win popular acclaim, it follows that economic advisers must become the 'slaves' of electorally oriented politicians rather than the reverse.

Comment: The authors quote extensively from my previous contributions to support this proposition (Jones and Cullis, 1993, pp. 66–7) and conclude that when economic advice was rejected by a Minister – the case in question being a strong criticism of the use of import controls – 'it was the economist's task to construct a "proof" for the politician's preferred policy'. I have read very carefully what I wrote on this matter and believe that I have not offered one shred of evidence to support this conclusion. Indeed, I was careful to point out that when advice was rejected, a Minister would simply 'instruct' his senior *administrators* to devise what he considered to be the appropriate policy. I can recall only one occasion in which a Minister asked me directly to 'rig' the evidence, to put it crudely, and I flatly refused.

Instead, I have repeatedly emphasized that there can be considerable competition in advice-giving provided by 'outside' economists who derive positive utility from being listened to by governments, even to the extent of providing it free. The authors' thesis would be better developed by reference to a Minister's ability to 'divide and rule' by being frequently in a position to examine alternative sources of economic advice and to choose the preferred option which supports his/her position. Even in the situation where those proffering economic advice offer no support for that position, (s)he can exploit the argument that economists only offered a 'one-sided' view of the 'true' situation. The Minister and his/her Cabinet colleagues need not feel obliged to accept that a necessary condition for the use of any instrument of economic policy must be the blessing of the economics profession (see further Chapter 22 in this volume).

Proposition 4: More 'openness' is required about the content of economic advice, and public disagreement amongst economists should be recognized. As a corollary to this, the 'frailty' (authors' word) of the advice behind political decisions should be made more obvious.

Comment: This argument rests on the strength of Proposition 2, which I have denied. It is extremely doubtful if a Minister would buttress his/her political position by emphasizing the 'certainty' of the economic analysis on which it is based. It is interesting to note – parenthetically – that recently the UK Treasury has taken to publishing its global economic forecasts based on stated government policies, alongside those made by independent private institutions. But what it has not done is to reveal the extent to which official thinking is modified by outside views, when it comes to advising Ministers on the economic implications of contemplated policy changes. Nor are the policy changes themselves revealed in detail in advance of the Budget, which would be a necessary condition for revealing the 'frailty' of advice. A cynic might argue that forecasting comparisons are more of a diversionary tactic designed to emphasize the 'frailty' of economic forecasting in general. (Cf. my comment on Proposition 3 above.)

Proposition 5: Politicians looking for support for their policies must leave economic advisers in the position of only offering advice which could be 'second best' – in the sense presumably that it is not the advice that the adviser could 'honestly' justify.

Comment: If this statement were true, then its implication would be that economists would trim their advice to the wishes of policy-makers if only to keep their jobs. In examining this contention, I make a distinction between economists employed as advisers who are employed by government within a professional cadre and those who are appointed as part of the entourage of particular Ministers.[1] The authors clearly have the former in mind. One must also be clear about what exactly 'economic advice' entails. Jones and Cullis are obviously concerned about the relation of economic advice to 'grand' decisions at the political level, rather than with the many routine but important tasks for which senior economic advisers will be responsible.

With the authors' contention before us that economic advisers are forced to be 'trimmers', I return to the examination of my original question about the adviser's motivation.

III. THE INTEGRITY OF THE ADVISER

I reject the proposition that it is in the interest of senior advisers to 'trim' their advice for the following reasons:

(i) While a Minister will prefer advice which goes with the grain of policy proposals, it is merely inconvenient if it does not. Official policy advice can be ignored, given the choice of alternative sources. Even then, the advice given by a senior economic adviser which is rejected may be worth studying carefully because it may marshal the arguments to be deployed against the Minister's position by his/her political rivals and in public debate of his/her proposals. The problem for the adviser is not that of being forced into 'slavery' but the effect on job satisfaction if advice is repeatedly ignored.

(ii) The trimming of advice to suit the predilections of a Minister can be a high-risk strategy for a utility-maximizing economist who is employed in a technical capacity. For one thing, the 'customer', that is the occupant of a Ministerial post, may change, and frequently; in the longer run, so may the political complexion of the government in power. A reputation for doctoring advice to suit a change in taste reduces its credibility, even when that advice is congenial to the new political incumbent. For another, where such an adviser were to run an economic service as part of the task of executing policies and reviewing how existing policy instruments work, his/her administrative counterparts would be less inclined to trust the technical results and any associated recommendations for change in bureaucratic procedures and practice. The consequences could be more serious than a loss of job satisfaction, if senior administrators are consulted on his/her promotion or continuation of appointment.

(iii) An economist interested in long-term prospects and job satisfaction will wish to keep options open about the pursuit of a career solely within government service. That being so, he/she will be particularly mindful of his/her professional reputation. While experience gained in government may enhance that reputation, particularly if it pays off in improving knowledge of how economic analysis may contribute to the study of political and bureaucratic motivation and action, it will be discounted if that reputation has been sullied by trimming. It may be granted that the experiences of those who admit to doctoring their advice to suit their political masters may have an anthropological interest, but the memoirs of rogues, however divertingly presented, usually have to be taken with large pinches of salt.

IV. CONCLUSION

Nothing in what I have said is meant to question the analysis of the dangers which beset economists who attempt to derive policy recommendations from a set of normative propositions and then enter the business of selling their ideas to policy-makers. Jones and Cullis make a highly commendable contribution to the study of the tastes and preferences of politicians for economic advice. What I question is their conclusion that government economic advisers must necessarily become politicians' slaves. If they do, then they cease to be economists.

NOTE

1. As Chief Economic Adviser to the Department of Trade and Industry, I attended in February 1974 the first meeting between senior officials and Mr Tony Benn, newly appointed Secretary of State for Industry, complete with his junior Ministers and personal political and economic advisers. Having explained his policy he asked for any questions. I did not realize that protocol required that none were put, but asked Mr Benn what Frances Cripps, his economic adviser, could do that I could not! Not a stickler for protocol himself, he regarded it as a perfectly fair question and explained the division of labour as follows: I would keep him informed of the economic situation and advise on the consequences of possible policy measures whereas Cripps as a committed Labour supporter would 'translate' that advice into a form compatible with Labour policy objectives. That things did not quite work out that way is narrated in Peacock (1991). That I was a disappointment to Mr Benn is clear from his published diaries (Benn, 1989, pp. 148, 152 and 191).

REFERENCES

Benn, T. (1989), *Against the Tide: Diaries 1973–79*, London: Arrow Books.

Jones, P.R. and Cullis, J.G. (1993), 'Public Choice and Public Policy: The Vulnerability of Economic Advice to the Interpretations of Politicians', *Public Choice*, 75, 1, January, 63–77.

Peacock, A.T. (1977), 'Giving Economic Advice in Difficult Times', *Three Banks Review*, 106. Reprinted in A.T. Peacock, *The Economic Analysis of Government*, Oxford: Martin Robertson, pp. 221–35.

Peacock, A.T. (1988), 'An Economic Analysis of Economic Advice-Giving', *Atlantic Economic Journal*, 16(3), 1–10.

Peacock, A.T. (1991), 'Economic Advice and Economic Policy', in D. Greenaway, M. Bleaney and I.M.T. Stewart (eds), *Companion to Contemporary Economic Thought*, London: Routledge, pp. 713–26.

Index